THE ENDURING DESERT

THE
ENDURING
DESERT

A DESCRIPTIVE BIBLIOGRAPHY

BY E. I. EDWARDS

Iza Ivan

FOREWORD BY RUSS LEADABRAND

THE WARD RITCHIE PRESS

1969

OTHER BOOKS BY E. I. EDWARDS

THE FINISHED PRODUCT

MOUNTAIN MEMORIES

THE VALLEY WHOSE NAME IS DEATH

DESERT YARNS

DESERT TREASURE

THE GIRL IN THE DOCTOR'S OFFICE

INTO AN ALKALI VALLEY

DESERT VOICES

LOST OASES ALONG THE CARRIZO

(EDITED BY) THE WHIPPLE REPORT

DESERT HARVEST

THE MYSTERY OF DEATH VALLEY'S LOST WAGON TRAIN

FREEMAN'S, A STAGE STOP ON THE MOJAVE

TWELVE GREAT BOOKS

Contents

Preface

———————————— ✖ ————————————

THE DESCRIPTIVE COMMENT appearing in this Bibliography must, of necessity, reflect a *personal* evaluation of the books and articles included in it. My purpose is not to influence readers into conformity with these individual likes and dislikes, but to incite interest in the items commented upon and perhaps encourage the reading of them.

Supplementing the bibliographical text with its more than two thousand items is the condensed gathering of journals and diaries recounting the early Southern California desert crossings. This important section lists—by author, title, desert area, and description—approximately one hundred fifty diaries and journals, together with the names of those publications in which they appear. Hopefully, *The Enduring Desert* will relate itself to the reference needs of student, researcher, librarian, writer, collector, and—perhaps most importantly—the casual reader who knows in his heart an abiding love for desert places and desert books.

The *book* listings in this Bibliography are not selective. Understandably, however, they cannot be all-inclusive; for no bibliographer is expected to know every published book containing material germane to his chosen subject. About the only qualification imposed upon a book is that some essential part of it have a direct bearing upon our Southwest deserts and, more specifically, the Southern California deserts. There are a few deliberate exceptions to this general rule. In the absence of basic California desert material, books on the Colorado River have been excluded—and for good and sufficient reason. I do not wish to intrude nor enlarge upon Francis P. Farquhar's selective bibliography—*The Books of the Colorado River and the Grand Canyon* (1953). Similarly, I have not penetrated too deeply into Kern County, although I have not altogether omitted its eastern portion that sprawls over the mountains onto the Mojave Desert. William Harland Boyd has turned in an excellent coverage in his *A Centennial Bibliography on the History of Kern County, California* (1966); and I have neither desire nor purpose to encroach too extensively upon his well-established domain.

Scientific and technical items are quite generally omitted. The few that are included denote the exception and not the rule. Newspaper items, unless available in book or magazine reprints, are excluded.

Unlike books, the listed *magazine* articles are chosen upon a selective basis. Obviously it would be difficult, if not utterly impossible, to locate all such items, even if one chose to do so. Of the relatively few appearing in this Bibliography, no pretense is made to having based the selection upon a qualitative appraisal. As a matter of fact, in making these selections the literary quality of a magazine article impressed me not in the least. My choice was in every instance an arbitrary one; but the rather nebulous guidelines governing selection were (first) the article's age, a conscious effort being exerted to locate early historical material; (second) a determination that the article contained desert material which did not appear in a book.

All books, unless otherwise noted, are in their first editions and, with few exceptions, in my own private collection. It may be well to remind the reader that the preponderance of desert books have not gone beyond their first editions. During recent years several of the older desert publications—Bartlett, Tyler, Cooke, Bell and others—have received a well-merited reprinting, thus making these scarce desert classics once more available.

Many writers appear concerned with defining, or establishing, precise geographical boundaries of desert areas. With the perplexing problem of where a desert begins and where it ends, I find little to interest me. When a mountain rises precipitously out of desert country, I may classify it as mountain or regard it as desert. Elevation, vegetation, lakes, rivers, cities, industries—all these have no significance for me when it comes to a determination of what is or is not a desert. Personally, I have yet to experience the slightest difficulty in recognizing a desert wherever or whenever I am fortunate enough to be on one—and this irrespective of anyone's definition of its precise boundaries. Similarly, in the selection of desert literature I choose not to concern myself with academic boundary resistances.

Over the past eleven years, immediately following the release of *Desert Voices*, a proliferation of desert books and magazine articles have come off the press. Several hundred of these more recent releases are included in this Bibliography, together with a reevaluation and revision in depth of the extensive coverage appearing in *Desert Voices*.

The Enduring Desert, therefore, is a new and enriched documentary treatise of California desert literature. The book is essentially a directional guide to the superb narrative of our desert country—its flowers and shrubs and trees and cacti, its birds and animals, its canyons and mountains and valleys, its old ghost-town mining camps, its sunrises and sunsets, its penetrant silences. It is an index to the history, drama, philosophy and adventure which are all inextricably woven into the pattern of our desert fabric by hundreds of devoted writers—many of them prominent, others not so well known; but each, to the extent of his or her ability, depicting some brilliantly conceived facet of the desert's romantic story.

Over the long years of close, personal contact with the desert, both as its guest and its resident, I have visited and explored many of the areas described in the books listed in this volume. In common with other desert lovers I have witnessed ancient landmarks vanish from the land. Much of the desert I once knew and loved has been submerged by the inexorable encroachment of the thing we loosely refer to as "civilization." Desert plants and animals are retreating before the inevitable deluge of homes and towns and industries, else they are being crushed by its unrelenting pressure.

Happily, the quiet, restful land that is so rapidly losing its physical character shall remain enshrined in the writings of these dedicated men and women whose creative interpretations are recorded in this book. Because of them the land and its memories shall forever live vibrantly within our minds and hearts—a viable, *enduring* desert.

E. I. EDWARDS

Foreword

BY RUSS LEADABRAND

THE DESERTS of California are a personal experience. Few people pass through them without some sort of positive comment. Some people are frightened by the desert, are uncomfortably awed by the open spaces, the great wash of wind, the towering sky.

Others exult in the room-enough. They find the desert a restoring domain, its distances reassuring, its muted colors stimulating, its silences satisfying.

I have long favored the deserts of California. I have probed their mysteries and have answered some of the come-and-look challenges of lost communities and forgotten mines. In seeking comrades in interest I found, through a book, E. I. Edwards.

The book was *Desert Voices*, an heroic bibliography of California desert literature. By reading this happy book it was possible to discover more about desert people, places and events than had ever been my luck before. I was enchanted with the book and was determined to meet the author and put questions—I had an endless list of them—to the man.

Desert Voices, I learned in short order, was not Edwards' first effort at desert bibliography. Before, in 1940, Edwards had offered the privately printed *The Valley Whose Name is Death*, a book devoted to the people involved in the tragic Death Valley struggle of 1849. The book also contained a large section on Death Valley literature. It was the first book of its kind and Edwards had every right to be proud of the kind things that collectors and desert buffs said about the book.

Then in 1948, a slimmer book, *Desert Treasure*, contained the basic germ of the idea for *Desert Voices*, a bibliography of Death Valley and general California desert items.

All three of the desert bibliographies went quickly out of print.

Edwards, as I discovered in those planned question and answer sessions, is a thorough and dedicated man. Even as *Desert Voices* was coming off the press he was mentally listing items that should have been in the book but weren't. Magazine articles, ephemera, lesser known works in some cases had to be left out. And there was more basic spade work to do, more desert to explore, more books to study. Edwards, now semi-retired from his demanding business activities, devoted more and more time to the challenge. He moved from Pasadena to Arcadia, finally to Yucca Valley, taking with him his incredible library. All the while he was listing new items, meeting new desert authors, talking, studying, writing.

Other books appeared with the Edwards byline. There was *Lost Oases Along the Carrizo*, a book about a southern desert puzzle that long intrigued the researcher. And there was a detailed bibliography in *Lost Oases*. *Desert Harvest* was a bibliography of a handful of special desert books that Edwards had high regard for. He wrote a stunning article, *The Mystery of Death Valley's Lost Wagon Train*, for the Westerner's Brand Book that I edited in 1964. He found time for other writing, playing with historic and geographic puzzles. But always the "new, big bibliography" was there on his desk, demanding his attention more and more.

I had no idea that the project was coming to fruition until 1966. Then Edwards, during one of the pleasant meetings we had when he came in from the desert, indicated that he was putting the big book together. In 1967 I had the opportunity to read the manuscript. It was big, but more than that, it was as close as you could come to offering a definitive desert bibliography.

Edwards, in a monumental effort, had combed out all the books, booklets, pamphlets, magazine articles, newspaper clippings, on the California desert and had put them together in a meaningful manner. He had commented on almost every one of these items, assigning it its place in the pageant of desert history and folklore, comparing this with that, relating this journal with that diary, attaching importance to this desert character, always with a central point of view.

Edwards is emphatic about the history that he reads. He dislikes sloppy history, he abhors historians who spend all their time in their typing chairs.

Now the big bibliography has become a book. It will not only stand out as a monument to E. I. Edwards, but it will indicate a high water mark in that special kind of book, the personal bibliography.

"A bibliography in the back of a book that contains no comments about the books listed means nothing," Edwards told me once. Readers will have no such complaint to make here. They will find *The Enduring Desert* a rich and satisfying desert experience. There is material here for a hundred monologs on desert history, folklore and traditions; enough material for dozens of magazine articles; endless newspaper items. There are other books that *The Enduring Desert* suggests. The book is a wellspring.

What after this?

"I'm all written out," Edwards confessed as he handed me the bulky manuscript of *The Enduring Desert*. Don't believe it. There are endless little puzzles and mysteries that have long piqued Edwards' fancy. There will be more articles and books from his desert-anchored typewriter.

You'll find a large number of old friends in *The Enduring Desert*. I counted many. Randall Henderson, the editor of *Desert Magazine* during its earlier days. Harold and Lucile Weight, they of the encyclopedic desert memories (and who write now all too little). Nell Murbarger, the delightful lady who makes ghost town exploring a lark. George Koenig, whose books and articles are all too few.

Students of desert history will find all the classic works listed here, and more. The listing of the articles of Philip Johnston suggests a Johnston book —nothing less.

Font, Anza, Williamson, Frémont, Walker, Manly, the names march off into the Zane Grey sunset that the old master painted for us so many times.

It is pleasant to think back and recall incidents along the birth of this, the big book. Edwards' enthusiasm is endless; he has often come to a meeting with enough enthusiasm to supply the two of us before the evening was over, to send me back to my less important writing chores all fired up with purpose and dedication.

His enthusiasm leaks out of many pages of the book. How else could you write such a giant?

Go now and enjoy *The Enduring Desert*. Read it at leisure as you would savor a fine wine or a rich steak. You'll find the rewards are without number.

Part One

BIBLIOGRAPHICAL SECTION

The Enduring Desert

— ✣ —

ADAMS, ANSEL

Death Valley. (See listing under Newhall, Nancy)

ADAMS, KENNETH C. (Edited by)

California Highways and Public Works. 1950. Sacramento. Centennial Edition. 168 pp. 8½ x 11. Replete with illus. Wrappers.

Of desert interest, in this account of the development of the State's highway system, are the following:

    Ch. 4, pp. 14-20, Anza Opens First Overland Route. (Alice F. Simpson.)

    Ch. 8, Part 2, pp. 39-41, Emigrant Trails of '49—Southern Route. (Alice F. Simpson.)

    Ch. 14, pp. 109-113, California Highways. (J. D. Gallagher.)

In the Gallagher article is a brief account of the highway program in Death Valley, including some discussion of the interesting old Eichbaum Toll Road. In this same section, reference is made to the wooden plank road across the Algodones Sand Dunes over the Yuma Sand Hills in Imperial County.

ADLER, PAT and WHEELOCK, WALT

Walker's R. R. Routes—1853. 1965. Glendale, California: La Siesta Press. 64 pp. 9 illus. 3 maps. Limited to 1000 copies. 5⅝ x 8⅝.

The book prints Captain Joseph Walker's "Statement" before the Senate Committee on Public Lands on March 24, 1853 regarding proposed routes for a railroad, most of them through Walker's Pass and east across the Mojave.

ADMIRAL, DON

Desert of the Palms. 1938. El Centro (now at Palm Desert), California: Desert Magazine Press. 55 pp. 25 pls. 5¼ x 8. Fldg. map of desert.

———

All books listed and evaluated in this Bibliography are in their first edition unless otherwise indicated.

Among other topics of interest, Mr. Admiral writes of the Colorado Desert's palms, its Indians, the Palm Springs-Indio Road, Palms to Pines Highway, Salton Sea, Carrizo Creek, Borrego Valley, Imperial Valley, Shrubs, Cacti, Wildflowers, Birds, Mammals, and Reptiles.

Palm Springs Desert Area and Vicinity. N.d. Palm Springs, California: *The Desert Sun.* 31 pp. Wrappers. 16 illus.

This is a booklet of carefully-assembled material on the desert in and around Palm Springs.

ADOLPH, E. F. and ASSOCIATES

Physiology of Man In the Desert—Survival In An Arid Land. 1947. New York: Interscience Publishers Inc. 357 pp.

"An exhaustive study of problems . . . of food and clothing in high temperatures, of stamina and training—of actual survival in lands of excessive heat and little water."

AIKEN, CHARLES S.

Surprise of the Desert, The. 1908. September issue of *Sunset.*

This is an early article on the Imperial Valley, with 23 pls., 1 map, and 1 full-page color illustration.

AIKEN, EDNAH

River, The. N.d. From reference given.

This reference is taken from Margaret Romer's *History of Calexico.* Of this item she says, "Its scenes are laid in Calexico and at the gap in the banks of the Colorado River. The book was written to idealize Mr. Cory, much to the indignation of Mr. Rockwood's friends. While not historically accurate, the book gives a very true presentation of early life, customs, and conditions in the town of Calexico in the early days. Mr. Cory is idealized in the leading part as 'Richard.' Mr. Rockwood is cruelly and unjustly characterized as the unsuccessful engineer called, in the story, 'Tom Hardin.' The other characters are all taken from life."

AINSWORTH, EDWARD MADDIN

Beckoning Desert. (1962.) New Jersey: Prentice-Hall, Inc. Illus. by Bill Bender. 264 pp. 6¼ x 9¼.

"Each man," writes Ainsworth, "saw the desert in his own way—and each translated its message for himself." Translations of the desert may vary significantly, but in their basic concepts they separate logically into two major group-classifications. One group envisions the desert as a vast playground, vibrant with the atmosphere created by plush night clubs, luxurious hotels, elaborate golf courses. To them the desert is a glorified fun-land spread rakishly beneath a clear desert sky. Ainsworth's book should commend itself to this group of desert lovers.

In fact, it would appear that Ainsworth chooses to identify himself with this group. "One thing," he writes, "impresses me more than any other. This is the desert's infinite capacity for providing the right setting at the right time for man's utilization of its resources and potentials. . . . As the eyes of millions from all around the world turned toward the California Desert, the importance of its contributions to a modern way of better living became more and more apparent."

The other group—those who are not so favorably impressed by these encroachments with their "contributions to a modern way of better living"—prefer a *virgin* desert, one that retains its *natural* beauty and rewards its visitors with the joy of *quiet* living. Moreover, these dedicated desert lovers steadfastly refuse to believe these "contributions" represent a "way of better living." A "modern" way, perhaps, and admittedly a *different* way; but not, as our popular author informs, a "better" way.

It may well be, then, that Ainsworth—with his choppy, single-sentence paragraphs and his melodramatic interludes—will have some appeal for the first group; rather less for the second group.

Much that the author has to tell has been told before; but Ed Ainsworth perhaps tells it better than most in this book. He knows his deserts and he knows how to write; although I doubt if he reflects the intimacy, in his writing, that he professes to share with his "beckoning desert." Possibly some will consider that he slants his book too generously toward Palm Springs, Palm Desert, and the Salton Sea, at the expense of other desert areas that are also "beckoning."

Eagles Fly West. 1946. New York: The Macmillan Company. 447 pp. 8⅝ x 5⅞.

This book, a novel, is based upon the engagement of Kearny's Army of the West with the Californians under Andrés Pico at the Battle of San Pasqual.

Five Acres of Heaven. 1955. Los Angeles: Lithographed by Homer H. Boelter. Wrappers. 30 numbered pp. 8 unnumbered. 6¾ x 10. Cover design and 46 illus. Also a reproduction, in color, of John W. Hilton's beautiful oil painting—"Joshua Tree Country."

This descriptive brochure of the High Desert country (Morongo, Yucca Valley, Joshua Tree and Twentynine Palms) is a generous presentation issue by Colonel and Mrs. E. B. Moore—who invested time and energy in locating homesteaders on "Five Acres of Heaven."

Golden Checkerboard. Ca. 1965 (no date shows in my Deluxe Edition). Palm Desert, California: Desert-Southwest, Inc. 195 pp. 100 numbered deluxe copies published in addition to the regular edition. 13 illus. 6¼ x 9¼.

Golden Checkerboard relates the tragic experiences of a small band of Agua Caliente Indians who occupied an area that, until recently, was a spread of barren desert sand surrounding some age-old hot springs at the base of Mt. San Jacinto. It describes the paradoxical predicament of this isolated group of Indians who were nearly destitute of even the basic necessities of life, yet were privileged to compute their actual monetary wealth in terms of millions of dollars.

Far back in 1876, during President Grant's administration, and more than fifty years before the region now known as Palm Springs held attraction for any considerable number of white men, the government granted alternate sections (640 acres each) of what was then worthless desert to this one small band of Indians.

However, although the Indians were technically the owners of these alternate sections, the land was held in trust for them by the federal government. They could not sell it; they could not lease it except for short-term periods that offered no possible inducement for development. To complicate an already deplorable situation, one of these alternate sections (Section 14) sprawled its unsightly squalor across the very heart of the plush desert region of Palm Springs. No paved roads penetrated it; to get from one segment of the city to another, it was necessary to drive completely around this unattractive square mile of Indian land.

Ainsworth describes the long, seemingly endless period of litigation that finally resulted in the break-through permitting the city to acquire by purchase the present airport section (Section 18) and to permit the Indians to grant long-term leases, and right-of-ways for improved roads, through Section 14—the mile-long eastern border of Indian Avenue. A further result of this break-through was to enrich the Indians. Ainsworth states that one little six-year old girl received $284,749.20 for her share of the airport section; other owners averaged $95,000 apiece. In addition, all members of the tribe receive perpetual income from leasehold rentals in Section 14.

It's an absorbing story Ainsworth tells; and an informative one.

Painters of the Desert. 1960. Palm Desert, California: Desert Magazine and Desert Printers, Inc. (printers). 111 pp. Foreword by Carl Schaeffer Dentzel. Has gone into reprint editions. 10 x 13½.

This is a gorgeous, delightful book. It is too lovely to be hidden from view in a bookcase; too precious to place carelessly where the unappreciative can get their hands on it. For *Painters of the Desert* is not for those who have failed to develop an understanding and appreciation of the beautiful.

Ed Ainsworth has brought out an enduring desert masterpiece in this attractive work. Thirteen notable artists, distinguished not alone by the quality of their work but by their innate knowledge of the desert, are selected to illustrate the book: Maynard Dixon, Clyde Forsythe, Jimmie Swinnerton, Nicolai Fechin, Carl Eytel, Paul Lauritz, Conrad Buff, Orpha Klinker, Don Louis Perceval, John Hilton, Bert Proctor, R. Brownell McGrew, and Bill Bender. Mr. Ainsworth has prepared an interpretive background sketch of each artist; numerous black and white illustrations and a dozen color plates illustrate the work.

Assuredly, one cannot find fault with Ainsworth's inclusion of these thirteen noted artists; but, like the books omitted from a bibliography, his omission of certain of our own personal favorites is bound to bring criticism. But it is Ed Ainsworth's book, and his is the privilege to include or omit as he thinks best.

ALBERT, HERMAN W.

Odyssey of a Desert Prospector. 1967. Norman: University of Oklahoma Press. The Western Frontier Library edition. 260 pp. 5¼ x 7¾.

The brief and unimportant mention of Death Valley Scotty and his castle (pp. 221-224) affords opportunity to call attention to this intelligently-written account of a prospector's colorful experiences in Nevada during the early 1900s. I would accord this book high rating among the books relating to Nevada's latter day mining boom. Beyond any doubt, it is one of the most entertaining books in my entire Nevada collection.

ALDRICH, LORENZO D.

Journal of the Overland Route to California & the Gold Mines, A. 1950. Los Angeles: Glen Dawson. 93 pp. 5½ x 8⅛. Fldg. pocket map. 330 copies.

The *Journal* was originally printed in 1851 by Alexander Kirkpatrick of Troy, New York. Mr. Glen Dawson indicates there are only three known originals. The chapter entitled—"Crossing the Gila River" (pp. 57-65) details the 1849 crossing of the Colorado Desert, and Aldrich was among the emigrants who followed this Southern route to the goldfields. His brief but illuminating account is one of the most delightful of the overland diaries.

Mr. Dawson has prepared and included in this volume a useful bibliography (pp. 87-93), listing some twenty-five diaries of emigrants traveling the Gila River Valley route to California.

ALEXANDER, J. A.

Life of George Chaffey, The: A Story of Irrigation Beginnings in California and Australia. 1928. Melbourne: The Macmillan Company, XV, 382 pp. Fldg. map and 6 page maps. 38 illus. 5¾ x 8¾.

Chaffey was one of the active participants in the Imperial Valley reclamation project. Ch. 20—"The Desert" (pp. 270-284), Ch. 21—"The Desert Conquered" (pp. 285-300), and Ch. 22—"The Master Builder" (pp. 301-312) have a direct bearing upon Imperial Valley. H. T. Cory contributes chapter 22, "The Master Builder."

ALTERGOTT, ALEXANDER

Economic History of the Valley of the Mohaves, etc. 1930. Los Angeles: University of Southern California, 132 pp.

"A history of the Colorado River Basin from the time of the aboriginal inhabitants to the present day. Included is an account of the origin and development of the town of Needles." (*From California Local History. A Centennial Bibliography.*)

AMERICAN POTASH & CHEMICAL CORPORATION

Story of the American Potash & Chemical Corporation. (1933.) One of the early issues of this illustrated brochure of the big chemical plant at Trona, on Searles Lake, in the Mojave Desert. 25 pp. 22 pls. 6¼ x 9¼. Wrappers. Successive editions (1935, 1937, and forward) have been issued, showing indicated revisions of content.

These booklets explain the manufacturing processes involved, together with the company's history and development. Some descriptive comment on the surrounding desert region is included.

ANDERSON, JEAN C.

Pacific Railroad Survey In California, The. July-December, 1853. 1948. September issue of the *Historical Society of Southern California Quarterly*.

This 18-page article should be read by one unfamiliar with the Railroad Surveys Program before he ventures into the original 13-vol. Survey Reports. It will give him an intelligent idea of what they are all about. Those desiring to limit their study to the surveys conducted in our Southwest desert areas will perhaps wish to confine their research to the major survey program supervised by Whipple and the one under the leadership of Williamson. Between them, the Mojave and Colorado deserts were quite thoroughly covered. Lt. Williamson, in particular, is worthy of study. He was under orders from the Secretary of War to conduct an independent survey within the State of California. Actually, it operated almost entirely in Southern California. The instant item will open the door of understanding to the characters, purposes and routes involved in the surveys.

ANONYMOUS

Beaumont, Formerly San Gorgonio. What Is It? Where Is It? (1886.) Published by the Southern California Investment Co. Los Angeles: Times Mirror. Illus. Fldg. map with text. (From Glen Dawson.)

Coachella Valley—The Key to Plants and Places of Interest. 1951. Indio, California: Date Palm Print Shop. 67 pp. 2 maps. 14 pls. Line drawings. 6⅛ x 9⅛. Wrappers.

This is a brochure, prepared by the Nature Study classes of the Coachella Valley Evening High School, with the arrangement of text designed for use in study courses.

Death Valley National Monument, Your Pictorial Guide. 1963. A Colour-picture Publication. Wrappers.

Some fifty colored photos (including the covers) are contained in this very attractive booklet. Brief, running comment and titles identify the pictures.

Death Valley Scotty's Castle. (1941.) Goldfield, Nevada: Castle Publishing Co. Wrappers. 75 pp. Illus. 6 x 8¼.

Perhaps no other publication gives so detailed an account of the castle's construction and its appointments.

Desert Cure, A. 1909. May issue of *Sunset*, this item being in reprint form. Pp. 517-524. 4 pls.

This is an account, duly authenticated by physicians, of a man who effected a cure for Bright's disease while living on the desert at Palm Springs. The item assumes some importance by depicting the initial stages of the development of Palm Springs.

(P. : : : : : : C.) *Early Freighting on the Salt Lake-San Bernardino Trail. 1853-1854.*

Appeared originally in the *Los Angeles Star* of February 18, 1854; later reprinted in the *Pacific Historical Review*, XI (March, 1942); in 1947 appeared as Appendix No. 1 in William B. Rice's *The Los Angeles Star*. (See listing under Rice, Wm. B. —*The Los Angeles Star*.)

The article consists of extracts from the Journal of P. : : : : : : C., describing a trip from Salt Lake to San Bernardino by the Reese brothers' caravan during the winter of 1853-1854. The train consisted of 24 wagons and 80 or 90 head of stock. Its purpose was to return with a supply of dry goods and groceries for the establishments in the Utah territory. The party encountered considerable trouble from the Indians and suffered heavy casualties among the live stock.

On their return trip the caravan pioneered a new cut-off and, as a consequence, fared badly. S. N. Carvalho, artist with the Frémont Expedition, met and described this returning caravan. (See listing under Carvalho, S. N.—*Incidents of Travel and Adventure*, etc.)

History of Old Government Road Across the Mojave Desert to the Colorado River, Including the Prehistoric. N.d. San Bernardino County Board of Supervisors. Duplicated. Cloth bound. LXV original full page photos, bound in, most of them signed by Walter Fiss. 4 blueprint maps, 3 of them folded. Brief bibl. Appendix with excerpts from Steward, Rogers, Whipple, Thompson, Van Dyke, Coues, and others.

Many of the photos are of petroglyphs in Newberry Mountains. Others are of petroglyphs in the vicinity of Piute Springs. (From Harold and Lucile Weight.)

Imperial Valley: 1901-1915. (1915.) Los Angeles: Kingsley, Mason and Collins Co. Wrappers. 32 pp. 5 x 7¾. 34 illus.

This is an early advertising medium extolling the wonders of the Imperial Valley, and tracing its development over a period of fourteen years. Harold Bell Wright contributes one of the two short descriptive articles. Mostly, however, the booklet is given over to its illustrations.

Inyo County, California (Inyo The Peerless). N.d. (ca. 1908.) Owens Valley Herald Print Shop. Copyrighted by Inyo Mines Syndicate. Pages not numbered. Double-page map of "Inyo County Cal. and Some Adjacent Territory." Nearly 100 interesting—and early—photographs. Decorative wrappers.

This is an early, scarce and much sought-after item. In addition to Owens Valley material, mention is made of Death Valley, Cerro Gordo, Bodie, Greenwater, Skidoo, and—in Nevada—Goldfield, Bullfrog, Manhattan, Round Mountain and Rawhide. An interesting article on Greenwater is included, authored by C. E. Kunze. Worth mentioning is the early photo of Skidoo.

Inyo County 1866-1966. 1966. Inyo County Board of Supervisors. 95 pp. Some 150 photographs and drawings. Wrappers.

Articles are authored by Dorothy C. Cragen, C. Lorin Ray, and others. Of more than passing importance, desertwise, is the article by Richard C. Datin, Jr., on "The Carson and Colorado R.R."

Joshua Tree. N.d. 9 pp. (unnumbered.) 15 photographs. Line drawings. Map. Pictorial wrappers.

This very attractive little booklet was either published or sponsored by the Joshua Tree Townsite Co., probably—judging from the photographs—in 1946; definitely not earlier. Three pages are given over to a description, both in text and photographs, of the Joshua Tree National Monument. Paper, photographs and text are of excellent quality.

Life of John Searles. 1906. San Francisco.

Credit for mention of this book goes to L. Burr Belden of San Bernardino. In a recent letter Mr. Belden writes: "This biography was printed in San Francisco and was at the binders when the great fire destroyed the entire edition. Six copies are said to have been given pre-publication distribution, largely to members of the Searles family in Oakland or vicinity. A former executive of the American Potash & Chemical Corporation at Trona told me of the work and had been allowed to read hurriedly a part of it. This was in 1944." Mr. Belden says further that the descendants of Mr. Searles, thus far contacted, have no knowledge of the book's existence.

Old Woman Springs. 1947. July-August issue of *The Desert Spotlight,* Illus.

This article is reprinted from the *Desert Grapevine,* Lucerne Valley, and is descriptive of the historic old desert ranch of Lucerne.

Sketches From the Journal of a Traveler, Overland to California. (See listing under Bieber, Ralph P.—*Southern Trails to California.*)

Story of Death Valley, Its Museum and Visitor Center. (1960.) Death Valley '49ers, Inc. 30 pp. 14 illus. Wrappers.

Horace M. Albright writes on "Creation of the Death Valley National Monument." Other articles included are: "The Death Valley '49ers, Inc.", "California's Share—A Gift To All the People", "The National Park Service In Death Valley."

Three Health Resorts. 1899. December issue of *Sunset.*

This early article, illustrated with two photographic plates, discusses Beaumont, Banning and Palm Springs in the days of their infancy.

ANTISELL, THOMAS

Geological Report. 1857. Washington, D.C. Vol. VII, *Pacific Railroad Surveys* assembled during the years 1853-1856. 8 colored lithographic pls.

Ch. 18—"Geology of the District from San Diego to Fort Yuma" (pp. 119-129), also Ch. 15—"Mohave River Valley" (pp. 97-106), have a direct bearing upon our California desert areas. Noteworthy are the careful descriptions given of the important watering places known as Alamo Mocho (or Mucho) and Cooke's Well, as recorded sometime between 1853 and 1856, or from eight to ten years after the initial passages of Kearny and Cooke. Again, as in Vol. V of the *Pacific Railroad Surveys,* a vague but certain reference is made to the High Desert country. (See listing under *Pacific Railroad Surveys.*)

ANZA, JUAN BAUTISTA DE, et al. (Edited by Bolton, H. E.)

Anza's California Expeditions. 1775-1776. (5 vol.) 1930. Berkeley: Univ. of California Press. Pls. Maps. Facsimiles. 6¼ x 9⅞. Each book contains approximately 500 pp. A Zamorano 80 item.

"A narrative of deep human interest, and profound significance. It brings together in one picture the pioneer work of soldier, missionary and colonist. It tells of the opening of a route of travel across the California mountains three quarters of a century ahead of the Forty-Niners."

Included in this important work are the diaries of Anza, Garcés, Díaz, Eixarch, Font and Palóu; likewise the narratives of Palóu and Maraga. One of the five volumes contains Dr. Bolton's introduction. Father Font's complete *Diary* (also published separately) occupies all of Vol. 4.

Captain Anza first crossed the Imperial Valley in 1774. Two priests (Garcés and Díaz), twenty soldiers, and perhaps ten others accompanied him on this first expedition which arrived at the San Gabriel Mission after 73 days travel. On his second expedition, in 1775-6, de Anza crossed with 240 men, women and children; 695 horses, mules and burros, and 355 head of cattle. Father Font was priest of the expedition.

Also published separately from the 5 vol. set is Vol. 1, appearing under the title —*Outpost of Empire.* (See listing under Bolton, Dr. Herbert Eugene.)

ANZA, JUAN BAUTISTA and FONT, FATHER PEDRO

An Early California Christmas: 1775. N.d. (1956.) Los Angeles: Homer H. Boelter. 40 pp. 9 x 9. End paper decorative maps and full color illustrations on every page. Each page over-printed upon a facsimile of the original Anza and Font diaries. Wrappers. Narrative by Lindley Bynum; decorations by Don Louis Perceval.

This attractive booklet is a masterpiece of the printer's craftsmanship and the designer's art. Displayed upon its pages is the record of an important historical enactment destined to become the opening scene in our far-flung drama of the California deserts.

ARCHER, FRED R.

In the Canyon of Red Rocks. 1925. February issue of *Touring Topics.* Illus.

This is one of the best descriptive articles presently available upon these picturesque formations. The Jayhawkers, Brier and Manly-Bennett parties of Death Valley fame are believed, by most authorities on the subject, to have passed through this spectacular canyon of the red rocks now traversed by the Bishop highway.

Monuments of the Gods. 1926. December issue of *Touring Topics.* Illus.

Here is an article, of more than transitory interest, relating to the area presently designated as the Joshua Tree National Monument. In the reading of it we miss the now-familiar names of "Yucca Valley" and "Joshua Tree." These thriving desert towns did not exist in 1926 when this early account was written. Instead we read of such vaguely-remembered locations as "Warren's Ranch and Warren's Well, where the staunch old teamster of the Chuckawalla Trail settled down to rest, and years ago wrested a ranch from the desert ground."

ARMIJO, ANTONIO

Diary: 1829-1830. 1947. San Marino: *Huntington Library Quarterly.* Vol. II, pp. 87-101. A translation of the original Spanish diary, with notes by L. R. Hafen. In Hafen's *The Old Spanish Trail* (1954).

Armijo's Expedition left Abiquiu November 7, 1829, arriving at San Gabriel January 31, 1830. Armijo transported goods from Mexico into California via the Old Spanish Trail.

ARNOLD, ADELAIDE WILSON

Son of the First People, A. 1940. New York: The Macmillan Company. 248 pp. Illus. 6 x 8¼.

This descriptive novel provides "a lively, vigorous adventure story and a fine picture of present day Indians," by the gifted author from Twentynine Palms. These "present day Indians" are the Cahuillas, about whom relatively little has been written.

ARNOLD, H. H.

Who Drew These Giants Along the Colorado? 1932. November *Touring Topics.*

These mysterious figures, discovered by an aviator flying over the desert region some 20 miles north of Blythe, are located just off Highway 95 within an area of about three square miles. The design of the several figures is not readily discernible except from the air. Three of these picture areas are now enclosed by protective fencing and may be conveniently located by a highway marker.

AUBREY, FRANCOIS XAVIER

Diary. (See listing under Bieber, Dr. Ralph P.—*Exploring Southwest Trails.*)

AUBURY, LEWIS E. (State Mineralogist)

Copper Resources of California. 1908. Sacramento: California State Mining Bureau No. 50. 366 pp. 75 pls. 11 fldg. maps. 6¼ x 9.

Pp. 298-346 are descriptive of mines in desert areas—Mono, Inyo, San Bernardino, Riverside, San Diego, and Los Angeles counties. Pp. 317-324, bearing upon the Greenwater activity, are of primary importance in their relationship to early desert history. Greenwater, a once-boisterous town on the eastern rim of Death Valley, has now completely vanished.

AUDUBON, JOHN WOODHOUSE

Audubon's Western Journal: 1849-1850. Being the MS. Record of a Trip from New York to Texas, and an Overland Journey Through Mexico and Arizona to the Gold-fields of California. 1906. Cleveland: The Arthur H. Clark Company. Introduction, Notes and Index by Frank Heywood Hodder. 249 pp. Fldg. map. Portrait of Audubon. Reproductions of 5 of Audubon's drawings. 6½ x 9¾.

The work originally appeared in 1852, published in New York by the author under the title *Illustrated Notes of an Expedition Through Mexico and California in 1849-50.* There were 48 pp. with 4 colored reproductions from the author's drawings. (Cowan P. 8; Wagner-Camp No. 208.) Says Cowan: "This work is excessively rare, not more than four or five copies being known to exist. Part 1 was all that appeared. It was issued in two styles—with plain and with colored plates." Part I was reprinted in 1915 by W. Abbott in 83 pp. and with the four plates much reduced. The *Journal* is partially reprinted in Valeska Bari's *Course of Empire.*

Most of Audubon's drawings and many of his notes were lost at sea, en route to New York. Some 37 of the drawings and several of his note books were mailed direct and, fortunately, arrived at their destination. The Southwest Museum came into possession of 34 of these most valuable drawings and, in 1957, the Book Club of California published them in a limited edition of 400 copies—beautifully done by the Grabhorn Press. The drawings are illustrative of passages in the *Journal,* and two or three relate to desert scenes.

The Audubon *Journal* contributes but little material that is directly associated with the California desert territory. Indirectly, however, it supplies an abundance of factual data on the 1849 gold rush movement via the Southern route, with its intimate descriptions of the emigrants congregated along the Colorado and Gila rivers.

Mystery has shrouded the unfortunate circumstances attending the Audubon expedition; but it is stated that cholera caused the death of a very considerable number of its personnel. Certainly there was gross mismanagement of the expedition; assuredly many of its number exhibited mental, physical or social incapacity for the rigorous undertaking. Jeanne Skinner Van Nostrand's article— *Audubon's Ill-fated Western Journey,* appearing in the December 1952 issue of the *California Historical Society Quarterly,* quotes from the *Diary of Jacob Henry Bachman,* a member of Audubon's group. This revealing paper sheds much light upon the Audubon expedition and its abstruse history. (See listing in this Bibliography.)

AULT, PHIL

This Is the Desert. (1959.) New York: Dodd, Mead & Company. Illus. by Leonard Everett Fisher. 175 pp. 6¼ x 9⅜.

Although a book written mainly for young people, *This Is the Desert* can be recommended to anyone in any age group who wishes to gain a comprehensive knowledge and a panoramic view of the desert and the desert's historic episodes.

AUSTIN, CARL F.

Coso Hot Springs—A Guide to Geology in Action. 1963. China Lake, California: The Maturango Museum, Inc. Publication No. 1, 21 pp. 4 illus. Charts. Location map showing access roads to the Coso Hot Springs Area. Wrappers.

The little booklet gives a Road Log covering the distance from China Lake to the Coso Hot Springs. This is not merely a mileage scale, but an interesting, descriptive narrative of each separate portion of the route. One section of the book is given over to a discussion of the Devil's Kitchen. The book reminds us that the Coso Hot Springs region lies within the restricted range areas of the United States Naval Weapons Center and can be entered by visitors only upon express permission.

Flock, The. 1906. Cambridge: Houghton, Mifflin and Company. Illustrated by E. Boyd Smith. 266 pp. Illus. 5¾ x 8¼. In its first state the publication date appears on the title page and corresponds with the copyright date.

The item presents a narrative of the sheep in California. In this book, as in her incomparable *Land of Little Rain*, Mary Austin writes charmingly, and in her own individual style. The flock, the herder, the dogs, the predators, the land itself —all are depicted in absorbing detail. In particular, the chapters on "The Flock" and on "Liers-In-Wait" are most delightfully done. The book—all of it—is an imperishable classic of the desert; make no mistake about this. A desert collection, to be at all adequate, must not omit *The Flock*.

Land of Little Rain, The. 1903. New York: Houghton, Mifflin and Company. XI, 282 pp. 6⅝ x 8⅝. Illustrated by E. Boyd Smith. Dark green cloth, with marginal sepia illustrations which appear both in the original and in several of the reprint editions. Subsequent editions of the same size and color designate the number of the reprint. Later editions have appeared in various sizes and colors. The true first shows the 1903 date on the title page.

Surely no one will urge denial to the assertion that *The Land of Little Rain* ranks among the all-time *great* books on California, and is an acknowledged classic of the desert. It was included, and properly so, among the Zamorano 80 listings. There are 14 tales in this book, all told in Mary Austin's inimitable style. Her locale is, as she describes it, "The country . . . between the high Sierras south from Yosemite—east and south over a very great assemblage of broken ranges beyond Death Valley, and on illimitably into the Mohave Desert."

The lasting appeal of *The Land of Little Rain* abides not so much in what the author tells as in the eloquent beauty she employs in the telling of it. As an example of her exemplary style, and her penetrant knowledge of the desert she describes, we read this passage from her first included story: "For all the toll the desert takes of a man it gives compensation, deep breaths, deep sleep, and the communion of the stars. It comes upon one with new force in the pauses of the night that the Chaldeans were a desert-bred people. It is hard to escape the sense of mastery as the stars move in the wide clear heavens to risings and settings unobserved. They look large and near and palpitant; as if they moved on some stately service not needful to declare. Wheeling to their stations in the sky, they make the poor world-fret of no account. Of no account you who lie out there watching, nor the lean coyote that stands off in the scrub from you and howls and howls."

Other great desert books have approached, but never quite captured, the peculiar charm of the Austin masterpiece. John C. Van Dyke's *The Desert* (1901) and Ida Strobridge's *In Miners' Mirage Land* (1904) nearly accomplished it; Miss Austin herself came pleasantly close to it in another of her fine desert writings— *The Flock* (1906).

There are fourteen desert tales included, the locale for most—but not all—of them being the Owens Valley country. Among the best are "Water Trails of the Cariso" and "The Scavengers."

Lost Borders. 1909. New York: Harper & Brothers. 209 pp. 7 illus. 5 x 7½.

This is a collection of 14 delightful tales of the desert by the one perhaps most gifted among those who write stories of our "silent land."

One-Smoke Stories. 1934. Cambridge: The Riverside Press. 295 pp. 5 x 7½.

Although these stories do not represent Mary Austin either at her best or even her near best, the book does bring us the atmosphere of the desert and—on occasion —the incomparable charm of Mary Austin. Including her introduction, there are forty of these desert tales. They are interesting, some of them; but the reader must never base judgment of Mary Austin upon the quality of these "One-Smoke" stories.

BACHMAN, JACOB HENRY (Edited by Van Nostrand, Jeanne S.)

Diary. 1942-December and 1943-March issues of *California Historical Quarterly*.

This article records the Audubon party's crossing of the Colorado Desert in October, 1849. Bachman, a member of this group, assists in clarifying the reasons for the many disasters attending Audubon on his overland journey to California.

BAGLEY, MRS. FRANK

Homestead Store. 1947. April issue of *The Desert Spotlight*. Illus.

The Bagleys came to the Twentynine Palms Oasis in 1927, a notably early year for settlers in the High Desert country, and established their pioneer market. This is the story of their experience—a story rich in material relating to early days of desert living.

BAILEY, DAVID

Llano's Withered Dream. 1963. May issue of *Desert*.

Capably and entertainingly assembled is this brief history of Llano's "Cooperative City" located on what is now Mojave Highway 138, stretching east from Palmdale toward Victorville (a short distance west of the point where 138 angles off southeast to Cajon Pass). This cult community flourished—in a desultory fashion—between the years 1914 and 1918. Bailey mentions that, in its hey-day, this Utopian experiment "had more than 60 different enterprises, including a sawmill, machine shop, bakery, hotel (the large ruin just north of Highway 138 was the hotel), commissary, laundry, quarry and limekiln, cannery, soap factory, tannery, and fish hatchery." The Colony boasted of two newspapers, 100 milk cows, 70 workhorses, two steam tractors. Mr. Bailey tells the fascinating story in this well-researched article, and further enhances its value by the inclusion of ten photos—some taken in the days of the Colony's existence, others of present-day ruins. (See listing under Hine, Robert V.—*California's Utopian Colonies*, and Conkin, Paul K.—*Two Paths to Utopia*.)

BAILEY, GILBERT ELLIS

California—A Geologic Wonderland. 1924. Los Angeles: Times-Mirror Press. 119 pp. 4⅝ x 7⅜.

This book affords a sensible presentation of the geologic wonders of Death Valley and other desert localities, together with its coverage of non-desert areas over the state. Pp. 55-58 refer to "Death Valley"; pp. 59-62 to "Why the Desert?"; pp. 93-96 to "Coral Reefs in Our Desert;" and pp. 97-101 to "The Salton Sea."

Saline Deposits of California, The. 1902. Sacramento: California State Mining Bureau Bulletin. No. 24. 216 pp. 24 pls. 5 maps (folders). 5¾ x 9.

The bulletin contains a vast amount of data, much of it non-technical descriptive material on California desert areas, particularly concerning the region in and near Death Valley.

BAILEY, L. R. (Edited by)

A. B. Gray Report. (See listing under Gray, A. B.)

Sylvester Mowry's Report On His March In 1855—From Salt Lake City To Fort Tejon. (See listing under Mowry, Sylvester.)

BAILEY, PAUL

For This My Glory. 1940. Salt Lake City: Bookcraft Publishing Co. 336 pp. Has gone into five editions (this entry being from the fourth edition).

This is one of Paul Bailey's great Mormon novels—intense, appealing, vibrant with its historic lore. Here is a gripping, fictionized account of the famous Mormon Battalion in its notable desert trek and its subsequent participation in California activities. Here, too, is a sympathetic evaluation of the Mormon pioneer movement in its dramatic westward surge.

Paul Bailey, author of many brilliant publications, brings us in his *For This My Glory* an enduring masterpiece of historical fiction. It was the Mormon Battalion, following closely behind General Kearny's Army of the West, who brought the first wagons into California. Of all that has been written of the Battalion and its indomitable non-Mormon leader, Col. P. St. George Cooke, no other account—not even among the diaries and journals of the participants—so graphically and dramatically etches the spirit and purpose of this achievement.

Sam Brannan and the California Mormons. 1943. Los Angeles: Westernlore Press. Distributed by Bookcraft Co. Salt Lake City. Copyright 1942-1943 by *Improvement Era Magazine*, and featured serially by them and also by the *Millennial Star* in Great Britain. 187 pp. 5¾ x 8¼. Has gone into several revisions.

Besides considering the activities of Brannan in California, the book has much to offer on the history of the Mormons in San Bernardino, and of the activities of the Mormon Battalion and its aftermath in this State.

The "special printing and enlarged edition" of 1953 (263 pp.), together with its reprints, not only provide much additional material but show a marked improvement in both style and content. This, by conservative appraisal, is the definitive work on Samuel Brannan.

Slavers In the Mojave. 1964. *Westerners, The* (Los Angeles Corral) *Brand Book* No. 11. 15 pp. 2 illus.

Mr. Bailey has prepared, for this special article, a careful study of the famous

Indian chief Walkara's horse-stealing activities in California. Even more importantly, he defines the relationship of Pegleg Smith and James Beckwourth—"a pair
of trappers and mountain men, who were now emerging as two of the most infa-
mous opportunists ever to turn traitor to their kind"—to the notorious Indian war
chief.

The "modus operandi" of the thieving bands was to raid the ranches of the Californians, driving the stolen horses over Cajon Pass. Says Mr. Bailey, referring to
one of these raids: "For magnitude and sheer audacity there has never been anything comparable to that night's Walkara-Pegleg raid on the *rancheros* of Southern California. At least five thousand horses were sent thundering through Cajon
Pass—of which less than two thousand were recovered by the aroused and fighting
Californios."

BAILEY, PAUL and HOLMES, ROGER

Fabulous Farmer. 1956. Los Angeles: Westernlore Press. 184 pp. 5⅝ x 8⅛. 10,000
copies.

In this story of Walter Knott and his extraordinary achievement at the Berry
Farm, Paul Bailey has woven excellent descriptive material into his relation of
Knott's many years as a homesteader on the Mojave. The final chapter in the book
(pp. 171-184) is devoted to Knott's restoration of the famous old ghost town of
Calico which he purchased and reopened for the enjoyment of the public.

BAILEY, PHILIP

Golden Mirages. 1940. New York: The Macmillan Company. 353 pp. 24 pls. 5⅞
x 8⅝. Words "First Printing" appear under copyright notice. 8 maps. 1 treasure
map. 1 drawing. Has gone into several editions.

Here is a book that rivets one's attention all the way from the artistic dust wrapper to the conclusion of the last chapter. *Golden Mirages* is a classic in the realm of
lost-treasure tales. There is much interesting material on the Lost Pegleg mine,
the fabled Lost Ship of the Desert, and the Carrizo Corridor. The book becomes
more delightful upon each successive reading.

BAILEY, RICHARD C.

Explorations In Kern. 1959. Bakersfield, California. The twenty-second Annual
Publication of the Kern County Historical Society. 81 pp. 43 illus. 6⅛ x 9¼.

Chapters of special desert interest—or, perhaps more accurately, chapters cited
from among those in a book whose *every* chapter reflects desert interest—include:
Rand Area, Ft. Tejon, Willow Springs, and Bird Spring Pass. Although not clearly
reproduced, the illustrations possess special historic appeal. Mr. Bailey's "explorations" invite reading for pleasure, for reference, for a more knowledgeable
approach to the study of a County with a captivating historical heritage.

Red Rock Canyon. 1964. *Westerners, The* (Los Angeles Corral) *Brand Book* No. 11.
9 pp. 2 illus. 1 map.

Millions of motorists drive swiftly through Red Rock Canyon, the scenic attraction north of the town of Mojave. Only a fortunate few know the background history of this oddly-shaped and brilliantly colored cliff.

Mr. Bailey dates these formations far back into the Tertiary period. Historically, he draws an association between this area and the escaping Death Valley parties. Next (during the 1890's), he alludes to the mining activity in the vicinity. This is followed by the stockmen's era, later by the road building activity and the aqueduct construction. The canyon's appeal to rockhounds, Indian-lore enthusiasts, and archaeologists receives proper attention. Old-timers, including "Burro" Schmidt and Charley Koehn, come in for well-deserved mention.

BAILEY, VERNON (As told to ULLMAN, WILLIAM)

Into Death Valley 50 Years Ago. 1940. December issue of *Westways*. Illus.

Mr. Bailey, the biologist, was a member of the noted Death Valley expedition of 1890-91. This article is source material, and of primary importance.

BALES, LEROY and MARGARET

He Belongs to the Panamints. 1941. November issue of *Desert*. Illus. Map.

The author relates the story of Pete Auguerreberry and his mine on the site of the once fabulous Harrisburg. Pete was one of Death Valley's colorful characters.

They Never Locked the Door of the Jail at Ballarat. 1941. May issue of *Desert*. Illus. Map.

This is the story of the ghost town of Ballarat, and its renowned one-time citizen —Chris Wicht.

BALL, SYDNEY H.

Geologic Reconnaissance in Southwestern Nevada and Eastern California, A. 1907. U.S.G.S. Bull. No. 308, 218 pp. Wrappers.

An abundance of material is supplied in this early U.S. Geological Survey Bulletin relating to the geologic study of Death Valley and the Panamint Range (pp. 195-211).

BANCROFT, HUBERT HOWE

Guide to the Colorado Mines. 1933. March issue of *California Historical Society Quarterly*. Vol. XII. No. 1.

Bancroft published his *Guide* in 1863, and accompanied it by a map which is of considerable importance. Published originally in wrappers, with 16 pages of subject matter, the *Guide* confines itself to the routes of travel and distances, together with helpful comments regarding water and forage. Only a few copies of the original *Guide* are known to exist today. The *Quarterly* article reproduces the map and reprints the text with its tables of distances and its descriptions of the several stations along the Old Bradshaw Stage route from San Pedro to the Colorado River. Through San Gorgonio Pass and into the Colorado Desert, the stops are all described—Agua Blanco (Whitewater), Agua Caliente (Palm Springs), Sand Hole, Old Rancheria, Canyon Spring, Tabaseca Tanks, Chuckawalla Well, Mule Spring, and on to Bradshaw's Ferry.

History of the Pacific States. (39 vols.) 1882-91. A. L. Bancroft & Co. Contents: Vols. 1-5, Native Races; 6-8, Central America; 9-14, Mexico; 15-16, North American States and Texas; 17, Arizona and New Mexico; 18-24, California; 25, Nevada, Colorado and Wyoming; 26, Utah; 27-28, Northwest Coast; 29-30, Oregon; 31, Washington, Idaho, and Montana; 32, British Columbia; 33, Alaska; 34, California Pastoral; 35, California Inter Pocula; 36-37, Popular Tribunals; 38, Essays and Miscellany; 39, Literary Industries. A Zamorano 80 item. (Cowan P. 11.)

Whether it be desert, mountain, lake or river, Bancroft describes it. No important character or event escapes his scrutiny. Any listing of desert material dares not omit the inclusion of Bancroft without impairing its effectiveness as a medium of reference.

BANDEL, EUGENE (Edited by Bieber, Ralph P.)

Letters and Journal of: 1854-1861. 1932. Glendale, California: The Arthur H. Clark Company. Vol. 2 of the Southwest Historical Series—*Frontier Life in the Army: 1854-1861;* 330 pp. 10 illus. 1 fldg. map of routes taken. 6⅜ x 9⅝. The illustrations, particularly those of Los Angeles in 1853 and Fort Yuma in 1852, are of special interest.

Eugene Bandel, a German, was—on occasion—a member of our Sixth Infantry. During his march across the mountains, plains and deserts of the Far West, this cultured young German wrote letters to his parents and friends in Prussia. The manuscripts were carefully preserved and later returned to him at his home in Benicia, California. His daughter, Olga, made it possible for these letters and the journal to enter the California State Library. Because of his educational attainments and his acutely-developed powers of observation the young Bandel etches accurate and vivid word-pictures of incidents, localities and people. California desert interest centers in his letters relating to the Mojave Expedition and the encampment in Southern California (pp. 247-293). The Mojave Expedition was occasioned by an unprovoked attack on the part of some Mojave and Walapai Indians against a party of California emigrants at Beale's Crossing on the Colorado River in the late summer of 1858. Lt. Col. Hoffman was instructed to conduct a punitive expedition against the Indians, and Bandel's company was one of the four units detailed for this service.

BANNING, WILLIAM and GEORGE HUGH

Dust of the "Swift Wagon." 1930. February issue of *Touring Topics.* Illus.

The Banning account tells of the days of the Butterfield Overland Mail. An added attraction to this excellent article are photographs of the original station at Vallecito, the old Warner's Ranch House, the ruins at Carrizo, Aguanga, and the picturesque Oak-Grove Station.

Wheel Tracks of the "Jackass Mail." 1929. November issue of *Touring Topics.*

An interesting, although sometimes confusing, account of the overland mail and passenger stages of James E. Birch, the Jackass Mail, and the Butterfield Line. Their route from San Antonio to San Diego crossed the Southern California desert from Fort Yuma to San Diego via Alamo Mucho, "Carissa" Creek, Lassator's, thence over the mountains to San Diego. The Butterfield Line continued on past Warner's Ranch to Los Angeles and San Francisco.

BARI, VALESKA

Course of Empire, The. 1931. New York: Coward-McCann. 368 pp. 16 illus.

Pages 95-130 reprint a portion of the *John Woodhouse Audubon Western Journal* under the caption "Overland by the Mexican Border Route." Unfortunately, its value is attenuated by the omission of those portions relating to the Colorado Desert crossing.

BARROWS, DAVID P.

Desert of the Colorado, The; On a Dry Trail. 1900. November issue of *Land of Sunshine.*

As in many of these early articles, age is the most commendable factor. Little, if any, new material is introduced, although we do catch intimate glimpses of the route stretching from Indio to the San Gorgonio Pass, as Barrows traveled it in 1897.

Ethno-Botany of the Coahuilla Indians of Southern California. 1900. Chicago. 82 pp. 6¾ x 9⅜.

In this early item Dr. Barrows describes the Indians (Cahuillas) of the desert interior of Southern California. A general description of the entire Colorado Desert area is also provided.

BARTLETT, JOHN RUSSELL

Personal Narrative of Explorations and Incidents in Texas, New Mexico, California, Sonora, and Chihuahua, Connected with the United States and Mexican Boundary Commission, During the Years 1850, '51, '52, and '53. 2 vol. 1854. New York: D. Appleton & Company. Vol. 1 shows XXII, 506 pp., 6 pp. of advertisements, unnumbered; 6 lithographs. Vol. 2 shows XVII 624 pp., 10 lithographs. 6 x 9. (Cowan P. 13; Wagner-Camp No. 234.) Attractively reprinted in 1965 by the Rio Grande Press.

The California desert material will be found in Ch. XXVI—"San Diego to Alamo Mucho," (pp. 109-133), relating to the general area of San Felipe, Vallecito, and Carrizo Creek. Mention is made of Kearny's battle at San Pasqual; also, Ch. XXVII—"Alamo Mucho to Ft. Yuma"—has material relating to our California desert interest. Says Cowan, "Mr. Bartlett's work is the best of its period." In this appraisal I enthusiastically concur. Bartlett was United States Commissioner at the time his book was written. Special attention is directed to the last nine pages of Vol. 2 (pp. 576-584) and their interesting reference to the Camel experiment.

BARTLETT, W. P.

Happenings. 1927. Los Angeles: Times-Mirror Publishing Company. 267 pp. 5⅜ x 7½. Publisher's name shown on second edition, but does not appear on the first; only the words "Porterville, California, 1927" show.

Mr. Bartlett has prepared a series of short sketches of Death Valley (pp. 15-113) and vicinity. The book makes for interesting reading.

More Happenings. 1928. Christopher Publishing House. 225 pp. 5⅜ x 8.
In this book the author assembles additional sketches of Death Valley (pp. 15-57) and surrounding desert regions, which are intended to supplement his first *Happenings* (1927). *More Happenings* fails to measure up to the standard set by the original.

BAXTER, DON J.

Gateway To California. 1968. "Compiled from a series of articles in P. G. and E. Progress." 47 pp.
Noteworthy are the book's illustrations—some thirty of them, depicting the more famous of the "pass" routes into California. Of desert interest are the sections on Tejon Pass, the San Carlos and Warner Passes, Cajon Pass, Walker Pass, and the San Gorgonio Pass. This is an attractive book, with much historic information of interest and value packed into its 47 pages.

BEALE, EDWARD FITZGERALD

Journal of the Expedition . . . From Missouri to California, in 1853. (See listing under Heap, Gwinn Harris.)

Uncle Sam's Camels. (See listing under Lesley, Lewis B.)

BEAN, LOWELL and LAWTON, HARRY

Cahuilla Indians of Southern California. 1965. Banning, California: Malki Museum Press. Pages (12) unnumbered. 8 illus. Wrappers.
This little brochure (Malki Museum Brochure No. 1) makes available a comprehensive history of the Cahuilla Indians and the Morongo Reservation. The two skillful authors—Bean and Lawton—have turned in a commendable job of assembling impressive historical material on the Cahuillas, including their social organization, culture and artistic expression, pottery, baskets, architecture, trade and commerce, weapons, clothing, games and music, and—finally—a gathering of interesting data relating to these relatively little-known Indians. The several photographs further enhance this attractive and useful booklet.

BEAN, LOWELL JOHN and MASON, WILLIAM MARVIN (Edited by)

Diaries and Accounts of the Romero Expeditions in Arizona and California: 1823-1826. (1962.) Palm Springs: Published by The Ward Ritchie Press of Los Angeles for the Palm Springs Desert Museum. 117 pp. 4 illus. End paper maps. 6¼ x 9. Foreword by C. E. Smith, Director of the Palm Springs Museum.
Of the 117 numbered pages, approximately 50 are given over to editorial comment, 22 to explanatory notes, 4 to the bibliography. Only 37 pages are required to contain the three short documents (Romero diary 11 pp., Estudillo diary 22 pp., the Gonzales account 4 pp.). The commendable feature of these documents is their

age. Romero's brief diary opens with an entry on June 8, 1823, closes on July 12 of the same year. The purpose of his exploratory expedition was to open a route of travel from Tucson (then in Sonora), across the Colorado Desert, and on "to the provinces of the Californias." He succeeded only as far as the Colorado River where, due to the perfidy of his Indian guides, he was forced into a temporary abandonment of his plans.

The Estudillo diary—the document with a direct bearing upon our Colorado Desert interest—opens at San Diego on a November 19, 1823, entry, and on November 27 an entry is recorded at the Mission San Gabriel, in Los Angeles. For the following month it is possible to follow Estudillo's movements with an assured certainty. The names he mentions are quite generally familiar to us—San Bernardino, Yucaipa, San Gorgonio, Agua Caliente (Palm Springs). From this point forward, however, the route followed by Estudillo is so vaguely described as to frustrate all effort toward accomplishing an accurate determination of it. The Editors bravely endeavor to identify his route; but, at best, their effort is conjectural. A cursory check of their section on Notes discloses over fifty instances where they have taken refuge behind such qualifying words as "probably," "possibly," "would appear," "would seem," "may suggest," "may indicate," "may have been," "likely," and so on. This is not to be construed as an indication of faulty editing; it merely points up the vagueness of the route descriptions. My personal opinion is that Estudillo followed rather closely the trail that later became known as the Bradshaw Road. Certainly there are passages indicating his presence at Canyon Spring, Tabaseca Tank, Chuckawalla Well and other water holes along the old trail. All this, of course, is mere supposition on my part. The meaning is too abstruse to permit of definite route orientation.

In any event, the Estudillo exploring group did not make it through to the Colorado River; although they must surely have been close to the attainment of their objective when they finally yielded to the urge to turn back and abandon further travel east.

BEATTIE, GEO. W.

Development of Travel Between Southern Arizona and Los Angeles as it Related to the San Bernardino Valley. 1925. *Historical Society of Southern California Annual Publications.* Fldg. map. Pp. 228-257.

The purpose of this article is to prepare a detailed tracing of the development of travel routes through the Colorado desert into the San Bernardino area. Emphasis is placed upon the Bradshaw Stage route. This is an early and important historical item.

(Edited by) *Diary of a Ferryman and Trader At Fort Yuma.* (See listing under Jaeger, L. J. F.)

Reopening the Anza Road. 1933. From the March issue of the *Pacific Historical Review*, pp. 52-71.

In this article Mr. Beattie describes the several attempts to reopen the route established by Anza in 1774, and abandoned in 1781 because of the hostility of the Yuma Indians.

BEATTIE, GEORGE and HELEN

Heritage of the Valley. San Bernardino: First Century. 1939. Pasadena: San Pasqual Press. XXV, 459 pp. 7 x 19. Bibliography (pp. 427-439). Reprinted in 1951 by J. A. Sullivan as No. 29 of Biobooks in an edition limited to 1000 copies. End paper maps. Illus.

Every once-in-so-often a great book makes its appearance. Beattie's *Heritage* is one of our truly great books on California, and its demonstrated value has already become cumulative in the scope of its appeal. Insofar as it is possible to achieve a truly developed work on a given subject, *Heritage of the Valley* has—I believe—accomplished just such a desideratum. Here is an account of San Bernardino and its surrounding territory—desert and valley—with complete utilization of every available contribution of source data. Among the more important chapters are those concerning the Mormon venture in San Bernardino and early travel through the Cajon and San Gorgonio Pass routes.

BELDEN, L. BURR

Death Valley Heroine and Source Accounts of the 1849 Travelers. (1954.) San Bernardino, California: Inland Printing & Engraving Company. First printing limited to 250 copies. 78 pp. 6¼ x 9¼.

The first 18 pages of this excellent book afford the reader a condensed account of the Death Valley venture of 1849. The author, a careful student of Death Valley history, has evidenced a faculty for achieving sensible coordination and integration of relevant source accounts. I perceive no important phase of the Death Valley story that Mr. Belden has neglected to penetrate in the preparation of his work. The value of the book is further enhanced by the inclusion—in most instances by an initial printing from original newspaper accounts—of the following source narratives:

1. Mrs. Juliet Brier—"Our Christmas Amid the Terrors of Death Valley." (*San Francisco Call* of December 25, 1898);
2. Mrs. Juliet Brier—"Mrs. Brier's Last Account." (Carson City, *Nevada News* of June 8, 1913);
3. Rev. J. W. Brier, Sr.—"The First Printed Account." (From Heap's *Central Route to the Pacific,* 1854);
4. J. W. Brier, Jr.—"True Story of the Perishing Emigrants." (*Inyo Independent* of July 26, 1884);
5. W. L. Manly—"Reply to the Brier Article." (*Inyo Independent* of August 30, 1884);
6. Thomas Shannon—"With the Jayhawkers in Death Valley." (*San Jose Daily Mercury* of November 16, 1903);
7. John Rogers—"John Rogers' Account." (*Merced Star* of April 26, 1894);
8. W. L. Manly—"Visit to a Pioneer." (*San Jose Pioneer* of July 15, 1895).

Death Valley's New Survey. 1954. November issue of *Westways.* Illus.

In this important study, Mr. Belden discusses the modern methods and equipment employed by the topographical engineers of the United States Geological Survey—jeeps and helicopters being used in the work.

Forgotten Army Forts of the Mojave. 1964. *Westerners, The* (Los Angeles Corral) *Brand Book* No. 11. 7 pp. 4 illus.

"In the lengthening shadows of the late afternoon a faint pair of wheel marks may be discerned leading in a general east-west direction across the center of the Mojave Desert . . ."—Thus does Mr. Belden begin his impressive article on the string of Army forts that stretched across the Mojave Desert during the 1860's. And these nearly-obliterated wheel marks, together with a few crumbling stone ruins, are the surviving physical evidence of Southern California's once principal transcontinental link with the East. It was known as the Old Government Road.

From Fort Mohave on west across the desert, fortifications were installed and troops maintained for protection against the Indians. Redoubts—more like stone corrals—were built at Bitter Spring and Resting Spring. A base camp—Camp Cady—was constructed near the present town of Daggett. Fort Beale was built in the Piute Mountains. A stockade with block houses was erected at Marl Spring. These, and the overall plan of fortification and troop protection, are capably discussed in this article.

Goodbye, Death Valley! The 1849 Jayhawker Escape. 1956. Palm Desert, California: Desert Magazine Press. 63 pp. 5 pen and ink illus. by Orpha Klinker (remarkably well done). 5½ x 8⅜. Publication No. 4 of the Death Valley '49ers. Wrappers.

Mr. Belden, perhaps our foremost living authority on early California history as it relates to the region in and around the San Bernardino area, has authored two of the relatively few outstanding books to be written thus far on the subject of Death Valley. The instant item is one of them; his *Death Valley Heroine* is the other.

Mines of Death Valley. 1966. Glendale, California: La Siesta Press. 31 pp. 12 photographs. 1 map. End paper maps. 5¾ x 8¾.

A delightful book, this. Good reading. Dependable information. Desert all the way through. A partial roll call of its fascinating chapters reads like this:

Salt Spring. At the southern end of Death Valley is a little oasis with brackish water in it. This marks the near site of Death Valley's first mine.

Gunsight. Perhaps the most romantically famous of Death Valley's mines. It's lost. People are still searching for it.

Panamint. Where they cast the produced silver into cannon balls weighing 700 pounds each. Too heavy for robbers to tote away.

Breyfogle. Another famous mine of the lost legion brigade.

Chloride Cliff. Where the first road was built.

Wingate Pass. "The Battle of Wingate Pass." This is one of Belden's most noted stories. Leading character—"Death Valley Scotty."

Greenwater. The late Senator Charles Brown was *the law* there in those early days.

Bullfrog. Scotty figures prominently in this.

Skidoo. They hanged the same man twice.

These are fair samples. There are plenty more to be had, just for the reading.

Old Stovepipe Wells. 1968. San Bernardino, California: Inland Printing and Engraving Co. 12 pp. unnumbered. 4 illus. 6 x 9.

This is Death Valley '49er Keepsake Publication 8, published for the occasion of the dedication of the Old Stovepipe Wells Monument in Death Valley on November 10, 1968. The book supplies the authentic historical background of Stovepipe Wells, as assembled by one of this desert's most distinguished historians.

Wade Story, The. 1957. San Bernardino: Inland Printing & Engraving Company. 15 pp. Photos of Mr. and Mrs. Wade. Wrappers.

Mr. Belden, in this paper, has again contributed pioneer effort in bringing this important relation of the Wade family to public attention.

BELL, MAJOR HORACE

On the Old West Coast. 1930. New York: William Morrow & Co. Edited by Lanier Bartlett. XIV, 336 pp. 55 pls. 6¾ x 9½. As a part of the first edition, 210 deluxe, numbered copies were run. Several editions have appeared.

This book—and I prefer it, even, to the author's *Reminiscences*—is referred to as the "Further Reminiscences of a Ranger." The fact that these yarns were not included among the original *Reminiscences* has tended to detract, somewhat, from their popularity. Irrespective of this, the reader will find them a source of entertainment; informative in portions of their historical reference. The photographic plates depict early-day scenes in and around Los Angeles. Of desert interest are his chapters—"Spit in the Mouth of Hell," pp. 194-206; "Oranges on Joshua Trees," pp. 267-280 (Widneyville-by-the-Desert); and "In Praise of the Mormons," pp. 293-296 (the Mormon Battalion). P. 150 contains a reference to Rev. Brier, of Death Valley fame, preaching in Los Angeles. The chapter on "Pegleg Smith, the Death Valley Party and John Goler's Mine," pp. 136-145, bears specific reference, in certain of its passages, to Death Valley.

Reminiscences of a Ranger, or Early Times in Southern California. 1881. Los Angeles: Yarnell, Caystile & Mathes, Printers. 457 pp. 6 x 9¼. A Zamorano 80 item. (Cowan P. 16.) Several reprint editions have appeared. The most recent of these is the Christmas presentation issue by the Advertisers Composition Company and printed by Anderson, Ritchie & Simon. Vol. 1 contains the first eight of the 37 chapters of *Reminiscences*. It appeared in 1965 in an edition of 1200 copies. Vol. 2, containing the next 14 chapters, appeared in 1966 in an edition of 1500 copies. Vol. 3, in an edition of 1500 copies, released in 1967, contains the remaining chapters. This is an unusually attractive set, and one greatly to be desired by every lover of fine books.

This is said to be the first book written, printed and hard bound in Los Angeles. Ch. 35 (pp. 407-425) gives Bell's account of "The Great Colorado Desert," "The Desert to be Filled with Water," "The Widney Sea," and "The Ship of the Desert." In this chapter we find the author's poem—"La Jornada de Muerte." Ch. 30 (pp. 336-349) contains the interesting legend of the lost city of Mojave; also, Bell's notable old poem—"The Phantom City." On p. 141, first edition, Bell makes a lone reference to the Death Valley Party by his mention of a "Rev. Briar" preaching the first Methodist sermon ever to be delivered in Los Angeles.

The character of Horace Bell would seem essentially to epitomize the spirit of early Los Angeles. He contrived to live more intimately, and more romantically, in the atmosphere of his times than perhaps any other person of that day. A little garrulous on occasions, never entirely reticent with respect to his own personal exploits, old Major Bell—from first to last—held the spotlight of interest in that day when Los Angeles was young.

BELL, JAMES G. (Edited by Haley, J. Evetts)

Log of the Texas-California Cattle Trail, 1854 A. 1932. *Southwestern Historical Quarterly* Reprint. 79 pp., including Introduction by Mr. Haley (4 pp.), and 1 p. of index.

This item is of significance in its relation to the Colorado Desert area. It is not generally known that for a period approximating 20 years, and beginning—perhaps—in 1853, Texas cattlemen drove large herds of cattle over the desert to the California markets. This industry, discontinued during the Civil War, was renewed—although less vigorously—after peace was resumed. Of all phases, or epochs, of our Colorado Desert history (Missionaries, Trappers, Soldiers, Gold Seekers, Surveyors) this segment having to do with the trail herd era has received least attention. I know of but two diaries (Bell and Erskine) that reflect any information of importance on this neglected subject.

The young Bell (he was only 22 at the time) was employed by a Mr. John James, owner of one of the many vast overland herds that reached their peak of prominence in the year 1854. Their trail followed the route of Kearny and Cooke (1846-47), and they entered California—over the Yuma Ferry—October 29, 1854. A fairly good description is given in this article of Warner's Ranch, Santa Isabella, the Indians at Warner's, and so on.

Mr. Haley, who edits this most interesting account, mentions that he had, for many years, endeavored to locate items relating to the cattle industry of the Southwest. Eventually—"a fragmentary transcript of the Bell Diary found its way into the Archives of the University of Texas. The remnants were thought to have been lost." Later, the original diaries were found to be in the possession of Mr. Ned C. Bell, nephew of the author. The diary begins June 3, 1854, at San Antonio. (See listing under Cureton, Gilbert—*The Cattle Trail To California 1840-1860.*)

BENEDICT, S. G.

Mapping Death Valley a Quarter Century Ago. 1931. November issue of *Touring Topics.* Illus.

Here is source material relating to Death Valley's early history and to one of the significant episodes in that history. The item discloses the experiences of a surveyor in the first topographic survey of Death Valley. The author assisted in the United States Geological Survey in the summer of 1905.

BENTON, F. WEBER

Desert, The: A Graphic Story in Verse of the California Sea of Sand. N.d. Los Angeles: Benton Publishing Company. 14 pp. unnumbered, including covers.

"Illustrated and printed from plates reproduced from original, hand lettering in artistic chirography, on sheets, all of wood from the desert Yucca tree, and bound together with Raffia strands."

BENTON, JOHN C.

Death Valley's National Monument: A Bibliography. (See listing under Voth, Hazel Hunt.)

BERGLAND, LT. ERIC

(See listing under Wheeler, Lt. George M.)

BERTON, FRANCIS (Translated and edited by Rudkin, Charles N.)

Voyage on the Colorado—1878, A. 1953. Los Angeles: Glen Dawson. This reprint is of the 1878 edition, and is limited to 300 copies. 101 pp. 10 illus. Several line drawings. 5¼ x 7½.

The author left San Francisco in April 1878, and crossed the San Joaquin and Merced Rivers, the Tehachapi Pass, the Mojave Desert, the San Fernando Valley, Los Angeles, San Gorgonio Pass, The Colorado Desert (with special mention of Seven Palms, Indio, and Dos Palmas). Pp. 14-15 (Mojave) and pp. 22-26 and 93-95 (Colorado) provide direct desert references. The account describes a trip along the Colorado aboard the steamer *Cocopah.*

BIEBER, DR. RALPH P. (Edited by)

Exploring Southwest Trails, 1846-1854. 1938. Glendale, California: The Arthur H. Clark Company. 383 pp. 6 pls. Map of routes taken. 6½ x 9⅝. Vol. 7 of the Southwest Historical Series.

In addition to the Introduction by Dr. Bieber, the book contains the *Journal of the March of the Mormon Battalion,* by Lt. Col. P. St. George Cooke (pp. 65-240); the *Journal of William Henry Chase Whiting* (pp. 243-350); the *Diary of François Xavier Aubrey* (pp. 353-383). The Aubrey *Diary* gives brief desert mention (Mojave) on pp. 357-358; also p. 379. (See listing under Cooke, P. St. George— *Journal of the March of the Mormon Battalion.*)

Frontier Life In the Army—being the Letters and Journal of Eugene Bandel: 1854-1861. (See listing under Bandel, Eugene.)

Southern Trails to California in 1849. 1937. Glendale, California: The Arthur H. Clark Company. Vol. V of the Southwest Historical Series. 386 pp. 6 illus. 1 fldg. map of routes taken. 6½ x 9⅝.

The section on the John E. Durivage "Letters and Journal" (pp. 159-255) is the book's most important contribution to the source records of overland travel via the southern route. (See listing under Durivage, John E.) The section containing

"Sketches from the Journal of a Traveler: Overland to California" (pp. 260-280) gives a short—but vivid—account of the desert crossing (pp. 272-277). The Alden M. Woodruff Journal—"Through Arkansas and Along the Canadian" (pp. 283-322) embodies a brief desert reference (pp. 321-322). (See listing under Woodruff, Alden M.)

Of particular value is the scholarly 45 page introduction to the volume, on pp. 17-62. Pp. 54-62 are replete with desert interest. Even in such a distinguished work, however, occasional errors creep in. About the last place one would look for a confusion of historical facts would be in Dr. Bieber's classic introduction. Yet on p. 55 I note this passage: "One group of emigrants, deserting the main trail near Mountain Meadow in order to reach the mines by what they thought to be a more direct route, soon lost their way and suffered indescribable hardships, a number perishing in the desert in southern California, which thereafter became known as Death Valley. Fatigued and emaciated but not disheartened, the argonauts eventually dragged themselves through Cajon Pass to Los Angeles." Couched in this one short passage is a veritable labyrinth of error. In the first place, the emigrants did not lose their way. They knew in which general direction they were traveling, and this is about the closest knowledge one can ever expect to have—even today—when wandering over a desert wilderness where there are no roads and no familiar landmarks. These emigrants were no more "lost" after turning off the main trail than they were while on it. True, they ran into a few mountain ranges and dry stretches which seriously impeded their progress; but at no time were they actually lost in the sense that they were wandering aimlessly to and fro. Second, the assertion that a "number" perished in Death Valley is erroneous. Only one emigrant of the entire 1849 group is known to have perished there. Third, these argonauts did not eventually drag themselves "through Cajon Pass to Los Angeles." A few did; but the majority continued either west over Walker's pass, or southwest through Soledad Canyon. Fourth, the inference is that, because so many perished in this desert, it "thereafter became known as Death Valley." The naming of Death Valley was not prompted by an assumption that people had perished there. The designation "Death Valley" derived from the belief on the part of the emigrants that this was a *dead* valley, a valley of *desolation* and *death* to all who might unduly linger within its lifeless borders. Fifth, to say these emigrants were "not disheartened" is to create a misconception of the entire venture. These people consorted with death every minute and every mile; and there was not a man, woman nor child among them who was not sick unto death with despondency. They continued moving forward only because they dared not turn back.

Further reference to the Colorado Desert may be found on pp. 272-277; also pp. 321-322.

BIGGERS, EARL DERR

Chinese Parrot, The. (1926.) Indianapolis: Bobbs-Merrill Company. 316 pp. 5¼ x 7⅝.

I regard this as one of the best of the exciting Charlie Chan mysteries. The yarn is written in a manner calculated to give one the *feel* of the desert.

BIGLER, HENRY W.

Extracts from the Journal of Henry W. Bigler. 1932. April, July and October issues of the *Utah Historical Quarterly.* Vol. 5, Nos. 2, 3, and 4. Parts of the Journal first appeared in the *Overland Monthly* in September, 1887; in 1962 Erwin G. Gudde republished the Journal under the title *Bigler's Chronicle of the West.*

This is the transcript from the Journal re-written and corrected in 1898 by Mr. Bigler. Reference made to the southern California desert area is of historical value. While no new material is disclosed, interesting sidelights are provided by the pioneer Bigler. Source information of this nature always merits respectful attention. Bigler was among a group that seceded from the original Sand Walking Company of 1849 and packed down Mt. Misery into Beaver Dam Wash in southwest Utah near the Nevada line. While in this canyon he carved his initials on a white rock. (See listing under Kelly, Chas.—*On Manly's Trail To Death Valley.*) It will be recalled that the members of this seceding contingent who did *not* turn back to the Spanish Trail, but continued obstinately on their westward trek, constitute the now-famous Death Valley Parties of 1849.

Journal. 1849. Pp. 142-180 in LeRoy and Ann Hafen's *Journal of Forty-Niners.*

The Bigler Journal, as recorded by the Hafens, begins October 8, 1849; extends through January 18, 1850.

BILLEB, EMIL W.

Mining Camp Days. 1968. Berkeley, California: Howell-North. 229 pp.

The basic value of this book reposes in its early-day photographs—over 200 of them. Much source material is made available on Bodie and the nearby *Nevada* towns of Aurora and Tonopah.

BLAKE, W. P. and CORY, H. T.

Imperial Valley and the Salton Sink, The. (See listing under Cory, H. T.; also refer to MacDougal, D. T.—*The Salton Sea.*)

BLAKE, W. P.

General Report. 1856. 33 Cong. 2 Sess. Sen. Ex. Doc. No. 78. Vol. III of *Pacific Railroad Surveys.*

In Part 4, pp. 51-56, Dr. Blake writes of the region extending from the Colorado River to San Pedro. (See listing under *Pacific Railroad Surveys.*)

Geological Report. 1857. Vol. V of *Pacific Railroad Surveys.*

(Cowan P. 19.) Cowan mentions that a number of extra copies from the official papers contained in Vol. V of the *Survey Reports* were run for Prof. Blake. From these assembled papers was prepared the volume listed by Cowan as *Report of a Geological Reconnaissance in California, etc.* Dr. Blake wrote the Geological Report, which is perhaps the most extensive and the most important portion of the entire *Report* as contained in Vol. V.

Pp. 85-88 are descriptive of the Cajon Pass. Pp. 89-94 take the reader over San

Gorgonio Pass into the Colorado Desert. And then—"after traveling about seven and a half miles over these long and barren slopes, we saw a green spot in the distance, and soon came to two large springs of water rising in the bare plain, not far from the foot of the mountain. One of these springs is warm, and forms a pool nearly thirty feet in diameter and three to four feet deep. The cold spring is not quite so large, and is only ten feet distant from the other. . . . A growth of rushes forms a narrow margin of green vegetation around the spring and its outlet. Willows and mesquite bushes grow there also, and I found a young *palm tree* spreading its broad, fan-like leaves among them. The surrounding desert, and this palm tree gave the scene an Oriental aspect." Thus Dr. Blake, and his 1853 description of Palm Springs, the now popular desert metropolis at the foot of Mt. San Jacinto.

Pp. 94-127 afford excellent descriptive accounts of the Colorado Desert—including the trail to Warner's, past Cooke's Well, Alamo Mocho, Carrizo Creek, Vallecito, and San Felipe. (See listing under *Pacific Railroad Surveys*.)

BLISS, ROBERT S.

Journal. 1931. July and October issues of *Utah Historical Quarterly* (Nos. 3 and 4).

Bliss was a member of the Mormon Battalion. He opens his Journal Tuesday, August 18, 1846; concludes it in the midst of an entry—even a word—on January 13, 1848. His record of the Colorado Desert crossing is brief—only 11 short entries (Mon. January 11 through Fri. January 22, 1847).

BLOOM, LANSING B. (Edited by)

From Lewisburg to California. (See listing under Chamberlin, Wm. H.)

BOELTER, HOMER H. and EDWARDS, E. I.

Desert Sanctuary. 1965. Los Angeles: Homer H. Boelter Lithography. 12 pp. unnumbered. Decorative wrappers.

Mr. Boelter has prepared five beautiful double-page and three single-page lithographs of desert scenes for this exquisitely fashioned booklet. The narrative—*Desert Sanctuary*—is by E. I. Edwards.

BOELTER, HOMER H. and HUSSEY, S. E.

Desert Thematic Portrait, The. (See listing under Hussey, S. E.)

BOLTON, DR. HERBERT EUGENE (Edited by)

Anza's California Expeditions (5 Vol.); *Font's Complete Diary*. (See listings under foregoing titles.)

Fray Juan Crespi, Missionary Explorer on the Pacific Coast 1769-1774. 1927. Berkeley: University of California Press. 402 pp. Maps and illustrations. 8 vols.

This item contains early source material, as it recounts the vicissitudes of the good Father's journey over Southern California. Father Crespi is the historically-renowned chronicler of the Portola expedition who gave us perhaps our earliest descriptive account of Los Angeles during that first week in August of 1769.

Outpost of Empire. 1931. N. Y. Alfred A. Knopf. xxi, 334, xvii pp. 66 illus. 6½ x 9⅝. Has been reprinted.

This is Vol. 1 of the five-volume set of *Anza's California Expeditions* (see listing in this Bibliography), the words "First Edition" appearing under the copyright notice. The book is essentially an introduction by Dr. Bolton to his translation of the several diaries in the other four volumes of the Anza set. The introduction relates to but one phase of de Anza's colorful career—his activities in California. Pp. 78-109 and 200-221 bear directly upon his California desert crossing.

BONSAL, STEPHEN

Edward Fitzgerald Beale, a Pioneer in the Path of Empire, 1822-1903. 1912. New York: G. P. Putnam's Sons. XII, 312 pp. 17 pls. 6 x 8⅞.

Ch. 2 "The War with Mexico" (pp. 9-24) contains an extract from Benton's speech before the Senate recounting the Battle of San Pasqual and the part Kearny, Beale and Carson played in this historic episode. A generous portion of the text is taken from the Journals of Heap and Beale. Included in Heap's account is Ch. 9 entitled "The Desert Journey" (pp. 147-173), detailing the trip from Parowan, Utah to San Bernardino, California (Aug. 4-22, 1853). The route was past Ojo de Archilete (Archilete's Spring), Amargosa, Agua del Tio Meso (Agua del Tomaso), "Mohaveh" River, Cajon Pass, and San Bernardino.

Ch. 11, "The Forgotten Camel Corps" (pp. 198-210), in which the author credits Beale and Carson with an unauthenticated exploration of Death Valley, contains material on Jefferson Davis' dramatic camel experiment.

BOWERS, STEPHEN

Reconnaissance of the Colorado Desert Mining District. 1901. Sacramento: California State Mining Bureau. 19 pp. Wrappers.

Material covered includes: Coyote Wells, Carrizo Creek, Fish Creek and Seventeen Palms Springs. These comprise the territory that had, at that time, been located for petroleum.

BOYD, JAMES and BROWN, JOHN

History of San Bernardino and Riverside Counties. (See listing under Brown, John.)

BOYD, WILLIAM HARLAND

Centennial Bibliography On the History of Kern County, California. 1966. Bakersfield, California: Kern County Historical Society. 49 pp. 6¼ x 9¼. The first 12 pages contain "A Synoptic History of Kern County by Ralph F. Kreiser."

In this twenty-eighth annual publication of the Kern County Historical Society,

Mr. Boyd includes approximately 100 books relating directly or indirectly to Kern County. Happily, this bibliography is not a mere listing by author and title, but provides useful commentary for every book mentioned. A title index would have been helpful.

Land of Havilah: 1854-1874. 1952. Bakersfield, California: The 14th annual publication of the Kern County Historical Society. X, 54 pp. 9 illus. 6¼ x 9¼.

The book tells the story of Keyesville, Kernville, and Havilah, in the Kern River country, California. Its content is of general desert interest, as it relates to a region which—in a degree—is essentially desert in character.

BOYLES, J. C.

He Witnessed the Death Valley Tragedy of '49. 1940. February issue of *Desert.* Illus.

Mr. Boyles narrates the story of Indian George of Death Valley who, as a boy, observed the emigrants of 1849 floundering in this pitiless wasteland sink.

BRAUNTON, ERNEST

Palm Springs Before the Dudes Came. 1934. November issue of *Westways.* Illus.

Here is a portrayal of early Palm Springs—"Indian rancheria, boom town, health resort, exclusive recreation mecca," together with a fascinating account of the long "extinct" village of Palmdale which at one time threatened to out-distance its nearby rival—Palm Springs.

BRAY, DORIS

Ballarat. (See listing under Hubbard, Paul B.)

BREWER, WILLIAM H.

Up and Down California. 1930. New Haven: Yale University Press. 601 pp. 63 illus. Has twice been reprinted. Edited by Francis P. Farquhar. 6¼ x 9¼.

In 1860 Josiah Dwight Whitney was appointed State Geologist and empowered to secure the aid of necessary assistants for the purpose of completing a Geological Survey of the State of California. William H. Brewer served as Whitney's "Principal Assistant." While engaged in his active survey work, Brewer found opportunity to prepare scientific reports, make current entries in his note books and—perhaps most importantly—write the letters included in this personal journal. Says Mr. Farquhar, in his capable Introduction: "These letters are the more remarkable in that they were written late at night by firelight or candle-light, sometimes in the blistering heat of a summer noon, sometimes in a leaky tent with cold wind and rain outside."

Brewer addressed the letters to his brother to read and hold in readiness for him upon his return from the Survey. It is improbable that he ever intended to publish them. In any event, prior to Mr. Farquhar's editing for publication in 1930, the letters remained as Brewer had written them during the 1860-64 Survey.

Of desert interest are his references to Fort Tejon on pp. 383-4, to the Mojave on pp. 388-394, to Mono Lake on pp. 415-420, and to the Owens Valley on pp. 534-539.

BREWERTON, LT. GEORGE DOUGLAS (Edited by Stallo, Vinton)

Overland with Kit Carson. A Narrative of the Old Spanish Trail in '48. 1930. New York: Coward-McCann, Inc. IX; 301 pp.; several illustrations; fldg. map; 6⅛ x 8¾. (Wagner-Camp No. 222.)

This account first appeared in the August 1853, issue of *Harper's New Monthly Magazine.* The young lieutenant left Los Angeles on May 4, 1848, for Independence, Missouri, via the Old Spanish Trail and the Santa Fe Trail. Kit Carson accompanied Brewerton as far as Taos. The route over the California desert was from the crossing of Cajon Pass northeast over the Mojave. Ch. 2—"From the Mojave to the Archilette" (pp. 53-56) is rich in its desert interest and also in its keen insight into Carson's personality and characteristics.

Ride With Kit Carson Through the Great American Desert and the Rocky Mountains, A. 1853. August issue of *Harper's New Monthly* and reprinted in book form in 1930 under the title *Overland with Kit Carson.* In addition to the title subject, both magazine and book contain "Incidents of Travel in New Mexico" and "In the Buffalo Country."

The route of Carson and Brewerton over the Old Spanish Trail crossed the Mojave Desert from Cajon Pass through the region of the present cities of Victorville and Barstow, and on through the present site of Las Vegas, Nevada. Brewerton prepared pencil sketches of the country traversed.

BRIER, REV. JAS. W.

Recommended Route to the Pacific. (See listing under Heap, Guinn Harris—*Central Route to the Pacific;* and Belden, L. Burr—*Death Valley Heroine.*)

BRIER, REV. JOHN WELLS

Death Valley Party of 1849, The. 1903. March and April issues of *Out West.* 11 pls.

This is the historically important source account of J. W. Brier, Jr. who, as a lad of six, was one of the original Death Valley pioneers of 1849. Brier's account derives mainly from information given him by his parents; not from his memory of the trip.

True Story of the Perishing Emigrants. From *Inyo Independent* of July 26, 1884. (See listing under Belden, L. Burr—*Death Valley Heroine;* also Long, Dr. Margaret—*The Shadow of the Arrow.*)

BRIER, MRS. J. W.

Last Account. Carson City News of June 8, 1913. (See listing under Belden, L. Burr—*Death Valley Heroine.*)

Our Christmas Amid the Terrors of Death Valley. San Francisco Call of December 28, 1898. (See listing under Belden, L. Burr—*Death Valley Heroine.*)

BRININSTOOL, E. A.

Desert Trek in 1904. 1952. November issue of *Desert.* Illus. Map.

A retrospective view is presented of the Colorado Desert as it appeared in 1904; also, there is an account of the difficult Devil's Canyon road from San Diego to Imperial Valley.

BROWN, JAMES S.

Life of a Pioneer. 1900. Salt Lake: Geo. Q. Cannon & Sons. 520 pp. 7 illus. 6 x 8¾.

Brown was a member of the Mormon Battalion, he and Bigler were with Marshall when the latter discovered gold, he was with the Jefferson Hunt Sand Walking Party (of Death Valley fame). Pp. 67-71 describe the Colorado Desert crossing of the Mormon Battalion; pp. 98-106 relate the thrilling gold discovery; pp. 127-129 mention the miraculous incident of the white gulls destroying the marauding crickets in Utah; pp. 130-144 are devoted to the desert crossing with the Jefferson Hunt Sand Walking Company. (This portion of the book—pp. 130-143—is reprinted by the Hafens in their *Journals of Forty-Niners.*) The book is scarce and important. It is reported that almost the entire edition was destroyed by water and mice. Its early Los Angeles and California material is inextricably threaded into the pattern of our State's historical lore.

BROWN, JOHN and BOYD, JAMES

History of San Bernardino and Riverside Counties (3 Vol.) 1922. Western Historical Association. Numerous illus. and photos.

Vol. 1, with XXVII and 602 pp., contains generous comment on towns and cities in the two counties, including several desert localities—Palm Springs, Banning, and others. Mr. Brown writes of San Bernardino County; Mr. Boyd of Riverside County. Vols. 2 and 3 are given over to biographical sketches of leading citizens of that day.

BROWN, JOHN S.

Salton Sea Region, California, The: A Geographic, Geologic, and Hydrologic Reconnaissance with a Guide to Desert Watering Places. 1923. Washington: U.S.G.S. Water-Supply Paper 497. XV, 292 pp. 3 detached end-pocket maps. 34 pls. and sketch maps. 5¾ x 9. Wrappers.

The four Water-Supply Papers: Brown (497), Mendenhall (224), Thompson (578), and Waring (338) compose the basic collection of California desert material as made available by the Government's Water Supply Paper publications. To students of desert literature the Brown Report is of major importance because of the diversification and the accuracy of its content. A careful study is prepared of the historical background of the entire Colorado Desert area; portions of the book are devoted to the climate, flora, fauna, and physiography of the region; sections are included on the geology, hydrology, and mineral resources; and pages 129-280 are given over to a detailed presentation of the several routes of desert travel. In this latter portion may be found valuable data on the Butterfield and Bradshaw trails, the Borrego, the sand dunes, and the Imperial and Coachella Valleys.

See also Brown's *Routes to Desert Watering Places in the Salton Sea Region, California*. U.S.G.S. Water Supply Paper 490-A. 1920. 186 pp. 2 fldg. maps. 6 pls. Wrappers. Contains descriptions, travel hints, road logs.

BROWNE, J. ROSS

Adventures In the Apache Country. A Tour Through Arizona and Sonora with Notes on the Silver Regions of Nevada. 1869. New York: Harper & Brothers. 535 pp., plus 4 pp. advertisements. 155 line illus. 4¾ x 7⅞. *Arizona Silhouettes* reprinted the portions of this book appertaining to Arizona. The California material was omitted. Dr. Horace Parker's *Piasano Press* has issued three beautiful reprints of Browne's writings: *A Peep At Washoe* and *Washoe Revisited* (1959), *The Coast Rangers* (1959), and *Illustrated Mining Adventures in California and Nevada* (1961).

Essentially, of course, this is a book *of*—and perhaps *for*—Arizona and Arizonans. However—and for this we shall be eternally grateful—California does come in for a quick sampler of the rich food Browne has heaped upon Arizona's table. And much that is said of California—again fortunately for our immediate purpose —relates to desert country. Chs. 2 and 3 (pp. 27-54) are priceless gems from the fabulous treasure-trove that is Browne. Both these chapters allude to the Colorado Desert. Again, in Chs. 38-41 (pp. 393-430), Browne comes out upon our deserts, this time in the region of the old hell-roarin' mining camp of Bodie. And what a guest he proves to be as he entertains us with his early-day descriptions of Bodie and her notorious "bad men." His chapters on "Bodie Bluff," "A Startling Adventure," "A Badger Fight," and the "Terrible Cloud-Burst" will—in the approved Browne fashion—grip the reader with an absorbing interest. Ch. 42 (pp. 431-444) gives an excellent account of Mono Lake as Browne came to know it back in 1863-64.

The chapter entitled "The Lost Ledge," being pp. 512-522, and contained in the section captioned "The Reese River Country," presents an interesting—though factually garbled—account of the movements of a "train of sixty wagons that left the Mountain Meadows for San Bernardino" in the year 1852. It is understandable how Browne, at such an early date, would so utterly distort the facts—for it is doubtful if any *written* record of the Death Valley parties of 1849 was existent at that time. It is patent, however, that he is endeavoring to describe the movements of these authentic parties of 1849—even to the inclusion of such participants as Towne and a Methodist minister. His chief effort is directed toward a relation of the experiences of three men—Towne, Farley and Cadwallader who, he claims, discovered a ledge of silver ore in Death Valley. Also, he contributes yet another version of the inscrutable Breyfogle, even averring that he knew the Dutchman when the latter was tax-collector of Alameda County.

An article by Browne, entitled "The Reese River Country," is included in *Harper's Magazine* for June, 1866. Although this early item does not contain the book chapter—"The Lost Ledge"—with its copious mention of Death Valley, it *does* print the name of this desert, mentioning (erroneously, of course) that Frémont passed through it. This magazine reference, therefore, discloses one of the earliest appearances of the name "Death Valley." Hittel, in his *Resources of California* (1863), gives us our earliest known *book* mention of the name; the newspapers *San Francisco Alta California* of April 12, 1861, and *Visalia Delta* of April 13, 1861, reveal what is perhaps the earliest *printed* designation of the name.

Report Upon the Mineral Resources of the States and Territories West of the Rocky Mountains. 1867. Washington: House Ex. Doc. 29. 5000 copies. 321 pp. 6 x 9⅛.

Desert interest is focused upon an article by Dr. John A. Veatch, pp. 179-187, entitled "Discovery of Borax in California." Also in 1867, in an edition of 10,000 copies (360 pp.), there was added to Browne's *Report* the *Report* of James W. Taylor. The book is entitled *Reports Upon the Mineral Resources of the United States.* Taylor's *Report* has to do with gold mines *east* of the Rocky Mountains.

BRUFF, J. GOLDSBOROUGH

Gold Rush. Being the Diaries of J. Goldsborough Bruff. (2 Vol.) 1944. New York: Columbia University. 1404 pp. Illus. & sketches. 6½ x 10¼. Limited to 1250 copies. A one-volume edition, abridged, was subsequently issued by *Biobooks*, in Oakland.

The first edition contains Death Valley material of primary importance—the diary of Louis Nusbaumer—entitled "A Little Light on Death Valley." These valuable data directly affect the history of those who made the "Long Camp," on the floor of Death Valley, and successfully account for the movements of such heretofore elusive characters as Nusbaumer, Hadapp, Culverwell, Fish, Graham (Isham), Smith (colored) and Schlagel. The discovery of this vital source material helps crystalize the component parts of the Death Valley personnel into an understandable entity. (See Long, Dr. Margaret—*The Shadow of the Arrow*—reprint edition.) For a definitive editing of the *original* diary of Nusbaumer, see George Koenig's superb study—*Valley of Salt, Memories of Wine* (listed in this Bibliography).

BUCK, FRANKLIN A. (Compiled by White, Katherine A.)

Yankee Trader in the Gold Rush, A. 1930. Boston: Houghton Mifflin Company. 294 pp.

Pp. 269-277 describe Buck's trip to Bodie and Mammoth City (in Mono County) in 1879.

BULLARD, WILLIAM C. (Chief Park Naturalist)

Death Valley National Monument—A Bibliography. 1963. Mimeographed unnumbered sheets.

This is a subject-classified listing (115 pages) of book, magazine and bulletin items relating to Death Valley. Sections cover General Works, Geology, Paleontology, Meteorology, History, Zoology (Archaeology, Ethnology, Pure Science, Invertebrates, Vertebrates, Birds, Mammals, Flora).

BURDICK, ARTHUR J.

Mystic Mid Region, The: The Deserts of the Southwest. 1904. New York: G. P. Putnam's Sons. IX, 237 pp. 2 pp. advertisements in back of book. 54 pls. (Almost uniformly, every third sheet is a photographic plate.) 5¾ x 8⅜.

Although a bit inaccurate in certain of his details as, for instance, when sketching the history of Death Valley, Burdick has turned in one of the all-time great desert items of California. A book whose substance is devoted entirely to the California deserts, and whose date of publication is 1904, is one we may safely assume to be a pioneer in its field. Therefore we dare not assess the value of its content too lightly. Burdick elaborates on desert plants, animals, Indians, basket-makers, burros, mining, borax, Death Valley, and below-sea-level journalism. Assuredly, the Burdick is a required item on any desert shelf.

BURMEISTER, EUGENE

Early Days In Kern. 1963. Bakersfield, California: Cardon House. 78 pp. 33 illus.

Mr. Burmeister's categorical presentation of names, places and events is a veritable compendium of Kern County information. The reader will encounter an almost unbelievable accumulation of facts—unbelievable because he is certain to wonder how such a vast accumulation of historical information could possibly be assembled within the physical limitations of a 78-page book. Anyone wishing a succinct encyclopedic coverage of early Kern County data will surely benefit from ownership of *Early Days In Kern.*

BURNS, HELEN

Salton Sea Story. 1952. Palm Desert, California: Desert Magazine Press. 30 pp. 11 pls. 2 maps. 5½ x 8½. Wrappers.

As one reads this fine account, it is with the sense of having gained precise information regarding the entire Salton Sea episode. Perhaps the most valuable section in the book is the one captioned "Appendix. Facts and Figures." Here may be found 25 items of top-level information.

BURNS, WILLIAM A.

Natural History of the Southwest. 1960. New York: George McKibben. 144 pp. plus index. Numerous photographic plates, several of them in color. Wrappers.

Contents of this excellent desert nature book include:
Story of the Southwest—William A. Burns
Trees, Flowers and Shrubs—Peggy L. Larson
Reptiles—William H. Woodin
Birds—Lewis W. Walker
Mammals—Lewis W. Walker

BURRELL, MRS. EDWARD

Across the Plains in 1849. From the *Enterprise* of Plainfield, Illinois and—later—the *San Jose Pioneer* of December 15, 1894.

Reprinted in Arthur Woodward's (or Manly's) *The Jayhawkers' Oath*; also in Dr. Margaret Long's *The Shadow of the Arrow*.

The Burrell letter is of major importance in Death Valley history, by reason of its valuable contribution of material affecting the Henry Wade party.

BYNUM, LINDLEY (Edited by)

Record Book of the Rancho Santa Ana del Chino, The. 1935. Los Angeles. John C. Fremont High School Vocational Printing Classes. Wrappers. 55 pp. Facsimile copy from page of the original Record Book. 6½ x 10. The copy under review is a reprint from the *Historical Society of Southern California Annual Publication*. 1934.

The del Chino Rancho of Isaac Williams was an important stopping place for the hordes of gold seekers coming over the Colorado Desert route in 1849-50. It also attracted large numbers coming into Los Angeles via the Cajon. The record book served as a register from 1849 to 1856. Many of the travelers registered their names here; several wrote brief accounts of their overland journey. This issue of the *Historical Society of Southern California Annual Publication* also contains Benjamin D. (Don Benito) Wilson's narrative—*Observations on Early Days In California and New Mexico*. (See listing under Cleland, Robert G.—*Pathfinders*).

CAIN, ELLA M.

Story of Bodie, The. (1956.) San Francisco: Fearon Publishers, Inc. XI, 196 pp. 71 pls. 6⅛ x 9¼. Published in hard and soft bindings.

The late Mrs. Cain, herself a long-time resident of the place, is peculiarly qualified to write this most nearly complete record of Bodie's dramatic history.

Story of Early Mono County, The. (1961.) San Francisco: Fearon Publishers, Inc. 166 pp. 66 photographic illus. 6¼ x 9¼.

Some there are who will contend that mountainous Mono County, with its lakes and streams, can scarcely qualify as desert country. This is probably true. At best it can make only a specious claim to this distinction. But I have tramped over areas of Mono County in the summertime that were as desertic as any country I have ever seen. Or so it appeared to me. The present item is early Mono County's number one book.

Ghosts walk in Mono; and Mrs. Cain gives her readers a spirited account of these once-boisterous mining towns of a day long gone: Dogtown, Monoville, Lundy, Bennettville, Masonic, Bodie, and Aurora. Aurora is actually in Nevada, but it was originally thought to be in California; was even the seat of Mono County for a time.

The illustrations—many of them early photographs of buildings and towns and people—enhance the book's value, both as a source of historical reference and as an item for pleasant reading.

CAINE, RALPH L.

Legendary and Geological History of Lost Desert Gold. 1951. Palm Desert, California: Desert Magazine Press. 71 pp. 8 pls. 7 maps. 5⅞ x 8⅞. Wrappers.

The locale of this book "comprises most of Imperial Valley . . . , all of Borrego Desert along with the Coyote, Vallecito, Fish, and southern part of the Santa Rosa mountains to the West." There are 16 tales of lost gold related in part 1; part 2 is "an attempt on the part of the author to correlate the many legends of lost gold with the geology of the region."

CALIFORNIA INTERSTATE TELEPHONE COMPANY

Romantic Heritage Booklets. 1961. Wrappers.

I can best identify these booklets by referring to them as "The Books for Which No Thanks Are Wanted." They were distributed without cost, presumably to those requesting them, with a printed insert informing that they came with the compliments of the company's President. There followed this somewhat mandatory admonition: "No acknowledgment necessary." Even though the grateful recipients were precluded from either a written or a vocal expression of their appreciation, I am sure all were happy to receive these attractive booklets.

The series—as I know them—consists of five separate items: Mojave River Valley, Upper Mojave Desert, Douglas-Alpine, Victor Valley, and Inyo-Mono. Included are references to early railroads, mining, borax, desert towns, Genoa, explorers, Victor Valley, Mono Lake, and other subjects of comparable interest. The booklets are replete with illustrative line drawings.

CALIFORNIA STATE CHAMBER OF COMMERCE— TRAVEL AND RECREATION DEPT.

Southern California Deserts. 1953-54. 30 pp. 10 pls. Sketches. 4 maps. 6 x 9. Wrappers.

This brochure consists of short, descriptive articles on the Imperial, Coachella, Palo Verde, Morongo, Yucca, Borrego, Mojave, Victor, Antelope, and Death Valleys; the Borrego State Park, Needles, Joshua Tree, Twentynine Palms, and the Joshua Tree National Monument.

CALVIN, ROSS

Lieutenant Emory Reports. (See listing under Emory, Lt. W. H.)

CAMP, CHARLES L.

Kit Carson In California. 1922. Reprint of the October issue of the *California Historical Society Quarterly*, 41 pp.

In this useful article, the author draws from available sources whatever material bears upon Carson's exploits and experiences in California. Desert references include mention of Carson's activities at Tejon; also his participation with Kearny at the Battle of San Pasqual.

Mr. Pegleg Smith. N.d. (1965.) San Francisco: Lawton and Alfred Kennedy. Limited to 200 copies. 10 pp. 1 illus. Decorative wrappers.

This is the authentic, definitive, impeccable account of that illustrious and notorious brother—Pegleg Smith—accomplice of the noble redskin, resolute, soberminded (except when likker muddled his brain which was mostly always), vacillating, unmitigated liar, famed discoverer of the three black-nugget buttes, and proud wearer of the pervasive peg leg. (All Clampers take note, and stock a copy of this scarce little item in your likker cellar.)

CAMPBELL, ELIZABETH W. CROZER

Archeological Survey of the Twentynine Palms Region, An. 1931. Los Angeles: Southwest Museum. No. 7 of the Southwest Museum Papers. Introduction by Edwin F. Walker. 93 pp. 48 pls. 1 map. 6½ x 10. Wrappers.

Mr. Walker's introduction (pp. 9-20) is a dependable local history of Twentynine Palms. The Campbell report itself is an intelligently-written paper on the archeology of the area.

Desert Was Home, The. 1961. Los Angeles: Westernlore Press. Foreword by Lloyd Severe. 265 pp. 39 illus. 5¾ x 8½.

Mr. and Mrs. Campbell moved to Twentynine Palms in 1924. About all there was in that early day was just the name—the name and one of the most healthful climates known to man. This book tells of their homesteading experiences, and of the early history of this High Desert town.

CAMPBELL, ELIZABETH W. CROZER and WILLIAM H.

Pinto Basin Site, The. 1935. Los Angeles: Southwest Museum Papers No. 9. 51 pp. 15 pls. 2 fldg. maps.

The archeological approach to the Pinto Basin is to identify it as "an ancient aboriginal camping ground in the California desert." The Pinto Basin is a part of the Joshua Tree National Monument.

CAMPBELL, ELIZABETH W. CROZER, et al.

Archeology of Pleistocene Lake Mohave, The. 1937. Los Angeles: Southwest Museum Papers No. 11. 118 pp. 57 pls.

One of the pioneer treatises on this region, the Lake Mohave paper is characterized by its thoroughness and its accuracy. The Campbells devote considerable attention to the documentation of evidence tending to support the theory that man existed on the North American continent during late Pleistocene times.

CANDEE, DR. JOEL G.

Letter of. 1954. (See listing under Foreman, Grant. *Marcy & the Gold Seekers.* pp. 170-173 and 326-333.)

Dr. Candee, the 45-year-old physician, was a member of the Knickerbocker

Company who left Fort Smith with twelve wagons and 75 men on March 26, 1849, and came into the gold fields via the southwest route over the Colorado Desert. Not the least conspicuous member of the Knickerbocker Company was the attractive 17-year-old daughter of Dr. Candee who "rode a beautiful black horse all the way to California" and "stirred the emotions of young emigrants and army officers."

CANNON, GEORGE Q.

Journal. 1869. Cannon's original journal made its initial appearance in the *Juvenile Instructor*, of which Cannon was both editor and publisher. This material was later reprinted in booklet form under the title *A Trip To California*. In 1954 the Hafens published extracts from the journal in their *Journals of Forty-Niners*.

CARDINELL, CHARLES

Diary. 1922. July issue of the *California Historical Quarterly* under caption— "Adventures on the Plains." Also reprinted in an edition of 150 copies.

Cardinell, a member of the Capt. Parker H. French Overland Expedition to California, came to the gold fields via the Southern route in 1850. His mention of the desert crossing is brief and vague, contributing little of value to our study. It is significant, however, that Cardinell accomplished much of his journey on foot and alone. He experienced and endured unbelievable hardships and suffering. His diary records, as do those of several other emigrants, that carcasses of dead animals were strewn over the desert and their stench was almost unbearable.

This material was assembled by the Society from those articles appearing in the San Francisco *Chronicle* under date of January 21, February 5 and February 16, 1856.

CARLING, JAMES L.

On the Trail of Willie-boy. 1941. November issue of *Desert*. Illus.

This article is among the more dependable of the several Willie-boy accounts. Willie-boy was a Paiute Indian about 26 years of age who, in 1909, killed his sweetheart's father—the Indian Mike Boniface—and then killed his sweetheart Isoleta (or Lolita, as some narrators call her). The killing of the girl occurred in the High Desert country near Twentynine Palms, thus instigating the most extensive manhunt ever attempted in this section of our deserts. The author of the article gets facts direct from Ben de Crevecoeur and Joe Toutain, both officers in the posse that finally caught up with the killer. Of added interest are the portraits of Isoleta Boniface and Willie-boy. (See listing under Lawton, Harry—*Willie Boy*.)

CARLSON, RAYMOND

Flowering Cactus, The. (1954.) McGraw-Hill Book Company, Inc. 96 pp. 9 x 11 ¾. Photographs are by R. C. and C. M. Proctor, with illustrations and designs by G. M. Avey.

This is a book of beautiful photographic plates, most of them in color. There is some descriptive comment, and the pictures all bear a caption. Essentially, however, it is a book of indescribable loveliness. Its exquisite colored photographs of cacti comprise a most attractive collection.

CARR, WILLIAM H.

Desert Parade. 1947. New York: The Viking Press. 96 pp. 74 pls. End-paper maps. 5⅝ x 8¾.

The book enumerates 22 species of mammals, 41 species of birds, 8 snakes, 9 lizards and tortoise, 11 spiders, scorpions and insects, 20 species of trees and shrubs, 18 wild flowers and weeds, 15 species of cacti. The excellent photographic work is by Marvin H. Frost. For quick reference value, and for choice and quality of illustrative material, this dependable book rates high commendation.

CARSON, KIT

Autobiography. 1935. (1856.) Chicago: Lakeside Press. XXXVIII, 192 pp. 4½ x 6⅞.

Perhaps the most reliable of all the accounts issued on the life and adventures of Kit Carson is his autobiography, as published by the Lakeside Press in one of their attractive little "Classics." Much California desert material is associated with the life and adventures of this frontiersman. Pp. 123-24, for instance, relate to Carson's desert trip with Lieut. Brewerton; pp. 108-118 narrate the scout's participation in Kearny's historic Battle of San Pasqual; and, of course, the narrative as a whole is replete with Carson's own references to his association with Frémont—often over California desert regions. Carson gives us a source reference of considerable importance relative to the Ewing Young fur-trapping expedition into California via the western end of the Spanish Trail. This was during the winter of 1829-30; and Kit was a member of the group. (See pp. 9-14). A most readable account of one of those heroic stalwarts in our country's era of overland expansion. Says LeRoy Hafen, in his *Old Spanish Trail,* "The basic account of Carson's career is his autobiography . . . and the best published version is edited by Milo M. Quaife." Dr. Hafen's reference is to the edition under comment—the Lakeside Classic.

CARTER, FRANCES

Bird Life At Twentynine Palms. 1937. Reprint from the September-October issue of *The Condor.* 10 pp. 3 illus.

This is merely a listing, with brief comment, of a number of birds observed in Twentynine Palms. Unfortunately, there are no photographs or line drawings of the birds; the listing itself is not alphabetical, thus making it quite inconvenient for purposes of reference.

CARUTHERS, WILLIAM

Loafing Along Death Valley Trails. (1951.) Palm Desert, California: The Desert Magazine Press. 186 pp. 17 pls. 6¼ x 9⅛. A second, and slightly revised, edition of this book was published in 1951 by the Death Valley Publishing Co. of Ontario,

California. Of this second edition, 100 copies (so I am informed) were issued in a special deluxe edition, beautifully done, containing 50 pls. and a full-page map of Death Valley.

This is one of the top-level items on Death Valley. In this fine book we read again of Aaron and Rosie Winters and their breath-taking discovery of borax, of old John Searles and his "lake of ooze," of the Indians, of desert gold, of Greenwater, Amargosa, Senator Charles Brown, "Dad" Fairbanks, Shorty Harris, and Death Valley Scotty. Caruthers ushers in a resurgence of glamour as he reactivates for his readers the romantic old ghost towns of this desert's fabulous mining era.

Long Man. 1943. May issue of *Desert.* Illus.

"Dad" Fairbanks—famous Death Valley character—is the "Long Man" of the narrative.

CARVALHO, S. N.

Incidents of Travel and Adventure in the Far West; with Col. Fremont's Last Expedition Across the Rocky Mountains: Including Three Months' Residence in Utah, and a Perilous Trip Across the Great American Desert, to the Pacific. 1857. New York: Derby & Jackson XV, 17-380 pp. 4 pp. advertisements at end. 5¼ x 7½. This first American edition shows the Frémont frontispiece, omitted in the London edition of 1856; also no dedication; also p. 251 shows no section heading "Mormonism." The most recent reprint is in 1954 by the Jewish Publication Society of America.

Carvalho was the artist with Frémont on his fifth and last expedition and provides our only descriptive source account of this venture. In his detailed relation (Ch. XXXVI, pp. 234-241) of their journey along that portion of the Old Spanish Trail extending into California, Carvalho presents what is perhaps the most vivid picture thus far available in any of the overland narratives bearing upon this segment of the trail.

Carvalho depicts, with an artist's true capacity for detail, the desolate route to Bitter Springs (about 20 air miles west of the present town of Baker): "Carcasses of dead horses and oxen strewed the way. Some were left to die, and others still warm, although dead. In the space of one mile I counted 40 dead oxen and cows; the air was foully impregnated with the effluvia arising from them. We also passed six deserted wagons, chairs, tables, and feather beds which were left on the road . . . At noon we arrived at Bitter Springs, the grounds about which were strewn with dead animals, and the polluted atmosphere at this time, one o'clock, p.m. ranges at 95° in the shade of our wagons, and is nearly unbearable. (June 1854.) This is a howling, barren wilderness; not a single tree or shrub for the last fifty miles, nor is there one in sight now. I did not observe during the last day's travel, a lizard or any sign of animal or insect life. There was plenty of food for wolves, but they dare not venture so far from water. These springs are not bitter, but possess a brackish taste. There are small springs in different places; the largest admitted one horse at a time to drink, the rest would have to wait until the water was replenished from the earth."

CAUGHEY, JOHN WALTON

Gold Is the Cornerstone. 1948. Berkeley: University of California Press. 321 pp. 5¾ x 8¾.

Dr. Caughey's book presents a complete integration of all factors, influences and personnel involved in the great migration of 1849. Ch. 7, "The Byways" (pp. 123-158), contains a description of the several routes over the Mojave and the Colorado, including that of the Death Valley trek. Pp. 301-314 give an excellent topical bibliography appertaining to the gold rush.

Indians of Southern California in 1852, The. 1952. San Marino: Huntington Library XXXIV, 151 pp. 2 pp. Bibliography. 6½ x 9⅜. Words "First Edition" appear under copyright notice.

The 1852 report of B. D. Wilson is here printed in book form for the first time. The text is prolific in its references to California desert Indians, and to regulations and procedures affecting them. Although credit is outwardly extended Mr. Wilson, it is the general consensus that Judge Benjamin Hayes is responsible for the actual preparation of this report. Discussion includes material on the Tulareños, the Cahuillas, the Luiseños and the Dieguiños.

(Edited By) *Rushing For Gold.* 1949. Berkeley and Los Angeles: University of California Press. Listed as Special Publication No. 1 of the Pacific Coast Branch of the American Historical Association. 111 pp. 7 x 10⅛.

Of the twelve articles in this book, two are of desert interest—"From Louisiana to Mariposa," edited by Robert Glass Cleland, and "Across Mexico In '49," by Glen S. Dumke. The item—"From Louisiana to Mariposa" is the Joseph Pownall diary. Pownall's account of the Colorado Desert crossing from Yuma to Warner's Ranch is brief and adds little of interest to our knowledge of the southern route. The following authorities contribute chapters to the book: Caughey, Paden, Wyman, Cleland, Dumke, Kemble, Lewis, Wheat, Rydell, Hunt, Baur, Carpenter. (See listing under Pownall, Joseph—*From Louisiana to Mariposa.*)

Southwest from Salt Lake in 1849 and the Jacob Y. Stover Narrative. 1937. June issue of *Pacific Historical Review.* This item is also published in reprint form; 17 pp., wrappers.

Caughey discusses the several groups that broke away from the original Sand Walking Company, and draws copiously upon the source authorities—Manly, Stephens, Brier, Colton, Stover, and others. The inclusion of the *Stover Narrative* probably denotes its first published appearance from the original manuscript. Subsequently, a portion of it was published (1954) in the Hafen's *Journals of Forty-Niners.* This item is rated high on the list of important Death Valley publications. It is perhaps not out of place to add that the original and its reprint are discouragingly difficult to locate. (See listing under Stover, Jacob Y.—*Narrative.*)

CHALFANT, W. A.

Death Valley; The Facts. 1930. Stanford, California: Stanford University Press. IX, 155 pp. 30 pls. 6¼ x 9. End paper relief maps. Has gone into several editions. (160 pp. and 32 pls. in the Third Edition.)

Chalfant's book is the recognized handbook of Death Valley and, as such, assembles a veritable treasure-trove of informative material. Its content features the Valley's geography, history, climatology, water, plants, animals, geology, mining, borax, novelties, perils, and man-made improvements. An essential item in any desert collection, the book supplies a comprehensive knowledge of its subject far beyond that to be obtained from any other single publication on this desert area.

My own personal evaluation of this item was expressed in *Desert Harvest* (1962): "Many great and enduring books have been written of this desert; but, to me, there are two of them that stand alone, distinctive and invulnerable. One of these is the Manly; the other, Chalfant's *Death Valley*."

Gold, Guns, & Ghost Towns. (1947.) Stanford: Stanford University Press. 175 pp. 7 x 10¼.

Garnered from the experiences and observations of an eventful life, Bill Chalfant ran columns of intriguing tales in his newspaper—the *Inyo Register*. Later, these were reprinted in the two books—*Outposts of Civilization* (1928) and *Tales of the Pioneers* (1942). Says Mr. Albright, in his Foreword—"Since both of these books are out of print it seems fitting . . . to issue this combined edition of the most distinctive and entertaining tales and sketches from the two books." And so we have *Gold, Guns, & Ghost Towns* with its vivid tales of Monoville, the Lost Cement Mines, Bodie, Aurora, Pioche, Bennettville, Lundy, Hamilton, Columbus, Mammoth, Shorty Harris, the Lost Ship of the Desert, Oliver Roberts, and many others. The 15 chapters relate mainly to ghost mining camps and characters of California and Nevada.

Outposts of Civilization. 1928. The Christopher Publishing House. 193 pp. 5½ x 8.

To date no revisions nor reprints have appeared of the book in its entirety. Certain of the tales have been reprinted, however, in the author's later book *Gold, Guns, & Ghost Towns*. The item is scarce, important, and a worthy addition to any desert collection. (There are 20 chapters included, eight of which have been reprinted in full, and four reprinted partially, in *Gold, Guns, & Ghost Towns*.)

Story of Inyo, The. 1922. W. A. Chalfant. 358 pp. 5½ x 7¾. Fldg. map of Inyo County. Revised Edition published 1933 with 430 pp. Index I to VIII. Publication date appears on title page of first.

Bill Chalfant, in this able treatise, provides carefully-documented material on Inyo County. The author expanded his Death Valley material into his later publication—*Death Valley: The Facts* (1930). Principal desert references in *The Story of Inyo* are as follows:

Chapter Title	1st Ed.	Rev. Ed.
Death Valley Party of 1849	Ch. 6	Ch. 8
Decade of Exploration	Ch. 7	Ch. 9
Coso and the Desert Camps	———	Ch. 10
Panamint	Ch. 24	Ch. 27
Other Mining Discoveries	Ch. 25	Ch. 28
Later Death Valley History	Ch. 26	Ch. 29
Death Valley Notes	App. D	App. C

Tales of the Pioneers. (1942.) Stanford: Stanford University Press. 129 pp. 7⅛ x 10¼.

To date these desert *Tales* have not been reprinted, except that five of the 18 chapters appear in *Gold, Guns, & Ghost Towns*.

CHALFANT PRESS–for SIERRA MEDIA, INC.

Ghost Town of Bodie, A California State Park. 1967. 120 pp. Soft bound.

The conspicuous feature of the book is its generous assortment of early photographs. Many of these are of outstanding quality. The text is composed largely of quotes from newspapers, arranged chronologically under sectional headings such as The Rise and Fall of Bodie, Stages and Freight Lines, Bodie Railway Rivalry, News Events, Entertainment, Indians, Chinese, Avalanche, Church, Cemetery, Badmen, Fire, and others.

CHAMBERLAIN, SAMUEL E.

My Confession. 1956. My copy, under review, is No. 32 of the special limited edition of 500 copies done by Harper & Brothers for the limited edition subscribers of Arizona Silhouettes; the first 50 done in full Arizona cowhide; X, 302 pp. 55 of the author's best illus., including 16 pp. in full color; end paper map; front cover design; 6½ x 9⅝.

The book is devoted mainly to an unorthodox narrative of the author's adventures while serving as an enlisted man in the Mexican War. A brief but significant reference appears on pp. 291-297 to an early crossing of the Colorado Desert made, apparently, in late April and early May of 1850. We find mention of "Cooks Wells," "Vallecita," and "San Phillippe." Realistic descriptions are given of the notorious Glanton gang of scalp hunters and its operations along the Colorado River. Interestingly, a casual reference appears (p. 259) to Lt. "Coutts" of early Colorado Desert crossing prominence. Lt. Couts was at that time serving in Mexico with Graham's Battalion.

CHAMBERLIN, WILLIAM HAYES (Edited by Bloom, Lansing B.)

From Lewisburg (Pa.) to California In 1849. 1945. January (pp. 14-57), April (pp. 144-180), July (pp. 239-268), and October (pp. 336-357) issues of the *New Mexico Historical Review*.

Chamberlin left Lewisburg, Pa., on Feb. 26, 1849, in company with five other young men, Robert B. Green (see listing in this Bibliography), David "Deacon" Howard, Cyrus Fox, S. Frederick Schaffle, and John Musser. Green and Howard, as well as Chamberlin, wrote of the trip. The Howard Diary is still in manuscript form. Chamberlin's letters appeared in the *Lewisburg Chronicle* in 1849-50; his Diary was published in the same newspaper in 1851. Later the *Lewisburg Saturday News* reprinted the *Chronicle* account. Mr. Bloom came into possession of the newspaper copies from a nephew of William H. Chamberlin, and gave the *Journal* its third printing—this time in magazine form.

The *Journal,* as indicated, occupies a total of some 133 pages of the *Review.* The description of the desert crossing, covering 11 pages, is of the Southern route, following Kearny's trail from the Colorado River crossing to Warner's Ranch. The desert crossing was accomplished during August 10-18, 1849.

This little-known *Journal* is unique in its descriptive appeal. Chamberlin had acutely-developed powers of observation and he gives us perhaps the best detailed description of the Colorado River crossing to be found in any of the overland diaries. It may be noted that his word pictures of the Indians are most colorful.

His dramatic style, as well as his capacity for picturesque description, is nicely portrayed in the following passage, written August 14, concerning their experiences at Cooke's "third" well: "It is situated in a large, deep ravine, but the supply of water was so scanty that we could get but a quart apiece for our animals, and none for ourselves. This place is a perfect Golgotha—the bones of thousands of animals lie strewed about in every direction, and a great number of carcasses of horses and mules that have died lately, pollute the atmosphere. Deserted wagons, harness, saddles, etc., add to this destructive and sickening scene. After draining the well to the last drop, we concluded it would be better to go ahead than to wait for it to fill up again. It was with great difficulty that we restrained our suffering animals from rushing into the pit headlong."

Chamberlin supplies interesting comment concerning the so-called "New River"—that providential overflow of the Colorado in 1849 that saved the lives of so many of the emigrants. His party had only three pints of water remaining when they came suddenly upon this apparent phenomenon.

The Chamberlin *Journal* makes reference, and in some detail, to the large number of Sonorans either traveling or encamped upon the desert in the course of their return from the gold fields to Mexico. We are told that these Sonorans gave "glowing accounts of the gold diggings, and had large quantities of the dust in their possession."

Chamberlin is one of the diarists who mention the "palmetto trees" of the little Palm Springs oasis in the Carrizo Corridor first noted by Pedro Fages and later by Lt. Col. Emory. On August 16 he records an earthquake shock—the same series of quakes, no doubt, as those referred to by Couts on September 22 and by Whipple on September 28.

CHAPMAN, ROBERT H.

Deserts of Nevada and the Death Valley, The. 1906. September issue of *National Geographic.*

Of no particular value to the student of Death Valley is the account on pp. 483-497, aside from the fact that it is one of the early printed descriptions of this desert.

CHAPPELL, MAXINE

Early History of Mono County. 1947. September issue of *California Historical Society Quarterly.* Vol. XXVI, No. 3. Pp. 233-248.

The article provides a comprehensive history of Mono Lake and the desert region surrounding it. (See listing under Cain, Ella M. *The Story of Mono County.*)

CHASE, J. SMEATON

California Desert Trails. 1919. New York: Houghton Mifflin Company. XVI, 387 pp. 35 pls. 5¾ x 8¾. The book has several times been reprinted.

This is, by a studied appraisal of values, one of the two outstanding books descriptive of the Colorado Desert, the other—obviously—being George Wharton James' *Wonders of the Colorado Desert.* All phases of desert life and desert conditions are ably covered. There are chapters on palm oases and canyons; on trees, shrubs, cacti, flowers, and Indian lore. There are early accounts of Palm Springs, Seven Palms, Thousand Palm Cañon, Salton Sea, Coachella Valley, Piñon Wells, Mecca, Figtree John's, Borrego Springs, Los Coyotes, Vallecito, Warner's Spring, Carrizo Creek Cañon, Agua Caliente, San Felipe, Imperial Valley, and the deceptive mirages. El Centro, Calexico, Holtville, Brawley, Shafer's Well, Corn Springs, Dale, and Twentynine Palms are accorded generous mention. Appendix A proffers hints on desert traveling; Appendix B lists and describes some 118 plants that are characteristic of the desert.

The book is well written; the material intelligently assembled. Here is no fictional account of the desert, nor one restrained and uncertain in its telling. *California Desert Trails* is well fortified with factual data gathered by a man-to-desert contact back in the year 1918, when the desert was still young in the knowledge of men. The book is indispensible to *any* library, large or small, whether for desert lover or desert stranger.

Our Araby: Palm Springs and the Garden of the Sun. 1920. Pasadena: Star-News Publishing Company. 83 pp. 9 pls. End pocket map. 4⅝ x 6⅞. Several reprint editions have appeared.

In *Our Araby* Mr. Chase has fashioned a delicately beautiful classic of Palm Springs. The main text is supplemented by a descriptive list of desert plants, and with a section on hints to desert motorists. Ch. 5 (pp. 39-51), presents an itinerary of trips into canyons and other points of interest—24 of them in all.

CHEESMAN, DAVID W. (Edited by Foy, Mary E.)

By Ox-Team from Salt Lake to Los Angeles: 1850. 1930. *Historical Society of Southern California Annual Publication.*

This is the memoir of David W. Cheesman, telling of his party's early-day experiences over the Old Spanish Trail written, apparently, just prior to Cheesman's death in 1884. Their route took them past Hernandez Springs, Mud Springs, and Bitter Springs as they traveled across the Mojave Desert.

CHICKERING, ALLEN L. (Edited By)

Bandits, Borax and Bears—A Trip To Searles Lake in 1874. (See listing under Leuba, Edmond.)

CLARK, ARTHUR H., JR.

Score of Years and Fourscore Issues, A. 1966. Los Angeles: Westernlore Press (printers). 8 pp. Wrappers.

This booklet classifies the issues of the quarterly publication known as the *Branding Iron*, together with the several *Keepsake* issues, published by the Los Angeles Corral of *The Westerners*. This convenient item lists alphabetically the names of the contributing authors with a notation of the issue to which each contributed. Also included is a Subject Guide, classifying subjects and indicating issue number.

CLARK, HOWARD D.

Lost Mines of the Old West. 1946. Los Angeles: Ghost Town Press. 64 pp. 5⅜ x 6⅞. Wrappers.

The author tells us this is the "authentic story of the 'Peg-leg' and 21 other stories of fabulous lost mines." While we may question the authenticity of *any* account relating to the enigmatic "Peg-leg," we certainly do *not* question the sustained interest stimulated by the reading of these lost mine yarns.

CLARK, MAY L. and COUZENS, TWILA G.

Yucca Valley and Its History. 1966. 25 pp. Wrappers.

In their Foreword the authors explain: "This paper came about through a request of the Parent Teacher Association . . . for third grade teacher research material which could be used to supplement their Social Science program . . . It has been our aim to stress the development and way of life of the area rather than its people . . ."

CLARKE, A. B.

Travels in Mexico and California, Comprising a Journal of a Tour From Brazos Santiago, Through Central America, By Way of Monterey, Chihuahua, the Country of the Apaches, and the River Gila, to the Mining Districts of California. 1852. Boston: Wright & Hasty. 138 pp. (Cowan P. 48; Wagner-Camp No. 210.) 4½ x 7½. Wrappers.

Clarke's description of the desert crossing is dramatically impressive. He and 45 others, all members of the Hampden Mining Co., left New York by boat to Mexico. On June 26, 1849, they crossed the Colorado River and started over the desert. On July 3 they arrived at Warner's. Death threatened them constantly, day and night, during this punishing mid-summer week on the relentless desert. Clarke tells of finding a water hole "eight feet deep with a dead horse and a few inches of water at the bottom." Later, they met "a poor old horse that had been left by someone. He looked at us a little and staggered on." At another time they "passed a poor mule with a saddle on, standing in the path, while a pack of wolves were howling for him over a neighboring sand hill. The whole distance we have passed carcasses of mules and horses . . . At least 30 or 40 a day."

CLARKE, DWIGHT L. (Edited by)

Original Journals of Henry Smith Turner. (See listing under Turner, Henry Smith.)

[49]

Stephen Watts Kearny—Soldier of the West. (1961.) Norman, Oklahoma: University of Oklahoma Press. 448 pp. 16 illus. Map. 6¼ x 9¼.

This is the definitive account of Stephen Watts Kearny, a man whose life's history and achievements are all but unknown to the vast majority of Americans. Mr. Clarke traces from its very beginning the brilliant career of this trained army man who led the Army of the West over the Colorado Desert and into the historic Battle of San Pasqual, then on through the trying ordeal of the court sessions resulting from his controversy with Frémont.

The Kearny book is a timely one; and the Clarke study fulfills a long-recognized need, not only in American history, but in its relation to the literature of our Southern California deserts.

CLELAND, ROBERT GLASS

An Exile On the Colorado. 1956. *Westerners, The* (Los Angeles Corral) *Brand Book* No. 6. 13 pp. 5 illus.

The article concerns Major Heintzelman, Lt. Sweeny, and Fort Yuma. There is mention of the Oatman tragedy, the Glanton gang, and the Garra revolt.

Cattle on a Thousand Hills, The: Southern California, 1850-70. 1941. San Marino: The Huntington Library. XIV, 327 pp. 4 pls. 6½ x 9¼. The book has been reprinted.

In connection with its study of the early ranchos, occasional reference is made to bordering desert areas and peoples—Warner's Ranch, Agua Caliente Ranch, San Gorgonio Ranch, the Cajon Pass, the Cahuilla Indians, and so on. Included in Dr. Cleland's distinguished book—in Appendix IV, pp. 306 to 315—is the letter of Mr. L. J. Rose, reprinted from the *Missouri Republican* of November 29, 1859. Rose was a member of the ill-fated group of emigrants who, in the latter part of August 1858, were set upon at the Colorado River by a horde of Mojave Indians. Several of their number were killed, and their livestock decimated. Later, a punitive expedition under Lt. Col. Hoffman was dispatched by the Government against the Mojaves.

Pathfinders. (1929.) Los Angeles: Powell Publishing Co. 452 pp. Fldg. map. End paper designs. 14 illus. 6¾ x 9⅝. "Of the Series California." This reviewed copy not identified as a first.

Beginning with the voyages of Cabrillo, we are given—in fast-moving sequence —the exploits of Drake, Vizcaíno, the men of the San Carlos, Portolá, Crespi, Garcés, Anza, Vancouver, Shaler, Jed. Smith, John Bidwell, John C. Frémont, Kit Carson, the Donner Party, and others. Ch. 7 "Conquerors of the Desert," (pp. 155-184), is rich in desert interest. Here we have the story of the de Anza expeditions, with their redoubtable Garcés and their intrepid Father Pedro Font.

The narrative of Benjamin D. (Don Benito) Wilson appears in the appendix (pp. 371-416). In this narrative (pp. 388-389) is related Wilson's experiences with Chief Cabezon and his Cahuilla Indians, during the latter part of 1845, when he set out through the San Gorgonio Pass to capture two renegade Indians who had taken residence with the Cahuillas. The Wilson narrative was reprinted in the *Historical Society of Southern California Annual Publication of 1934.* (See listing under Bynum, Lindley—*Record Book of the Rancho Santa Ana del Chino.*)

CLEMENS, SAMUEL L.

Roughing It in California. (See listing under Twain, Mark.)

CLEMENTS, LYDIA

Indians of Death Valley, The. (1953.) Hollywood: Hollycrafters. 23 pp. 5 illus. 5½ x 8½. Wrappers.

This book may well be reckoned essential Death Valley material. The author goes all the way back to the Ice-Age man, following through a study of Prehistory Indians with their petroglyphs and maps, on down into the period of historic times with a discussion of Indian relics—jewelry, tools, pottery and basketry. Mention is made of the first recorded contact of the Indians with the white man; also of their habits and their dwellings. Finally, the author extends her scope to include a study of present-day Indians, their education and culture.

CLEMENTS, THOMAS

Geological Story of Death Valley. (1954.) Publication No. 1 Death Valley '49ers, Inc. Printed and distributed by Desert Magazine Press at Palm Desert, California. 52 pp. 17 pls. 1 map. 5½ x 8½.

Valuable information is made conveniently available to the reader in this quick reference booklet. Dr. Clements, in his expository treatise, achieves the enviable distinction of having presented a technical subject in a style completely understandable to the lay-reader.

CLYDE, NORMAN

High-Low. 1930. November issue of *Touring Topics.* Illus.

The author describes his descent from Mt. Whitney's 14,496-foot altitude to the near-lowest spot in America—over 280 feet below sea level—on the floor of Death Valley (Bad Water). The entire descent occupied only 7 hours. (Refer to Neill C. Wilson's *Telescope Peak From Death Valley.*)

COCKERELL, T. D. A.

Colorado Desert of California, The: Its Origin and Biota. 1945. June issue of *Transactions Kansas Academy of Science.* Vol. 48, No. 1. 39 pp. 12 pls.

Among other sections in this well-written account are included: Formation of the Colorado Desert, Lake Cahuilla, Desert Endemics, Mojave-Colorado Area, Plant Association, Wild Bees, Climate, People of Colorado Desert, and Salton Sea.

CODY, IRON EYES

"Little White Chieftain." 1963. *Westerners, The* (Los Angeles Corral) *Brand Book* No. 10. 40 pp. 46 reproductions of Clarence Ellsworth's paintings.

Iron Eyes Cody prepared the running text to the Clarence Ellsworth folio of paintings—forty-five of them reproduced in sepia, one in a large folding reproduction in color of Ellsworth's famous painting, "The Buffalo."

The Editor of *Brand Book* No. 10, in his capsule presentation of Iron Eyes' exceptional article, writes: "No one is better qualified to write of the life and accomplishments of Clarence Ellsworth than Iron Eyes Cody, who was his close friend and next door neighbor. Their relationship resembled that of father and son. . . . A generous portion of the article is given over to a taped recital by Mr. Ellsworth of his life and experiences, with particular emphasis upon his interest in art and the gradual development of this exceptional talent."

COKE, MR. and MRS. LARRY

Calico. 1941. Barstow: *Printer Review.* 57 pp. Illus. 4¼ x 6⅜. Wrappers.

Who could better write of the famous old ghost town known as Calico than its longtime residents, Larry and Lucille Coke? It's all here—the story of the silver boom, the discovery, the mining era, the big fire, the eventual decline. The book contains short biographical sketches of notable old-time characters—J. A. Delameter, Charles Henry Colton, Charley Williams, Madame DeLill, and others. Among its 22 photographic plates are some rather unusual pictures—in particular one of Mr. and Mrs. Delameter and one of Aaron and Rosie Winters (of Death Valley borax prominence).

COLLIER, JAMES

Adventures of James Collier, First Collector of the Port of San Francisco. (See listing under Foreman, Grant.)

Collier came to San Francisco via the Southwest trail in 1849.

COLTON, JOHN B.

Death Valley Mines, The. From *San Jose Pioneer* of December 15, 1895.

Reprinted in Arthur Woodward's (or W. L. Manly's) *The Jayhawkers' Oath.* Colton was one of the original Jayhawkers of Death Valley fame.

Interview With. From *San Francisco Bulletin* of February 4, 1903. Reprinted in Dr. Margaret Long's *The Shadow of the Arrow.*

The venerable Colton, one of the heroic Jayhawkers of Death Valley, was unfortunate in having been interviewed by a reporter whose impertinence eclipsed his better judgment.

COMFORT, H. G. (Compiler) and ROGERS, BILL (Photos)

Camera Shots of Ghost Cities of California and Nevada. 1941. Shafter, California: Shafter Press. 30 pp. 48 pls. 5½ x 7½. Wrappers.

The several photographs are of special interest.

CONKIN, PAUL K.

Two Paths To Utopia. (1964.) 212 pp. 5¼ x 9¼.

The book goes into considerable detail regarding the experimental socialist utopian colony of Llano, in the Mojave Desert. There are two major divisions to the book: Part One—The Brethren Known As Hutterites; Part Two—Llano Del Rio. It is Part Two that relates the book to our Southern California desert interest.

Llano was established in 1914 by a socialist lawyer, Jeb Harriman. From a nucleus of five people, Llano knew—for a short time—its maximum membership of 1100. Almost from the beginning the colony was an economic failure. As early as October 1917 the equipment and industries of the colony started the move from California to Louisiana. By 1920 the Llano colony had about passed out of existence.

The author suggests that Llano did not overlook the cultural aspects of her existence. It developed park and play activities, held open forums on intellectual and even controversial topics, housed a library of over 5000 volumes, maintained good schools, enjoyed dancing. On the other hand, it devoted little time and thought to religious matters. Significantly, the colony contained a relatively large number of men and elderlies. Not many who came remained for any great length of time. The esoteric colonists could not adjust to this new and peculiar way of life. So the utopian concept died for the very obvious reason that it lacked the capacity to live.

(See listings under Bailey, David—*Llano's Withered Dream;* also Hine, Robt. V. —*California's Utopian Colonies.*)

CONKLING, ROSCOE and MARGARET

Butterfield Overland Mail, The. (3 vol.). 1947. Glendale, California: The Arthur H. Clark Company. Vol. 1, 412 pp.; Vol. 2, 446 pp.; Vol. 3, Charts, Maps and Illustrations. 6½ x 9½.

The Conklings have prepared an exhaustive treatise of the historic Butterfield route (1857-1869), a portion of which extended through our Southern California deserts. "The Route and Stations on Division VIII—Through California From Fort Yuma to Los Angeles," pp. 193-253 in Vol 2, provides a desert reference of immediate interest. The magnitude of its scope, and the almost insuperable odds against recovery of the Butterfield's long neglected and romantic past, cause this narrative of the colorful stage line to become one of the truly important literary contributions to the history of the West.

CONKLING, ROSCOE P.

Butterfield Overland Mail in California, The. 1949. Los Angeles: *Westerners, The* (Los Angeles Corral) *Brand Book* No. 2.

The Conkling article, descriptive of the Overland Route generally, and the California portion of it in particular, may be found on pp. 17-23 of the *Brand Book.* The article has 4 illus.

CONROTTO, EUGENE L.

Lost Desert Bonanzas. (1963.) Palm Desert, California: Desert Printers. 278 pp. Maps by Norton Allen. 7 x 10¼.

Conrotto has "boiled-down" some 112 lost mine stories that had appeared over the years in *Desert* Magazine. As far as capable condensation will permit, each of these skeletal remains suggests a tale of absorbing interest.

CONSTANS, BERNICE R.

Songs of the Sands. 1937. 28 pp. 8 full-page reproductions of photographs taken in the California deserts. 7⅞ x 10. Wrappers.

This attractive booklet contains eight poems of the desert.

COOKE, P. ST. GEORGE

Conquest of New Mexico and California, The. 1878. G. P. Putnam's Sons. 307 pp. Fldg. map. J. A. Sullivan reprinted the Cooke in one of his Biobooks in 1952 in a limited edition of 600 copies. This reprint, under review, contains 165 pp., fldg. map, 4 colored lithographs from the *Pacific Railroad Survey*, Vols. 5 and 7; measures 7 x 10. Horn and Wallace came out with a most attractive facsimile edition in 1964, containing 307 pp., with a foreword by Philip St. George Cooke III.

Chs. 3 and 4—"The Infantry March to the Pacific" and "California" (pp. 66-137), detail the march of the Mormon Battalion over the Colorado Desert. (Cowan P. 55; Wagner-Camp No. 165.) Colonel Cooke's narrative takes on added interest in view of the fact that it represents the viewpoint of the non-Mormon leader of the historic Mormon Battalion. (Pp. 125-262 reflect the Colorado Desert material in the Horn and Wallace reprint.)

Journal of the March of the Mormon Battalion, 1846-1847. 1846-1847. Sen. Ex. Doc. 31 Cong. Spec. Sess. Included in Dr. Ralph P. Bieber's *Exploring Southwest Trails 1846-1854*, being Vol. 7 of the Southwest Historical Series, Glendale, California: The Arthur H. Clark Company. 1938.

That portion of the *Journal* relating to the Battalion's march across the Colorado Desert to San Diego, via Carrizo, Vallecito, and Warner's Ranch, appears on pp. 200-240 of the Bieber reprint. The *Journal* of Col. Cooke, the non-Mormon leader of the Mormon Battalion—all members of which, save one, were Mormons —provides the basic account of the Battalion's march across the desert to San Diego. There are several source accounts of this historic episode—Cooke, Tyler, Standage, Bigler and others; but the Cooke narrative is distinguished not alone by the keen perceptiveness of its author, but also by the refinement in composition that so conspicuously sets it apart. The *Journal*, couched in the cherished traditions of military exactness, does not once fail to bear evidence of the writer's capacity for appropriate and precise expression.

As a leader, Cooke was resolute in his purpose and frequently inexorable in the enforcement of it. Not once, so far as we know, did he relax his authority over the men. In the initial stages of their march this authority was regarded by some as extreme and coercive; but, as the journey progressed, distaste for the commander became subordinated to a growing respect—both by the men and by the leaders of the Church. Cooke, also, experienced a complete reversal of his early estimate of the qualities and qualifications of the men. Distrust, lack of confidence, exasperation over their desultory obedience to military discipline—these eventually gave way to a surge of admiration for the men of the Mormon Battalion. Cooke incited courage by being himself courageous; he commanded respect and loyalty by virtue of example. For instance, when a narrow defile was encountered that negatived possibility of wagon passage, it was Cooke who—without a word—secured an axe and "pounded, broke, split and hewed the rocks to increase the opening" so the wagons could go through.

Report of His March From Santa Fe, New Mexico to San Diego, Upper California. 1847. Pp. 549-562 of Lt. Col. W. H. Emory's *Notes of a Military Reconnoissance* (House Ex. Doc. No. 41). Reprinted in the January 1954, issue of the *Utah Historical Quarterly*.

Pp. 558-560 supply Cooke's report to General Kearny of the Mormon Battalion's march from the Colorado River crossing to San Diego. In this brief account the energetic Cooke tells much, and he tells it well.

COOLIDGE, DANE

Death Valley Prospectors. 1937. New York: E. P. Dutton & Company. 178 pp. Illus. 5¾ x 8⅜. Words "First Edition" appear under copyright.

Coolidge sketches in bold strokes the activities of notable Death Valley characters—Breyfogle, Smitty, Lemoigne, Shorty Harris, Death Valley Scotty. The author tends toward the racy and melodramatic, as distinguished from the more conservative style and factual concern of the historian.

Fighting Men of the West. 1932. New York: E. P. Dutton & Company. 343 pp. Illus. 6 x 8¾. Death Valley reference pp. 303-336. Words "First Edition" appear under copyright notice. Even in its reprint editions this book is hard to come by.

Our desert reference alludes to Walter Scott (Death Valley Scotty). Coolidge summarizes in one discerning paragraph what may serve as a sensible conclusion to the long-drawn controversy as to whether the inscrutable Scotty had a mine, or if he was merely a four-flusher, drawing imperiously upon his millionaire partner, Johnson. Says Coolidge—"There are those who will swear that Scotty never had a mine, but he must be crazier than he looks to roam Death Valley for forty years and not pick up some gold. Shorty Harris found four mines in less than forty years, among them the Bullfrog and Harrisburg, and Scott has traveled farther and seen more. He has chosen to be mysterious, keeping his diggings a secret, and he has a rich partner who stakes him; but it is reasonable to suppose that, despite his evasive talk, he did discover a very rich mine. No man would squander money the way he did without some color to show for it."

Scotty's Castle. 1939. March issue of *Westways.* Illus.

Few writers are better equipped than Dane Coolidge to write on the subject of Scotty and his fabulous castle on the outskirts of Death Valley.

Death Valley and the Creek Called Furnace. (1962.) Los Angeles: The Ward Ritchie Press. IX plus 60 pp. with an additional 32 unnumbered pages of photographic plates by Ansel Adams. Foreword by Lawrence Clark Powell. 7½ x 10½.

This book reprints the Death Valley portion of Corle's earlier (1941) *Desert Country*. The superb photographic plates by Ansel Adams lend character, and cause the book to become an identity rather than just another reprint.

Desert Country. (1941.) New York: Duell, Sloan & Pearce. 357 pp. 6 x 8¾. Words "First Edition" appear under copyright notice. End paper maps. There are several reprint editions.

The book, in its entirety, is devoted to the subject of deserts—deserts in California, Nevada, Utah and Arizona. California deserts are featured on pp. 3-65, under the section heading "Mojave is Mojave." Here, among other subjects of even interest, is an article on Calico, another on Twentynine Palms, another on the Mitchell Caves in Providence Mountain. In another section of the book, captioned "Though I Walk Through the Valley of the Shadow of Death" (pp. 267-316), may be found a reasonably accurate account of Death Valley—its history, its geological background and physical attractions, its borax industry, its near-by ghost town of Skidoo, and its Death Valley Scotty. Portions of the section on "Fourth Estate" (pp. 202-224) relate to the California deserts, as do parts of the section on "Legendry" (pp. 225-234 and 250-265).

In general, *Desert Country* is accurately and entertainingly written. By all odds it may be considered one of California's great books of the desert; a book that is certain to endure.

Fig Tree John. 1935. New York: Liveright Publishing Corporation. 318 pp. Republished in February of 1955, in a boxed deluxe edition of 550 copies, by The Ward Ritchie Press.

A novel of Indian life around the Salton Sea area.

Gila, The: River of the Southwest. 1951. New York: Rinehart and Company, Inc. 402 pp. Illustrated by Ross Santee. 5¾ x 8¼. One of the "Rivers of America" series.

Always the Gila River must be closely associated with the historical background of the Colorado Desert. For this was the route they followed—Kearny, Emory, Cooke, the Forty-Niners: west along the Gila to its mouth; across the Colorado; over the treacherous desert; through Carrizo, Vallecito, and Warner's; thence to San Diego or Los Angeles. In his book, Corle coordinates the history of this great westward surge with his story of the Gila.

Corle has turned in a brilliant contribution to the history of Arizona in his absorbing narrative of the Gila. Anyone interested in pursuing his study of the engaging historical background of the Colorado Desert should accept—as his initial project—the reading of *The Gila*. It is this region round-about the junction of the Gila and Colorado Rivers that provided the springboard approach to a precipitous plunge into the vast desert area spreading monotonously to the west. It was here that the southern-route emigrants of 1849—and even the missionary explorers who came earlier—paused to consolidate their energies for the huge adventure that lay before them.

The Gila, Martin's *Yuma Crossing*, and Wallace's *The Great Reconnaissance* constitute that effective triumvirate of books descriptive of the geographic and historic significance of the region where the Gila joins its waters with the Colorado. It was here, at this precise point, that vital incidents of far-reaching consequence transpired which influenced immeasurably the development of our southern deserts and—for that matter—of the entire State of California.

Mojave. (1934.) New York: Liveright Publishing Corporation. 272 pp. 5½ x 7¾.
The book contains 14 stories, each replete with the penetrant tang of the desert. The first yarn, "Listen, Desert," is—if a purely personal opinion may be ventured— a masterpiece of desert literature.

CORNELL, RALPH D.

Conspicuous California Plants. 1938. Pasadena: San Pasqual Press. 192 pp. 46 pls. 6¾ x 9¾. Limited to 1500 copies.
Pp. 20-29 and 121-160, with 14 full page pls., constitute the desert section of this fine book—a book, by the way, that will add character and charm to any library.

CORY, H. T. and BLAKE, W. P.

Imperial Valley, The and The Salton Sink. 1915. San Francisco: John J. Newbegin XIII, 1-61 pp., 1204-1581 pp. 6⅛ x 8⅞. Eight photographs in front on unnumbered pp. 1 pl. Numerous maps and diagrams.
Part I (pp. 1-35) provides a non-technical discussion by Dr. Wm. P. Blake, he of the *Pacific Railroad Surveys* in the early 1850s. Part 2 (pp. 37-51) contains abstracts of scientific monographs by W. H. Ross and Godfrey Sykes concerning the Salton Sea. Part 3 (pp. 53-61) is by H. T. Cory. Part 4 (pp. 1204-1571) is a technical article by H. T. Cory, and Part 5 (pp. 1572-1581) is likewise authored by H. T. Cory.

COUES, ELLIOTT (Translated and edited by)

On the Trail of a Spanish Pioneer: The Diary and Itinerary of Francisco Garces (Missionary Priest), in His Travels Through Sonora, Arizona, and California. 1775-1776. (2 Vol.) 1900. New York: Francis P. Harper. Limited to 950 copies. Vol. 1—312 pp.; Vol. 2—313-608 pp. 18 maps, views and facsimiles. 6½ x 9¼. (Cowan P. 94.)
The Garcés *Diary*, as translated from the Spanish and edited by Dr. Coues, contains considerable material bearing upon the missionary's route over the Southern California deserts. Dr. Coues's theory that Garcés came through the San Gorgonio Pass has since been discarded for one favoring the San Carlos Pass. This work is a desert item of importance.
Says Dr. Coues, in his Introduction, "On his [Garcés'] fourth expedition, in 1774, he accompanied Captain J. B. de Anza to the Californian mission of San Gabriel on the return from which he took a turn on his own account to one of the

Yuman tribes on the Colorado. . . . In 1775-1776 . . . Garcés started with Anza's celebrated expedition for the establishment of a mission and colony at San Francisco in California . . . but separated from the main party at Yuma, at the junction of the Gila and Colorado, then went to the mouth of the latter river, returned, went up the Colorado to Mojave, thence across California to San Gabriel, thence by way of Tulare Valley back to Mojave, thence to Moqui and back again to Mojave, thence down river to Yuma, and so on up the Gila to his post at Bac." (See listing under Galvin, John—*A Record of Travels In Arizona and California*.)

COULTER, DR. THOMAS

Notes on Upper California, a Journey from Monterey to the Colorado River in 1832. 1951. Los Angeles: Printed for Glen Dawson. 40 pp. 5 x 7¼.
    "Coulter made the first botanical exploration of the California deserts and many plants, including the Coulter Pine, are named for him." (From Glen Dawson.) Coulter's original notes were accompanied by what may well be the earliest map of a region later to become the nearly exact route of the Butterfield line.

COUTS, LT. CAVE JOHNSON

From San Diego to the Colorado in 1849. The Journal and Maps of Cave J. Couts. (Edited by William McPherson.) 1933. Los Angeles: The Zamorano Club. XXVII, 78 pp. 3 maps. 5 x 6½. The Arthur M. Ellis Memorial Edition, limited to 130 copies.
    Two editions of this important *Journal* have been published. The Arthur M. Ellis Memorial Edition is done in full grain leather with an "In Memoriam" section to Arthur MacDonald Ellis authored by J. Gregg Layne; a "Tribute" by William Webb Clary; a "Eulogy" by Robert Ernest Cowan. J. Gregg Layne writes the preface to the *Journal*; the Notes are prepared by William McPherson. The Memorial Edition, while bearing the publication date of 1933, is—in fact—identical to the so-called First Edition published in 1932. The Zamorano Club merely picked up 130 copies of the first edition, added the memorial articles, and bound them in full leather. (It has been anonymously stated that only 50 of these copies were bound in full leather and printed on a special grade of paper.)
    Says Mr. Layne in his Preface—"The Diary is of especial interest not alone for the many details of life and conditions it depicts, as well as the numerous persons mentioned, but for the fact that it is one of the few early diaries of an expedition going east from California." Pp. 6-25 bear directly upon this West-to-East desert crossing.
    Couts served with Graham's Battalion as a lieutenant of the First U. S. Dragoons; also in the Boundary Survey until 1851. In 1849, he conducted the Whipple Expedition from San Diego to the Colorado, being in command of its military escort. Lt. Whipple's project was to assist in the survey of the new boundary between the United States and Mexico. The impetuous Couts etches graphic word pictures of people and places. Of collateral interest is the purely incidental contact established between Couts—the east bound traveler—and the "swarms" of west

bound emigrants enroute to the gold fields over the uncertain trails of Emory and Cooke through the tortuous desert areas of Southern California. Couts shared no community of interest with these emigrants in their absorbing urge to arrive at the gold fields. They merely annoyed him with their endless inquiries; exhausted him with their ceaseless requests for "way-bills" (a western colloquialism for written travel information). And so it is that these two sets of contemporary accounts— Couts's and the gold seekers'—so utterly divergent in their basic concept and in their objective approach, yet so closely interrelated in their focal bearing upon one single, historic event, present an intimate word-picture of that revealing pageant of human emotions and human operations. For the expressions of the emigrants, in their journals and letters and diaries, see listing under Foreman, Grant—*Marcy & the Gold Seekers*. Reference is also made to Lt. Whipple's report of this expedition. (See Whipple, Amiel Weeks—*Report of Lieutenant Whipple's Expedition from San Diego to the Colorado, 1849*.)

It is not always possible to demarcate the basically essential from the purely decorative aspects of history, even in retrospective appraisement. The story of Mary Conway is illustrative. Mary was the attractive seventeen-year-old daughter of one of the emigrants—a Dr. Conway. She was the eldest of ten children. As one writer puts it: "[Mary] rode a beautiful black horse all the way to California; for ten months was the cynosure of many admiring eyes. She stirred the emotions of young emigrants and army officers. . . ." Her beauty and personality set her apart as someone quite special. Unquestionably, Mary Conway supplied an aura of romance among the emigrants at Camp Salvation that may have been equally as beneficial as the life-saving water so miraculously provided for them. Even the sophisticated Lt. Couts became victim to her charm. "I had a delightful time with the interesting Miss Mary," he writes, "for whom I have been saving a bottle of molasses and a lump of sugar since three weeks. I found more than anticipated, though she had been so highly spoken of by all who had passed. Had the pleasure of her and her mother's company with me on the 25th and 27th; could not tear myself away until seeing them some miles from camp. An angel in such wilds! Farewell, Miss Mary! May you wed your true love, and the Lord take a liking to you."

Journal (Hepah, California). 1961. Tucson: Arizona Pioneers' Historical Society. Designed and printed by Lawton Kennedy. Edited by Henry F. Dobyns. Limited to 750 copies. 113 pp. plus eight unnumbered pages of index. Contains selection of eight maps from the manuscript map journal of Couts. Complete fldg. map of Couts's journey; 4 sketches by Samuel E. Chamberlain; portrait of Couts. 7¼ x 10½.

The *Journal* records the 1848-49 march from Monterrey, Nuevo León, Mexico to Los Angeles. The expedition was under the command of Major Lawrence P. Graham for whom Lt. Couts had little or no respect, classifying him as one "of a weak mind stupified by whiskey. . . . He arrived here drunk; is now drunk and will leave here drunk and will be drunk as long as mules last to haul the sutler's whiskey."

On November 28, 1848, they crossed the Colorado. In the process of doing so,

Couts almost drowned. On the night of December 2 they arrived at the Carrizo and rested here a day before proceeding up the Corridor past Vallecito and on to Warner's Ranch.

Nine months later Lt. Couts crossed the Colorado Desert again; but this time his route was from West to East. Couts was in command of the military escort accompanying Lt. Whipple who was in charge of the survey party.

It is unfortunate the voluble Couts did not have more to say of the desert crossing from the Colorado River west to Warner's. It is patent he saw no purpose in so doing. "The desert passed over," he laconically states, "has been described by many." And he lets it go at that. One cannot equate his reference to "many" with actual fact. In 1848 only a minimal number of such descriptions had been written. In 1849-1850, when the vast hordes of gold seekers swarmed across this desert, the number of descriptive accounts proliferated into an almost unbelievable quantity. Significantly, the existence of the Couts journal—prior to its publication—was largely unknown.

COUZENS, TWILA G. and CLARK, MAY L.

Yucca Valley and Its History. (See listing under Clark, May L.)

COVILLE, FREDERICK VERNON (Jointly with MORTON, C. V.)

Botany. 1935 (June 15 and July 15). Journal of the Washington Academy of Science. 1936 (March 15 and May 15). Journal of the Washington Academy of Science.

The foregoing have been issued in reprint form. They supply material supplementary to the 1893 edition of *Botany of the Death Valley Expedition*.

Botany of the Death Valley Expedition. 1893. Washington: U. S. Government Printing Office. 363 pp. 6½ x 10. Large fldg. map of California, Nevada, and Utah. Wrappers.

Twenty-one elaborate plates of Death Valley flora are included in the back section of this rare old book on Death Valley. It is said Coville lists 136 separate species of plants to be found in the Valley in 1892.

COX, CORNELIUS C. (Edited by Martin, Mabelle Eppard)

From Texas to California in 1849: Diary of C. C. Cox. 1925-1926. July and August (1925) and January (1926) issues of *Southwestern Historical Quarterly* (Texas).

Cox is another of the 1849 emigrants who found their way to the goldfields via the Southern route, across the Colorado Desert. Owen C. Coy, in his *The Great Trek*, quotes copiously from the Cox *Diary*.

COY, OWEN C.

Battle of San Pasqual, The. 1921. Sacramento: California State Printing Office. 18 pp. 1 pl. 2 maps. 6 x 9. Wrappers.

"A Report of the California Historical Survey Commission with Special Reference to its Location." An act of the California State Legislature provided for the acceptance of one acre of land, presumably the site of the historic battle of San Pasqual; also for the preparation, by the Historical Commission, of a descriptive narrative of the battle with a determination of the exact location of its several engagements. The brochure appears to accomplish its objective, succinctly and accurately. Lt. Emory's account of the battle is freely drawn upon. Quoted, also, is General Kearny's official report of the battle under date of Dec. 12, 1846.

Great Trek, The. (1931.) Los Angeles: Powell Publishing Co. 349 pp. Illus. 6½ x 9⅝. This copy not identified as a first.
Coy's book favors us with a composite picture of the great westward movement, strengthened by extracts from diaries of the several overland groups. Of desert interest are pp. 253-262, quoting from the diary of Cornelius Cox as he describes the journey over the Colorado Desert. Similarly (pp. 265-280), "The Death Valley Trail" touches upon the adventures of the Death Valley contingent. Included in this section is an excerpt from the diary of Judge Walter Van Dyke; also a short excerpt from the Benjamin Hayes *Diary.*

CRAFTS, MRS. E. P. R.

Pioneer Days In the San Bernardino Valley. 1906. Redlands: Kingsley, Moles & Collins Co., printers. 214 pp. 35 early photographs of people and places. 5¾ x 7¾.
Ch. 11 (pp. 114-120) discloses an intimate picture of Indian life and character, the Indians being the desert Cahuillas and their noted chief—Cabazon. Ch. 11 (pp. 21-26) tells of the early Mormon pioneers, with some reference to Capt. Jefferson Hunt and the Death Valley Party, and more particularly to the Brier family. Mrs. Crafts's book makes for interesting reading, and it may well be considered one of the more important among the relatively few source records available concerning the early history of the San Bernardino Valley. The author moved into the Valley in 1854, at the age of 29; lived there for the remainder of her long, eventful life. Her book, now quite scarce, was written in her 80th year.

CRAMPTON, FRANK A.

Legend of John Lamoigne. 1956. Denver: Sage Books. 32 pp. 12 interesting pls. of early desert scenes. 1 line map. 5½ x 8½. Wrappers.
The author, himself an early pioneer of the Death Valley region, supplies interesting comments on one of the Valley's famous prospectors—old John Lamoigne. In November 1956, the author issued a book descriptive of his early experiences in the Nevada gold fields—*Deep Enough* (Denver: Alan Swallow. 275 pp.; 59 photographic illustrations; 5¾ x 8⅝). The final chapter in this book (pp. 252-275) is the material contained in the *Legend of John Lamoigne.* The story of Lamoigne's "castle" at Garlic Springs sounds a bit fantastic, even for Death Valley. Interesting, also, is the author's reference to the early *supply center* of Ballarat as the "old Panamint Silver Mining Camp."

CRAWFORD, THOMAS EDGAR

West of the Texas Kid, The. (1962.) Norman: University of Oklahoma Press. Edited by Jeff C. Dykes. 202 pp. 5¼ x 7¾.

California desert material may be found in abundance in the final section of this exciting book—"Death Valley Ways, 1906-1910" (pp. 173-200). There is some unusually good descriptive writing on the Mojave Desert, particularly in the Panamint area. One of the chapters relates the author's mining experiences in and near Death Valley; another—and perhaps the most important—tells of Ballarat and a few of the incidents occurring there. This account, written by an on-the-scene observer, is one of the most intimate records available concerning the day-by-day life in the old supply camp during the peak of its activity.

CREMONY, JOHN C.

Life Among the Apaches: 1849-1864. 1868. San Francisco: A. Roman & Co. Reprinted in 1951 by Arizona Silhouettes, Tucson. Reprint edition limited to 750 copies. 322 pp. Illus.

In Ch. 9 mention is made of Lt. Whipple, and the singular and fortuitous incident of the eclipse of the moon. In Ch. 10 we find some account of the Colorado River crossing and the march into the desert, past Carrizo Creek and Vallecito.

CRESPI, FATHER JUAN

Fray Juan Crespi, etc. (See listing under Bolton, Herbert E.)

CRISFIELD, J. W.

Colorado Desert. 1862. (April 23.) House Report No. 87, 37th Congress.

Under joint resolution of the California legislature, passed April 12, 1859, the United States was asked to donate and cede to California a tract of land known as the Colorado Desert. The reason for the resolution was to cede to O. M. Wozencraft and his associates enough land to enable them to bring in water from the Colorado River to accomplish Wozencraft's dream of a vast reclamation project in the Imperial Valley. Included in the Report are letters from Capt. H. S. Burton, Major Emory, R. C. Matthews, A. B. Gray, E. F. Beale, J. J. Abert, O. M. Wozencraft and others. The Report covers 26 pages, and provides a most interesting and unusual concept of the Colorado Desert area and an altogether intriguing bit of early desert literature. Incidentally, the bill covered by this Report was favorably received by the Federal Government but, before action could be taken, the attack on Ft. Sumter occurred and the great project of reclamation lay dormant for many years to come.

CRONISE, TITUS FEY

Natural Wealth of California, etc., The. 1868. San Francisco: XVI, 696 pp. H. H. Bancroft Co. 10¼ x 7½. A portion of the first edition carries 16 pls. (Cowan P. 60.)

Death Valley is mentioned in the chapters on San Bernardino and on Inyo

Counties, with conflicting dimensions given of the Valley. Desert material is to be found on pp. 94-103, 117-120, 280-288. The Cronise gives us one of our earliest published *book* references to Death Valley, naming it as such.

CRONKHITE, DANIEL

Death Valley's Victims. 1968. Verdi, Nevada: Sagebrush Press. IX 33 pp. 3 additional pp., not numbered, captioned "About the Author." 12 illus. 6 x 9. Edition limited to 225 deluxe copies and 750 copies in wrappers.

This book is noteworthy for at least two reasons. So much has been written of Death Valley that any author who can produce a book containing virgin material on this muchly-exploited desert has truly accomplished something new under the sun. Author Cronkhite has done just that. His entire subject matter relates to those who have met death on the sands of this desert land. The arrangement is chronological, extending from 1849 through 1966.

The other reason that gives this book some claim to distinction is that it is handset—"Every letter has been set and justified in a composing stick by the author."

The photographic reproductions are remarkably well done, and the subjects intelligently selected.

CROTSENBURG, MAXINE and CAL

Gateway to the Hi-Desert—A History of Morongo Valley. N.d. ca. 1958. 14 pp. unnumbered. 14 photographs. Wrappers.

Maxine Crotsenburg writes the first article—"Picture Frame For Morongo Valley;" Cal Crotsenburg authors another contribution to the plethora of literary outbursts that have already appeared and, unfortunately, will likely continue to appear, concerning the ubiquitous Willie-Boy. There are short columns telling of 29 (sic) Palms, Pioneer Town, Yucca Valley, and Joshua Tree. Outstanding are the photographs contained in this scarce booklet of our High Desert country.

CROWDER, FARNSWORTH

Mojave—Perennial Frontier. 1937. June issue of *Westways.* Illus.

The Crowder article reviews recurrent boom days in old Mojave—that once boisterous town which still bravely endures and holds great promise for future development.

CULLIMORE, CLARENCE

Forgotten Fort Tejon. 1941. Bakersfield, California: Kern County Historical Society. 88 pp. 19 illus. Wrappers.

This is one of the most thorough, and assuredly one of the best, of all accounts presently available of Fort Tejon. The author demonstrates a remarkable facility for researching pertinent material. Of more than passing interest is his account of the exhuming of Peter Lebec's skeleton; also the chapters—"Plan and Construction of Fort Buildings," and "The Ruins Tell Much Regarding Construction."

CURETON, GILBERT

Cattle Trail To California. 1953. June issue of *Historical Society of Southern California Quarterly.*

This article describes one of the early (1840-1860) cattle drives from Texas to California.

CUTTS, JAMES MADISON

Conquest of California and New Mexico by the Forces of the United States, in the Years 1846 and 1847. 1847. Philadelphia: Carey & Hart. 264 pp. 2 engravings. 4 line maps or plans. 4½ x 7⅜. (Cowan P. 61; Wagner-Camp No. 131.)

Quotations from the diary of Capt. Abraham Johnston and from reports of General Kearny appear in portions of the text. Some mention is made on pp. 173-174 of the Battle of San Pasqual; pp. 192-194 supply quotations from Johnston's diary descriptive of the desert crossing; p. 196 quotes from one of Kearny's reports of the Battle of San Pasqual. In its relation to California desert material, little of value is contributed by this early book. Such inclusions as may be found are usually in the nature of quotations from original sources.

DALE, EDWARD EVERETT

Indians of the Southwest, The. 1949. Norman: University of Oklahoma Press. 283 pp. 32 pls. 5 maps. 6¼ x 9¼.

Ch. 6, "The Indians of Southern California, 1868-1903" (pp. 80-94), refers to the Indians of the California deserts, mainly the Mission and the Coahuilla.

DALE, HARRISON CLIFFORD

Ashley-Smith Explorations and the Discovery of a Central Route to the Pacific 1822-1829. 1918. Cleveland: The Arthur H. Clark Company. 352 pp. 6¼ x 9¾. A Zamorano 80 item. Revised, and published by The Arthur H. Clark Co. in 1941, with 360 pp., fldg. map, and page map, 3 illus. 6½ x 9⅝. Original journals edited by Mr. Dale.

Jedediah Smith is the first known white man to come into California via the overland route from the east, crossing the Mojave Desert into Los Angeles. This book contains the Ashley narrative (pp. 117-161); the Smith narrative (pp. 186-194); the first and second journals of Harrison Rogers (pp. 197-271).

DAVIDS, ARLETTE (Preface by De Montherlant, Henry)

Rock Plants. (1948.) New York: The Hyperion Press. 10¼ x 13½.

The book includes 32 full-page plates of desert cacti exquisitely done in color by the artist Davids.

DAVIS, ALFRED

Death Valley. 1907. July issue of *Overland.*

The *Overland* article tells of two men being overcome by heat on the floor of Death Valley.

DAVIS, ARTHUR P.

New Inland Sea, The. 1907. January issue of the *National Geographic,* Vol. XVIII, No. 1. Pp. 37-49. 8 illus.

This is the transcript of an address to the Society, on November 23, 1906, by the Assistant Chief Engineer of the U. S. Reclamation Service. It furnishes an excellent interpretive discussion of the great break in the Colorado. The photographic illustrations present an effective visual portrayal of this disastrous inundation of our desert farm lands.

DAWSON, E. YALE

Cacti of California. Berkeley: University of California Press. 64 pp. 47 colored plates; many pen drawings. Wrappers.

Some forty varieties of cacti are discussed. The author's style is not too technical for the lay reader to understand and enjoy. His descriptions, coupled with the illustrative pen drawings and the beautiful color plates, give the book considerable merit in its field. Not only desert lovers, but desert travelers should fortify themselves with a copy of this interesting item before venturing out upon the desert.

DEATH VALLEY EXPEDITION

North American Fauna No. 7. 1893. Washington: Government Printing Office. 393 pp. Illus. Fldg. maps. 6¼ x 9¾. Wrappers.

This early, scarce item—companion volume to *Coville's* Botany—is devoted to a survey of parts of California, Nevada, Arizona and Utah. It is stated that Part I, comprising the general report (itinerary, description of the region, and discussion of life zones) and the reports on mammals, was never issued.

The contributing authorities and their respective subjects are as follows: A. K. Fisher—Birds; Leonard Stejneger—Reptiles and Batrachians; Chas. H. Gilbert—Fishes; C. V. Riley—Insects; R. E. C. Stearns—Mollusks; C. Hart Merriam—Desert Trees and Shrubs; C. Hart Merriam—Desert Cactuses and Yuccas; T. S. Palmer—List of Localities.

DeDECKER, MARY

Mines of the Eastern Sierra. 1966. Glendale, California: La Siesta Press. 72 pp. 14 photographic illus. Maps. Line drawings.

Historic mining centers in Mono and Inyo Counties are discussed briefly. Of desert interest are to be noted, among others, Coso, Lundy, Dogtown and Cerro Gordo.

DEKENS, CAMIEL (As told to Patterson, Tom)

Riverman—Desertman. 1962. Riverside, California: Press Enterprise Company. 111 pp. 8 illus. Wrappers.

Whenever Tom Patterson chooses to author, co-author, or edit a book, the result is invariably rewarding to the reader. In co-authoring the Camiel Dekens book his task was not an easy one. "Dekens," Mr. Patterson reminds us, "has his individual way of speaking and does not organize his reminiscing. . . . I wrote his story as simply as I could and checked the provisional text with him for correction and elaboration."

There is much about Ehrenberg, the once-active mining town on the Arizona side of the Colorado; and of Blythe, the city on the California side; and of Rice in the days when it was a town of some consequence. More significantly, the book relates the development of agriculture in the Palo Verde Valley. Dekens was there from 1907, almost at the beginning of its irrigation project. And in those days "Palo Verde Valley was a place where men came who wanted to stay lost."

The several recounted anecdotes and experiences are entertainingly told.

DELAMETER, JOHN A. (As told to Hogg, John Edwin)

My 40 Years Pulling Freight. 1930. August issue of *Touring Topics.* Illus.

A series of interesting desert incidents enliven the freight trail experiences of El Oso Viejo (the Old Bear). The relation of these fugitive adventures, fallible though they may sometimes be, is an important one. For this is source material, and the period of its availability is limited by the life-span of those who participated in the events described.

DELAMORE, H. E.

Desert Lands of California, The. 1912. October issue of *Travel.*

Of first importance are the early desert photographs—eight of them—including one of "The Twenty-Nine Palms." The article itself provides one of our early printed accounts of Twentynine Palms and the High Desert country. The item, generally, represents the desert as such a desolate and dangerous area that few readers would care to venture upon it. Irrespective of this, much sensible information is made available concerning our California desert regions—including Death Valley.

DE NOGALES, RAFAEL

Memoirs of a Soldier of Fortune. 1932. New York: Harrison Smith Inc. XVI, 380 pp. 3 pls. 8 x 8⅝. Lowell Thomas writes an introductory tribute to Nogales.

In this exciting adventure narrative, we find Nogales in the Nevada-California desert country in 1906-1907. Ch. V, "Nevada Days" (pp. 91-111), tells of Goldfield and Rawhide; also of Panamint Canyon where he found two prospectors dead in their tent as the result of emptying the contents of a bottle of 2x horse linament in an effort to quench their thirst—which it did, and effectively. Likewise, we are given the account of the captured coyote with a stick of dynamite tied to its tail. Bets were placed upon the unfortunate beast's endurance, and how long it would take him to "blow up." In Ch. VI, "The Old Payne Mine" (pp. 112-116), we are given an early view of Keeler and its immediate vicinity. Pp. 102-106 bring together the adventurous Nogales and the notorious Scott of Death Valley. The former indicates a decided antipathy for Scott; and, so far as I know, these two venturesome characters never did compose their differences.

DERR, PETER

Account of Experiences of Peter Derr of Humboldt County, California, Who Came Through On the First Train South From Salt Lake to California. 1954. These "Experiences" (1880) are in manuscript form in the Bancroft Library, and printed in LeRoy and Ann Hafen's *Journals of Forty-Niners*. They were (according to the Hafens) originally obtained by one of historian Bancroft's interviewers.

The so-called Gruwell-Derr Wagon Train left Salt Lake a week or so in advance of Jefferson Hunt's Sand Walking Co. (1849). Although casual references are made to this group in contemporary accounts, the reports of Peter Derr and J. D. Gruwell provide our only specific information—and this is meager enough. Derr mentions there were 23 wagons. (Addison Pratt, in his *Diary*, states there were 50 wagons.) The company suffered hardships and hunger; were finally overtaken and furnished succor by the Hunt train. (See listing under Gruwell, J. D.)

DILLON, RICHARD H. (Edited by)

Gila Trail. (See listing under Harris, Benjamin B.)

DIVISION OF MINES, DEPARTMENT OF NATURAL RESOURCES

Evolution of the California Landscape. (See listing under Hinds, Norman E. A.)

Geology of Southern California. 1954. California State Printing Office. 5000 copies. Issued as Bulletin 170. Consists of an Index, 10 Chapters, 5 Geologic Guides, and a separate envelope containing 34 Map Sheets; the whole comprising 16 booklets, soft bound, each measuring 8½ x 10. The booklets and the envelope of Map Sheets come packed in a cardboard slip case.

The work is concerned largely with a study of California desert regions. Its photographic plates are of outstanding merit; particularly the aerial views. Though a bit technical in the scope of its coverage, the text is not without its appeal to the lay reader.

DIX, R. S.

Death Valley. 1891. August issue of *The Chautauquan*. Pp. 629-633.

Although sometimes over-dramatic and even mawkish in his style, Mr. Dix's article is of more than collateral importance due largely to its age. Although factually unreliable, it bears a date three years in advance of Manly; one full year prior to that of Spears. In any event the article merits this short quotation: "As far as the eye could reach, there was nothing but gleaming white splendor; not a trace of vegetation, not a creature to break the solemn silence which pervaded the place like a benediction; nothing but white everywhere, dotted here and there with twinkling pools of water. . . . Burning salt marsh at its bottom, pathless tracts of salt and borax just above, then the thorny bush, and yet higher the mournful stunted pine, all under the glare of a blazing sun, unrefreshed by brook or pond, and enlivened only by scorpion and snake; and last of all, the bones of hundreds of lost travelers bleaching in one's path."

DIXON, BEN F.

Camp Salvation. 1965. San Diego.

The title is extended by the following: *First Citizens of Calexico. An Oasis On the Gold Rush Trail.* Further comment on the title page reads "No. 10, The Benjamin Franklin Junior Historical Series. A Bookshelf of American Genealogy."

In the great gold rush over the Colorado Desert in the year 1849, the lives of hundreds—perhaps even thousands—of emigrants were probably saved by the sudden appearance of a sizable body of water in the hot, burning sands of the desert. The *source* of the water was easily explained—an overflowing of the Colorado River. The *presence* of a lake of water at this very crucial period impressed many as being more than just a natural phenomenon. It bordered on the miraculous. Lt. Cave Couts, in command of the military escort for the Whipple Survey, shared this opinion. "This particular place of the river," he writes, "favored with such luxuriant grass, can only be the work of an Invisible Hand to aid the thousands of distressed emigrants. I have called it Camp Salvation."

The challenge of determining the precise geographical location of the historic "Camp Salvation" was accepted by the author of this discerning study. Ben Dixon has done his work well. By an intelligent correlation of all available data, he arrived at what surely appears to be a logical conclusion to this problem: "On the official map of the boundary, the long sought site was specifically identified between two boundary monuments at New River, and just north of the boundary line [between the United States and Mexico]. This conclusively placed the location within the present corporate limits of the City of Calexico."

Besides a generous assortment of maps, there are included reproductions of 34 photographs of early-day people and places. This collection has outstanding reference value.

Recently a suitable commemorative marker was placed in Rockwood Plaza at Calexico. On it is inscribed:

CAMP SALVATION

Here on September 23, 1849, Lieut. Cave J. Couts, Escort Commander, International Boundary Commission, established Camp Salvation. From September till the first of December 1849, it served as a refugee center for distressed emigrants attempting to reach the gold fields over the Southern Emigrant Trail.

DOBIE, J. FRANK

Coronado's Children. Tales of the Lost Mines and Buried Treasures of the Southwest. (1930.) Dallas: Southwest Press. XV, 367 pp. 6½ x 9½. End paper map. Done in black cloth, with design of treasure chest stamped in gold. The first edition must not be confused with the Literary Guild copy that comes in yellow cloth. Ramon F. Adams, in his *Six Guns & Saddle Leather*, mentions that the distinguishing mark of the first issue is the omission, in the author's dedication, of the word "clean" from the portion of the sentence reading—"a *clean* cowman of the Texas soil."

The Death Valley reference is limited to a discussion of the Breyfogle mine (Ch. 11, pp. 208-214). The story differs essentially from most other versions. The book itself is one of the best ever written on the subject of lost mines and buried treasure.

DOBYNS, HENRY F. (Edited by)

Journal of Cave Johnson Couts. (See listing under Couts, Lt. Cave Johnson.)

DODGE, NATT N.

Flowers of the Southwestern Deserts. 1951. Globe, Arizona: Southwest Monuments Association. Gila Pueblo. 112 pp. Wrappers.

There are 100 drawn plates, by Jeanne R. Janish, depicting 145 desert plants.

Poisonous Dwellers of the Desert. 1947. Globe, Arizona: Southwest Monuments Association. Gila Pueblo. 48 pp. Wrappers.

This book is a compendium of important information concerning these less desirable neighbors of our desert region.

DOUGLAS, JACK

Gold In Lost Mines. 1951. 36 pp. Wrappers.

Those interested in the lore of lost mines will wish to examine this little item. It is not pretentious; and it reads well.

DRISKILL, EARL C.

Death Valley Scotty Rides Again. (1955.) Death Valley: Stovepipe Wells. 59 pp. 5 pls. End paper map. 6 x 9. Wrappers.

"Tales told by Death Valley Scotty, winter of 1952-1953, at Scotty's Castle." The author was manager of the Castle during this period, and Scotty's close companion.

DUMKE, GLENN S. (Edited by)

Mexican Gold Trail. (See listing under Evans, W. B.)

DUNHAM, WAYLAND D.

It's a Date. 1948. Pasadena: The Publication Press. 159 pp. 18 pls. End paper maps. 5¾ x 8¾.

The book describes date culture in the Palm Springs—Coachella Valley area of California. Included are 13 pages of date recipes. An item well worth having in one's collection.

DURIVAGE, JOHN E.

Letters and Journal. 1937. Included (pp. 159-255) in *Southern Trails to California in 1849.* Southwest Historical Series Vol. V, edited by Ralph P. Bieber and published in 1937 by The Arthur H. Clark Company of Glendale, California. This particular section is captioned—"Through Mexico to California."

That portion of the section which deals exclusively with the Colorado Desert crossing may be found on pp. 226-244. The *Journal* originally appeared in the *Daily Picayune* (New Orleans) in the issues of August 7, September 23, and October 11, 1849.

The arduous trek over the Colorado desert was accomplished late in the month of June 1849, when the heat, at times, was intolerable. Grant Foreman tells us, in his superb work—*Marcy & the Gold Seekers,* that the temperature along Carrizo Creek was 110° in the shade. Durivage's route over the desert followed closely that of Kearny and Cooke (1846-1847). The author is infectious in his style, and candid in his portrayal of the odious trail conditions.

"On every side," he writes, "the eye encountered objects attesting the distresses and misfortunes of parties who had preceded us. Every few yards on each side of the road, marking the trail plainly, were dead mules by scores, saddles, bridles, blankets, broken trunks, bags, pantaloons, packs, cantinas, and all sorts of articles." When the arroyo was discovered, "literally covering the ground were dead mules, fragments of harness, gun barrels, trunks, wearing apparel, barrels, casks, saws, bottles, and quantities of articles too numerous to mention. The hot air was laden with the fetid smell of dead mules and horses, and on all sides misery and death seemed to prevail." The Durivage ranks among the best of the Colorado Desert journals.

DURYEA, EDWIN, JR.

Salton Sea Menace, The. 1906. January issue of *Out West.*

This article is illustrated with a generous collection of photographs of the rising inland sea and the heroic efforts taken to check the flow of water. It is well written, supplying important data assembled during the 1905-1906 break in the Colorado River that formed the present Salton Sea.

DWYER, RICHARD A. and LINGENFELTER, RICHARD E.

'Nonpareil' Press of T. S. Harris, The. (See listing under Lingenfelter, Richard E.)

DYKES, JEFF C. (Edited by)

West of the Texas Kid, The. (See listing under Crawford, Thomas E.)

EARLE, W. HUBERT

Cacti of the Southwest. 1963. Phoenix. Science Bull. No. 4. Arizona Cactus & Native Flora Society, Inc. 112 pp. Map. Approx. 125 photographs (by author). 6 x 9⅛.

Among the considerable number of items in my cacti collection, Mr. Earle's book is far and away the favorite because it is indubitably the most useful. Useful to me, certainly, because I can understand what I read and see illustrated in it. The book is concerned mainly with the classification of cacti, its distribution, structure, flowering and fruit.

EARLY, LEE and MORHARDT, 'AIM

Western Men and Desert Gold. 1954. Bishop, California. Wrappers.

The little booklet consists of stories, songs and poems of Death Valley and vicinity.

EATON, WALTER PRICHARD

Boy Scouts in Death Valley. (1939). Boston: W. A. Wilde Co. 307 pp. Illus. 5½ x 7¾.

The first section of this book tells the story of the Death Valley trek in 1849, and its outstanding character—William Lewis Manly.

ECCLESTON, ROBERT

(Diary of) Overland to California on the Southwestern Trail. 1849. 1950. Berkeley: University of California Press. Edited by George P. Hammond and Edward H. Howes. Bancroft Library Publication No. 2. XVIII, 256 pp. 6⅝ x 10⅛. 2 fldg. maps. Limited to 750 copies. Publication date appears on title page of first.

This is the first published appearance of what is perhaps the most spirited and colorful item among the contemporary diaries and journals prepared by those emigrants of 1849-50 who followed the Southwest Trail. Unfortunately, the diarist ends his account at New River—only a short distance west of the Colorado River. Unfortunately again, for our purpose, the diary devotes itself mainly to the party's route through Texas.

Eccleston was a member of the Frémont Association, one of the groups specially organized to engage in mining on a cooperative basis. Their route followed, mainly, that established by Cooke and his Mormon Battalion. In the Burro Mountains of New Mexico the Frémonters effected a cut-off to Tucson, thereby accomplishing a ten-day reduction in trail time from the Cooke route, with a corresponding saving of some 150 travel miles. This cut-off segment was quite generally followed in later years by the Butterfield Overland Stage line, the Southern Pacific Railway and, finally, by our modern transcontinental highways. The picturesque former Texas Ranger and all-time celebrated adventurer, Col. "Jack" Hays, was one of the leaders of this group.

Pp. 241-247 offer brief comment on the California portion of the trail. Even this concise recital reflects something of the characteristic vigor and enthusiasm of the youthful narrator, to whom the entire overland journey was one huge adventure—glorious.

Note: In 1957 the University of Utah Press came out with a second volume of the diaries of Robert Eccleston—*The Mariposa Indian War 1850-1851*, edited by C. Gregory Crampton.

EDGERTON, LUCILE SELK

Pillars of Gold. 1941. The Grosset & Dunlap reprint shows 403 pp.; is 5¼ x 7¾.

This is a novelized account of gold-rush travel to the Arizona—La Paz fields, emphasis being given the Southern route over the Bradshaw Road.

EDWARDS, CHARLES LINCOLN

Jose—A Story of the Desert Cahuilla. 1930. Los Angeles: City School District. 21 pp. 4 illus. 6 x 9⅛. Wrappers.

The story is of the Cahuilla Indians, and contains descriptive material on the

Devil's Cactus Garden which extended from the base of Mt. San Gorgonio. The Twentynine Palms area also comes in for a fair share of comment.

Story of the Colorado Desert, A. 1928. Los Angeles: City School District. 16 pp. Wrappers. 6⅛ x 9⅛.
Material is arranged for juvenile study of the Colorado Desert.

EDWARDS, E. I.

Death Valley's Neglected Hero. 1966. *Westerners, The* (Los Angeles Corral) *Brand Book* No. 12. 15 pp. 4 photographs. 1 drawing by Homer H. Boelter.
This article is an attempt "to position John Rogers (who, with Lewis Manly, saved a party of men, women and children from almost certain death in Death Valley) by elevating him to his rightful status, both as an individual and as a participant in the Death Valley affair. For it is time, and long past time, that recognition be extended this man whose contribution to California history is in every respect comparable to that of Manly."

Desert Christ Park. 1966. From special publication—*Remembrances of the High Desert.* (See listing under Evans, Carolyn and Wilson, Joan.) 4 pp. 10 photographs.
The article reviews the interesting history of the creation of this beautiful and unusual park which "remains, and probably will continue to remain, Yucca Valley's outstanding attraction."

Desert Harvest. 1962. Los Angeles: Westernlore Press. 128 pp. 8 photographs. Limited to 600 copies. 6 x 8½.
Quoting from the dust jacket review: "Recently Mr. Edwards was asked to name the twenty-five books he would choose to retain from his desert library were he to dispose of all volumes other than this narrow choice. He was not asked to name his *favorite* books; nor, for that matter, the books he would care to *recommend*. The suggestion was to name strictly those he would choose to retain. This book is the synthesis of twenty-five years of exploring and writing about the Southwest deserts. Distilled into it is the wisdom and experience of a man who owns one of the largest private collections of Southwest desert books, and who has written four valuable desert bibliographies, all of them scarce and wanted volumes of desert literature."

Desert Sanctuary. (See listing under Boelter, Homer H.)

Desert Treasure—A Bibliography. 1948. Los Angeles: Edwards & Williams. 42 pp. XI. 6¼ x 8½. 250 copies.
The book contains a chronological listing—by author, title and description—of 445 California desert items, with an additional 65 items listed in an inserted supplement.

Desert Voices: A Descriptive Bibliography. 1958. Los Angeles: Westernlore Press. Foreword by Harold O. Weight. Limited to 500 copies. 215 pp. 9 photographs by Harold O. Weight. 6⅝ x 9⅝.
From the dust jacket review—"In *Desert Voices*, a labor of years, Mr. Edwards

has answered a great and accumulated demand with this first comprehensive reading bibliography of the California deserts—a work vast in scope, with over 1500 separate citations and comments on the staggering amount of material that has been written pertaining to this dramatic and mysterious area of the Great West. Through years to come it will stand as the definitive work on this subject . . . *Desert Voices* truly is a course in desert appreciation."

Desert Yarns. 1946. Los Angeles: The Ward Ritchie Press. 41 pp. 5⅝ x 8⅞. Limited to 250 copies.

Says the author, in his preface, "These yarns are real; they tell of some fugitive adventure—some typical desert experience—that occurred on the wide stretches of the great Mojave along the road that leads to Death Valley. And a few of them—perhaps *most* of them—tell of the region in and around our 'beloved desert', out at Twentynine Palms, and of the really fine desert folks who dwell there."

Freeman's: A Stage Stop On the Mojave. 1964. Glendale, California: La Siesta Press. 47 pp. 16 photographs, 2 maps, line drawings. Wrappers.

The book supplies a background history for what was once a flourishing establishment known as Coyote Holes, located near what is now called "Freeman Junction" on the Mojave Desert where the Walker Pass road to Bakersfield turns off the Bishop Highway (State 14). The early historic photographs are of special value. There is much material on the famous highwayman, Tiburcio Vasquez, and his Mojave Desert raids from nearby "Robbers' Roost." These oddly-placed rocks are plainly visible from the highway.

Into An Alkali Valley—The First Written Account of Death Valley. 1948. Los Angeles: The Ward Ritchie Press. 8 pp. 5¾ x 8¾. Wrappers. Limited to 250 copies.

Contained in this book is the story of the Death Valley parties of 1849, together with an account of the first written description of Death Valley. Included is that portion of Sheldon Young's "Log," detailing the experiences of the Jayhawkers in Death Valley for the week from December 24 to December 31, 1849. The Sheldon Young "Log" supplies the first written description of Death Valley, the author referring to this desert as "an Alkali Valley."

Lost Oases Along the Carrizo. 1961. Los Angeles: Westernlore Press. Foreword by Harold O. Weight. Companion volume to *Desert Voices*. Limited to 500 copies. XVI plus 126 pp. 8 photographs by Harold O. Weight. End paper maps by Norton Allen. 6⅝ x 9⅝.

From the author's opening paragraph: "This is the story of an isolated Corridor in one of the most desolate sections of the Colorado Desert. It is the story, too, of a remote little palm tree oasis that long ago flourished there—just midway in the Corridor. On at least four separate occasions epoch-making history surged westward through this particular segment of desert to enact drama of profound importance in the long-range development of California." The Carrizo Corridor, located in the Anza Desert, is on the early southern emigrant route from the Colorado river crossing to Warner's Ranch, past Carrizo Creek, Vallecito and San Felipe Valley.

Pages 53-104 contain a descriptive bibliography of the Colorado Desert, classified according to groups, places and events. A chronological listing has been prepared, additionally to the regular author alphabetical arrangement.

Mystery of Death Valley: How It Was Named. 1962. *Westerners, The* (Los Angeles Corral). *The Branding Iron.* No. 61, June. 5 pp. 1 photograph. (*The Branding Iron* is the Los Angeles Corral's quarterly publication.)

This is a researched study to ascertain the person or group responsible for giving Death Valley its melancholy name.

Mystery of Death Valley's Lost Wagon Train, The. 1964. *Westerners, The* (Los Angeles Corral). *Brand Book* No. 11. 60 pp., including 5 pp. of Bibliography. 9 photographs, 1 line drawing by Don Perceval. 200 copies bound separately from the *Brand Book.*

Quoting the author's opening paragraph: "To my knowledge, no definitive account of Death Valley's lost wagon train has ever been written; yet any serious approach to this desert's fascinating history cannot entirely escape consideration of it. The possibility of the one-time existence of a lost wagon train with its attendant horrors of suffering and death should not be shrugged off as mere sensational nonsense; neither should it merit credibility solely on the basis of its emotional appeal. After being ignored for well over a hundred years it is time the numerous references to abandoned wagon trains and bleached human bones receive intelligent evaluation, either to establish their absolute truth or to expose their inherent error. This paper is a documented study written in the hope of accomplishing that purpose. In its preparation some twenty-five early accounts have been selected and examined from among a hundred or more consulted."

Twelve Great Books. 1966. *Westerners, The* (Los Angeles Corral). Published as *Westerners' Keepsake No. 80.* Foreword by Paul D. Bailey. 46 pp. Printed by Westernlore Press (Los Angeles).

The "Twelve Great Books" refer to the twelve *Brand Books* published to date by the Los Angeles Corral of *The Westerners.* In addition to the descriptive introduction to the *Brand Books* the material is divided into three sections:

1. Alphabetical Classification of Articles by Books, showing by author and article the content of each of the twelve books;
2. Alphabetical Classification of Articles by Authors;
3. Subject Guide, classifying articles by subject matter, with reference to book and page numbers.

Valley Whose Name Is Death, The. 1940. Pasadena: San Pasqual Press. 122 pp. 7 x 9¾. Edition limited to 500 copies, irrespective of the book's printed limit notice of 1000 copies. Additionally, six full-leather bound copies were issued as gifts.

Part One of this work is an attempt to coordinate the source accounts affecting the identity of the several parties who crossed Death Valley in 1849. Part Two (pp. 71-122), presents the first and—with the exception of the author's *Desert Voices* and this present volume—the only descriptive bibliography of Death Valley literature. Nearly 600 items are conveniently classified by author, title and description, together with critical comments upon the content and upon the relative significance of most of the items listed.

(Edited by) *Whipple Report, The.* (See listing under Whipple, A. W.—*Journal of An Expedition From San Diego to the Rio Colorado.*)

EDWARDS, W. E.

Desert Deluge, A. 1927. February issue of *Touring Topics.* Illus.
An exciting and realistic account of a sudden flash flood on the desert.

EGAN, HOWARD

Pioneering the West: 1846 to 1878, etc. 1917. Richmond, Utah: Howard R. Egan Estate. 302 pp. Approx. 54 illus. Several line drawings. 5¼ x 7⅝. Pp. 169-176 relate to the Mojave Desert crossing. Portions of the diary are reprinted in the Hafens' *Journals of Forty-Niners.*

The Sand Walking Company, of which the now-famous Death Valley groups were an integral part, moved out of Salt Lake in the fall of 1849. A few days behind it came the Pomeroy wagon train that left Salt Lake on November 3, 1849. The Egan Party made its departure from Salt Lake on November 18, 1849, with three wagons and fifteen head of stock. They overtook, and passed, the Pomeroy wagon train.

ELLENBECKER, JOHN G.

Jayhawkers of Death Valley, The. 1938. Marysville, Kansas. 130 pp. 6⅛ x 9⅛. Wrappers.

Contained in this remarkable book are numerous photographs of the Death Valley pioneers and their descendants. Shortly before his death, Mr. Ellenbecker prepared a five-page, double-column supplement to his book.

The author's effort is concentrated upon a study of group personnel—who they were, whence they came, and their subsequent history after crossing Death Valley. As a result, the book is a thesaurus of information concerning these pioneers. Only the most acutely-developed acquisitive sense could ever have induced the author to venture upon such an extensive undertaking as this. He contacted, personally, every known descendant of every known pioneer. He met with them at their reunions; he fraternized with them in their homes. He despaired at no lead—however tenuous—to accomplish his avowed purpose of running to earth any scrap of information that chanced to present itself. The task to which he assigned himself was a stupendous one; the result was successful, even beyond his own fondest expectation.

To be sure, Ellenbecker perhaps accorded deferential treatment to his beloved Jayhawkers; but many of the others were remembered also—Manly, Bennett, the Briers. The end result is an imperishable *personal* record of the majority of those intrepid pioneers who immortalized Death Valley. Of further value is the inclusion of several source records—the *Diary* of Asa Haynes, L. Dow Stephen's letter of January 28, 1895 addressed to the Jayhawkers, and one of Mrs. Brier's letters.

This book has long since gone out of print and is now hard to come by. If ever an item merited reprinting (and perhaps re-editing) it is John Ellenbecker's classic of Death Valley.

ELLERBE, ROSE L.

History of Temescal Valley. 1920. *Historical Society of Southern California Annual Publications*. XI: pp. 12-23.

"The Temescal Valley, in Riverside County, heads in Lake Elsinore, drops to the southwest, and opens out on the plains where Corona and the Arlington district of Riverside flourish." This is a brief but well assembled local history.

ELLIOTT, WALLACE W.

History of San Bernardino and San Diego Counties. 1965. Riverside, California: Riverside Museum Press. Introduction by Harry W. Lawton. 204 pp. "Illustrations descriptive of its Scenery, Farms, Residences, Public Buildings, Factories, Hotels, Business Houses, Schools, Churches, etc., from Original Drawings, Including Biographical Sketches."

The present volume is a reprint of the 1883 original, published by Wallace W. Elliott & Co., 106 Leidesdorff Street, San Francisco. The full page map of California in 1882 is reproduced in color.

There is much of southern desert interest in this huge old record book of 1883. In glancing over the table of contents, references are noted to many interesting localities and topics—Death Valley, First Settlement by Mormons, Overland Mail, Stages, San Bernardino County, the now-ghost town of Calico, San Timoteo Canyon, San Gorgonio Pass, Temescal Tin Mines, Colorado Desert, Temecula Hot Springs, Fort Yuma, and others.

Mr. Lawton's helpful Introduction supplies a back drop to the scenes the reader will witness as he turns his attention to the *History* itself. In essence, the Introduction is also a history—a history *of* these fascinating County Histories of the 1880s. Pointing out that Elliott's *History* has assumed classic proportions in its importance to local history collectors, Mr. Lawton reminds us that we can "be grateful that he operated at his particular moment in time. He caught the pastoral essence of San Bernardino, Riverside, and San Diego counties just as the great land boom began, rendering scenes that would vanish before the end of the decade."

EMORY, WILLIAM H.

Lieutenant Emory Reports. (1951.) Albuquerque: University of New Mexico Press. 208 pp. 6¼ x 9⅜.

This is the first reprint of the 1848 Emory: *Notes of a Military Reconnoissance*. The large folding map of the first edition, divided into six sections, is reproduced in the reprint. Each map section precedes that portion of the text to which it relates. The introduction and 12 pages of notes are by Ross Calvin. The notes supply 153 references which significantly clarify the text. Subdivision 5 (pp. 141-166) follows the march of Kearny's Army of the West across the Colorado Desert—all the way to Warner's "Rancherie," and the bathing pools at Agua Caliente. Subdivision 6 (pp. 167-176) describes the Battle of San Pasqual.

Notes of a Military Reconnoissance, from Fort Leavenworth, in Missouri, to San Diego, in California, Including Part of the Arkansas, Del Norte, and Gila Rivers. 1848. Washington. Of the two editions printed, the Senate Ex. Doc. 7 shows 416 pp., 26 pls. of scenery and portraits, 14 pls. of botany, 3 plans, 1 large fldg. map in map pocket in some of the copies. 5¾ x 9. The House Ex. Doc. 41 shows 614 pp. and contains additional reports by Lt. J. W. Abert (pp. 417-548), Capt. A. R. Johnston (pp. 564-614), and Col. P. St. George Cooke (pp. 549-563). There are 21 pls. of scenery, 3 pls. of fossils, 2 small maps. Emory's 1848 Report was first reprinted (1951) by the University of New Mexico Press, Albuquerque. A Zamorano 80 item. (Cowan P. 77; Wagner-Camp No. 148.)

Emory was with the advance guard in Kearny's Army of the West. Upon the discovery of gold, his Report became immediately popular, as it afforded the first and only description of the Southern route west to Santa Fe, supplying detailed information relative to watering places, roads, deserts, Indians, plant and animal life. Pp. 100-113 describe the trek over the Southern California desert country to San Diego, and include an eye-witness account of the historic Battle of San Pasqual by an active participant.

Some indication of how highly this book of Emory's was prized by the gold seekers is unintentionally supplied by one of these self-same emigrants (John E. Durivage). While struggling across the treacherous desert, according to Durivage: ". . . not-withstanding we left every article we thought we could possibly dispense with at the Colorado, we deemed it necessary to make still further sacrifices. Away went a bag of beans; out tumbled a suit of clothes; Major Emory's Report and a cannister of powder followed suit; a case of surgical instruments followed; and a jar containing five pounds of quick-silver with a small bag of bullets brought up the rear."

Emory's large-scale map was the first ever made of the entire distance. For adverse critical comment relative to this elaborate map, see H. M. T. Powell's *The Santa Fe Trail.* For adverse critical comment regarding Emory, see Powell's *The Santa Fe Trail* and Dwight L. Clark's *Original Journals of Henry Smith Turner.*

United States and Mexican Boundary Survey. 1857. Vol. 1—Washington: 34th Cong. 1st Sess., Vol. 14, House Ex. Doc. 135. Part 1: XVI, 258 pp., 80 pls., 2 maps; Part 2: VIII, 174, pp., 21 pls., map. (Wagner-Camp No. 291.) Appears in two, sometimes three, volumes.

Also printed as Sen. Ex. Doc. 108; 9 x 11½. Same as House edition except for imprint and pagination. Part 1, by Lt. Col. W. H. Emory, pp. 1-73, gives his personal account, general descriptions, and so on; Lt. Michler's report occupies pp. 74-80 and pp. 101-124; Dr. Parry's reconnoissance, pp. 125-129. Additionally, there are sections giving distances, astronomical and geodetic work, and meteorology.

Part II contains geological reports by Dr. Parry and assistant Arthur Schott, notes by W. H. Emory, a report on paleontology and geology by James Hall, a description of cretaceous and tertiary fossils by T. A. Conrad.

ERKSON, ALEXANDER C.

Account. 1894. (See listing in Manly, W.. L.—*Death Valley in '49*; Hafen, LeRoy and Ann—*Journals of Forty-Niners.*)

On the occasion of the 1849 westward defection movement, all but seven wagons turned westward from the original Sand Walking caravan (some 100 wagons in all) and proceeded on the disastrous cutoff that led a portion of them into Death Valley. At Mt. Misery several groups packed down the gorge and later followed the trail of Hunt and the seven wagons on the Old Spanish Trail that led over Cajon Pass and into San Bernardino. The majority of the seceding group, however, (from 60 to 65 wagons) turned back from Mt. Misery to the Old Spanish Trail. They did not overtake Hunt, but they followed his lead safely to their destination. No journal nor diary is presently available recording the experiences of this main body of the Sand Walking Company, other than the brief account of Alexander C. Erkson, as recorded by Manly in his book on the Death Valley episode.

Erkson very casually tosses out a tempting morsel to all of us who love to search out old trails. "On my way back from Mt. Misery," he writes, "I climbed up on a big rock and inscribed the date—Nov. 10, 1849." (Hopefully, I shall one day find that rock.)

ESTUDILLO, DON JOSÉ MARÍA

Diary. (See listing under Bean, L. J.—*The Romero Expeditions.*)

EVANS, CAROLYN and WILSON, JOAN

Remembrances of the High Desert and the Communities of Morongo Valley, Palm Wells, Yucca Valley, Pioneertown, Landers, Joshua Tree and Twentynine Palms. 1966. Yucca Valley, California: Artcraft Print Shop. 49 pp. Many photographic reproductions. Advertisements. Double-page map of area. Decorative Wrappers. Vol. 2. (Vol. 1, entitled *Yucca Valley*, follows.)

Short articles appear on the history of Yucca Valley, Morongo Valley, Palm Wells, Landers, Joshua Tree, Pioneertown and Rimrock, Twentynine Palms, Mines of the High Desert, Parks and Recreation, Hi-Desert Nature Museum, Desert Christ Park, Camino d'Oro and Pioneer Loop, Joshua Tree National Monument, and Mission Creek Indian Reservations. The early photographs are of recognized historical value.

Yucca Valley—A Glimpse Into the History of (including Morongo Valley, Palm Wells and Yucca Mesa, California). 1965. Yucca Valley, California. Artcraft Print Shop. 64 pp. Many photographic reproductions. Advertisements. Vol. 1. (See Vol. 2 in above listing.) Decorative wrappers.

Articles include Yucca Valley Post Office, Our High Desert Heritage—First Pioneers, Prospectors and Gold Mines, Ranchers and Rustlers, The Homestead

Years, Building a Town, Palm Wells, Yucca Valley Airport, The Changing Face of a Town, Yucca Valley Recreation and Park District, Hi-Desert Schools, Yucca Valley Sheriff's Office, Yucca Valley Fire District, Hi-Desert Memorial Hospital, Hospital Guild, Morongo Valley, Yucca Mesa, Hi-Desert Wildlife, Indians of the High Desert, Willie Boy. As in Vol. 2, the feature of outstanding importance is the collection of early photographs assembled for this attractive publication.

EVANS, JOHN HENRY

Charles Coulson Rich—Pioneer Builder of the West. 1936. New York: The Macmillan Co. 400 pp. 5⅞ x 8⅝. The words "First Printing" appear under copyright notice.

The section of importance to students of desert (Death Valley) history (pp. 179-194) is the reference to the Smith Party, the Flake-Cannon-Rich Party, and those others who packed down Mt. Misery into the Beaver Dam Gorge.

EVANS, W. B. (Edited by Dumke, Glenn S.)

Mexican Gold Trail. 1945. Los Angeles: Huntington Library. Printed by The Ward Ritchie Press. 340 pp. 6¼ x 9¼.

This is the Journal of a forty-niner. Of special significance is the newly revealed Death Valley material, pp. 254-255 and 259, which providentially accounts for the movements and ultimate fate of two of the Death Valley groups of 1849 whose experiences have heretofore posed an inscrutable mystery to students of Death Valley history. (It is my belief that these two groups were the "Georgians" and the "Mississippi Boys.") Additionally, pp. 160-173 supply a lucid account of the Evans party's early crossing of the Colorado Desert on their way north to the gold fields.

EWING, BELLE C.

I Remember. 1947. September issue of *The Desert Spotlight.* Illus.

Eugene Van Deventer, in the early seventies, drove freight from Spadra to Prescott—400 miles—over the Bradshaw Trail. This article describes the desert route through Banning, Whitewater, Agua Caliente (Palm Springs), El Toro, Dos Palmas—and on to Ehrenberg.

FAGES, PEDRO

Diary of Pedro Fages. The Colorado River Campaign: 1781-1782. 1913. May issue of Publications of the Academy of Pacific Coast History. Vol. 3, No. 2. Translated and edited by Herbert Ingram Priestley. 101 pp. Verso in original Spanish; recto in the English translation.

The Yuma Indians staged their savage revolt against the Spaniards in the summer of 1781. Soldiers, missionaries and settlers were massacred, including Fathers Garcés, Díaz, Moreno and Barreneche. Lt. Col. Fages was sent out in command of a punitive force, and his *Diary* is here published for the first time. Fages and his soldiers are supposed to have been among the first Europeans to travel over portions of the Colorado Desert country, including the region in and around Vallecito

(Little Valley) in the Carrizo Corridor. Fages reputedly gave the place its present name. The *Diary*, as translated, does not permit quick orientation of Fages' exact route.

The Fages *Diary* contradicts the prevalent notion that Col. Emory's reference—on November 29, 1846—to a palm tree oasis about midway along the sixteen miles of sandy desert between Carrizo Creek and Vallecito is our first mention of Washingtonia palm trees in California. On April 17, 1782, Fages writes: "We set out from this place in the afternoon, traveling six leagues (15 mi.) west along the same dry stream and halted on one bank of it at sundown, *at the Three Palms,* where there was little pasture for the animals, and poor water." Again, on April 18, he writes: "We set out from this place in the morning, following the same dry stream, winding to the westward. After we had gone four leagues (10 mi.), we found a small spring of good water, near which there were *three or four very tall palm trees* on our right."

FAIRBANKS, H. W. and STORMS, W. H.

Old Mines of Southern California. (See listing under Storms, W. H.)

FAIRBANKS, RALPH J. "DAD" (As told to Hogg, John Edwin)

My 73 Years on Southwestern Deserts. 1930. June issue of *Touring Topics.* Illus.

Living close to the heart of the desert for so many active years, Fairbanks was familiar with the essential characteristics of Death Valley and its surrounding areas. He knew the desert's sinister forebodings, its somber colorings, its melancholy desolation, its vibrant stillness. He held bivouac with its terrors, tested its challenges, insulated himself against almost every unrelenting force the desert could muster against him. It is as though he had taken measure of the desert, and the desert—in turn—had come to accept him as fit companion to the stuff of its mountains, its soltitudes, and its sands. Here is source material from one who stands high among the truly great pioneers of our southwest desert area.

FAIRCHILD, MAHLON DICKERSON

Trip to the Colorado Mines in 1862, A. 1933. March issue of *California Historical Society Quarterly.* Vol. XII. No. 1.

This article is an excerpt from Fairchild's reminiscences, describing early Los Angeles (1862) and a trip to the Colorado River mines along the Bradshaw Trail. Included is important material on the old stage stations and water stops—the Indian villages, Martinez, Dos Palmas, Tabaseca Tanks, and Chuckawalla Well. Fairchild's mention of the epidemic of measles at the Indian villages is of special interest.

FARNHAM, THOMAS J.

Travels in the Californias, and Scenes in the Pacific Ocean. 1844. N.Y.: Saxton & Miles. 416 pp. 1 map. 1 pl. (Wagner No. 107). The book has been several times reprinted, including an abridged edition in *Biobooks.*

P. 324 makes brief mention of an abortive attempt by a "Captain Young" to cross the Mojave Desert with 20 men and 20 mules. The animals all died, and five of the men perished. The survivors abandoned their effort and returned to Salt Lake. Says Farnham—"This was the last attempt to explore this awful waste. And long will it be, ere man can know the silent gloom and horrors of its awful depths."

Pp. 312 *et seq*, relate an account of a "Doctor Lyman, of Buffalo" who, in 1841, supposedly crossed the Mojave along the Spanish Trail route to Los Angeles. No material of importance is introduced, either in the Young or the Lyman references. Their substance is attenuated, in a measure, by the grandiloquence of the author which connotes a glorification, rather than an unembellished recital, of the incidents described.

FARNSWORTH, HARRIETT

Remnants of the Old West. (1965). San Antonio: The Naylor Company. 139 pp. 23 illus. 6 x 8½.

California, Nevada and Arizona share honors in Mrs. Farnsworth's book. And mostly all of it is desert. The first chapter—"Historic Willow Springs"—is good Mojave Desert material; even more interesting is the chapter—"William Seliger of the Mojave." Nor is Death Valley neglected in this book of "Remnants." Mention of it includes the chapters—"Dolph Nevares of Death Valley" and "Death Valley Authentics" (Adolph Nevares, Johnny Mills, and the old Indian Shoshone Johnny).

Kern River Valley comes in for passing notice. And so does that ancient and always honorable order of E Clampus Vitus with its Credo Quia Absurdum. Speaking of a certain woman, the author writes: "She had the distinction of being the first and only woman, at the time, to be granted membership in Death Valley's famed E Clampus Vitus group." Now I shall not attempt to explicate this rather questionable passage; for, grievous though it may be to contemplate even the *possibility* of a woman ever having been admitted into our sacred sanctuaries, there is no accounting for what an ebullient group of Clampers may do nor how they may choose to do it. But what I cannot rationalize with "Clamfact" is the author's reference to this dear lady being granted membership "in Death Valley's famed E Clampus Vitus group." I thought I knew a thing about Clampers, and I have heard comment from time to time concerning Death Valley. But any mention of a "Death Valley's famed E Clampus Vitus group" implies connotations of perfidious shenanigans, and most certainly evokes grave suspicions of misconduct and foul play amongst the brethren.

Despite all this, Harriett Farnsworth's *Remnants of the Old West* is a book every one (even "famed" Death Valley Clampers) should read and own.

Willow Springs—Oasis of the Mojave. 1947. February issue of *Westways*. Illus.

The importance of this well-written article stems from the fact that it affords material on a once little-known, and almost forgotten, historic spot on the vast Mojave. Willow Springs, with its interesting old rock structures, is but a short distance west of the settlement of Rosamond—midway between Lancaster and Mojave. In 1862 Willow Springs became a stopping point for stages and freight wagons. In 1876 the railroad diverted traffic, but mining operations guaranteed some activity to this secluded oasis.

FARQUHAR, FRANCIS P.

Books of The Colorado River and The Grand Canyon. A Selective Bibliography. 1953. Los Angeles: Glen Dawson. Designed and printed by Ward Ritchie. Dawson's Early California Travels Series XII. 75 pp. 1 illus. 5¼ x 7½.

Everyone is entitled to his likes and dislikes. In a bibliographical collection far more extensive than I can reasonably justify, Mr. Farquhar's book is one of my high-ranking favorites. The office of the bibliographer is to disseminate information *about* books; to make of his bibliography a *creative* effort that will instruct and inform. Mere book listings repel me. Anyone can prepare a list of books and authors. I approach a bibliography to learn something of the *nature* and *substance* of a book; not merely its name and author. Mr. Farquhar's book *tells* me something; quickens my urge to know more of an author and his work. He is responsible for the acquisition of many fine books in my own private collection.

The 125 included books in his Colorado River item are arranged in chronological order. Incidentally, with the exception of a few notable publications that can be related directly to our California deserts as well as to the Colorado River, I have purposely avoided duplicating Mr. Farquhar's chosen entries. He is our unquestioned authority on books of the Colorado River, and there is no point in repeating here what he has made so conveniently available.

et al. *Camels In Western America.* (See listing under Gray, A. A.)

(Edited by) *Up and Down California In 1860-1864.* See listing under Brewer, Wm. H.)

FARR, F. C. (Edited by)

History of Imperial County, California, The. 1918. Berkeley: Elms & Franks. 526 pp. 7 x 10. Pp. 311-516 comprise a section devoted entirely to biographical information.

Frequent mention of desert country in Imperial County is included. The historical account is drawn mainly around the life and experience of prominent individuals in the area.

FARRER, WILLIAM

Diary. 1954. Pp. 193-218 in LeRoy and Ann Hafen's *Journals of Forty-Niners.*

The Farrer *Diary,* as recorded by the Hafens, begins October 11, 1849; extends through December 9, 1849. Farrer was with the Flake-Rich party of Mormons who cut off from the Hunt wagon train and packed down Mt. Misery into the Beaver Dam Canyon. Henry Bigler was also a member of this group.

FARWELL, J. M.

Narrative of. 1940. In Walter B. Lang's—*First Overland Mail, The: Butterfield Trail.*

Farwell writes one of the leading contemporary accounts of passengers traveling over the Butterfield Stage Line during its two and one-half years' operation
from September of 1858 until March of 1861. Among all the Butterfield passengers, Farwell writes the best descriptive account of the little *Palm Springs* oasis,
midway along the Carrizo Corridor.

FEDERAL WRITERS PROJECT OF THE WORKS PROGRESS ADMINISTRATION

Death Valley: A Guide. 1939. Boston: Houghton Mifflin Company. XV, 75 pp. Pls.
Fldg. map. 6¼ x 9½. Done in both cloth and wrappers.

Outlined in this important publication are 20 suggested tours of the Valley; together with informative material on its 2,981 square miles of National Monument, 500 of which are below sea level. Of outstanding value are its superb photographic plates.

Old West, The; Pioneer Tales of San Bernardino County. (1940.) San Bernardino:
The Sun Company. 53 pp. 11 illus. 6 x 9. Wrappers.

In compiling these yarns of the Old West, acknowledgment is extended to the
following contributors: C. J. Daley, Abe Delameter, Ed Stiles, Lee Yount, Bert
Doty, Dix Van Dyke, L. V. Root, Art Huffman, Edwin Booth, Grant Holcomb,
George Miller, William Talmadge, Jim Craig, John Duxter, Bill Keys, Emma
Jackson, Bob Grier, and Jim Mitchell. We find assembled for our pleasure a treasure-trove of lively anecdotes. The contents are segregated into sections relating
to frontier days in San Bernardino, life in Calico, the Mojave Desert, the Indians,
and several miscellaneous subject headings.

FERGUSON, MELVILLE F.

Motor Camping on Western Trails. (1925.) New York: The Century Co. XIX,
300 pp. 56 pls. End paper maps.

Chs. 18-19 (pp. 243-272) give an early—though desultory—account of Palm
Springs, the Imperial Valley, and a portion of the Mojave Desert.

FERRIS, ROXANA S.

Death Valley Wild Flowers. (1962.) Death Valley: Death Valley Natural History
Association. Drawings by Jeanne R. Janish. 141 pp. Numerous pen and ink
sketches.

Unquestionably this is a flower guide that merits highest commendation. The
drawings are notable for their clarity in depicting plant detail. Unfortunately,
some readers depend quite largely upon color as an aid to their identification of
flowers (or cacti, trees and birds). I am referring now to the novice; to one not
interested in, nor familiar with, a technical knowledge of botany. To such a reader, colored plates would be most helpful.

An index is provided, making available both the scientific and common street-
corner-English names. This is a help. The book's Introduction estimates between

500 and 1000 species of plants to be found in the Death Valley National Monument, and mentions the interesting fact of the "occurrence of a few species that grow there and nowhere else."

FINKENBINDER, C. E.

Mojave Desert Trails. 1940. Barstow, California: Barstow Printer Review. 72 pp. Pls. 6 maps (by Jack Renie).

The item describes points of interest over the great Mojave—Death Valley, Calico, Mitchell's Caverns, Hoover Dam, and others.

FISHER, LILLIAN E. (Edited by)

Colorado River Campaign; Diary of Pedro Fages. (See listing under Priestley, H. I.)

FISK, O. J. (As told to Johnston, Philip)

Ghosts of Greenwater. 1940. November issue of *Westways.* Illus. Map.

In this article Johnston supplies a source account of early life in the once boisterous mining camp of Greenwater, on the eastern rim of Death Valley.

FITCH, GEORGE HAMLIN

Where the Date Palm Grows. 1900. August issue of *The Land of Sunshine.* Vol. 13. No. 3. 136-142 pp. 4 pls.

The author gives us this early view of Palm Springs, its Indians and some of its palm canyons in the near-by San Jacinto Mountains.

FLEMING, A. M.

Gunsight Mine, The. 1929. Boston. 209 pp.

"True story of early mining in California, mostly in Death Valley; prospecting in the High Sierras, etc." (Reference from Mr. Dick Mohr.)

FLETCHER, COLIN

Thousand Mile Summer, The. 1964. Berkeley: Howell-North Books. 210 pp. Approx. 40 photographs; end paper maps of route.

A pleasantly entertaining book. The author, an Englishman, decided to walk from one end of California to the other. He did just that, starting at the southern boundary near Yuma (at Algodones, Mexico); emerging at the Oregon State line. His route took him along the Colorado River through Earp, past the Parker Dam, to Needles, Baker, Death Valley, the Panamints and Bodie. These were the desert areas traversed along his chosen route to California's northern border.

FLETCHER, ED

Memoirs of Ed Fletcher. 1952. Privately printed. XV, 751 pp.

Ch. 6—"Historic Warner Ranch"—delivers basically sound material of desert interest, and this interest is implemented by the inclusion of 14 illus., many of them early and little known.

FLORIN, LAMBERT

In Mr. Florin's books the ghost town enthusiast can find material abundantly sufficient to satisfy his most exigent demands. First and foremost, Mr. Florin is a master-photographer, and his photographs of historic old ghost town buildings capture all the flavor and atmosphere of his chosen subject. A concomitant pleasure, in all his books, derives from his editorial and descriptive comment. His books are not merely photographic treasures; they rank among the best historic writings available on the ghost towns of the West. Mr. Florin is an astute student of his chosen subject and qualifies as one of its foremost authorities.

The author-photographer travels far afield in the Western United States and Canada. To date, seven uniformly-sized books have been issued in his ghost town series, all published by the Superior Publishing Company of Seattle, all measuring 8⅝ x 10¾, and housing from 176 to 192 pages each. No ghost towns are duplicated in any of the books. The series includes:

    No. 1—Western Ghost Towns—1961
    No. 2—Ghost Town Album—1962
    No. 3—Ghost Town Trails—1963
    No. 4—Ghost Town Shadows—1964
    No. 5—Ghost Town Treasures—1965
    No. 6—Boot Hill—1966
    No. 7—Tales the Western Tombstones Tell—1967

For their Southern California desert interest, three of his seven books qualify for inclusion in this Bibliography. The other three, while generous in their display of California ghost town subjects—particularly those in the Mother Lode region—do not relate specifically to our southern desert areas.

Mr. Florin's books, consistently, are dedicated to David C. Mason, M.D., "whose assistance has made the series possible."

Boot Hill.

From the dust jacket of this book we learn more of this versatile man who has done so much to vitalize and re-activate our vanishing ghost towns. We know him as a proficient writer and photographer. Now we learn he is a florist by profession, a rockhound, can recognize the notes of most birds of the desert and forest, knows the names and characteristics of many of the mountain wild flowers.

Boot Hill, while not following a digressive trend from the central theme of ghost town lore, introduces a new and essentially different approach. This time Florin takes his readers directly to a ghost town's *Boot Hill*. This is, oddly enough, a sensible procedure. One of the first places a confirmed ghost town lover attempts to locate is the old cemetery. Happily, Mr. Florin provides an excuse, albeit an exiguous one, to include *Boot Hill* among our listings: he devotes two or three pages to Bodie. There is considerable material on our neighboring states of Nevada,

Arizona and Idaho. His most recent book—Tales the Western Tombstones Tell—
follows the pattern of *Boot Hill.*

Ghost Town Treasures.
  Tropico, Gold Camp, Randsburg, Garlock and Johannesburg are featured.

Guide To Western Ghost Towns, A.
  In 1967 there appeared the ghost town *Guide.* It is keyed to the general series;
is uniform in size, except it contains only 96 pages; is available in both hard and
soft bindings. This book is indispensable to the ghost town buff.

Western Ghost Towns.
  Included are photographs of scenes in Cerro Gordo, Swansea, and Ballarat. As
in all his books the *visual* concept made possible by the artistic ability displayed in
his photography is implemented by his careful historical accounting. There is
much on the ghost towns of Arizona and Nevada.

FONT, FATHER PEDRO

Complete Diary (Translated and edited by Bolton, Dr. H. E.) 1933. Berkeley:
University of California Press. 552 pp. 35 pls. 6¼ x 8¾.
  This is the "Long" (or "Complete") *Diary* of Father Font, being some five times
the length of the "Short" *Diary* and based upon it. The Font *Diary,* as here listed,
is a separate publication comprising Vol. 4 in the five-volume set of Anza's California Expeditions (1774-1776), edited by Dr. Bolton and published in 1930. Says
Dr. Bolton of the Font *Diary*—"In spite of his [Font's] illness and his temperament, or because of them, he wrote a superb diary—one of the best in all Western
Hemisphere history, it is safe to say." Chs. 6 and 7 (pp. 122-160) specifically describe the expedition's experiences in crossing the Imperial Valley. Father Font was
the priest accompanying de Anza's second expedition (1775-76) across the Colorado Desert. One can safely recommend Font for sustained interest, thrills, entertainment, temper, courage, robust character, and valuable historical information.

FORD, WALTER B.

She Found Happiness In Her Desert Paradise. 1947. February issue of *The Desert
Spotlight.*
  Fourteen miles from the town of Daggett, in the Mojave Desert, is a place
known as Willis Well. A graded road leads up to a 4000 foot elevation. The chief
attraction at Willis Well is a huge rock wall "that extended back from the road
several hundred feet, then continued at a right-angle to the mountain of boulders
that we were approaching. Back of the main wall, another wall continued to a
rocky abutment, forming a small enclosure. . . . The walls contain approximately
115,000 cubic feet of stone."
  And these walls were built by one lone woman, living with a sick husband up
in the lonely Ord Mountains. They moved there in 1915; and it required some ten
years to accomplish her gigantic task. The story is a fascinating one and Mr. Ford
tells it well. (See listing under Johnston, Philip—*The Woman of Ord Mountain.*)

Adventures of James Collier, First Collector of the Port of San Francisco. 1937. Chicago: The Black Cat Press. 61 pp. 6⅝ x 9½. Edition limited to 250 copies.

Collier and his party were among the 1849 westward-bound emigrants who came into the gold fields via the southern route—across the Colorado River westward over the Colorado Desert. The book concerns itself mainly with Collier's experiences at San Francisco in his official capacity as Collector of the Port. Pp. 24-28 inform of his desert crossing.

Mr. Foreman presents such material as he could collect on James Collier. Considering the fragmentary data available, he did a pretty good job of it. There is considerably more mention *of* than *by* this man Collier. H. M. T. Powell, in his diary, indicates that Collier followed the mountain route out from the Carrizo Corridor, his trail leading up through a canyon, over the mountains, finally bringing him to San Diego. Thus he would not have followed the sandy wash up the Carrizo Corridor; but would have skirted the mountains to the west, by-passing Vallecito, San Felipe Valley, and Warner's.

Marcy & the Gold Seekers. The Journal of Capt. R. B. Marcy with an Account of the Gold Rush over the Southern Route. 1939. Norman, Oklahoma: University of Oklahoma Press. Words "First Edition" appear under copyright notice. 433 pp. 6 illus. Fldg. map of Southern Route of the 49ers to California. 5½ x 7¾.

Mr. Foreman's book represents a work of considerable merit, reflecting information that could be assembled only as the result of intensive research and laborious effort. The true value of the book is expressed in the vast round-up of letters, documents, journals, diaries, and comments actually written by the 49ers who ventured into the gold fields along the Southern desert route of Kearny and Cooke. Foreman parades a wealth of exciting material, garnering his rich harvest of source information from such groups as those of Washington, Buford, Gildersleeve, Birge, Hawkins, Havilah Mining Company, Clarksville Company, Little Rock Company, the Quaker—Charles Pancoast—and his company, Dr. Joel Candee and the Knickerbocker company, Aldrich, Audubon, Collier, and numerous others.

Chs. 11 and 12 (pp. 279-338) reflect material bearing upon our immediate desert interest. Specifically, in a portion of the Alden M. Woodruff account of the adventures of the Little Rock Company (pp. 283-284), mention is made of the route through Carrizo Creek, Vallecito and San Felipe. Similarly, in the account of Dr. Joel G. Candee of the Knickerbocker Company (pp. 330-332), we find reference to precisely this same portion of the trail. Passages from Audubon's *Journal* are likewise included (pp. 316-318).

A fundamental work this, and one of recognized importance because it is designed to supplement all that has elsewhere been written of the dramatic Gold Rush chapter in California history. The book exhibits much that has heretofore been denied us, presenting a composite picture of the parties, groups, divisions, and companies of those who also journeyed to the gold fields in 1849, but who chose to follow—as their route of travel—the trail that led over the treacherous desert areas of Southern California. Mention should be made of the Lt. Cave

Couts' *Journal* (see listing in this Bibliography), with the recommendation that it be read in conjunction with the Marcy; for here is a narrative that differs essentially from all other contemporary accounts. Lt. Cave Couts was *not* one of the emigrants and he was *not* traveling from east to west but from west to east. His comments concerning the "swarms" of emigrants who besieged him for trail information and travel advice ("way-bills") are most revealing—and thoroughly entertaining. Says Couts, while languishing in a shade temperature of 110 degrees (it was September)—"Have been troubled nearly to death by emigrants inquiring the route to Los Angeles and San Diego. If I have made one I have made a hundred way-bills for them." Rarely are we privileged to enjoy such a diversification of viewpoint as that presented in this one isolated facet of our great westward surge of empire during that epochal year of 1849.

(Edited by) *Pathfinder in the Southwest. A. The Itinerary of Lieutenant A. W. Whipple During His Explorations for a Railway Route From Fort Smith to Los Angeles in the Years 1853-1854.* 1941. Norman: University of Oklahoma Press. XV, 298 pp. 7 illus. Fldg. map. 6¼ x 10⅛. Words "First Edition" appear under copyright notice. (Wagner-Camp No. 265.)

Mr. Foreman here reproduces, with careful editing and annotations, the Whipple account in Vol. 111 of the *Pacific Railroad Surveys.*

Ch. 15—"From the Colorado River to the Mormon Road" (pp. 248-264), and Ch. 16—"From the Mormon Road to the Pacific" (pp. 265-279), cover Whipple's route after leaving the Colorado to his arrival in Los Angeles via the Mojave Desert and Cajon Pass.

FOWLER, HARLAN D.

Camels to California. 1950. Stanford: Stanford University Press. 93 pp. 18 illus. End-paper maps. 7¼ x 10¼.

The singular episode of the camels in America, instigated by the then Secretary of War—Mr. Jefferson Davis, is closely associated with California's desert history. The chapter on "Camels at Fort Tejon" (pp. 63-73) bears a direct reference to the desert route leading to Cajon Pass. (For a more detailed description of the camel brigade and the unfortunate aftermath attending it, see listing of *Uncle Sam's Camels*, under Lesley, Lewis B.)

FOX, MAUDE A.

Both Sides of the Mountain. (1954.) Palm Desert, California: Desert Magazine Press. 132 pp. 8 pls. 6¼ x 9¼.

The author and her husband moved to Yucaipa Valley, in Southern California, in 1919. From this vantage point she observed a phenomenal development over the years on "both sides of the mountain"—the Valley side and the Desert side. To those of us who love the desert there comes a poignant regret that Mrs. Fox had so little to say with regard to the *other* side of the mountain—the *desert* side. Only in a relatively small segment of her present narrative does she become historically articulate desert-wise. Here and there we find choice morsels: a visual account of early Palm Springs, a quick reference to the historic Warren's Well, the story of

Willie Boy—the Indian youth who ruthlessly murdered his sweetheart and her father, thus precipitating the greatest man hunt ever staged on the High Desert country in and around Twentynine Palms. Of purely collateral interest, and of baroque substance, yet closely woven into the fabric of desert history, the Willie Boy story has become an integral factor in whatever quantum of dramatic lore our High Desert area can muster.

Hidden Valley. 1946. July issue of *The Desert Spotlight.* Illus.

Historical reference of some importance is made available in this article to an unique valley in the Joshua Tree National Monument. Reportedly, the Hidden Valley was at one time a hide-out for horse thieves.

Thar's Gold in Them Thar Hills. 1946. July issue of *The Desert Spotlight.*

The article relates the story of early mining activities in what is now the Joshua Tree National Monument.

FOY, MARY E. (Edited by)

By Ox-Team from Salt Lake to Los Angeles. (See listing under Cheesman, David W.)

FRASHER, BURTON

Portfolio of Desert Area Photographs from 1920 to 1939. 1964. *Westerners, The* (Los Angeles Corral) *Brand Book* No. 11. 20 pp.

A remarkable gathering of early-day photographs, chosen from a collection of several hundred assembled by the dedicated photographer Burton Frasher "who drove the sandy washes into Death Valley first in 1920 and continued his visits for 30 years." As Westerner Russ Leadabrand—Editor of *Brand Book* No. 11— points out: "Burton Frasher may not have been the first man there, but in many cases he was the first man there with a view camera." (See listing under Leadabrand, Russ—*Photographer of the Desert.*)

FREEMAN, BARNARD B.

Canyon of the Martyrs. 1941. December issue of *Westways.* Illus.

This is a short, but interpretive, item on a little-known desert wonderland— Afton Canyon, or Caves Canyon, as it is sometimes called. This gorge is some 40 miles east of Barstow, and was discovered by Father Garcés on March 9, 1776. It was he who gave it its name.

FRÉMONT, JOHN CHARLES

Report of the Exploring Expedition to the Rocky Mountains in the Year 1842, and to Oregon and North California in the Years 1843-44. 1845. Washington: U. S. Senate. Perfect copies run 693 pp.. 22 pls., 2 fldg. maps, 2 page maps, 1 large fldg. pocket map of Oregon and California. Two editions were issued by the Government—one by order of the Senate, the other by order of the House. Each edition ran 10,000 copies, the texts being identical except that the House edition omits the astronomical observations. A Zamorano 80 item. (Cowan P. 91; Wagner-Camp No. 115.) Several reprint editions have appeared.

Fremont conducted five exploratory expeditions. The first of these (1842) did not touch California. The second (1843-44), on its return from California—according to J. Gregg Layne—"left Sutter's Fort and proceeded south through the Sacramento and San Joaquin Valleys, through Tehachapi Pass and across the Mojave Desert to the head of Cajon Pass, where it followed the Old Spanish Trail to its pass through the Wasatch Mountains." The third expedition (1845)—again according to Mr. Layne—moved "south past Mono Lake and through present Owens Valley in California, . . . then through Walker Pass into San Joaquin Valley." The fourth expedition (1848-49)—that clumsy, blundering, disastrous expedition where men floundered in snow at temperatures 20 degrees below zero and were forced to eat the scabbards of their hunting knives, and where eleven of them eventually perished—this fourth expedition ultimately headed southwest and thence west to the Gila River. They moved along the south bank of the Gila to the Colorado which they crossed and continued northwest over the desert via Warner's Ranch to Los Angeles. On the fifth, and last, expedition the party fetched up along the Kern River, a ways south of Walker's Pass; but not, however, until Frémont implored his men to swear they would not resort to cannibalism.

Many and varied are the articles written *by*—and particularly *about*—the controversial "Pathfinder." In this Bibliography I list but one as being sufficient to tie in the excursive pilgrimages of the quixotic Frémont with our desert theme. His *Report of the Exploring Expedition* (covering his first two expeditions) is a great book and an important one. It constitutes an early narrative of overland adventure; and, as such, it infused tremendous enthusiasm into the hearts of men everywhere to consort with excitement and danger by venturing out upon the vast surge of westbound migration. Moreover, the book is well written. And to the dynamic Frémont must go the credit for the writing of it; *not* to his wife, Jessie, as so many critics insist. Conceivably she aided in the preparation of the book, but Frémont and Frémont only could actually have written it. There is no point in denying him the signal honor of having compiled one of the earliest and best written of all our overland narratives. Mrs. Frémont composed, to a large extent, the one volume *Memoirs*—wherein is entered some account of the third expedition.

In the course of his Second Expedition travels, Frémont came onto the Mojave Desert through Tehachapi Pass; crossed south and eastward over it until he struck the Old Spanish Trail which he continued to follow to his ultimate destination. Kit Carson and Alex Godey were with him.

Some readers discern a possible reference to the High Desert country in and around Twentynine Palms. However, the party did not directly explore this region; actually passed well to the north of it.

On his return from the ill-advised Fourth Expedition the impetuous "Pathfinder" crossed the Colorado Desert. On the Fifth Expedition he again traveled a portion of the eastern Mojave, along the Old Spanish Trail. But of that devastating Fourth Expedition and the equally discouraging Fifth, he has little or nothing to say. And small wonder. For about all that remained to Frémont after these disastrous failures were the lingering memories of his fragmented dream of empire.

FROTHINGHAM, ROBERT

Trails Through the Golden West. 1932. New York: Robert M. McBride & Co. 272 pp. Illus. Words "First published March 1932" appear under copyright notice. 5¾ x 8⅜.

Pages 135 to 167 touch on Death Valley.

GALLAGHER, J. D.

California Highways. From Ch. 14 of *California Highways and Public Works.* (See listing under Adams, Kenneth C.)

GALVIN, JOHN (Edited by)

Record of Travels In Arizona and California 1775-1776, A (See listing under Garcés, Francisco.)

GARCÉS, FATHER FRANCISCO

On the Trail of a Spanish Pioneer. (See listing under Coues, Elliott.)

Record of Travels In Arizona and California 1775-1776, A. 1965. San Francisco: John Howell. Designed and printed by Lawton and Alfred Kennedy. Limited to 1250 copies. Introduction and editing by John Galvin. IX plus 116 pp. Fldg. map of Garcés travels. Fldg. map (Font's). 5 colored illus. 6 sectional drawings. 2 appendices. 9½ x 13¼.

This book may claim merit for a craftsmanship that is commensurate with the historical value of its text. Garcés began the exploratory venture detailed in this diary on October 21, 1775. The diary concludes with his entry of September 17, 1776. During this period he covered over 2000 miles. His journey entailed travel over deserts, mountains, and along rivers. The reader can trace his course past Tubac, the ruins at Casa Grande, the Colorado River and into California. On his return trip he saw the Grand Canyon. Unfortunately, as Mr. Galvin explains, Garcés was not a naturalist. He leaves us little or no description of the country over which he traveled, nor of the animals and birds he saw there. Landscapes meant nothing to him. His work was with the Indians; and concerning them his writings were understandably effusive.

GARDNER, ERLE STANLEY

Desert Is Yours, The. 1963. New York: William Morrow & Co. 256 pp. No index (nor is one needed). Approximately 150 photographs, including 9 colored plates. 6½ x 9½.

Mr. Gardner pictures the desert as he is able to see it from helicopters, airplanes, 4-wheel drives, Pak-Jaks, super sand buggies, trailers, and air-cooled two-wheel power scooters. Some of us are still old fashioned enough to do much of our exploring in a more intimate manner—perhaps even by *walking* a little, now and then. By such an approach we establish a physical, man-to-desert contact and bring ourselves into closer rapport with the desert's certain appeal.

Gardner's relation of lost mine hunting for the Pegleg, the Dutchman and others, holds interest. Chapter One, "A Look at the Real Desert," is Erle Stanley Gardner—experienced desert man and close companion of the waste lands—at his literary best.

Neighborhood Frontiers. (1954.) William Morrow & Co. 272 pp. End paper design. Pls. 6¼ x 9½.

The subject matter in this book is divided into five sections: Desert Country, Puget Sound Country, Yucatan Peninsula, Yaqui River, Barranca Country. The section on Desert Country extends from p. 15 to p. 116, and contains 17 desert plates (2 additional desert plates are to be found elsewhere in the book). The desert interest that might otherwise attach to Ch. 1 (pp. 15-52), in what started out to be a description of Quail Springs, largely dissipates itself in an extraneous account of one Samuelson. I am at a loss to understand why this Samuelson narrative, seemingly so utterly foreign to the subject of deserts, was ever injected into the desert section in the first place, or into any other section of the book for that matter. Desert lovers, generally, would appreciate more of Quail Springs; less—much less—of Samuelson.

GIFFEN, HELEN S.

Camp Independence. 1942. December issue of *Historical Society of Southern California Quarterly.* 15 pp. Line drawing showing ground plan of Camp Independence.

Camp Independence was established in Owens Valley on July 4, 1862 (hence its name). Its purpose was to afford protection from the Indians. The instant article records the several Indian uprisings and the role played by the soldiers stationed at the army camp. The Owens Valley earthquake of 1872 destroyed most of the original buildings; the new post was entirely rebuilt by 1875. This article gives the specifications for the several buildings. The Camp was finally abandoned in July of 1877. Eventually the land was thrown open to settlers; the buildings were either destroyed or carted away. None presently remains at the site of the old post.

GILBERT, E. M.

Panamint Legend. (1957). Los Angeles: The Hesperus Press. 16 pp. 9 line drawings by author. Wrappers. 5 x 7½. Typography by Stanley H. Gunderson.

I consider this the outstanding account, among those examined, of the Racetrack Dry Lake west of Stovepipe Wells, in Death Valley. This is the spot with its bewildering mystery of the sliding rocks. What force or agency causes them to slide over the surface of this dry lake? Are they pushed by human hands? Does the wind blow them back and forth over the slippery lake bed? Mr. Gilbert presents a reasonable and convincing theory; and he presents it in a charming and readable style.

GILBERT, HELEN M.

Over the Plank Road to Yuma. 1962. February issue of *Desert* Magazine. Four interesting photos; map.

The article states that the first plank road was built in 1915 and financed mainly by public subscription; but in 1916 the California Highway Commission built the improved plank road at a cost to the State of $35,000. The road extended for 7½ miles. Re-planking was necessary within a year. The first pavement came in 1926. (See listings under Weight, Harold O.—*Lost Gold of the Great Dunes;* Imperial Valley Pioneers—*The Valley Imperial;* Adams, Kenneth—*California Highways and Public Works;* Taylor, O. and E.—*Across the Sand Dunes To Yesterday.*)

GLASSCOCK, C. B. and KUNZE, T. E.

Death Valley Chuck-Walla, The. 1907. Greenwater, California. 56 pp. (Vol. 1, No. 4.) 4¾ x 6½.

There were ten issues, altogether, of this now-evasive magalet. They were published semi-monthly in the old boom mining town of Greenwater, now entirely disappeared, on the eastern edge of Death Valley. The year was 1907. The first issue (Vol. 1, No. 1) was dated January 1. Its circulation extended to every State in the Union. It boasted twenty subscribers on Wall Street. On the front cover (Vol. 1, No. 4) are printed these words: "A magazine for men. Published on the desert at the brink of Death Valley. Mixing the dope, cool from the mountains and hot from the desert, and withal putting out a concoction with which you can do as you damn please as soon as you have paid for it. . . . Price ten cents." On the inside of the front cover (Vol. 1, No. 4) we find this choice tid-bit of boom-town arrogance: "The Theme of the Chuck-Walla. The men and the mines, the life and the lore, the wealth and the wisdom of the Western desert comprise the theme of the *Chuck-Walla.* Born on the desert, and versed in all things of the desert, it carries to the world the knowledge of what is here. If you don't like it, don't read it. If you do read it remember these facts: What it says is true; what it does is honest; it will call a liar a liar, a thief a thief, or an ass an ass, as is justified, and if you don't like it you may kick and be damned. Its editors are its owners, and will do as they see fit with their own, restricting themselves only in-so-far as they are restricted by their demand for the truth, the whole truth, and nothing but the truth, and their wish to give the devil his due."

When Greenwater quit, everything quit—including the *Chuck-Walla.* Its life tenure was five months, or ten issues. And now those issues are so scarce that it appears impossible to locate one. I know of the existence of only six, although there probably are more—somewhere. I hope so.

GLASSCOCK, C. B.

Gold In Them Hills. (1932.) New York: The Bobbs-Merrill Co. Inc. XIII, 17-330 pp. 15 illus. End-paper maps. 6 x 8⅞. Words "First Edition" appear under copyright notice. The book has gone into reprint editions.

Although mainly a book on Rawhide and other Nevada areas, choice material on the early mining fields surrounding Death Valley is made available to the reader, particularly in the chapter on Greenwater. The author's comments on Greenwater are neither languid nor verveless. They couldn't possibly be—and for two excellent reasons: first, Glasscock wrote them; second, he helped make Greenwater. His name is consonant with its glamorous, but short-lived, existence. And when its precipitant finale was ushered in, Glasscock dead-headed out of the region on "Uncle Billy's Chug-Chug." But he was there "to the last man," having experienced its exhilarating hey-day and likewise the abrupt invasion of those forces which contributed to its sudden demise.

Here's Death Valley. (1940.) New York: The Bobbs-Merrill Company. The words "First Edition" appear below copyright notice. XIV, 329 pp. 22 pls. 6 x 8¾. End paper maps. Several reprint editions have been published.

The author was, himself, one of the old Ghost-City pioneers, having published the *Death Valley Chuck-Walla* at Greenwater in 1907. He utilizes every opportunity to collect interviews from old-time desert characters, gathering tales of innumerable incidents that lend vitality to the narrative. The reader is favored with intimate descriptions of the old mining towns of Panamint, Darwin, Bullfrog, Rhyolite, Beatty, Greenwater, Harrisburg, Skidoo and Leadfield. And, of course, Scotty figures prominently, as does the old Greenland (Furnace Creek) Ranch, and also the borax industry. No other book written of this desert excels *Here's Death Valley* in readability; few, if any, are more historically sound.

GODWIN, WALT

Ghost Town Romance. 1947. April issue of *The Desert Spotlight.*

An unusual, and particularly fascinating story this, with its locale at the site of the old ghost town of New Dale, a few miles east of Twentynine Palms. Here is an incident told simply, yet convincingly; and one that is scheduled to stir the imagination. (What a plot for a movie!)

GOETZMANN, WILLIAM H.

Army Exploration In the American West 1803-1863. 1959. New Haven: Yale University Press. 509 pp. 14 text maps; 5 fldg. maps in back cover pocket. 27 illus. 6½ x 9½.

In his preface Mr. Goetzmann writes: "The Topographical Engineers performed heroic deeds . . . were just as colorful and as human as any group of explorers whose deeds history is likely to record." In this high estimate I enthusiastically concur. Whether the author has succeeded in elevating the engineers to this glorified status is a question that can best be resolved by each individual reader as he attempts to relate the book to his own preferences.

Mr. Goetzmann approaches the development of his premise in a scholarly fashion that is likely to appeal to the academic community. Similarly, those who are less concerned with actual epic experiences than with a cultural dissertation upon the over-all aspect of the survey program will find this well-documented book to their liking.

GOLDER, FRANK ALFRED; BAILEY, THOS. A.; SMITH, J. LYMAN

March of the Mormon Battalion from Council Bluffs to California, The. (1928.) New York: The Century Company. XIII, 295 pp. Map. 8 pls. End paper maps. 5½ x 8. Words "First Printing July 1928" appear under copyright notice.

The account is taken from the *Journal* of Henry Standage, a private in Company E of the Battalion. The Mormon Battalion arrived in California in January 1847, six weeks after the arrival of General Kearny and the Army of the West. They followed—with little deviation—the latter's trail across the Colorado desert. Under the leadership of Col. P. St. George Cooke they succeeded in bringing the first wagons across the southern desert country. Other documents are included in the Golder book, telling of the organization and the early days of the Mormon Church. In this 295-page book, only 100 pages carry the *Journal*; and even in this one-third portion of the book numerous letters and narrative material are sandwiched among the *Journal* entries. Pages 281-288 list the names of officers and members of the several companies of the Battalion.

GONZALES, RAFAEL

Account. (See listing under Bean, L. J. *The Romero Expeditions.*)

GOODMAN, JESSIE H. (Edited by)

Overland In 1849: From Missouri to California By the Platte River and the Salt Lake Trail. An Account from the Letters of G. C. Pearson. (See listing under Pearson, G. C.)

GOODMAN, JOHN B. (Edited by)

Over the Salt Lake Trail In the Fall of '49. (See listing under Lorton, Wm. B.)

GOULDING, JAMES E. (Transcribed, with Foreword and Notes by CHICKERING, MARTHA A.)

Founding of a Mojave Desert Community, The. 1948. June issue of *California Historical Society Quarterly*. Vol. 27, No. 2. Illus.

The desert community referred to in this article is the one presently known as Lucerne Valley, in San Bernardino County. It was founded by Mr. Goulding in 1897.

GOWER, MARY LILLIAN and PAULSON, GOLDIS

Death Valley Natural Bridge. 1939. September issue of *Desert*. Illus.

The article informs of the discovery and location of the picturesque natural bridge in Death Valley, in a canyon on the west side of the Black Mountains.

GRACY, DAVID B. and RUGELEY, HELEN J. (Edited by)

From the Mississippi to the Pacific: An Englishman in the Mormon Battalion. (See listing under Whitworth, Robert W.)

Letters of. 1959. Los Angeles: Glen Dawson. Introduction and Notes by LeRoy R. Hafen. Limited to 250 copies. Printed by The Ward Ritchie Press. 50 pp. 5¼ x 7⅜.

Granger was associated with the group who traveled from Salt Lake with the Jefferson Hunt wagon train in the fall of 1849. He was among those who defected from the train and started on the disastrous western cut-off. He was also with those who turned back at "Mount Misery" in the hope of rejoining the Hunt train. (The approximate 27 wagons that did not turn back at "Mount Misery," but continued their westward course, constituted the now-famous Death Valley Party of 1849.) In the wake of the Hunt party, Granger followed the trail across the Mojave Desert and over Cajon Pass to San Bernardino and Los Angeles. He refers to the water supply at "Vegas" (Las Vegas), Cottonwood Spring, "Willow Spring" (Stump Spring), "Hernandez Spring" (Resting Spring), the Archillette Springs, the Amargosa River, Salt Spring, the "Augua de Tomaso" (Bitter Spring), and the Mojave River.

Most of the "letters" in the book bear reference to Granger's life and experience in California. He practiced law in Los Angeles, was elected District Attorney, moved to Oroville where he was twice elected to the state legislature. Later he became Receiver of the U. S. Land Office.

GRANSON, EVE

Desert Mavericks. 1928. Santa Barbara. Hubbard.
The item consists of short verses, illustrated by line drawings of desert animals.

GRANT, U.S. IV.

Midsummer Motoring Trip. 1961. Reprint from the March issue of the *Historical Society of Southern California Quarterly*. 12 pp.

Inserted in my presentation copy from Dr. Grant is a 1913 folding map of the Salton Sink region. The map was not included in the regular issue of the Quarterly. Also included are two mimeographed pages of "Notes and Comments On Place Names to Accompany *A Midsummer Motoring Trip*."

This "saga of impetuous youth" relates to an early desert camping trip (1913) by Dr. Grant and his brother into the heart of the Imperial Valley region. 1913 was a pioneer year for this desert; and the boys attempted their arduous trip in "a stripped-down, two-seater, Overland automobile." The trip started from San Diego, via the inland route to San Bernardino and a few days of fishing at Big Bear Lake. In entering the desert area they drove through Banning and Whitewater into the Coachella Valley, but not until they "went on toward a small settlement called Palm Springs, an oasis directly at the foot of the lofty San Jacinto Mountains." They touched at Indian Wells, Indio, Coachello and Thermal, past the Salton Sea and Figtree John's place (Figtree was then reputed to be 91 years of age).

There follows a fascinating account of the boys' assorted experiences in this wild desert land. And some of these experiences—including the stalled car episode—were harrowing ones. Dr. Grant's descriptions of infant Palm Springs and Figtree John are among the highlights of this delightful narrative of early desert travel adventure.

GRAVES, JACKSON A.

California Memories. 1930. Los Angeles: Times-Mirror Press. 330 pp. plus 16 unnumbered pp. 50 pls.

Ch. 37 (pp. 303-319) relates to Death Valley; and Ch. 27 (pp. 215-223) contains appropriate material under the caption—"Touring the Owens River Valley."

GRAY, A. A.; FARQUHAR, FRANCIS P.; LEWIS, WM. S.

Camels In Western America. 1930. Reprint from the December issue of the Quarterly of the *California Historical Society*. 48 pp. 6 reproductions from Edward Vischer. Reproduction of the title page of the Charter of the American Camel Company (1854). Bibliography.

Mr. Gray has prepared the title article—"Camels in California"; also the article on "The Dollart Case." Mr. Farquhar writes on the subject of "Camels In the Sketches of Edward Vischer." The exhaustive nine-page bibliography on Camel Experiment material is assembled by Mr. Lewis. Camel shipments arrived in the United States during the years 1856 and 1857. A portion of the animals were driven to Fort Tejon, in California. Eventually, three were taken into Death Valley by one of the exploring parties. The unfortunate camel experiment, championed by Jefferson Davis, was short lived. (See listing under Lesley, Lewis B.—*Uncle Sam's Camels*.)

GRAY, A. B. (Edited by Bailey, L. R.)

Report. 1963. Los Angeles: Westernlore Press. 240 pp. 36 illus. Limited to 900 copies. End paper maps. 5¾ x 8¼.

L. R. Bailey edits this report of the railroad survey along the 32nd parallel and supplies the informative bibliographical notes. The Third Division, embracing the region from the confluence of the Gila and Colorado rivers to San Diego or San Pedro on the Pacific coast, ties in the report directly with our Southern California desert area. The survey was in 1854; their route followed the Kearny-Cooke-Emigrant route, dipping south along the Colorado river from Fort Yuma into Mexico, thus circumventing the sand dunes. The approximate 85 miles over the treacherous desert brought them to water at Carrizo Creek, thence up the corridor past Vallecito and Warner's ranch. It is interesting to note Gray's enthusiasm for his projected railroad route over the burning sands of the Colorado Desert. He writes: "The four times that I have traversed this so-called desert (January, June and October) we experienced no sickness, nor any trouble except for want of water." This reference to the Colorado being a "so-called desert" is so palpably erroneous that the reliability of his entire report becomes suspect. Gray was not only optimistic and enthusiastic; he was guilty of gross deception. He *knew* better than to write such misleading and dangerous comment. He does, in fact, all but pass over the desert crossing entirely. He gives only a meager description of this segment of the survey; the inference being that he was more diligent in *avoiding* mention of it than he was in factually describing it. He appeared deliberately to ignore it, except to insist it was the natural locale for a railroad.

Included in the A. B. Gray *Report* are the Reminiscences of Peter R. Brady. His reference to the Colorado Desert is both quantitatively and qualitatively so insignificant that I see no purpose in further mention of it.

GRAY, FRED (As told to Johnston, Philip)

Memories of Ballarat. 1940. September issue of *Westways*. Illus.

Ballarat is the old ghost town northeast of Trona, in the Panamint Valley. The article narrates the colorful history of this old-time supply center that flourished in the late nineties.

GREEN, ROBERT B. (Edited by Oliphant, J. Orin)

On the Arkansas Route to California in 1849. 1955. Lewisburg, Pa. The Bucknell University Press. IX, 87 pp. Mr. Oliphant's Introduction and Notes to Introduction, pp. 3-26. End paper maps. 7⅛ x 10¼.

From Lewisburg, Pa., on Feb. 26, 1849, these six young men departed in their wagons westward to the gold fields—Robert B. Green, David "Deacon" Howard, Cyrus Fox, Wm. H. Chamberlin, S. Frederick Schaffle, and John Musser. Their California desert crossing, pp. 73-80, followed the Kearny route from the Colorado River crossing to Warner's Ranch. Three of them wrote of their trip—Robert B. Green, Wm. H. Chamberlin (see listing in this Bibliography), and David "Deacon" Howard. Howard's notes are available only in transcript form, and this imperfectly done. The University gives us our first published appearance of Green's *Journal*, and Mr. Oliphant does a superb job of editing it. Mrs. Clara P. Hall, in a letter to the author of this present Bibliography, states that only 350 copies were printed; and the University has decided not to print additional copies. Some 320 copies were distributed to friends of, and donors to, the University, while a few other copies were sent to selected libraries in California and Arkansas.

Says Mr. Oliphant, in his Introduction, "Green was neither solemn nor reticent. Sparkling humor and stinging sarcasm inform his writing. Moreover, his style, like his emotion, runs freely. With jaunty carelessness he 'roughs up' his mother tongue, and with artless skill he manhandles Spanish words. And with equal freedom he passes judgment on persons . . . In brief, he recorded in his Diary both happenings and opinions that most diarists on such journeys would think it proper not to record."

Green says precisely, and without literary adornment, the thing he has to say. There is no hedging, no studied effort to create atmosphere. An example in point is his description of the Indians along the route. What he says is as vividly naked as the savages themselves. And as unpredictable. I consider the Green item the most delightfully distinctive Journal in my entire collection.

GREENWOOD, ROBERT

California Outlaw, The—Tiburcio Vasquez. 1960. Los Gatos, California: The Talisman Press. 296 pp. Photographic illus. 6¼ x 9¼.

Much of Vasquez' activity was centered in Southern California; some of it—like the stage coach raid at Coyote Holes—was out on the open desert. Coyote Holes, or Freeman Junction as it is now called, is located on the Bishop highway at the point where the Walker Pass road turns off west to Bakersfield. The bandit struck here on February 25, 1874.

Mr. Greenwood prints the 1875 George Beer's account which, according to him, is the best contemporary book on Vasquez. (See listing under Edwards, E. I.—*Freeman's, a Stage Stop on the Mojave.*)

GREY, ZANE

Death Valley. 1920. May issue of *Harpers.* Illus.

This item appeared later (1922) in book form—"Tales of Lonely Trails"—together with other sketches by the author. An early, mediocre item.

Wanderer of the Wasteland. 1923. New York: Harper & Brothers. 419 pp. 5⅛ x 7⅝.

This is Zane Grey's novel with its locale in Death Valley; at least it is given the Death Valley setting about halfway through the book (p. 156); and it pretty well remains there, except for occasional trips to other desert areas.

Grey managed to get all fouled up on the Death Valley historical angle. "Seventy Mormon gold seekers," he writes, "had wandered into this red-walled, white-floored valley, where sixty-eight of them perished. The two that escaped gave this narrow sink so many hundred feet below sea level the name Death Valley!"

All of which comes reasonably close for Zane Grey. And it is to be remembered he wrote this book at a relatively early date—for Death Valley literature, that is.

GRIERSON, EVELYNE BOYNTON

I Paint the Ghost Towns. 1962. Palm Desert, California: Desert Printers, Inc. Pages are unnumbered, but there are close to 50 of them. Decorative wrappers.

Indeed this artist *does* "paint the ghost towns," and she paints them artistically, beautifully and—of superlative importance—authentically. If one has ever been in any of the ghost towns she paints, he finds no necessity to refer to the title of her painting. She faithfully reproduces on canvas the charm and the detail of our boisterous old mining towns of yesteryear.

California is not omitted from her choice assemblage, and shares comparable honors with Nevada. Bodie is not forgotten; neither is Cerro Gordo. Ballarat, Gopher Gulch, and Randsburg are honored by inclusion.

Each painting, together with its location, is described briefly but adequately by the artist-author.

GRIFFIN, JOHN S., M.D.

Doctor Comes to California, A. 1943. San Francisco: *California Historical Society.* Special Publication No. 18, being a reprint from the *California Historical Society Quarterly.* Vol. XXI. Nos. 3 and 4, and Vol. XXII, No. 1. 97 pp. 1 pl. 7⅛ x 10⅝.

This is the diary of John S. Griffin, rated Assistant Surgeon with Kearny's Dragoons during the years 1846-1847. Dr. Griffin was a participant in the historic Battle of San Pasqual, and his is one of the two complete diaries of General Kearny's march from Santa Fe to San Diego with his Army of the West (the other being Emory's *Notes of a Military Reconnoissance*), and of their memorable engagement with the Californians at the Battle of San Pasqual. This book contains the noted Emory map, from his *Reconnoissance* (1848), separated into four convenient full-page sections, and tracing the route of Kearny's march from Santa Fe to San Diego and Los Angeles. The introduction and notes of the reprint are prepared by George Walcott Ames, Jr.; the foreword by George D. Lyman, M.D. Dr. Lyman's "Foreword" supplies one of our best descriptive accounts of the Battle of San Pasqual.

Incidentally, the first published appearance of portions of Dr. Griffin's diary may be found in the Warner, Hayes, Widney *An Historical Sketch of Los Angeles County, California* (1876). (See listing in this Bibliography.)

GRUWELL, J. D.

Account. 1954. Original manuscript (Oct. 18, 1887) in Bancroft Library. Printed in LeRoy and Ann Hafen's *Journals of Forty-Niners.*

This *Account*, together with that of Peter Derr, supplies our only participant-record of the so-called Gruwell-Derr wagon train that left Salt Lake a week or so in advance of the Jefferson Hunt Sandwalking Company (1849). Members of this group, with their 23 (or possibly 50) wagons, felt they could not afford Jefferson Hunt's guide service and decided to venture the overland journey without him. They suffered severe hardship; were finally overtaken by Hunt who extended them aid. (See listing under Derr, Peter—*Account of Experiences*.)

GUDDE, E. A. and E. K. (Translated and edited by)

Exploring With Frémont. (See listing under Preuss, Charles.)

GUINN, J. M.

Las Salinas (The Salt Pits). 1907-1908. *Historical Society of Southern California Annual Publication.*

This short article refers to a little-known incident in California history. About the year 1815—and once every spring thereafter until the early '30s—an expedition of wooden-wheel carretas, a detail of Mission Indian ox-drivers, and a squad of caballeros from the pueblo guards acting as escort, set out from Los Angeles pueblo to the sink of the Colorado Desert. Their trail led through the San Gorgonio Pass to what is now the Salton Sea. This "jornada para sal"—the journey for salt—

required about one month. In the early '30s salt works were established at the Salinas, in or near the present site of Redondo, where a lake was formed by the waters from salt springs. Mr. Guinn states that he could find no record of these desert treks for salt in any of the historical accounts. He gained his information from an early pioneer.

HAENSZEL, ARDA M., KNIGHT, EMILY M., SMITH, GERALD A.

Historic Chronology of San Bernardino County. 1962. San Bernardino: Summer issue of the *Quarterly* of the San Bernardino County Museum Association. 36 pp. Wrappers.

The Chronology opens with a 1772 entry; closes with an entry in 1962. Here is a convenient summation of what occurred, and when, in the 190-year span of San Bernardino County history.

HAFEN, LE ROY (Edited by)

Letters of Lewis Granger. (See listing under Granger, Lewis.)

HAFEN, LE ROY and ANN (Edited by)

Journals of Forty-Niners, Salt Lake to Los Angeles. 1954. Glendale, California: The Arthur H. Clark Company. 333 numbered pp. Fldg. map of the routes of the Forty-Niners: Salt Lake to Los Angeles. 8 pls. 6¾ x 9¾. The book is Vol. 2 of the Far West and the Rockies Historical Series 1820-1875. 1000 copies.

The basic value of this book asserts itself in the impressive number of travel accounts it contains, many of which are here published for the first time. Included are journals, diaries, and contemporary records of such pioneers as Sheldon Young, Addison Pratt, James S. Brown, Henry W. Bigler, Charles C. Rich, James H. Rollins, William Farrer, George Q. Cannon, Jacob Y. Stover, and others. These men were all associated, in one capacity or another, with the now-famous 1849 emigrant train from Salt Lake to California, some of whom arrived at their destination by way of San Bernardino; others by way of Death Valley. While the existence of much of this material has been generally known, now—for the first time—it is made readily available to both students and lay-readers. The 26-page section of this book devoted to its historical background and summary presents an intelligent interpretation and evaluation of the source material contained. The Hafens also include portions of the four accounts descriptive of the Pomeroy wagon train expedition that followed the Sand Walking Company along the Old Spanish Trail —Van Dyke, Seeley, Hogan, and Pettit. Additionally, they present the *Diary* of Howard Egan, whose party left Salt Lake shortly after the Pomeroy wagon train, and who overtook and passed it on the trail. (These several Journals and Diaries are separately listed in this Bibliography.)

Old Spanish Trail—Santa Fe to Los Angeles. 1954. Glendale, California: The Arthur H. Clark Company. 377 pp. with five unnumbered pp. showing contents of "The Far West and the Rockies Historical Series (1820-1875)" of which the present item is Vol. I. 18 pls. 1 fldg. map of routes taken. 6½ x 10¾. Limited to 1000 copies.

Under the section entitled "Contents of the Series," we read the following: "Here is presented for the first time a complete history of one of the notable pioneer trails of America. This picturesque route extended over mountains and deserts to tie together the frontier outposts of Santa Fe and Los Angeles. Included in this volume are scores of extracts from contemporary records. The rare diaries of Antonio Armijo and of Orville Pratt are given in full." Additionally, there are extracts from the Lt. George W. Brewerton article—*A Ride with Kit Carson*, etc., from *Harper's Magazine*. The trail routes and experiences of early day travelers over the Santa Fe trail are carefully detailed—Escalante, Garcés, Jedediah Smith, Frémont, Brewerton, Carson, and others.

Supplement to Journals of Forty-Niners. 1961. Glendale, California: The Arthur H. Clark Company. Pp. 15-124 contain the supplemental journals and diaries of Forty-Niners; pp. 125-360 contain the General Analytical Index to The Far West and Rockies series (15 vol.). 6⅝ x 9⅝.

Included are travel accounts, supplemental to Vol. 2 of the Series—*Journals of Forty-Niners;* also the accounts of one additional wagon party (the Huffaker Train). The material in this *Supplement* includes:

1. First Company of Packers—
   Chas. V. Stuart's Trip
   Statement of W. C. Randolph
   Account of Judge H. S. Brown

2. Gruwell-Derr Wagon Train—
   Jacob Gruwell's Report to Hayes
   Mr. Shearer's Journal
   Pearson's Recollections

3. Travelers With Hunt's Wagon Train—
   Dr. C. N. Ormsby's Letter
   Lewis Granger's Letter
   Leonard Babcock's Recollections
   Letter of W. B. Lorton

4. Additional Account of the Pomeroy Train—
   Hamelin Journal

5. The Huffaker Train—
   The Thomas Kealy Letter
   Moody's Reminiscent Account
   Journal of Albert K. Thurber

(Reference should be noted to listings in this Bibliography under Granger, Lewis; under Lorton, W. B.; and under Pearson, G. C.)

HAGER, ANNA MARIE and EVERETT

Cumulative Index: Westways-Touring Topics 1909-1959. 1961. Los Angeles: Automobile Club of Southern California. Foreword by Patrice Manahan. 505 pp. 6¼ x 9⅜.

The book's subject matter is arranged under an alphabetical listing of authors, artists, photographers, and subjects. Identification by month, year and page number provides instant reference to the issue in which the desired material appears. Students, writers, researchers, casual readers even, will find this book a source of helpful information. It provides the key—the "Open Sesame"—to the treasure that awaits the reader in the voluminous run of *Touring Topics—Westways*. This timely publication is a working addition to any library, large or small.

The Historical Society of Southern California Bibliography. 1958. Los Angeles: The Historical Society of Southern California. 183 pp. 6¾ x 10⅜.

The first section of the book classifies by volume and part the *annual* publications of the Society, beginning with Vol. 1, Part 1, 1884. The contents of each volume are listed under chronological arrangement. The second section continues the same classification arrangement for each *quarterly* publication, beginning with Vol. XVII, No. 1, of March 1935. The third section provides an author index, listing articles alphabetically by authors. Quick identification is made available by date, volume, part, page, and page of bibliography. Section four employs an identical arrangement for title listing.

The Historical Society of Southern California Topical Index of All Published Works 1884-1957. 1959. Los Angeles: The Historical Society of Southern California. 305 pp. 6¾ x 10⅜.

This companion volume to the *Bibliography* supplies information on any particular topic covered in the magazine. A further section provides an author index; still another sets up a topical index of the illustrations used.

Like the *Cumulative Index*, these two bibliographical studies open wide avenues of approach to the riches of the Historical Society's unique publications. Because of the generous and untiring effort of the Hagers, this tremendous accumulation of valuable research material has suddenly become accessible to those who have a necessitous purpose for immediate reference to it.

HALL, SHARLOT M.

First Citizen of Prescott, Pauline Weaver, Trapper and Mountain Man. N.d. (1929.) *Prescott Courier Print.* 28 pp. 2 pls. 6¼ x 9½. Wrappers.

This is an enlightening account of the life and activities of Pauline Weaver, "free trapper, fur trader, empire builder, patriot," with an introduction by Alpheus H. Favour. Weaver was born in Tennessee in 1800; died at Camp Verde June 21, 1867. In California he was granted 2800 acres of land in San Gorgonio Pass, near the site of the present City of Banning. Weaver joined the Mormon Battalion on November 28, 1846, Kearny having sent him to act as their guide. In 1853 he was living in a small adobe ranch house at the top of San Gorgonio Pass.

HALL, THORNE

Odyssey of Death Valley. 1962. Santa Barbara: Pacific Coast Odyssey Publications. 36 pp. 29 photographic illus. Interesting double (center) page map of Death Valley. Wrappers.

Perhaps most important among the photographs are those taken in Panamint City and Skidoo. In the text are sections on Panamint City, Death Valley Scotty, Borax, the Jayhawker Saga, and Death Valley. The early history of Death Valley, as recorded in the "Jayhawker Saga," is somewhat garbled in a few relatively unimportant instances.

HALL, WILBUR JAY

Story of the First Decade In Imperial Valley. (See listing under Howe, Edgar F.)

HALLIDAY, WILLIAM R.

Adventure Is Underground. 1959. New York: Harper & Brothers. XVIII plus 206 pp. 63 illus. 5 maps. 5¾ x 8⅝.

This is "the story of the great caves of the West and the men who explore them." With the exception of Carlsbad, the Texas bat caves, and the caves of the Black Hills, the book concerns itself with Western speleology. The author has visited all the great caves of the West; has assisted in their first systematic explorations.

Two Mojave Desert caves receive attention: the Mitchell Caverns and their neighboring cave—Cave of the Winding Stair. These are located in the Providence Mountains some twenty miles from the desert town of Essex. (See pp. 1-14). Crystal Cave, on Kokoweef Peak, is also brought under discussion (pp. 27-35).

This is a book teeming with the excitement of high adventure. It covers its chosen subject thoroughly and entertainingly; even breathlessly.

HAMLIN, EDITH

Death Valley. (See listing under Newhall, Nancy.)

HANKS, HENRY G.

Death Valley and Its Tragical History. (From San Francisco Bulletin of February 10, 1869.) (See listing under Long, Dr. Margaret—*The Shadow of the Arrow.*)

Second Report of the State Mineralogist: 1880-1882. 1882. Sacramento. 226 pp. 6 x 9.

Pp. 227-240 yield significant desert material under the section entitled—"Mud Volcanoes and Colorado Desert."

Third Annual Report of the State Mineralogist. 1883. Sacramento. Part I—26 pp.; Part 2—111 pp., 20 line drawings. 5¾ x 9. Wrappers. The *Report* also appears in hard binding, with a folding map of the borax regions.

Part 2, entitled "Report of the Borax Deposits of California and Nevada," contains material of pronounced desert value. Pp. 29-37 give one of our very earliest printed accounts of Death Valley—an account antedating the Spears by 9 years, the Manly by 11 years. Included are important data concerning early Death Valley exploring parties: Dr. Darwin French and his party of 15 men (1860), Dr. S. G. George and his group (1860), a party of 8 or 10 Mexican Miners (1861), and the Hugh McCormack party (1861). Borax activities in Death Valley are discussed in some detail, with considerable attention given the Eagle Borax Works.

Mr. Harold O. Weight, in his capable publication—*20 Mule Team Days In Death Valley*—reprints, for the first time, the Death Valley portion of the interesting old Hank's article.

HANNA, PHIL TOWNSEND

Aboriginal Derelicts of Death Valley. 1929. February issue of *Touring Topics*. Illus.
This article describes the Digger Indians and their very low state of civilization.

Beauty and the Beast. 1928. December issue of *Touring Topics*. Illus.
Mr. Hanna mentions that Death Valley's 134° temperature on July 10, 1913, is the highest officially recorded temperature in the world, exceeding the Sahara maximum by 7°. On that same day, Los Angeles registered 89°, San Bernardino 105°, and Imperial Valley 119°. The average annual precipitation in Death Valley is 1.79 inches, the season of rain being from January to March. The author further discusses why, with an ample supply of water in their canteens, desert wanderers have sometimes been found dead or dying from thirst. Contrary to the popular belief that a chemical reaction sets in from the metal in the canteen, science explains the cause as being due to the body's inability to "transfer ingested water to the pores with sufficient rapidity to reduce the body temperature."

et al. *Death Valley Tales*. 1955. Palm Desert, California: Desert Magazine Press. 59 pp. Line drawings. Wrappers.
This little item is Publication No. 3 of the Death Valley '49ers, Inc. Its contents are:
When Death Valley Took Its First Toll—Hanna
Hungry Bill Talks—Wheat
The Battle of Wingate Pass—Belden
When Manly Returned to Death Valley—Woodward
The Story of "Cap" Lemoigne—Nosser
The Law at Greenwater—Brown
Mule-Skinning in 1904.—Gibson
So None Died of Thirst—Hilton
Charles Alvord, His Rescue and His Murder—Walker

Mysterious Desert Palm, The. 1928. April issue of *Touring Topics*. Illus.
This is Mr. Hanna's account of the California desert palm. As a matter of record, the "29 Palms" oasis is *not* "475 miles east of Whitewater." A typographical error, no doubt.

Something Different in Deserts. 1928. March issue of *Touring Topics*. Illus.
This article describes the Amargosa Desert.

Wells of Santa Rosa of the Flat Rocks, The. 1928. January issue of *Touring Topics.* Illus.

This article describes the Yuha basin region, in Southern Imperial County, and its peculiar sandstone concretions.

HANNUM, ANNA P. (Edited by)

Quaker Forty-Niner, A. (See listing under Pancoast, Chas. E.)

HARPER, OLIVE

Through Death Valley. 1907. J. S. Ogilvie Publishing Co. 124 numbered pages, the first page being designated as No. 9. Preceding it are 6 unnumbered pages. Four numbered pages of advertisements appear in the back of the book. 4¾ x 7⅛. Wrappers.

The advertisements in the back of the book are lurid and sensational, particularly those referring to the four books—"How to Woo," "Courtship and Marriage," "The Lovers' Companion," and "The Popular Letter Writer." Another page "by the popular author of 'A Bad Boy's Diary' extolls the 'Blunders of a Bashful Man.' " And, finally, there is featured the useful publication—"A Hundred Ways of Kissing Girls, or the History of a Kiss." *Through Death Valley* is a melodramatic "Novel Founded on Joseph Le Brandt's Successful Drama of the Same Name." This item is early and scarce; few collectors know of it. Unfortunately, only its age and scarcity commend it.

HARPER'S WEEKLY

Mining Issue. 1908. April 11 issue of *Harper's Weekly.* Illus.

The entire issue is devoted to the early Nevada mining fields. The articles, and particularly the advertisements, in this early item—written at the heyday of the mining boom—cause it to be greatly coveted by desert collectors. Strictly speaking, it does not relate directly to California deserts; but the proximity of these Nevada areas to our California desert regions suggest its inclusion in this listing.

HARRINGTON, M. R.

Pass Into Yesterday. 1952. November issue of *Westways.* Illus.

This article relates to the San Fernando—or Frémont—Pass. Appropriate illustrations enliven the text.

Pinto Man at Little Lake. 1950. September issue of *Desert.* Illus. Map.

Here is presented plausible evidence of the one-time existence of the Pinto man who supposedly lived on the California deserts thousands of years ago.

Pinto Site at Little Lake, California, A. 1957. Los Angeles: Anderson, Ritchie & Simon. VI, 91 pp. 54 photographic illus.

This item, No. 17 of the Southwest Museum Papers, is an archaeological study of the region in and around Little Lake, on the Bishop Highway in the Mojave Desert.

HARRINGTON, MARK W.

Notes on the Climate and Meteorology of Death Valley, California. 1892. Washington: U. S. Dept. Agr. Bull. No. 1. 50 pp. 5⅞ x 9¼. Wrappers.

This is one of the very early items on Death Valley, written by the then Chief of the Weather Bureau.

HARRINGTON, R. E.

Souvenirs of the Palm Springs Area. 1962. Simi, California: (Printed by) Peg Wilson. 68 pp. Approx. 65 photographic illus. Numerous sketches and maps. 6¼ x 9⅛.

Mr. Harrington's book has the benefit of two confluent advantages: his innate knowledge of the area described (he was integrally a part of much that he writes about), and his early-day photographs that lend *visual* support to the written history. His "Palm Springs Area" is more extensive than the words indicate. The book encompasses, in addition to Palm Springs, the Salton Sea-Coachella Valley area where, far back in 1907, he was working as a ranchhand. 1907 was an early year for this region. It was essentially an undeveloped, sparsely populated land; a land young and primitive when measured by a white man's knowledge of it.

Most of the photographs are pictures the author had taken as a boy: pictures of early desert roads, of the flooding waters from the Colorado that poured over present Salton Sea into the age-old Cahuilla basin, of the beginnings of Palm Springs, of Indian life and culture. Happily, Mr. Harrington's own participation in the events he describes is made incidental to the basic theme of his narrative, thus subordinating purely personal experience to the more important historical narration.

There are all too few such books as this being written today. There will be even fewer as time goes on; because much that is written into them is the stuff and essence of which history itself is made, and those qualified to write of it are already few among us.

HARRIS, BENJAMIN BUTLER

Gila Trail, The. 1960. Norman: University of Oklahoma Press. Edited by Richard H. Dillon. XV plus 175 pp. 12 illus. Map. 6¼ x 9¼.

Printed for the first time from the original manuscript, this "reminiscence" rates high among available source records having to do with the early Colorado Desert crossings. The narrator is one of the relatively few educated emigrant journalists, and history benefits as a result. Although Harris wrote of his experiences "forty years, six months and four days" following his crossing of the Colorado River into California, he recalled fascinating bits of trail lore that escaped his trail comrades. One of these is his absorbing description of a mirage in the Carrizo Corridor; another, of his party's fortunate avoidance of a flash flood in this same Corridor; still another of a singular diversion engaged in by certain of the emigrants wherein "dead animals lined the road, and being dry, had been stood on all four feet by irreverent humorists in ghastly mockery and gloomy fun." The ultraperceptive Harris does not neglect mention of the providential "New

River" that suddenly flowed out upon the desert, thus saving the lives of perhaps thousands of emigrants; nor of the little *Palm Springs* oasis midway in the Carrizo Corridor; nor of the attitude of the Indians in the vicinity of the Colorado River crossing, prior to the arrival of Lt. Couts' military escort with the Whipple Survey Party. Any objective assessment of the diaries and journals of this place and period will almost certainly accord impressive rating to the Harris account.

Harris, who "formed one of a horseback party, each with at least one pack mule, . . . left Panola County, Texas, on March 25, 1849." Pp. 85-94 relate to the Colorado Desert crossing—from the river to Warner's Ranch. It is regrettable that the author did not extend his faculty for descriptive detail even more generously to this particular segment of his overland journey to the mines.

HARRIS, FRANK "SHORTY" (As told to Johnston, Philip)

Half a Century Chasing Rainbows. 1930. October issue of *Touring Topics*. Illus.

Shorty Harris was the typical jackass prospector, disposing of his strikes as soon as he made them; some profitably, some as the result of clever bargaining on the part of his purchasers. But it all figured to the same end result—days of peak living far up in the heights of popularity and acclaim, then broke and drifting aimlessly back along the lonely trek, hell-bent on the quest for gold. This item assembles important material—source material. Shorty Harris is gone now; but his personal narrative remains for all time, replete with its historic lore.

HARRIS, LEWIS BIRDSALL

Overland By Boat to California In 1849. 1949. September issue of the *Historical Society of Southern California Quarterly*. Edited by Aurora Hunt.

This is the novel account of the 1849 desert crossing on horseback and in the "old green boat-wagon" of Harris, his wife, and their two Negro slaves—Bob and Jane. Cornelius C. Cox and James McAllister completed the personnel of this group. Mention is made, in one of Harris' letters, of the historic *Palm Springs* oasis midway in the Carrizo Corridor. In another letter—written to a brother by Harris while at *Camp Salvation* on the Colorado Desert, October 21, 1849—he mentions his "wife's health has been excellent all the way, and she has made most of the trip so far on horseback. Although the wagon is fixed up very comfortable and pleasant, still she prefers the saddle unless the sun is too hot." Of some interest, in this regard, is C. C. Cox's comment in his *Diary* (see listing under Cox, Cornelius C.—*From Texas to California in 1849*) that—on December 1 of the same year— Mrs. Harris "presented her other half with an heir."

John W. Audubon, in his *Journal* (see listing under Audubon, John Woodhouse—*Audubon's Western Journal*), mentions Harris and his boat wagon. Says Audubon: "We had the use of a boat in the crossing, which belonged to a Mr. Harris who came from Texas, near Houston. It was really a large wagon body, made into a scow, and very useful we found it; Mr. Harris treated us with the greatest kindness, and aided us with provisions to the best of his abilities, and we most sincerely wished him and his amiable wife all happiness and comfort." His fellow-traveler, Cox, describes the boat-wagon in similar fashion, mentioning that both ends of the water-tight bed were turned up, with oars carried on the side.

The instant item informs that Harris, in 1851, was Sheriff of Sacramento County; in 1852-53, Clerk of the County; elected Mayor of Sacramento in 1856; and, later, served as Deputy Secretary of State.

All readers, I am sure, will share my enthusiasm for Aurora Hunt's superb editing accomplishment in putting together this Harris material.

HART, HERBERT M.

In 1963 the first in a series of books on Western forts, by Mr. Hart, came off the press. Mr. Hart is accomplishing for his study of forts a similar objective to that attained by Mr. Florin in his study of Western ghost towns (see listing under Florin, Lambert). Published through 1967 are:

No. 1—Old Forts of the Northwest (1963)
No. 2—Old Forts of the Southwest (1964)
No. 3—Old Forts of the Far West (1965)
No. 4—Pioneer Forts of the West (1967)

The format of these books follows that of Lambert Florin's books on ghost towns. Both series are published by the Superior Publishing Company of Seattle; both are the same size—8½ x 10¾; both have about the same number of pages—approximately 192 each. Both have attractive dust wrappers, illustrated by photographs. And just about here the similarities cease. The one is of ghost towns; the present series is of forts.

The first volume—Old Forts of the Northwest—contains no material relating to Southern California deserts.

Old Forts of the Far West.
Words "First Edition" appear. This book is prolific in its Southern California desert material: Camp Independence, a discussion of the Column from California, Fort Yuma, the Mojave Desert Forts and Camps of Piute, Rock Springs, Marl Springs, Soda and Cady. From 2 to 4 pages are allotted each post and an abundant supply of photographs is made available. Only one suggestion: an orientation map for each fort, camp, post and cantonment would be helpful to the reader. Granted, there are convenient "To Get There" paragraphs; but these should be implemented by area maps.

Old Forts of the Southwest (1850-1890).
Words "First Edition" appear. Pp. 62-64 present some material on Fort Tejon, a diagram of the Fort, seven excellent photographs. Its inclusion in this Bibliography is indicated—and perhaps justified—by Fort Tejon's relation to the Camel Experiment.

Pioneer Forts of the West.
Words "First Edition" appear. Pp. 170-171 give an interesting account of Camp Wright in Southern California in the Warner's Ranch-Oak Grove area.

HAWORTH, AL

Liquid Wealth from a Desert Dry Lake. 1950. August issue of *Desert.* Illus.

This article records the interesting story of Trona, and the operations of the American Potash & Chemical Corporation on Searles Dry Lake in the Mojave.

HAYES, JUDGE BENJAMIN

Pioneer Notes from the Diaries of (1849-1875). 1929. Los Angeles. Privately printed. 307 pp. 16 pls.—many of them illustrative of early historic scenes. 6¼ x 9¼.

Judge Hayes lived from 1815 to 1877. He arrived in Los Angeles in 1850 having started from Independence on September 10, 1849. The name of Judge Hayes is frequently mentioned by the emigrant parties of those 49ers who followed the Southern route. Descriptive of his journey from the Mimbres River to Warner's Ranch, Judge Hayes wrote a separate diary in later years that would fill perhaps a hundred printed pages. Excerpts from the diary appear in Owen C. Coys' *The Great Trek.* Pp. 42-47 of the present item give only a quick summation of this diary. The regular narrative is resumed on p. 48, under date of Jan. 13, 1850 (at Harazthy's camp). From this point the party soon arrives at Warner's ranch, following the route of Col. Cooke. Beginning on p. 49 (Jan. 14) and extending to p. 68, we have Judge Hayes' impressive description of Warner's Ranch, Agua Caliente, and Temecula. This is reprinted, in its entirety, in Joseph J. Hill's conclusive work on Warner's Ranch. The remainder of *Pioneer Notes*, while not directly applicable to the subject of deserts, gives one of the best pictures anywhere available of early Los Angeles.

HAYNES, ASA

Diary. 1938. (See listing under Ellenbecker, John—*Jayhawkers of Death Valley.*)

"Old Cap. Haynes" (who was not so old in fact, but who perhaps seemed ancient to his more youthful companions) was one of the leaders of the 1849 Death Valley group known as the Jayhawkers.

HEALD, CHAS. L.

Cathedral Town On the Mohave. 1939. October issue of *Desert.* Illus.

Mr. Heald narrates the story of the "Pinnacles"—those peculiar formations representing the handiwork of millions of microscopic bits of primitive plant life known as algae. "Cathedral Town," with its picturesque minarets, rises from the former bed of prehistoric Searles Lake near the town of Trona. (See listing under Johnston, Philip—*Stone Castles Reared by Plants.*)

HEAP, GWINN HARRIS

Central Route to the Pacific; from the Valley of the Mississippi to California: Journal of the Expedition of E. F. Beale, Superintendent of Indian affairs in California, and Gwinn Harris Heap, From Missouri to California, in 1853. 1854. Philadelphia:

Lippincott, Grambo and Co. 136 pp. 46 unnumbered pp. of advertisements. (Several variants appear in the advertisements.) 13 tinted lithographs. 6 x 9. (Cowan P. 107.) Reprinted in 1957 by The Arthur H. Clark Company, Glendale, California, and edited, with introduction and notes, by LeRoy and Ann Hafen. 346 pp.

This is the journal of the E. F. Beale-G. H. Heap expedition from Missouri to California in 1853. The most significant desert reference may be found printed as an appendix to the book itself (pp. 133-136), and relates to an account given by the Rev. James W. Brier—one of the original pioneer emigrants who crossed Death Valley in 1849. His is perhaps the earliest published account of Death Valley although, in the writing of it, Brier assigns no name to this desolate region. Singular, indeed, is the concept of this loquacious preacher of Death Valley notoriety who, having himself suffered intolerably from the hardships of the trail, and having observed the constant agony inflicted upon his wife and children, still could muster the temerity to recommend this identical route as a feasible roadway to the Pacific.

In his distinguished work, *Death Valley Heroine*, pp. 39-41, Mr. L. Burr Belden reprints the Brier article.

Ch. VI, "Passage of the Deserts" (pp. 98-111), is descriptive of a midsummer's crossing of the Mojave Desert (August 6-22). Heap writes vividly, and with consummate skill. The following is typical: "The solitude was unrelieved by the song of bird or the chirp of insect; the mournful murmur of the breeze, as it swept over the desert was the only sound that broke the silence. In many places a deceptive mirage spread fictitious lakes and spectral groves to our view, which a puff of wind, or a change in our position, suddenly dissolved. . . . The pale moon, occasionally overshadowed by clouds, threw a ghostly light over the desert, and skeletons of animals glistening in her beams, strewed the way, adding horror to the scene." The Amargosa (Bitter Creek), Agua del Tio Meso (the Spring of Uncle Meso), and the "River Mohaveh" are described in minute detail. So likewise, is the Ojo de Archilete (Archilete Springs—now called Resting Spring) and the springs presently known as Salt Springs.

Of Agua del Tio Meso, better known today as Bitter Spring, the author writes as follows: "This spring is named after an Old Mexican called Meso, who was styled Tio, or uncle, on account of his age. He discovered it when he and his party were nearly perishing with thirst. Their happy deliverance was celebrated by a great feast; he washed and dressed himself, and rambled about the place singing until he fell dead, killed by a stroke of apoplexy. Two peons, abandoned on the desert by their master, reached this spring after their party had left for the Mohaveh. Unable to proceed farther, they both died of starvation, and the next travelers who encamped there, found their skeletons locked in each other's embrace, as if they had expired in the act of devouring one another . . . The Agua del Tio Meso is an oasis; for, although a wretched spot, it is the only resting-place in the desert between the Amargosa and the River Mohaveh. We were glad to leave it."

Of all the journals and diaries telling of the Mojave Desert crossing, none appears comparable to the Heap in sheer readability and in picturesque descriptive quality.

HEFFERNAN HELEN; RICHARDS, IRMAGARDE; SALISBURY, ALICE

Desert Treasure. (1939.) San Francisco: Harr Wagner. 298 pp. A subsequent printing (1955) shows 309 pp.

"A story of adventure and the Mohave Desert, its people, plants, and animals; with work plans for reading, comprehension, word pictures, word building and word clues." (John D. Henderson.) The book is a juvenile, capably written and illustrated with interesting photographs.

HEFFERNAN, DR. W. T. and ROCKWOOD, C. R.

Personal Recollections of the Early History of Imperial Valley (by Heffernan), and *Born of the Desert* (by Rockwood). (See listing under Rockwood, Charles Robinson.)

HEINLY, BURT A.

Carrying Water Through a Desert: The Story of the Los Angeles Acqueduct. 1910. July issue of the *National Geographic.* Pp. 568-596. 19 illus. 1 map.

This is an early article concerning a significant episode in the history of Los Angeles. A liberal amount of desert atmosphere is created.

HENDERSON, RANDALL

In J. Wilson McKenney's *Out West Journal,* only recently issued, (see listing in this Bibliography) he includes an article, authored by himself, entitled "Desert Editor." He refers, appropriately enough, to the man who was associated with him as his partner in organizing and publishing the now-famous *Desert Magazine—* Randall Henderson. Their first issue came off the press in November 1937. They turned out 7,000 copies. When Mr. Henderson wrote his final editorial some 25 years later, the magazine's circulation had climbed to over 32,000.

The names *Desert Magazine* and *Randall Henderson* were synonymous. Both the magazine and its editor had transcended the status of individuals. Each had become an institution.

The almost incalculable number of articles written by Mr. Henderson for *Desert,* and his desert classic—*On Desert Trails, Today and Yesterday*—will endure proudly and for all time as his monument. No man could ask for a nobler recognition of his dedicated effort.

Desert Cavalcade of Imperial Valley. 1948. March 11-13. El Centro (now at Palm Desert), California: Desert Magazine Press. 36 pp. 53 pls. Wrappers.

This attractive publication is made distinctive by the inclusion of an article by Harold O. Weight, entitled—"They Blazed the Desert Trail." (See listing under Weight, Harold O.) Actually, two articles appear under Weight's name, the other being "They Brought Water to the Desert." Much factual information on Imperial Valley is disclosed throughout the entire magazine.

Desert Was Our Beat, The. 1964. *Westerners, The* (Los Angeles Corral) *Brand Book* No. 11. 19 pp. 2 illus. Line drawings by Don Perceval.

This article by the former owner-publisher of *Desert* Magazine pulsates with the "feel" of the desert—as do all the books and articles authored by this knowledge-able desert explorer and writer. In the *Brand Book* article he tells of the pioneer days of Desert Magazine. In November 1937, with 618 paid subscribers, a print-ing plant, and $6,000, the popular *Desert* Magazine had its inception.

In referring to the several early writers and would-be writers for *Desert*, Mr. Henderson reveals the criterion for article-acceptance that proved cohesive with the good common sense that characterized both the man and the magazine: "Also, there were scholarly essays, very correct, but without a spark of human interest. Gradually, we became convinced that it would be easier to make writers of desert people than to instill the feel of the desert into professional writers whose manu-scripts were plotted in the more sophisticated regions beyond the far horizons." How regrettably tragic that some of our current magazines and quarterly journals lack the business acuity to employ this same principle!

As a desert Bibliographer, I accept this as complete vindication for my own atti-tude as I attempt to evaluate desert books. I know I must be biased, for I am in-clined not to assess an author's work entirely and irrevocably upon the basis of its literary merit, its stilted academic phrases, its precisely correct diction and its studied effort to appear "scholarly." I probe the book to ascertain if its author came to know the desert from actual physical contact, or if he was content to wear out the seat of his academic pants in some plush library, skimming the cream from another's hard-earned harvest; and all because he was morally and physically afraid to get a little trail dust on his boots. Library research is important and neces-sary, but physical man-to-desert contact is absolutely indispensable to good desert writing. It is such as these whom Mr. Henderson encouraged to write for *Desert*—Weight, Murbarger, Hilton, Kelly, and others like them who shared intimate camaraderie with desert places.

He Built Scotty's Castle. 1952. September issue of *Desert*. 8 illus.

Matt Roy Thompson, the noted engineer, designed Death Valley's famous castle and directed the building of it. The construction and furnishings are described in this article. Interesting photographs accompany the text.

On Desert Trails, Today and Yesterday. 1961. Los Angeles: Westernlore Press. 357 pp. 31 photographs. Designs by Don Louis Perceval; maps by Norton Allen. 5¾ x 8½.

In this book Mr. Henderson has endeavored to synthesize his many years of diversified desert experience. The book tells of trail adventure and explorational work in California, Arizona, Utah, and Mexico. Even the distant Sahara receives mention. Notable desert characters are introduced into the narrative, and consid-erable space is devoted to a discussion of Indian characteristics, ceremonies, and living conditions. Interesting episodes are narrated, including the author's visit to the skeletal remains of Lt. Ives' historic old steamboat—the *Explorer*; the mysteri-ous and unsolved disappearance of the young desert artist—Everett Ruess; the saga of Death Valley's inimitable Scotty and his world-famous castle. The author is at his best in such chapters as "Gold, Men and Burros," "Campfires in Sage and Sand," and "Phantom Treasure in the Desert."

As in almost every good book, certain errors—typographical or otherwise—are discernable. For a writer of lesser stature than Mr. Henderson, the detection of a few misstatements might well be passed over without comment. But what Mr. Henderson writes is apt to be accepted categorically as fact, and the following must not be accepted in this fashion for the very good reason that they are *not* fact. (1) Henry Washington did *not* bestow upon Twentynine Palms its disgustingly unoriginal and unromantic name. Some authorities doubt that he ever actually visited this part of the High Desert. Be that as it may, the best name this prosaic surveyor could muster, in writing his survey notes on May 16, 1855, was "a small cluster of cabbage palmetto." (2) The name "Boulder Dam" was *not* changed back to "Hoover Dam" during the Republican administration of President Eisenhower, but during the Democratic administration of President Truman, the date being April 30, 1947. (3) The palm trees in Mountain Palm Canyon are *not* likely the palm trees seen and visited by "an advance detachment" of General Kearny's troops. I even doubt there is any authentic historical record in support of the *existence* of "an advance detachment" in that segment of Kearny's Army of the West that entered the Carrizo Corridor. Furthermore, Emory doesn't record having seen or having visited any palm trees up in Mountain Palm Canyon. The palm tree oasis Emory (and Captain Johnston) visited and described was the little *Palm Springs* oasis that once existed mid-way along the Carrizo Corridor, whose trees were "projected" against a background of mud "cliffs."

These irregularities are of trivial dimension. The book achieves a unique blending of many facets of the desert's appeal. Only one whose philosophy is attuned to the vagarious moods of this rugged land could so adroitly write of it and give interpretation to it. The author's knowledge derives from his intimate physical contact with the desert, and from a sympathetic appreciation built into his many years of desert living, desert exploration, and desert writing. "The desert," says Mr. Henderson, "is harsh and may be cruel to the imprudent, mysterious to the unknowing, fascinating to those who delve behind the mask of austerity, but never hostile to those who come with prudence and humility."

Sun, Sand and Solitude—Vignettes From the Notebook of a Veteran Desert Reporter. 1968. Los Angeles: Westernlore Press, Illus., 206 pp. plus 18 unnumbered pp. displaying 12 colored pls. by Ralph D. Cornell, Harry Vroman, and Robert F. Campbell. Desert sketches by Norton Allen. 6½ x 9½.

Mr. Henderson's "Vignettes"—some 150 of them—are avenues of philosophical approach to desert lands and desert adventuring. He writes in the intimate, informal style of a desert friend and companion with whom one may share pleasant conversation around a camp fire.

Sun, Sand and Solitude is a book we dare not permit to associate with other books on a crowded book shelf where all too often an item loses character and identity. It merits a conspicuous position on the living room table where it is instantly available whenever the reading urge beckons. For this is a book designed to be read not once, but again and yet again; sometimes for quick reference to a favorite passage, sometimes for an entire evening's retreat into quiet desert enjoyment. Whatever the motive, to read this book is to break bread with "Mr. Desert" himself. No man among us is more knowledgeable, desertwise, than he; none is better qualified to communicate this knowledge to others.

Another notable feature of this fine book is its exceptional beauty. Its publishers can know a real pride in the craftsmanship that fashioned such an attractive volume.

They Guard the Caves in Providence Mountains. 1939. March issue of *Desert*. Illus. Map.

This is *Desert's* story of Jack and Ida Mitchell, and the spectacular caverns in Mojave's Providence Mountains. (See listing under Mitchell, Jack.)

Trail to 49 Palms. 1940. December issue of *Desert*. Illus.

The author regards the 49 Palms Canyon as one of the three most picturesque palm canyons in the southwest. At the time of his first visit (1938) he counted 40 old trees and 15 younger ones. This oasis is located within the Joshua Tree National Monument area, and some six miles distant from Twentynine Palms. An approximate two-mile hike is required in order to reach it.

Waterhole on the Old Bradshaw Trail. 1947. January issue of *Desert*. Illus. Map.

Primarily this is the story of the oasis at Dos Palmas; but the article further tells of the historic old Bradshaw Trail route through San Gorgonio Pass to Ehrenberg. Mr. Henderson mentions that the original two palms at this oasis have increased to a total of twenty-seven. (Note: This was 30 years ago. There were considerably more than twenty-seven when I recently revisited the oasis.)

We Found the Sheep-Hole Palms. 1942. February issue of *Desert*. Illus. Map.

George Wharton James, in his *Wonders of the Colorado Desert* (1906), mentions the eixstence of two small groups of palms in Sheep Hole Wash. The location of this oasis remained a mystery until Desert Steve Ragsdale led a group of Sierra Club hikers, among whom was Mr. Randall Henderson, to this long-lost site.

Wild Palms of the California Desert. (1951.) Palm Desert, California: Desert Magazine Press. 32 pp. 1 map. Wrappers.

The following chapters are contained: (1) Where Wild Palms Grow, (2) Waterfall in Palm Canyon, (3) Paradise in Andreas Canyon, (4) Dripping Springs in Fern Canyon, (5) Tapestry in Eagle Canyon. Concerning the palm canyons in our deserts, this is the best item I have read. Certainly no one is better qualified to write on the subject of palm oases in Southern California than the distinguished former editor of *Desert Magazine*.

and McKENNEY, J. W. *There Are Two Deserts.* 1937. November issue of *Desert*. Illus. Repeated in the November 1958, issue.

This is the beautifully written editorial appearing in Vol. 1, No. 1 of *Desert*. One desert is the hard, desolate land the stranger sees as he speeds across its barren wastes. The other—the *real* desert—is the one seen by the more perceptive visitor who can look beyond and beneath the mask. This other desert is the one folks learn to love.

HILL, JOSEPH J.

History of Warner's Ranch and Its Environs, The. 1927. Los Angeles. Privately printed. The Special Deluxe Edition is limited to 300 copies, each housed in a slip case, and intended for presentation only. A Special Edition indicates a limitation of 1000 copies; still other issues bear no limitation notice. The Deluxe Edition measures 8⅛ x 11. The Special and the Regular (no limitation copies) measure 7¾ x 10¾; run X, 221 pp.; 11 pls.

The story of Warner's Ranch is closely interwoven with the history of the Southern California desert. It was along the Carrizo-Vallecito-San Felipe-Warner Ranch route that Kearny and Emory forged a trail in 1846-1847 with their exhausted Army of the West. Here, too, passed the Mormon Battalion with their wagons, under the leadership of the militant Cooke. The glamorous old ranch became a well-known station site for the Butterfield Overland Stage line. In practically every account of these early-historic desert episodes, this ranch of Warner's figures prominently as a beckoning caravansary to the weary traveler. Hill gives us a clearly defined account of it. Included are the source descriptions of Emory (pp. 114-118), of Cooke (pp. 118-119), of Tyler (pp. 119-120), and—most detailed of all—the 1850 account of Judge Benjamin Hayes (pp. 121-145).

HILL, R. T.

Southern California Geology and Los Angeles Earthquakes. 1928. Los Angeles: Southern California Academy of Science. 232 pp. 38 pls. Maps. 3 fldg. maps in back. 5⅝ x 8.

Part 3 to 6 (pp. 63-226) contain Southern California desert material.

HILTON, JOHN W.

Henry Kaiser Came to the Desert for Iron. 1949. March issue of *Desert.* Illus.

John Hilton wanted to call this article "The Sleeping Giant;" but the title didn't pass censorship. I think the publishers missed a good bet when they discarded this intriguing title and substituted such a commonplace designation in its stead. The article tells of Kaiser's development of the iron ore deposits in the Eagle Mountains.

This Is My Desert. 1960. Reprinted from *Arizona Highways* for March, 1960. 6 pp. text. 13 colored reproductions of Hilton canvasses; 5 pen sketches; 22 photographs; color reproductions of paintings on front and back covers.

Reproductions in color of some of Hilton's more notable paintings include: Whispering Canyon, Verbena Time, Papago Gold, Desert Flames, Four Peaks, Banners of Spring, Candles of the Lord, Canyon Mouth, Giants in the Moonlight, Morning Star, Sundown Splendor, Festive Mood, Picacho at Sundown, Candles in the Big Church, and Bahia de Los Angeles. The text is one of the most appealing tributes to the desert to be found listed in this Bibliography.

Wells of the Ancient Cahuillas. 1936. March issue of *Westways.* Illus.

The author discloses the locations of several early desert wells of the Indians.

The versatile Hilton—artist, author, musician, lecturer, gemologist, geologist, and on, ad infinitum—is also an authority on the Indians of the Southwest.

HINDS, NORMAN E. A.

Evolution of the California Landscape. 1952 (December). San Francisco: Department of Natural Resources; Division of Mines; Bull. 158, 240 pp. 115 photograpic pls. of mountains, valleys, deserts—many of them aerial views. Numerous sketches, charts and diagrams. 3 map charts in cover pocket. 8⅝ x 10¼. 10,000 copies.

This is a desirable book, ably illustrated by an array of interesting plates. Applicable to the deserts are text and illustrations on pp. 87-108. The chapter on Basin-Ranges (pp. 61-86) also contains desert material, profusely illustrated.

HINE, ROBERT

California's Utopian Colonies. 1953. Henry E. Huntington Library & Art Gallery. (1966 Yale University Press Paperback reprint—XI, 209 pp.; 9 illus. 1 location map.)

Treatment extends to six principal Colonies, and to ten others which the author groups under the very appropriate chapter caption "Colonies in Short and After a Fashion." In this latter group his six-page discussion of the Mormons in San Bernardino is clearly of desert interest. Briefly he tells of the Mormons coming into the Valley in 1851 and being called back to Salt Lake in 1857, largely because of a growing apostasy in the Church.

Of major interest, desert-wise, is the eighteen-page chapter on the interesting Llano del Rio Colony in Antelope Valley on the Mojave Desert just north of the San Gabriel Mountains. (See listing under Conkin, Paul K.—*Two Paths To Utopia.*)

HOBBS, CAPTAIN JAMES ("of California")

Wild Life in the Far West: Personal Adventures of a Border Mountain Man. 1872. Hartford: Wiley, Waterman & Eaton. 488 pp. 33 illus. 6 x 8½. There is at least one reprint; perhaps more.

The publishers naïvely state, in their Introduction: "Had as many words been used to say as little as there are in many books, it would have required several volumes the size of this to have contained the account of the author's experiences."

In this scarce old item the author recounts his experiences with Indians, with Pegleg Smith, and with the Mormons. He relates his long and intimate friendship with Kit Carson, his contact with James Kirker, his activities as freighter and trader in Mexico, his interview with Santa Ana, and his association with—and service under—Col. Doniphan. We find him at Fort Yuma, and are given a magnificent word picture of his Colorado Desert crossing in 1850; we note his visits to San Francisco and the gold country; and—once again—we travel with him into Mexico, this time during the period of the French invasion, and are favored with a vivid account of the Maximilian execution. His excellent telling of the Indian attack upon an emigrant train is followed in quick order by an early portrayal of the Owens River country, and of the Cerro Gordo mines in 1868.

About the same year he travels into Death Valley, and supplies information of a most startling and unusual nature. He tells of a lost emigrant party who perished there in 1852—all but one survivor, that is. Hobbs states, unequivocally, that he met this man who—in turn—informed him of the elusive Gunsight Mine. And this is not all. Down in Death Valley, he avers, he saw with his own eyes the remnants of this train—and the skeletons. He saw something else in Death Valley, also. He saw a group of dead Indians, and he is implicit in his conviction that they had been poisoned with strychnine as an act of revenge by a party of white men.

Mono Lake, Aurora, Virginia City, Arizona, Mexico—none of these is neglected. His book guarantees a captivating experience in exciting reading—from the author's novel method of curing snake bite to the sordid murder of "Hog" Rogers by one who posed as a minister.

Always the question persists—is Hobbs an actual character or merely a fictional creation of some imaginative writer? Are we being deluded by his adventure tales into the belief that they actually occurred? Or, assuming the identity of such an equivocal character, was he victim of an errant imagination? Despite his assertiveness, and his certain knowledge of the historical background of many of the incidents he describes, did he *actually* participate in these ventures or must we interpret them as being apocryphal both in their substance and in the authenticity of his claim to active participation in them? In all our California desert literature, Hobb's book will probably continue to remain—as it remains today—the great imponderable of the imponderables.

I have been unable to identify Hobbs by reference to any of his contemporary writers. I have found not the remotest mention of such a man; and this is odd when we consider the great diversity of his experiences, and the vast number of people—some of them prominent—whom he claimed to know and with whom he is supposed to have associated. It would appear that some one, some where, would make at least cursory mention of so adventurous a gentleman as "Captain James Hobbs." Perhaps someone has, and the reference has escaped attention. The publishers, in their Introduction, add this further comment: "One thing the author wishes distinctly understood; he has in no case 'drawn upon his imagination for his facts.' There are a few incidents given upon what he considers reliable information, and they are so designated; but nearly all is from his own experience. As he never contemplated the publication of his adventures, he kept no diary or record of events, but relies entirely upon his memory, which prevents his giving exact dates in all cases." (For further commentary on the Hobbs' book, see Edwards, E. I. —*The Mystery of Death Valley's Lost Wagon Train*.)

HOGAN, GOUDY

Extract From Journal of. 1954. (See listing under Hafen—*Journals of Forty-Niners*, and Van Dyke, Walter—*Account*.)

This extract, together with the accounts of Van Dyke, Seeley, and Pettit, relates to the Pomeroy wagon train expedition over the Old Spanish Trail route across Cajon Pass to San Bernardino in 1849.

HOGG, JOHN EDWIN

Fossil Hunting About Carrizo Creek. 1929. October issue of *Touring Topics.* Illus.

Mr. Hogg's account sheds interesting light on the coral reef in the Imperial Valley mountains, indicating that the ocean once covered a portion of Southern California.

(As told by Delameter, John A.) *My 40 Years Pulling Freight.* (See listing under Delameter, John A.)

(As told by Fairbanks, Ralph J.) *My 73 Years on Southwestern Deserts.* (See listing under Fairbanks, Ralph J.)

HOGNER, DOROTHY CHILDS

Westward, High, Low, and Dry. (1938.) E. P. Dutton & Company. 310 pp. Cuts. End-paper maps. 6¾ x 9⅝. The words "First Edition" appear. Desert references on pp. 228-275.

There is occasional mention of the desert; but the Death Valley reference (pp. 253-275) is somewhat disappointing. The author arrived rather late in the season for tourists; camped for a few hours; then hurried on. She did not really *see* Death Valley; and this is deplorable—in view of her demonstrated capacity to present a really fascinating description of whatever appeals to her. But in the superficial view she had of Death Valley it was impossible for her to become sensible to its indescribable charm. She bravely endeavored to come under the spell of its fascination; but hers was an apathetic interest, and hers an enthusiasm curtailed— I think—by a weariness from travel and an absorbing passion to return home.

Her account of desert territory is not restricted to Death Valley. The desert reference includes material on "Potash Town," referring—of course—to Trona, on Searles Lake; "Mojave;" "Ghost Towns;" the sand dunes out of Yuma; the Coachella and Imperial Valleys.

HOLMES, ELMER WALLACE, et al.

History of Riverside County, California, With Biographical Sketches of the Leading Men and Women of the County Who Have Been Identified With Its Growth and Development from the Early Days to the Present. 1912. Los Angeles: Historic Record Co. XII, 5-783 pp. 31 pls. 8 x 11.

Pp. 174-217 contain early material on San Gorgonio Pass, Banning, Beaumont, Whitewater, and general area. A discussion of "Days of the Stage Coach" is included. Pp. 218-252 bear reference to San Jacinto Valley, with generous comment on "Vallecitos."

HOLT, WM. F.

Memoirs of a Missourian. (1942.) 128 pp.

Holt was one of the promoters and founders of the Imperial Valley development. Included in the book is some account of the history of Imperial Valley from 1900 to 1942. Also included are chapters on the "Early Development of the Colorado Desert," "Founding of El Centro," "Desert Tragedies," and others. It is reported that Harold Bell Wright fashioned the leading character—Jefferson Worth—in his popular novel, *The Winning of Barbara Worth*, after his good friend Wm. F. Holt.

HOOVER, MILDRED B. and RENSCH, H. E. and ETHEL G.

Historic Spots In California. (See listing under Rensch, H. E. and Ethel G.)

HOUSTON, ELEANOR JORDON

Death Valley Scotty Told Me. (1954.) Louisville, Kentucky: The Franklin Press. 106 pp. 6 pls. Numerous sketches. End paper map. 6 x 8½. Wrappers. The book has been reprinted.

The book contains a collection of some 17 yarns, as told to the author by Walter Scott.

HOWE, EDGAR F. and HALL, WILBUR JAY

Story of the First Decade in Imperial Valley, The. 1910. Imperial, California: E. F. Howe and Sons. 291 pp. Illus. 6½ x 9¼.

The photographic illustrations lend an immediate interest. The material made available by this early account is of primary importance to the student of desert history. The item is definitely a collector's "must."

HOYT, FRANKLYN

He Discovered the Dead Sea of the Cahuillas. 1956. July issue of *Desert* Magazine. 4 pp. 3 illus.

This is the story, well told, of the 1853 Railroad Survey party under Lt. Williamson. Dr. William P. Blake, geologist and mineralogist, was a member of this survey group. Coming down San Gorgonio Pass, one of the first places of interest described is Agua Caliente—later to be known as Palm Springs. The group continued down the Coachella and Imperial Valleys, later going into the Carrizo Corridor and on to Warner's Ranch. Mr. Hoyt, in this article, gives emphasis to the activities of Dr. Blake. (See listing under *Pacific Railroad Surveys*—Vol. V.)

HUBBARD, PAUL B.; BRAY, DORIS; PIPKIN, GEORGE

Ballarat 1897-1917. Facts and Folklore. (1965.) Lancaster, California: Paul B. and Arline B. Hubbard. 98 pp. 22 illus. Maps. Wrappers.

Assisted by Doris Bray and George Pipkin—*and* Arline B. Hubbard who prepared the very attractive charcoal cover-sketch—Paul Hubbard has done more in this book to restore the old supply town of Ballarat than any other person I know. Not a physical restoration, but a permanent restoration of its memory. His effort effectually illustrates the meaning behind the title of this Bibliography—*Enduring Desert.* For here is a classic example of an historic old desert town that has been saved from oblivion, and will *endure*, because of the material assembled in this book. The buildings of Ballarat may continue to erode into the desert from which they long ago took substance and form. But Ballarat will *endure*, even without physical semblance. And thus has another segment of our desert heritage been made secure while yet there was time and opportunity.

"The span of life in Ballarat is measured by its post office, established July 21, 1897, and discontinued September 29, 1917. It had a lively 20 years. . . . Ballarat started its life with two saloons being moved to the townsite. The last enterprise to die as the town passed into ghostly status was a saloon. A sadly lacking and probably direly needed institution was a *church*."

A fascinating book to read is this saga of old Ballarat; and a prideful addition to any desert library.

Garlock Memories. 1960. Ridgecrest, California: Hubbard Printing, Inc. 44 pp. 14 illus. 2 maps. Wrappers.

The book commends itself immediately because of its attractive format. The outside cover sketch by Arline B. Hubbard is beautifully and artistically done.

Garlock, once called "Cow Wells," is located roughly midway along the paved road branching off the Bishop highway to Randsburg. Garlock is a short distance off this road. Originally, "Cow Wells" was a desert water hole. Then, with the discovery of the famous Yellow Aster Mine in nearby Randsburg, the population escalated to a significant six or eight hundred inhabitants. This was in 1896. Later in that same year—April 10—the Garlock post office was established.

The author reminds us that, so far as a town with a future is concerned, Garlock died in 1899. There were recurrent periods of animation, however; particularly when the Southern Pacific extended its tracks from Mojave to Keeler. This period of revival, Mr. Hubbard writes, "provided the old deserted buildings with transient tenants, but not for long." For a time Garlock supplied the milling service for Randsburg's Yellow Aster. In the early '20s the post office was re-established. On June 30, 1926, however, it closed for the second and last time. The fading remains of only a few buildings identify the old town today.

HUDSON, TOM

Three Paths Along a River. The Heritage of the Valley of the San Luis Rey. (1964.) Palm Desert, California: Desert-Southwest Publishers. XI plus 245 pp. Illus. by H. R. Love. End paper maps. 6⅜ x 9⅜.

Part One—The Land of the Indians; Part Two—Spanish and Mexican Eras; Part Three—The American Era; Part Four—Symposium. These are the divisions of the book. In Part Two is some mention of de Anza's desert crossing; also material on John Trumbull Warner and his historic Warner's Ranch. Part Three reviews briefly the march of Kearny and the Army of the West; also the story of the Battle of San Pasqual is retold and considerable material is included on the Mormon Battalion. Part Three covers quite thoroughly the trail of the Jackass Mail and the Butterfield Stages from Warner's Ranch through the Carrizo Corridor.

Mr. Hudson clarifies his position in the preface: "No claim is made to having unearthed hitherto unknown sources of knowledge." Perhaps not; but he has done an excellent job assembling and reviving those sources of knowledge that may have grown dim in our memories.

HUFFORD, D. A.

Death Valley: Swamper Ike's Traditional Lore: Why, When, How? 1902. Los Angeles: D. A. Hufford & Co. 43 pp. 10 pls. 4½ x 7½. Wrappers.

An early and peculiar account by one who claims to have journeyed into Death Valley shortly after the turn of the century. My personal opinion is that its contents border on the apocryphal. Some of the weird incidents described would impress one as being in the nature of desert aberrations.

HUGHES, JOHN T.

Doniphan's Expedition; Containing An Account of the Conquest of New Mexico; General Kearny's Overland Expedition to California; Doniphan's Campaign Against the Navajos; His Unparalleled March Upon Chihuahua and Durango; and the Operations of General Price at Santa Fe. With a Sketch of the Life of Col. Doniphan. 1847. Cincinnati: J. A. and U. P. James. (Original edition in pictorial wrappers.) 9-144 pp. Other editions appeared: 1848, with 407 pp; 1850, with 13-407 pp. (Cowan P. 115; Wagner-Camp No. 134.)

Hughes, the author, accompanied Doniphan on the latter's notable expedition. Chs. 13, 14 and 15 (pp. 222-254) have material applicable to the operations of the Army of the West. Ch. 13 recounts the story of Kearny's battle at San Pasqual.

HUGHES, TOM

History of Banning and San Gorgonio Pass. (1938.) Banning, California: Banning Record. IV, 213 pp. 62 photographic illus.

This book, now difficult to locate, assembles important historical material regarding a region about which relatively little has been written. The text is in two parts. Part I is a chronological listing of important historic events during the period extending from 1774 to 1938; Part 2 is given over mainly to interesting stories of the region, and to biographical sketches of the early pioneers.

HUNGERFORD, JOHN B.

Slim Princess, The. 1956. Reseda, California: Hungerford Press. 36 pp. 29 illus. plus front and back cover illus. 2 maps. Wrappers. 5½ x 8½.

This delightful, nostalgic item informs us liberally concerning the Southern Pacific's narrow gauge, operating from "Owenyo to Keeler and Keeler to Laws and return to Owenyo." Mr. Hungerford has chosen a subject that has been too often neglected by desert writers, and he handles his subject well. For his readers the author has snatched from oblivion a vital chapter in California's desert history. This book is companion to the author's earlier release—*Narrow Gauge To Silverton.*

HUNT, AURORA

Army of the Pacific, The: Its Operations in California, Texas, Arizona, New Mexico, Utah, Nevada, Oregon, Washington, Plains Region, Mexico, etc. 1860-1866. 1951. Glendale, California: The Arthur H. Clark Company. 455 pp. 20 illus. Fldg. map of routes. 6½ x 9¾.

This is an exhaustive treatise of the organization, movements and accomplishments of the Army of the Pacific—that division of the Union troops which, from 1860 to 1866, "was composed entirely of volunteers who fought over a territory one-third larger than the total area of all the seceded states." Desert-wise, the activities of the Army of the Pacific assume importance. A camp and supply base was established at Warner's Ranch in October of 1861. The site of the Camp was about one mile from the old Warner adobe house, and bore the name of the General— George Wright.

Overland By Boat To California In 1849. (See listing under Harris, Lewis Birdsall.)

HUNT, ROCKWELL D.

California in the Making. 1953. Caldwell, Idaho: The Caxton Printers, Ltd. 325 pp.

Reference is made on pp. 107-116, to "William Lewis Manly, Hero of Death Valley," and on pp. 241-242, to "Hero of Death Valley." The book contains 23 articles by Dr. Hunt. Hunt knew Mr. Manly; was, in fact, his neighbor for a season. Substantially a repetition of the Manly reference appears in Dr. Hunt's *California's Stately Hall of Fame*, and in the April 1943 issue of *Ghost Town News*. (See, also, the listing under Hunt, R. D.—*Personal Sketches of California Pioneers I Have Known.*)

Personal Sketches of California Pioneers I Have Known. 1962. Stockton, California: University of the Pacific. Limited to 500 copies. 109 pp. Pen sketches. 6¾ x 10.

In the front of this book I filed a clipping from one of the Los Angeles papers, dated March 2, 1966. The clipping contained Rabbi Magnin's column—Eternal Light. I am sure Rabbi Magnin will understand and approve my purpose in quoting a portion of his beautiful tribute: "A few weeks ago my friend, Prof. Rockwell Hunt, passed away. He lived into the deep 90s, but was young at heart. While he specialized in the history of California, his interests embraced the whole world. Every Christmas came his message which was a choice bit of philosophy. It was a little lantern lighting up a path into the New Year."

Dr. Hunt's books affect me in much the same way—like "a little lantern lighting up a path. . . ." As in Rabbi Magnin's Christmas message, sometimes the light would shine from one of Dr. Hunt's characteristic philosophical observations; often it would reflect from some obscure historical material. This is true in the instance of his *Personal Sketches of California Pioneers I Have Known.*

One such relevant "Sketch" is that concerning one of Death Valley's foremost heroes—William Lewis Manly (pp. 49-58). Reading this chapter approaches the equivalent of meeting Mr. Manly in person, for Dr. Hunt *knew* him personally; was his near neighbor in San Jose. What a remarkable portrayal Doctor Hunt gives of this great Death Valley character: "In the small college community, I observed, from time to time, an older man, quiet in manner, with a noticeable stoop and patriarchal beard, as he came to the post office and store, just across the street, sometimes apparently without a spoken word to those who might happen to be standing by. In the course of time I learned the name of the man. It was Mr. Manly. A little later I found it to be William Lewis Manly, a California pioneer, who had entered California in 1849. I became interested. I had only recently been reading a book with the title *Death Valley in '49.* Then I became somewhat excited on learning that the old man who was coming over to the post office so casually and disappearing almost totally unobserved was the author of that book, and that the book itself was nothing other than his own life story."

Although not pertinent to our subject of deserts, the other California Pioneers whom Dr. Hunt knew and tells about include John Bidwell, Moses Schallenberger, Martin Briggs, Daniel McLaughlin, Virginia Reed Murphy, Cornelius Cole, Edwin Sherman, John Braly, Charles Prudhomme, Emanuel Speegle. Not alone because of my interest in Manly and Death Valley, but because of Dr. Hunt's intimate personal characterization of *all* these notable California pioneers, I know a sincere fondness for this fine book.

HUNTINGTON, ELLSWORTH

Death Valley and Our Future Climate. 1916. May issue of *Harpers.* Illus.

The article emphasizes the part Death Valley now plays, and the bearing it may eventually have, upon our climate.

HUSSEY, JOHN ADAM

Kit Carson at Cajon—Not Tejon. 1950. March issue of *California Historical Society Quarterly.* Vol. XXIX, No. 1.

This article (pp. 29-38) endeavors to prove that Kit Carson was at Cajon Pass—and *not* Tejon Pass—during "the greater part of the winter" of 1847-48, when he was in command of a detachment of 25 men who were assigned the task of making it impossible—or unprofitable—for Indians to drive herds of stolen animals through the pass.

HUSSEY, S. E. (Commentary), and BOELTER, HOMER H. (Photography)

Desert Thematic Portrait, The. 1945. Hollywood: Homer H. Boelter. 28 pp. End paper designs. 8⅝ x 11¼.

There are 26 beautiful full-page photographs of the desert, with another—in color—showing on the front cover. Mr. Hussey's commentary has captured, in words, the deep mysteries of the desert: "For who that has looked upon her sparkling nights but has entered into dreams with her? . . . has beheld in dream the multitudinous fall of stars, and heard old whispers of abandoned trysts?"

HUTCHINSON, TED and McCAIN, A. D.

Rattlesnake Recipes. 1950. Barstow, California. 16 pp. Sketches. 5½ x 8½. Wrappers.

This is a humorous item of "Mojave Masterpieces."

IACOPI, ROBERT

Earthquake Country. 1964. Menlo Park, California: Lane Book Co. A *Sunset* Book. The words "First Edition, first printing" appear opposite title page. 192 pp. Profusely illustrated with photographs, diagrams, maps. 8½ x 11⅛.

The photographs—all of them, and particularly those showing earthquake damage—are of exceptional interest. Dr. Charles F. Richter, in his foreword, sets the tempo for this unusual book: "Mr. Iacopi has written a factually sober—and sobering—book." Every page of this important item is both instructive and interesting. Desert mention is prominent throughout and receives direct treatment in the section "Exploring the Southern San Andreas Fault: Salton-Imperial Basin, Indio to San Gorgonio Pass, San Bernardino Area, Cajon Canyon to Palmdale, Palmdale to Gorman" (pp. 64-101).

IMPERIAL VALLEY PIONEERS

Valley Imperial, The. 1956. 72 pp. 12 illus. Map. Wrappers. 6¾ x 10.

Elizabeth Harris, the Historian of the Imperial Valley Pioneers, has accomplished much in the preparation of this historically-informative booklet. The lead article, her own by the way, is entitled "The Coming of the Strong Ones," and presents brief biographies of the "strong ones" whose pioneer effort contributed immeasurably to the development of the Imperial Valley. Another article—"Early Roads the Hard Way"—gives a comprehensive account of the several roadways that have penetrated the Algodones Sand Dunes. Earl V. Northrup's article—"Authentic Location of Butterfield Overland Stage Trail"—supplies a condensed tracing of the old Butterfield route. In January of 1958 a second historical volume was published. Although interesting and well-written, it falls below the first publication in its historical value.

INGERSOLL, LUTHER A.

Century Annals of San Bernardino County: 1769-1904. 1904. Los Angeles. 887 pp. Numerous pls. and illus.

The book contains occasional references to desert country in both the Mojave and the Colorado Deserts, through the Cajon Pass and the San Gorgonio Pass. Chs. 3 and 10 display an abundance of desert material. The book consists quite largely of biographical sketches.

INGLES, LLOYD GLENN

Mammals of California and Its Coastal Waters. (1954.) Stanford, California: Stanford University Press. XIII, 396 pp. 49 pls. 25 pictorial keys. 6¼ x 9¼.

This book was originally published (in 1947) as *Mammals of California*, and reprinted (in 1948). This present item is a revised edition, with an Appendix containing additional material. The main text provides a detailed description of the animals included—their habits, characteristics, and so on. Of assistance to the novice, as a means of identification, are illustrations of footprints and of fecal droppings.

INYOKERN–CHINA LAKE BRANCH OF THE AMERICAN ASS'N. OF UNIVERSITY WOMEN

Indian Wells Valley—A Handbook. 1948. China Lake, California. 78 pp. 17 pls. Numerous sketches. Vicinity map. 5 x 7½. The book has been issued in revised editions in 1953, 1960, and 1967.

Early history, plant life, birds and animals, planned sight-seeing trips, first-aid treatments, and other associated subjects are discussed. This book offers information concerning a desert region about which relatively little has been written.

IRELAN, WILLIAM (State Mineralogist), et al.

First Biennial Report (being the eleventh report issued). 1893. Sacramento. 612 pp. Numerous pls. and maps.

The sole purpose for including this *Report* in our Bibliography is to cite that portion relating to the Calico Mining District (pp. 337-349) by W. H. Storms and, more particularly, to the article on the Salton Lake region (pp. 387-393) by E. B. Preston. Some readers may not be aware that a lake existed in the ancient Salton Sink bed only a short time prior to the big break of the Colorado River in 1905-06 that formed our present Salton Sea.

IVES, J. C.

Report of Exploration for a Railway Route. (See listing under Whipple, A. W.)

IVINS, ANTHONY W.

Traveling Over Forgotten Trails. III—Indian Revenge, and a Brother's Devotion. 1916. May issue of *Improvement Era.* Vol. XIX. No. 7.

This is an account of Edwin E. Woolley who brought the remains of his brother, Franklin B. Woolley, across the desert from California to Utah in 1869. Franklin had been killed by Indians. The article contributes an intimate word picture of this section of the Mojave desert in 1869. It has been reprinted in Preston Nibley's *Pioneer Stories* (1940), pp. 181-191.

JACKSON, HELEN HUNT

Ramona. 1884. Boston: Roberts Brothers. 490 pp. 5¼ x 7½. A Zamorano 80 item. (Cowan P. 119.) Many reprint editions have been published.

Here we encounter the supreme achievement in novel-writing, provided we regard popularity as an indication of supreme achievement. For surely no novel ever enjoyed greater historic importance—in California, at any rate—than our beloved *Ramona.* Frequent reference to desert scenes and incidents is integrated with the plot; and the plot itself finds much of its locale in and around Temecula, the San Jacinto-Hemet Valleys, and the Coahuilla country.

JACKSON, JOSEPH HENRY

Bad Company. N.d. (Circ. 1949.) New York: Brace and Company. Words "First Edition" appear on copyright page. XX plus 346 pp. 18 illus. 6 x 8¾.

The author makes it clear that his comments on highwaymen mentioned in this book are to be regarded as sketches and not detailed biographies. Four of these sketches were published some ten years earlier under the title—*Tintypes in Gold*. The present volume considers such notorious California outlaws as Joaquin Murieta, Tom Bell, Rattlesnake Dick, Black Bart, Dick Fellows, and Tiburcio Vasquez. Of desert interest are the depredations of Tiburcio Vasquez. (See listing under Greenwood, Robert—*California Outlaw*; Edwards, E. I.—*Freeman's: A Stage Stop on the Mojave*.)

JACOBS, LOUIS L. (As told to Jacques, Jean)

Oasis Boomtown. 1941. December issue of *Westways*. Illus.

Oddly enough, this little two-page article is one of our early printed historical accounts of Twentynine Palms. It is told by one who was himself among the original settlers, having come into this virgin desert in 1909. He served as Justice of the Peace from 1931-1934.

JACQUES, JEAN

Land of Little Rain. 1941. November issue of *Western Trailer Life*. Illus.

This is an article on Twentynine Palms, and a fairly good one. Although the name of our queenly oasis at Twentynine Palms—"Marrah," or "Mara"—may signify "land of little rain," even this circumstance seems not sufficient to justify using a title made famous by Mary Austin in her incomparable desert classic.

(As told by Jacobs, Louis L.). *Oasis Boomtown*. (See listing under Jacobs, Louis L.)

JAEGER, EDMUND C.

Art in a Desert Cabin. 1948. September issue of *Desert*. Illus.

This is perhaps our most informative article on Carl Eytel, desert artist and illustrator of George Wharton James' monumental work—*The Wonders of the Colorado Desert* (1906). The author, Dr. Jaeger, was both friend and companion of the artist for many years. Included is a reprint of Elwood Lloyd's *Of Such As These Is the Spirit of the Desert*. (See listing in this Bibliography.)

California Deserts, The. (1933.) Stanford: Stanford University Press. 207 pp. End paper maps. Illus. and Sketches. 5⅝ x 8. Rev. 1938; 3rd prtg. 1941; 4th prtg. 1946; 5th prtg. 1948; 3rd Ed. 1955.

This book is, as it purports to be, a handbook of the deserts of California. Its chapters relate to the desert's past, its physiographic aspect, weather, climate, insects, snails, fishes, frogs, reptiles, birds, mammals, aborigines, botany, fungi, ferns, grasses, shrubs and trees. This is the book one should slip into his pocket when he goes out upon the desert.

Denizens of the Desert. 1922. Boston: Houghton Mifflin Company. 299 pp. 25 pls. 5⅝ x 8⅛. Reprints have followed the first edition.

Dr. Jaeger has written an entertaining account of desert wild life, discussing

28 species of animals. The author later expanded this work in *Our Desert Neighbors*.

(Edited by) *Desert in Pictures, The.* 1955. (May or June). Palm Springs: Palm Springs Museum. 42 pp. 53 pls. 1 portrait. Outside cover pls. 6½ x 10. Wrappers.
  The book is composed of desert photographs with brief, accompanying comment.

Desert Wild Flowers. (1940.) Stanford: Stanford University Press. XII, 322 pp. 24 pls. End paper designs. 5¾ x 8½. The book has gone into reprint editions.
  Some 764 separate species of desert flowers are described, illustrated by pen sketches.

Ghost That Refuses to Die, The. 1954. August issue of *Desert.* Illus.
  Dr. Jaeger tells the story of old Hesperia, in San Bernardino County; and writes entertainingly of its historically famous hotel (now destroyed). Built in the 1880s, the hotel was long a well-known landmark on the Mojave desert.

Monument of the Joshuas. 1955. May-June issue (Vol. 8, No. 3) of *Pacific Discovery.* Illus.
  Here is a capable description of the Joshua Tree National Monument. Fourteen excellent photographic plates by Don Ollis illustrate the article, and represent what is perhaps the best published collection of photographs on this particular region.

Naturalist's Death Valley, A. 1957. Palm Desert: Desert Magazine Press. 68 pp. 11 photographic illus. Numerous pen sketches by the author. 5½ x 8½. Wrappers.
  This item is publication No. 5 of the Death Valley '49ers, Inc. Dr. Jaeger ably presents first-hand material with respect to Indians, mammals, birds, reptiles, insects, trees, flowers and fossils.

North American Deserts, The. 1957. Stanford: Stanford University Press. VII. 308 pp. 6¼ x 9¼.
  The book is replete with photographs of the desert areas covered—Chihuahuan, Sonoran, Sahuaro, Yuman, Colorado, Vizcaino-Magdalena, Gulf Coast, Mohave, Great Basin, and Painted. Pp. 166-355 are given over to line drawings and descriptions of desert insects, reptiles, birds, mammals and plants. It is this second section of the book that causes it to be outstanding among desert publications. Of not so much importance, perhaps, is the type of material introduced—for much of this same material is available elsewhere and from many sources. What is important is the fact that Dr. Jaeger makes all this diversified desert information available *in one volume.*

Once Upon a Time We Had a Railroad. 1950. April issue of the *Palm Springs Villager.* Illus.
  Of pronounced interest is Dr. Jaeger's account of the attempted settlement of Palmdale (or Palm Dale), near Palm Springs, where the Smoke Tree Ranch is now located. They had a railroad there once—an engine, three flatcars, and two street cars. And it by-passed Palm Springs.

Our Desert Neighbors. (1950.) Stanford: Stanford University Press. X, 239 pp. 36 pls. Drawings. End paper maps. 5⅞ x 8⅝. The book has gone into a reprint edition.

The habits, characteristics, and physical description of thirty species of desert animals and bird life are presented. Additionally, chapters are devoted to insects, lizards, snakes, and the desert tortoise. Dr. Jaeger employs a non-technical style in his writing, thus enabling the lay-reader to understand and enjoy what he reads.

Where Burros Collect the Garbage and No One Pays Rent. 1955. March issue of *Desert.* Illus.

An early description is drawn in this article of the near-ghost town of Darwin, California, and its inhabitants.

JAEGER, L. J. F. (Edited by Beattie, G. W.)

Diary of a Ferryman and Trader at Fort Yuma: 1855-6. 1928 and 1929. *Historical Society of Southern California. Annual Publication.*

Jaeger owned and operated the ferry at Fort Yuma on the Colorado and he is believed to be the author of this fragment of a diary found—in 1913—in an old trunk "amid debris on the bank of the Jurupa water ditch running through the deserted settlement of Agua Mansa, southwest of Colton." Entries dating from December 20 through December 30, 1855, describe, in succinct fashion, a trip across the desert from Fort Yuma to Los Angeles.

JAMES, GEORGE WHARTON

Heroes of California. 1910. Boston: Little, Brown, and Co. 515 pp. 5⅝ x 8⅜. Illus.

Desert material is contained in Ch. 4—"The Indefatigable Hero, Captain De Anza;" Ch. 11—"The Generous Heroes of Death Valley, Manly and Rogers;" Ch. 12—"The Unknown Heroes of Death Valley;" Ch. 13—"The Watchful Hero Scouts, Carson and Beale;" and Ch. 38—"The Reclamation Heroes of the Colorado Desert, Wozencraft, Rockwood and Chaffey."

The Death Valley reference, based upon an account by Robert E. Rinehart appearing in the Los Angeles *Times* for Sunday, August 16, 1908, recites the story of *another* wagon train—a lost caravan—which attempted to cross Death Valley in the summer of 1850, or about six months later than the epochal migration of 1849. The author (Rinehart) admits that little is known of this doomed train, *every* member of which is said to have perished. No one knows from whence these people came, who they were, nor how great was their number. The casual reader will experience difficulty in reconciling the disparity between the *known* fact of only one emigrant having perished in Death Valley in 1849, and the conception prevalent among so many writers (not authorities on the subject, however) that a large number of deaths occurred there. Many are the chimerical tales of emigrant wagons being lowered over cliffs into Death Valley, and of camp equipage being strewn across its floor. It must be borne in mind that any story, however fantastic, gathers unto itself a certain realistic flavor merely by the process of repetition. And the very name—*Death Valley*—lends credence even to the most extravagant and incongruous yarns concerning its mystery and adventure. It is not generally known, however, that this desert's melancholy christening was intended to supply a name descriptive of the dry and barren valley in which the emigrants *lived*—not *died*—during that interminable ordeal at the *Long Camp*. The purpose motivating this somber designation was not to imply that any deaths had occurred there, but rather that the Valley itself appeared devoid of life. To the emigrants who bestowed its name, the place was a *dead* valley; a valley of death to anyone or anything venturing to remain too long within its desolate confines. (See listing under Edwards, E. I.—*The Mystery of Death Valley's Lost Wagon Train.*)

Tourists' Guide Book To South California. 1895. Los Angeles: B. R. Baumgardt & Co. 458 pp. Fldg. map of Los Angeles. Nearly 150 photographic pls. and line drawings (I counted 139). 16 pp. of advertisements in back. 5 x 7¼. Wrappers.

The book contains extracts from the Griffin *Diary*, together with James' description of the Battle of San Pasqual (pp. 56-64). Ch. 8 tells of the Salton Sea Basin, Indio, Seven Palms, Palm Springs, Banning and Beaumont. Pp. 229 *et seq*, mention Palmdale, Lancaster, Rosamond, Mojave, Goler, Cameron, and the Mojave desert generally. Ch. 21 discusses the territory from the Needles to San Bernardino, on the Santa Fe Railway, with some discussion of the Calico Mining District, Barstow, "Victor," and Hesperia.

The historical value of this book must not be minimized. Few people know of the curious little *Tourists' Guide*. It represents a prodigious undertaking, and a tremendous expenditure of effort. James includes early-day descriptions of towns and historical events that are not ordinarily available. In 1904 the published volume *Traveler's Handbook to Southern California* (see listing) repeats much of the material contained in the *Tourists' Guide*. The *Handbook*, however, lacks many of the interesting and early photographic plates appearing in the earlier book.

Traveler's Handbook to Southern California. 1904. Pasadena: George Wharton James. 507 pp. 4¾ x 6⅛.

Ch. 25—"From the Colorado River to the Pacific Ocean on the Southern Pacific" (pp. 282-296)—reflects material on the desert towns of Ogilby, Old Beach, Imperial, Brawley, Calexico, Eastside, Salton, Volcano Springs, Indio, Palm Springs, Banning and Beaumont. In Ch. 27—"From Los Angeles Over the Tehachapi Mountains On the Southern Pacific Railway" (pp. 324-326)—we read an early account of Palmdale, Lancaster, Rosamond, and the Mohave desert. Ch. 32—"From the Needles to San Bernardino on the Santa Fe Railway" (pp. 364-377)—speaks of Needles, Calico Mining District, Daggett, Barstow, Victor, Hesperia, Summit, Cajon, Irvington and San Bernardino. Also, in this chapter, is to be found some comment on Death Valley. Pp. 45-56 describe the Battle of San Pasqual with a lengthy quotation from the diary of Dr. John S. Griffin. Much of the material in this book is contained in the author's earlier *Tourists' Guide Book To South California.*

Wonders of the Colorado Desert, The. (2 vol.) 1906. Boston: Little, Brown, and Co. Vol. I contains pp. I-XLIV and 1-270. Vol. II contains pp. I-XIV and 271-547.

8⅞ x 6. The illustrated sketches are by the noted artist, Carl Eytel. Vol. I has 15 pls. and one full-page color painting (by Eytel); also 173 illustrations. In addition there are two small maps, and one large folding map of the Colorado desert. Vol. II has 17 pls. and 164 illustrations, together with seven maps and designs. The first edition must be in two volumes with medium blue cloth sides with gold cover design and gray back strip; publication date—1906—appears on title page of each volume. Dust jackets were provided for the first edition.

This item, long out of print even in the re-print editions, remains—after all these years—the classic and definitive account of the Colorado desert. Here is a closely-integrated presentation of the desert's history, its inhabitants, its plant and animal life, its physical characteristics, its every imaginable facet of interest. In the quality of its realistic approach to the subjects covered, in the appeal of its versatility, and in the extensiveness of its scope, James' superlative effort stands majestically alone. No other item on the Colorado desert, with the possible exception of J. Smeaton Chase's *California Desert Trails* (1919), can even remotely approach it.

Carl Eytel's sketches contribute measurably to the book's appeal. There are, significantly, 337 of these remarkably accurate desert illustrations, which lend effectiveness to the work and vitalize its content.

A rash of literature, sensible and otherwise, has appeared concerning the *Mojave's* chief romantic appeal—Death Valley. The Colorado Desert's somewhat restricted literary adornment stems, in a measure at least, from the very obvious fact that Mr. James has neglected to leave much about which others can write. Few, indeed, are the literary crumbs of omitted comment—even upon the most isolated portions of this desert—that have fallen from his richly laden table. He has doubtless inspired many with the *urge* to write, but has effectually denied them sufficient virgin material with which to accomplish this urge. For although his book is essentially pioneer effort, he has successfully exhausted nearly every phase of his subject—every trail, every experience, every incident, every locality, every aspect of desert life, custom and adventure. Fortunate indeed is the present-day writer who finds, in the Colorado Desert, one stone unturned, one pathway untrodden, one sunset unrecorded, one mystery unexplored, one venture unattempted. It is all there—all minutely observed and all eloquently detailed by the incomparable James.

Of primary appeal to those whose devotion to the desert leads them most often to the High Desert Country of Morongo, Yucca, Joshua Tree, and Twentynine Palms—the chapter "A Pasear from the Garden of Eden by Way of Morongo Pass and Twenty-nine Palms to Indio" (pp. 473-485) affords, so far as I can determine, our first printed eye-witness account of this region and certainly one of the earliest appearances of the printed name "Twenty-nine Palms." (It's spelled "Twentynine Palms" now.) This initial description, although far too meager to satisfy our avid desires, is yet adequate and reliable; and the telling of it is superbly done. There is abundant material on Palm Springs, Indians of the desert, desert canyons, the Butterfield Overland Mail, Date-Palm culture, desert ranches, mines, rivers, et cetera.

JAMES, HARRY C.

Cahuilla, The. 1960. Los Angeles: Westernlore Press.

The story of Southern California's Cahuilla Indians is authentically told in this book. Mr. James, well qualified to write as an authority on the subject, has assembled a vast reservoir of information in this definitive treatise.

JAMES, JOSEPH F.

Colorado Desert, The. 1882. January issue of *The Popular Science Monthly.*

This six-page article is typical of a number of these desert travel items that may be discovered from time to time in early magazine releases. The James' article, while not introducing new material, provides an early traveler's reaction to our desert as it was before civilization moved in. The narrative is spiced by an undisguised contempt for our desert lands. His "protracted journey," as he chooses to term it, "occupied four weeks." It "gave me an excellent chance to see it (the desert) and its worst aspect." Its "worst aspect" quite appalled Mr. James. "It is hard to imagine anything so fearful as the reality, and unless one can see the ground and feel the sand, and experience a heat of 120° in the sun, one can have only a poor conception of the desert."

The author mentions, and all too inadequately describes, the several stations along the railroad: Whitewater, Seven Palms, Dos Palmas, Frink's Spring, Volcano, Flowing Well, Mammoth Tank, Mesquite, and Cactus. Remember—this was far back in 1882.

JAMES, T. E. and STRETCH, R. H.

U. S. Government Bulletin. 1874. Senate Report of 43 Congress, 1st Session. March 19, 1874.

This article toys with the puerile idea of "turning the waters of the Gulf of California into the Colorado Desert and Death Valley." This is one of the earliest printed accounts of Death Valley.

JOHNSTON, CAPT. ABRAHAM ROBINSON

Journal. 1848. Washington: House Ex. Doc. Cong. I Sess. No. 41. Pp. 564-614. This Journal (in the House, but not the Senate document) is appended to Lt. Col. W. H. Emory's *Notes of a Military Reconnoissance from Fort Leavenworth to San Diego. 1846-1847.*

The Johnston *Journal* is quoted in James Madison Cutt's *"The Conquest of California and New Mexico, etc."* It may be noted, in passing, that the Johnston *Journal* is included in The Arthur H. Clark Company's "Southwest Historical Series," Vol. IV; but this *Journal* does not contain entries relating to the California desert crossing.

Direct reference to the desert crossing appears on pp. 610-614. Johnston takes a dismal view of California—and little wonder, considering the type of country over which the Dragoons had passed.

Speaking of the men of the Army of the West, Johnston remarks—"Poor fel-

lows! they are well nigh naked—some of them barefoot—a sorry looking set. . . .
They will be ready for their hour when it comes."—As, indeed, they were—only
six days later, at the historic Battle of San Pasqual. Johnston himself was killed
there. His last journal entry is dated December 4, 1846. He was shot—and killed
instantly—at daybreak on December 6.

JOHNSTON, PHILIP

Prior to January 1934 the Automobile Club's publication *Westways* was known
as *Touring Topics*. Then, as now, this remarkable magazine—while not devoted
exclusively to the subject of deserts—always accorded generous mention to them.

Some of the best articles ever written about our California deserts were authored
by Philip Johnston during the 1920s and 1930s. My problem, in putting together
this section of the Bibliography, was to determine the Johnston articles I should
omit. There just wasn't sufficient space to enter them all, even though their subject
matter and readability qualified their inclusion.

Mr. Johnston went directly to the *source* to obtain his material. His articles are
not a re-hash of something that had already been written; for Johnston did not do
things the easy way—like playing the role of copy-cat in some plush library, skimming the cream from the actual *physical* research of another. Johnston and his
fellow-writers—Hanna, Hogg, and Archer salvaged from almost certain oblivion
much valuable desert history direct from the men who had helped *make* that history: Dad Fairbanks, John Delameter, Ed Styles, Shorty Harris, Dix Van Dyke,
and others.

Along the Eastern Rim of Death Valley. 1937. January issue of *Westways.* Illus.

Along the eastern rim of Death Valley, Mr. Johnston takes his readers to the
sites of old Greenwater, Shoshone, Tecopa Hot Springs, Resting Springs, and on to
Death Valley itself.

America's Great Natural Chemical Crucible. 1927. September issue of *Touring
Topics.* Illus.

The article conveys informative data concerning the borax industry in Death
Valley, Searles Lake, and surrounding territory. Its brief descriptive comment is
slanted toward Death Valley. Much is included on the 20-Mule Team borax
transportation.

Ancient Houses On a Hilltop. 1931. March issue of *Touring Topics.* Illus.

A group of ruins located upon the summit of a volcanic mountain range on the
Mojave bears a striking parallel to Arizona's Cliff dwellings. These ruins lie only
a few miles distant from one of our State highways. Their location is beyond Saltdale and Garlock on the road to Randsburg, a relatively short distance north of
Saltdale near the Holland Mine holdings.

Arid Outposts of Carrizo. 1934. January issue of *Westways.* Illus.

This is an article, capably written, on the historic route of Kearny's Dragoons,
the Mormon Battalion, and the old Butterfield Stage Line through Carrizo, Vallecito, and Warner's.

Borrego Valley, a Desert Sanctuary. 1935. April issue of *Westways*. Illus.

Mr. Johnston sketches the history of Borrego Valley from 1774, when de Anza first glimpsed it. The article emphasizes the scenic grandeur of this desert area.

California's Garden of the Gods. 1934. April issue of *Westways*. Illus.

This noteworthy article, having to do with the Joshua Tree National Monument in the High Desert country, was written before the region was declared a monument by President Roosevelt on August 10, 1936. The author discusses the mining activities in this area; also he tells the story of prospector Johnny Lang, the gentleman whose grave presently adorns the roadside on the approach to Salton View.

Cities That Passed in the Night. 1927. April issue of *Touring Topics*. Illus.

A lively account is presented in this item of the once boisterous cities of Bodie, Aurora, and Rhyolite—now forlorn ghosts of the desert.

Crystal Caverns of the Mojave. 1933. August issue of *Touring Topics*. Illus.

This article concerns the Mitchell Caverns, in the Providence Mountains, some 16 miles north of the town of Essex on U. S. 66. (See listing under Mitchell, Jack.)

Days and Nights in Old Panamint. 1928. November issue of *Touring Topics*. Illus.

This is an engrossing article on old Panamint, the city that once, with her 3,000 population and 10 saloons, was the metropolis of Inyo County. Now only an occasional prospector adorns its deserted streets, and the buildings have been reduced by cloudbursts and vandals to mere wraiths of a ghost city. As late as the winter of 1966 the old landmark stack was still standing, but in a weakened condition.

Dead Volcanoes on the Mojave. 1929. March issue of *Touring Topics*. Illus.

Amboy Crater and Mount Pisgah, extinct volcanoes on the Mojave Desert, are capably described in this article. These two cones are located within a few miles of one another on U. S. 66.

Death Valley Canyons. 1934. March issue of *Westways*. Illus.

This article portrays the scenic wonders of Death Valley's canyons, many of them now made accessible to the motorist. Among others mentioned are Titus, Grotto, Mustard, Corkscrew, Twenty-mule-team, and Echo.

Derelicts of the Colorado Desert. 1928. February issue of *Touring Topics*. Illus.

This is one of Johnston's top-level articles. His "Derelicts" describe factually and with sustained interest some of the old deserted mining camps in California and Arizona. Calico, Dale, La Paz, Picacho, and Tumco are included.

Forgotten Rendezvous. 1936. April issue of *Westways*. 2 pp. 4 illus. Map.

The "Forgotten Rendezvous" of Philip Johnston is the picturesque Corn Springs oasis, once a popular stopping place for those traveling one of the routes leading to and from California in their horse-drawn conveyances. On the Blythe-Indio Highway, at a point some ten miles east of Desert Center, a rough, seldom-traveled dirt road winds south through mesquite and cholla to the Chuckwalla mountains. The beautiful Corn Springs oasis abides there; also, the area surrounding it abounds in petroglyphs—ancient rock writings of a mysterious people long disappeared.

In describing the oasis Johnston writes: "The tall, native palms clustered above the spring; the picturesque cabin tenanted by occasional gold-seekers; the mysterious rock-writings of a vanished race that appear on the surrounding boulders— all of these combine to make Corn Springs one of the most enchanting retreats to be found in the Colorado desert."

Mr. Johnston, no doubt curtailed by space limitations, does not write his usually revealing article in this instance. For a better description of Corn Springs—this time in 1918—I quote from J. Smeaton Chase in his delightful *California Desert Trails*: "We (his horse Kaweah and himself) kept on . . . to a group of small palms and mesquite which gave notice of water. Among them was an old cabin, and near by it a spring. . . . In a walk down the cañon I noticed near the spring a fine exhibition of Indian picture-writings. The figures were scratched in firm outline on the faces of smooth slabs of rock, and stood out white against the red of the granite as clearly as if done but a year or two ago. . . . The presence of the house was explained by my coming upon an abandoned mine. The place has evidently long been the haunt of prospectors. On the door was roughly painted the invitation: 'Come in and camp: Wood and Water Free.' Above the fireplace was a square of pasteboard with 'Hotel de Corn Springs' . . ."

A year or so ago I made my most recent visit to this secluded oasis. The spring was either thoroughly choked with debris, else it had dried up completely. Vandals had burned one of the lovely groups of palm trees, and the cabin was either burned or deliberately destroyed. The more accessible rock paintings were defaced by vandals or interspersed with intolerable name-scribbling by present generation knotheads whose mental acuity has not developed into even embryonic proportions.

Much of the pristine beauty of the isolated oasis remains, however: several groups or clusters of lovely palm trees, the rocks with their mysterious petroglyphs and pictographs, the indescribable charm of the natural wilderness setting.

(As told by Fisk, O. J.) *Ghosts of Greenwater*. (See listing under Fisk, O. J.)

Great Cat of the Desert. 1940. October issue of *Westways*. Illus.

This is the story of Cronise Valley—the Valley that lies in the shadow of the Cat. "Sheltered in a cove and protected from the gales, lay a huge sand dune. More than a thousand feet high, it bore the outline of a giant cat—ears, head, rotund body, and tail—sitting alert and watchful over the valley below." Cronise Valley, a farming community in the early 1900s, became isolated by floods until today much of it is virgin wilderness. Cat Mountain, incidentally, is on the north side of the highway, sixteen miles west of Baker.

(As told by Harris, Frank "Shorty".) *Half a Century Chasing Rainbows*. (See listing under Harris, Frank.)

Hot Times in Old Cerro Gordo. 1936. July issue of *Westways*. Illus.

The Cerro Gordo mining district, high in the mountains and located not far to the northeast of Keeler in the Owens Valley region, was discovered in 1865. With a production record of $17,000,000 in lead and other ore, this district became, for a season, one of the State's most active mining centers.

In Quest of the Lost Breyfogle. 1929. February issue of *Touring Topics*. Illus.

This is another—and one of the best—of the many articles that have appeared on the subject of Breyfogle and his elusive mine.

(As told by Van Dyke, Judge Dix.) *Law On the Desert.* (See listing under Van Dyke, Judge Dix.)

(As told by Gray, Fred.) *Memories of Ballarat.* (See listing under Gray, Fred.)

Mysterious Mono. 1934. August issue of *Westways*. Illus.

Mono Lake and the region surrounding it are well described in this interesting article.

(As told by Van Dyke, Judge Dix.) *Old Times In Daggett.* (See listing under Van Dyke, Judge Dix.)

Prehistoric Pageantry in Stone. 1933. October issue of *Westways*. Illus.

Interesting material is supplied in this article regarding the ancient rock-writings to be found in the Argus Range of the Mojave desert.

River of Bitterness. 1939. April issue of *Westways*. Illus.

The word "Amargosa" denotes "bitter" and the Amargosa River is just that. In fact, it is more *bitter* than it is *river*. Some 40 miles south of Beatty it ceases to be a river and gets itself completely lost in a region known as Ash Meadows. The author favors us with a quotation of considerable length from Gwinn Harris Heap, bearing upon this portion of the Old Spanish Trail.

River Upside Down, A. 1929. November issue of *Touring Topics*. Illus.

This is an account of the Mojave River and its historic importance. Says Mr. Johnston, regarding this unusual river: "Rising and sinking in the same county, with a length of but ninety miles, yet having a relatively large annual flow, it is one of the outstanding enigmas of the desert country."

(As told by Stiles, Ed.) *Saga of the Twenty Mule Team.* (See listing under Stiles, Ed.)

Silver and Calico. 1934. November issue of *Westways*. Illus.

Johnston's account of Calico, the famous old mining camp of the 80's, is one of the most fascinating articles thus far examined on the early history of this now-popular ghost town.

Skidoo Has 23'd. 1936. March issue of *Westways*. Illus.

At the top of this article is a photograph of the old ghost town of Skidoo in its 1905 heyday, with buildings that housed 700 inhabitants. Below this picture is another of the *ghost* of Skidoo, with its three forlorn remnants of what once were buildings. Only one of these three buildings remained when I last visited the old camp in the late fall of 1964.

Stone Castles Reared by Plants. 1936. March issue of *Westways*. Illus.

This article describes the peculiar formation known as the "Pinnacles" near the town of Trona, on one of the approaches to Death Valley. Early freighters referred to the site as "Cathedral Town."

When fresh water filled the Searles Lake Basin to an approximate depth of 600 feet, these picturesque towers and minarets were being patiently builded by their tiny artisans—the microscopic "Cryptzoön," or blue-green algae. First, there was the huge Owens Lake, of which the present namesake is but a shriveled remnant. This immense body of fresh water overflowed into Indian Wells and Salt Wells vicinity, thence into the Searles Lake Basin, thence into the Panamint Basin, and finally into the sink of Death Valley. In a reverse order these lakes retreated into their drying process. When lo! from above the surface of slowly-receding waters in old Searles Lake, there appeared this fantastic wonderland of subterranean architecture. Scientists have calculated that Searles Lake was fresh during the height of the Babylonian civilization. The ancient shore line of this once proud body of water is readily discernable today, out-flung as though in triumphant confirmation of that day when nature generously smiled on the valley we now call Death. (See listing under Heald, Chas. L.—*Cathedral Town On the Mohave.*)

To the Roof of the Panamints. 1927. October issue of *Touring Topics*. Illus.

Mojave, Randsburg, Salt Wells Valley, China Lake, Trona, Ballarat, Indian Ranch, Wildrose Canyon, Telescope Peak—all these localities and many others are ably discussed, both descriptively and historically. This ranks among the author's best written articles.

When the Kern Bore Gold. 1927. November issue of *Touring Topics*. Illus. 4 pp. 7 photographs.

In this early article, Johnston discusses the Kern River towns of Kernville (formerly Whiskey Flat), Keysville, Quartzburg (ruins), and Havilah.

Woman of Ord Mountain, The. 1936. September issue of *Westways*. Illus.

This is the story of a woman and her husband who made their home on the desert; and how the woman, unaided, built her rock walls on the desolate slope of Ord Mountain, in the desert country between Victorville and Daggett. For ten years she worked at clearing her land of boulders and constructing her walls of stone. Why did she do this? The reason gives substance to one of the most fascinating stories ever to come out of the desert. And Johnston tells that story—superbly. (See listing under Ford, Walter B.—*She Found Happiness In Her Desert Paradise.*)

JONAS, CHAS. H.

Walled Oasis of Biskra, The. (1928.) Los Angeles: Hoag & Ford (advertising); Kellow-Brown (Lithographers). 16 pp. Map. 9 lithographic pls. 4 sketches. 9¼ x 12¼.

This item is an invitingly designed real estate brochure, attempting to promote the development of one of the Coachella Valley oases north of Indio and a short distance south of the Thousand Palms Oasis. The idea was to construct a walled shopping and hotel center resembling an Algerian oasis. A unique concept; a scarce and coveted desert item. (I have been informed that this lovely oasis was only recently burned by vandals.)

JONES, HARLOW WELLESLEY

Casa de Mud. 1946. April issue of *The Desert Spotlight*. Illus.

The article supplies data concerning the Old Adobe building (originally the oldest in Twentynine Palms, but now removed) at the Oasis of Mara. To those of us who knew this old adobe and its history so intimately, its destruction was a saddening experience.

Morongo—Nature's Air Cooled Valley. 1946. August-September issue of *The Desert Spotlight*. Illus.

Morongo Valley, in the High Desert country, is the subject of this *Spotlight* article.

Mysterious Giant Rock. 1946. May-June issue of *The Desert Spotlight*. Illus.

Frank Critzer lived in a cave at Giant Rock (near Yucca Valley) during World War II. An air of mystery pervaded the place; and when armed deputies came to investigate, Critzer set off a home-made bomb, destroying himself and wounding some of the deputies. It is supposed he was acting in the capacity of a German secret agent. The article contains two interesting photographs—one of Critzer in his rock-walled living room; the other of the huge rock. (See listing under Pratt, Helen—*Mystery of Giant Rock*.)

Pinto Basin Gold. 1946. October issue of *The Desert Spotlight*. Illus.

This article gives the history of mining activities in the Pinto Basin country near Twentynine Palms before, and immediately following, its inclusion in the Joshua Tree National Monument.

Wheels Still Turn at Amboy, The. 1946. July issue of *The Desert Spotlight*. Illus.

The beginnings of Amboy, on Highway 66, are shrouded in uncertainty. No one seems to recall when and by whom the town was first established. Mr. Jones writes an interesting summation of the history of the place.

JONES, IDWAL

Journey With Funsten. 1952. October issue of *Westways*. Illus.

This article tells something of the experiences of the Death Valley expedition in 1891. Funsten—later to become prominent in military annals—accompanied Coville, Palmer and others on this epochal expedition to Death Valley. (See listing under Coville—*Botany*; also under Death Valley Expedition—*North American Fauna*.)

JONES, NATHANIEL V.

Journal. 1931. January issue of the *Utah Historical Quarterly*.

Jones, a member of the Mormon Battalion, describes their California desert crossing in six entries, extending from January 11 through January 21, 1847. Jones is one of the few journalists who mention the "Palm" or "Palmetto" oasis in the Carrizo Corridor.

JONES, STANLEY A.

Caverns In the Sky. 1946. August-September issue of *The Desert Spotlight*. Illus.

The Mitchell Caverns in the Providence Mountains are described in this early article. The area is now a State Park. (See listing under Mitchell, Jack.)

JOSHUA TREE TOWNSITE CO.

Joshua Tree. N.d. (circ. 1946). Los Angeles. 9 pp., 15 photographs, 3 line drawings. map. Wrappers.

This little advertising brochure is a beautiful item and, in its relation to the High Desert area, both an early and a scarce one. There is no mention in it of Yucca Valley—and, I suppose, for a very good reason. At that early date there was scarcely enough of Yucca "Village" to rate even casual mention.

To us old timers out here on the High Desert, this coveted little item—so very attractively designed—holds nostalgic meaning. There is a photograph of Joshua Tree in 1944; another taken two years later. The second section of the book is given over to a description, with photographs, of the Joshua Tree National Monument.

This is one of those rare little items that would afford pride and pleasure in mere possession, even though there were no other reason apparent to justify ownership.

KEAGLE, CORA L.

Tale of the Mono Rail. 1944. May issue of *Desert*. 5 illus. 1 map.

This is, historically, an important desert item; and it supplies some evidence of a careful documentation of the data applicable to this singular project undertaken in a remote canyon in the Slate Range, far out on the Mojave Desert. Valuable, also, are the photographic illustrations accompanying the article. The Mono Rail was an elevated road constructed by the American Magnesium Company to transport magnesium sulphate "from the Trona railroad out through Layton Canyon on the Slate Range, east across Wingate Valley, through Wingate Pass in the Panamint Mountains to the deposit south of the pass, a total distance of 29 miles."

KEELER, CHARLES A.

Southern California. 1899. Los Angeles: Passenger Department of Santa Fe. 141 pp. Pen sketches. 5½ x 7½. Wrappers.

The first two chapters—"The Desert" and "San Bernardino Valley" (pp. 11-34) —contain early desert material.

KEGLEY, HOWARD C.

Good Samaritan of Death Valley, The. 1912. November issue of *The Illustrated Outdoor World and Recreation.*

This article relates the story of Lou Westcott Beck, known as "The Good Samaritan of Death Valley." He is noted for his unremitting effort to place directional water signs over Death Valley in this early day of its history. Whenever and wherever he found a human skull, there he would heap together a pile of rocks in a pyramid several feet high, and anchor to it a directional sign locating the nearest water. Coupled with his sign-posting activities, Beck is conspicuous for his efforts in rescuing prospectors who had lost their way in this unmarked desert wilderness. Of a piece with Beck in this great humanitarian venture, and sharing honors with him, was his big St. Bernard dog "Rufus."

Other articles on Beck may be found in (1) the December 1912, issue of *Boy's Life*—"Boy Scout Sign Boards in the Desert," an anonymous item; (2) an article by Beck himself—"Robbing the Desert of Its Menace," in an early issue (January of 1913 or 1914) of *Popular Mechanics*; (3) an article by Louise George—"A Desert Savior and His Dog," in the March 19, 1921, issue of *California Life*; (4) another by Kegley—"Lou Westcott Beck, the Good Samaritan of Death Valley," in the September 1913, issue of *American.*

KELLY, ALLEN, et al.

Construction of the Los Angeles Aqueduct. Final Report. 1916. Los Angeles: Department of Public Service. 332 pp. 23 maps in pocket. 14 maps and profiles. Numerous pls. 8 x 11.

This item describes the desert region along the course of the Los Angeles Aqueduct.

Imperial Valley. N.d. (probably in 1913). 16 pp. 15 pls. 1 map.

This is an advertising folder issued by the Board of Supervisors of Imperial County. There is a description of the Valley itself, with some detail on the cities or towns of Imperial Junction, Brawley, Imperial, Holtville, Seeley, Calexico, Heber, and El Centro.

KELLY, CHARLES

On Manly's Trail to Death Valley. 1939. February issue of *Desert.* Illus. Map. Reprinted in *Desert's* September 1962 issue.

To students of Death Valley history, and to many who entertain but a casual interest in the subject, this magazine article assumes major importance. On November 3, 1849, the pioneer Henry W. Bigler, a member of the now-famous Hunt wagon train that headed over the Old Spanish Trail toward San Bernardino, wrote in his journal—"I cut the first three letters of my name on a rock, and the date . . ." The historian Kelly, 89 years later, went out in search of these initials. He found them; and, in the process, established beyond all doubt the exact situs of the spot referred to by those early-day pioneers as "Mt. Misery" which their records describe as "a bluff seemingly a thousand feet to the bottom, and straight up and down."

There were originally 107 wagons in this fateful emigrant train of 1849 that headed toward the California gold fields via San Bernardino. Somewhere near the site of the present town of Enterprise, in Southwestern Utah, 100 of the wagons turned west, hoping to effect a more direct route to the gold fields. After about three days they came to the abrupt edge of a vast table land, and looked below "seemingly a thousand feet to the bottom." A man might work his way down on foot; possibly on horseback. But with a wagon—never. Accordingly, 60 or 70 wagons turned back to the Old Spanish Trail; several were abandoned at the edge of the cliff; still others—some 25 of them—finally succeeded in working their way either *down* or *around* the gorge to continue along their westward trek. This latter group constituted the memorable Death Valley contingent of 1849.

Bigler was one of those who packed down Mt. Misery onto the canyon floor. Someplace on a wall of this canyon, or wash, he carved his initials. The date— November 3, 1849. No one knew precisely the location of Mt. Misery, although students conjectured it was the ridge or plateau on the eastern rim of Beaver Dam Canyon. By locating these initials, therefore, Mr. Kelly accomplished absolute identification of Mt. Misery as "the high ridge east of the Bowers ranch at the head of Beaver Dam Wash." Little wonder the memory of this spot was etched so sharply into the consciousness of the Death Valley pioneers. Says Kelly—"We drove back toward White Rock Wash, but before reaching the rim, turned on a very dim trail, which soon led to the brink of the wash. Straight down it ran, apparently into the bowels of the earth, the longest, steepest, narrowest trail we had ever encountered in many years of desert travel."

In describing the suspense-packed discovery of Bigler's initials, Mr. Kelly writes—"Breaking through the sagebrush and bushes at the base of the cliff, I glanced along the smooth surface and almost the first thing that met my eye were the dim but perfectly legible letters 'H. W. B.' carved in the center of a smooth panel, seven feet from the ground. . . . The letters are about six inches high, and were originally very carefully and deeply cut, but have been severely eroded during the 89 years. The date, which Bigler says he cut along with his initials, is so far gone that it does not show in the photograph, only traces of the figures remaining. But the finding of these initials establishes the accuracy of his (Bigler's) old record and indicates clearly the route of the 49ers after they left the Old Spanish Trail."

In late August of 1966, in company with Dr. Melvin E. Gainder, the author of this Bibliography "took to the road" in the effort to locate and see for himself the historic Bigler initials. The trip down into the deep canyon, the miles of rough going through thick underbrush and along the precipitous cliff edges in a frantic search for the age-old initials, the inexpressible thrill when they were finally located—all this would make quite a story in itself. By actual measurement the Bigler initials were found to be 3½ inches in height—with the letter "B" measuring four inches. Mr. Kelly's estimate of six inches is a bit too high.

We also located two other carvings in this immediate sector, each only a few feet on either side of the Bigler initials. Just around the Bigler panel to the right were the initials "JP," possibly those of Joseph Peck, a fellow member with Bigler of the

Flake-Rich Company of Mormons. There is evidence of tracings following these initials, probably a surface scratching of the last name. Unfortunately, these had so eroded over the past 117 years as to become undecipherable.

A few feet to the left of the Bigler initials—on an adjoining cliff panel—I discovered something else that, along with the "JP" monogram, was apparently overlooked by Kelly and the other two or three known exploring parties who had visited the initals ahead of us. At first I thought it was the Masonic emblem (without the central letter "G"); later I learned the square and compass were also symbols of the Mormon faith. In the Hafen book—"Documentary Account of the Utah Expedition" (Far West and Rockies Series Vol. VIII, 1958), on page 181 there is a photograph of "Governor Brigham Young." He is shown wearing—on his white shirt front—an emblem identical in appearance with the carving I saw on the sheer white cliff of Beaver Dam Canyon.

Salt Desert Trails. 1930. Salt Lake: Western Printing Co. 178 pp. 34 pls. End-paper map. 6⅜ x 9¼. Publication date appears on title page.

Mr. Kelly explains that the present Great Salt Lake, in Utah, is but an insignificant remnant of a once mighty inland sea of fresh water, currently referred to as Lake Bonneville. Where Salt Lake City now stands, this ancient lake measured over 1,000 feet in depth. For many miles west of the present saline waters of the Great Salt Lake extends a desert of semi-dry salt, absolutely barren of vegetation. This is the floor of what was once the larger half of Salt Lake. Across the seemingly endless monotony of this Salt Desert traveled many of the California emigrant parties—Hastings, Jed. Smith, Clyman, Frémont, Bartleson, Russell, Young and Harlan, the Donner Party, Stansbury, the Beckwith Survey group, the Simpson Survey party, and Rishel. Some mention is included in *Salt Desert Trails* of Death Valley (pp. 113-114). (Reference is here made to Mr. Kelly's article, *Treasure Hunt on the Salt Desert,* appearing in the December 1946, issue of *Desert.*)

KENDIG, FRANCIS

Climbing Mount San Gorgonio. 1927. February issue of *Touring Topics.* Illus.

Strictly speaking, San Gorgonio is *not* a desert, but a mountain. However, San Gorgonio and its fellow-portal, San Jacinto, are so closely associated with desert country that one should feel remiss in his effort to record desert material were he to omit this distinctive article. After all, when is a mountain not a mountain—but a desert? Or, where does a desert end—at the foot of a desert mountain, or at its summit? No matter. The Kendig article merits inclusion, and so I include it.

KENNAN, GEORGE

Salton Sea, The: An Account of Harriman's Fight With the Colorado River. 1917. New York: The Macmillan Company. 106 pp. 9 pls. Map. Sketches. 5½ x 8⅜.

The book ably presents the role of the Southern Pacific in the memorable fight against the Colorado River break in 1906-1907. The content of the book is sectionalized as follows: The Salton Sink, The Creation of the Oasis, The Runaway River, The Saving of the Valley, The Recompense.

In Kennan's later work—*E. H. Harriman: A Biography* (2 vol.), 1922, Chs. 23 and 24 (pp. 88-173) relate to the Imperial Valley.

KETCHAM, WALTER E.

Bright-Eyed Dipodomys. 1933. January issue of *Touring Topics.* Illus.

As the result of his intimate study of the characteristics of the Dipodomys, out on his Rancho at Twentynine Palms, the late Mr. Ketcham became a recognized authority on the little Kangaroo Rat of the desert.

Dipo, the Little Desert "Kangaroo." 1940. October issue of *The National Geographic.* 14 pls.

This entertaining article denotes an intimate study of the life habits of the kangaroo rats, as the author observed them at his "Rancho Dipodomys" out on the desert at Twentynine Palms. The author of this Bibliography has spent many a delightful evening at this Rancho watching the show put on by the little Dipos as they enjoyed the grain thrown to them on the patio floor. They would freely come onto the palms of our hands to gather the food offered them. When their cheek pouches were filled to capacity they would scamper off a few feet on the desert, swiftly bury their food in a shallow hole, then return later at night after we had vacated the patio, dig up the grain and carry it out on the desert to their nearby burrows.

KING, CLARENCE

Mountaineering in the Sierra Nevada. 1935. New York: W. W. Norton and Company, Inc. Reprint of the 1871 Edition, edited and prefaced by Francis P. Farquhar. 320 pp. 8 pls. 6 x 8¾. A Zamorano 80 item. (Cowan P. 130.) Several reprint editions have appeared.

In the first chapter of the book—"The Range"—on pp. 32-44, King describes his desert horseback ride in early May of 1866, from the Colorado River westward along the road from La Paz to San Bernardino. This ride over miles of dreary desert, on through the Cabezon Country and over the San Gorgonio Pass, is significant for two reasons. First, it occurred in an early day (as we reckon time on the basis of a white man's knowledge of a thing); second, the description he gives of that desert ride is remarkably well done. King could write; and this account of his long desert ride finds him in excellent form.

It seems appropriate, just here, to remark that King's *Mountaineering* is one of the great books of all time. It has tremendous fascination for the reader. Little wonder that the compilers of *Zamorano 80* were unanimous in their determination to place it high on their selective list of California's 80 best books.

KIRK, RUTH E.

Death Valley. (See listing under Newhall, Nancy.)

Exploring Death Valley: A Guide For Tourists. 1956. VI, 82 pp. 42 pls. 11 line maps. 5¼ x 9. Wrappers. Revised and reprinted.

This is our most recent guide book, to date, of the Death Valley country. Its photographic plates deserve special mention; and the book's content gives evidence of extensive and painstaking effort.

Where Hungry Bill Once Lived. 1953. March issue of *Desert.* Illus.
   Hungry Bill's spring-watered ranch is located in a remote canyon of the Panamints. It is well described in this article.

KNIGHT, CLIFFORD

Affair at Palm Springs, The. 1938. New York: Dodd, Mead & Company. 303 pp. 5¾ x 8.
   A detective story, thoroughly entertaining and with a wealth of local color, is provided by Mr. Knight. It's a good yarn; and it captures the "feel" of its desert setting.

Affair in Death Valley, The. 1940. New York: Dodd, Mead & Company. 270 pp. 5⅞ x 8.
   Aside from being an entertaining yarn, this detective story successfully catches the atmosphere of Death Valley. The book deserves a front row position in any Death Valley collection.

KNIGHT, EMILY M., et al.

Historic Chronology of San Bernardino County. (See listing under Haenszel, A.)

KNOTT'S BERRY FARM

Calico Ghost Town. 1952. Knott's Berry Farm. 56 pp. 49 pls. 5½ x 8½. Wrappers.
   Walter Knott had but recently acquired the interesting old ghost town of Calico when this item was written. This folder indicates his over-all plan of restoration.

KOCH, FRED W.

Through Death Valley. 1893. June issue of *Sierra Club Bulletin,* Vol. I, No. 2.
   Written many years ago—and representing one of the earliest printed records of the Mojave Desert—Koch's article covers "a brief account of a trip from Daggett to Furnace Creek." No new material is introduced, but the item is important because of its early publication date. The year 1893 places it one year before Manly's *Death Valley In '49;* only one year following Spear's *Illustrated Sketches.*

KOENIG, GEORGE (Edited by)

Valley of Salt, Memories of Wine—A Journal of Death Valley, 1849. 1967. Berkeley: Friends of the Bancroft Library. Foreword by J. S. Holliday; 3 photographs by Ansel Adams; route map by Robert Becker. 68 pp. 7¼ x 10½. This being Number 15 in the series of Keepsakes issued by the Friends of the Bancroft Library for its members. Designed and printed by Lawton and Alfred Kennedy.
   The book reprints the *original* journal of Louis Nusbaumer, one of the gold-seeeking emigrants who crossed Death Valley in the winter of 1849-1850. The

Nusbaumer journal first appeared in print in *Gold Rush: The Journals of J. Goldsborough Bruff*, in 1944. It was reprinted in 1950 in Dr. Margaret Long's revised edition of *The Shadow of the Arrow*. Both these appearances are extracts from the original, based upon a 1933 translation by Nusbaumer's daughter. The present translation, as Mr. Koenig informs in his excellent Prologue, "was checked against the original journal, corrected and completed, including those fragmented portions which she (the daughter) understandably noted as 'pages missing.'" The original journal to which Mr. Koenig alludes "actually comprises two small pocket note books, approximately 7 x 3¾ inches."

The story of Koenig's extensive search for the original note books, and the rather involved process of acquiring them, would rival in interest the journal itself. After completing purchase of these valuable documents, he made it possible for the Bancroft Library to secure them for their extensive collection of gold rush diaries and letters.

Important as is the Nusbaumer journal (and I would rate it among the three most significant source documents authored by the Death Valley Forty-niners), were it to stand alone—completely unbuttressed by the capable editing of George Koenig—it would convey little or no meaning to the average reader. It is only as Koenig intelligently correlates it with contemporary records, and with its proper historic and geographic environment, that it takes on meaning and vitality as an integrated segment in the over-all pattern of Death Valley history.

A careful student of Death Valley, Mr. Koenig has applied himself to an intensive study of Nusbaumer, the German emigrant whose impact upon this desert's early history is of recognized impressiveness. Koenig is perhaps our most knowledgeable authority on the relatively unknown Nusbaumer; and his superb editing of this difficult journal elevates it to a conspicuous position among the West's important historical papers.

Zeroing In On the Gunsight. 1964. Los Angeles: June issue of *The Branding Iron*, the quarterly publication of the Los Angeles Corral of *The Westerners*.

In this article we find a refreshingly different approach to the possible location of the enigmatic Lost Gunsight Mine of Death Valley lore. Mr. Koenig disdains the unenviable reputation of being merely an arm-chair historian. He *knows* the Mojave desert; and this knowledge does not derive exclusively from books that others have written. He has traveled its jeep trails, its Honda trails, its early historic areas where there *are* no trails. He has followed the routes of the Death Valley Forty-Niners from "Mount Misery" all the way to Los Angeles. He does not maunder, nor express himself equivocally, in his written or verbal discussions of early Death Valley history.

KRAUTTER, FRANCES C.

Story of Keeler, The. 1959. Owens Inyo Company. Pages unnumbered (32). 45 photographs. Wrappers.

Keeler was the southern terminus of the Carson & Colorado Railroad. The author states that at one time the place was called Hawley. Then a Captain Keeler became active in the town's development and the name soon changed from Hawley to Keeler. The Carson and Colorado Railroad was brought in during 1883. The town's population attained a peak of 7500; presently numbers less than one percent of this figure.

Some information is given of the boat transportation, mentioning several of the boats by name, including the Bessie Brady and the Molly Stevens. Large scale commercial shipping on Owens Lake is said to have existed in 1882. There is considerable material on the Carson & Colorado; also on the mining operations at Cerro Gordo.

The photographs are of unusual historic interest; the book is replete with stories of people and incidents in the life-span of Keeler. Unfortunately, this otherwise attractively printed and well-written booklet is victim of occasional errors, typographical and otherwise. Competent editing would have obviated this fault.

KROEBER, A. L.

Handbook of the Indians of California. 1925. Washington. 995 pp. 83 pls. 78 text figures. Fldg. map. Published as Bull. 78 of the Bureau of American Ethnology of the Smithsonian Institute. XVIII. Has been reprinted.

The portions of this book relating to the Chemehuevi Indians (pp. 593 et. seq.) and to the Mohave Indians (pp. 726 et seq. and 754 et seq.) are of importance in view of their desert interest. The book, as a whole, is considered standard authority on the subject of Indian tribes in California.

KRUTCH, JOSEPH WOOD

Desert Year, The. 1951. New York: William Sloane Associates, Inc. 270 pp. 5¾ x 8½. The book has gone into several reprint editions.

Desert Year is a book of prose sketches with general desert interest. It is well written, and qualifies as one of the more reliable desert publications.

Voice of the Desert, The—A Naturalist's Interpretation. (1955.) New York: William Sloane Associates, Inc. 223 pp. 16 pls. 5¾ x 8½. Several reprint editions have made their appearance.

The author takes a leisurely approach to his own scholarly interpretation of the desert. The title designation insists that his is a *naturalist's* interpretation. It *is* this—and more. Basically, it is the *philosopher* who unfolds the desert before us.

Desert lovers will enjoy this book. And, from the reading of it, the non-desert lover may achieve the inspiration that—eventually—will kindle respect and admiration for our "quiet land;" perhaps even an urge to venture out upon it. The following is typical: "Nothing, not even the sea, has seemed to affect men more profoundly than the desert, or seemed to incline them so powerfully toward great thoughts, perhaps because the desert itself seems to brood and to encourage brooding. To the Hebrews the desert spoke of God, and one of the most powerful of all religions was born. To the Arabs it spoke of the stars, and astronomy came into being."

Aside from its purely philosophical appeal, the book is revealing in its presentation of the desert's plants, birds, insects and animals. In this connection the chapter on "The Mouse That Never Drinks," referring to the Kangaroo Rat, is by far the most intelligent and the most entertaining I have ever read on the subject. It is unfortunate, however, that the author refers to the Kangaroo Rat (Dipodomys) as a mouse. And with all due respect to Dr. Krutch, I know it to be a fact that the Dipo can—and will—bite if occasion demands. Also, I know it can—and will—drink water. Perhaps it doesn't *require* water, but the species *Deserti-Deserti* for one—can and will drink it; or, at any rate, make a very convincing performance of doing so.

KUNZE, T. E.

Death Valley Chuck-Walla, The. (See listing under Glasscock, C. B.)

KYNE, PETER B.

Parson of the Panamints. 1929. New York: Cosmopolitan Book Corp.
    An interesting novel of the Panamint desert country.

LABBE, CHARLES

Rocky Trails of the Past. 1960. Las Vegas, Nevada. 222 pp. 24 illus. Map. Wrappers.
    In my explorations of old ghost mining camps, I have found Mr. Labbe's book most helpful. It is always with me on my trips into the Nevada and Southern California ghost town mining areas.
    The book is mainly on Nevada, although some twenty-five or thirty California mining towns are included in the study. The author's primary interest appears to be in the history of mines and early mining operations. Even though incidental, his ghost town information is of pronounced value. And it is reliable.

LAMB, TAZE AND JESSIE

Dream of a Desert Paradise. 1939. June issue of *Desert*. Illus. Map.
    This is the story of Dr. Oliver Wozencraft who initially crossed the Southern California desert in 1849. He is reputed to be the first man to devise and submit a plan of irrigation for the Colorado desert.

LANG, WALTER B.

First Overland Mail, The: Butterfield Trail. 1940. 163 pp. 6 illus. 1 map. 5⅞ x 9. Wrappers. Also appears in cloth.
    There are two books in the series—St. Louis to San Francisco, and San Francisco to Memphis; but the one concerning the route from St. Louis to San Francisco (1858-1861) presently invites attention. In 1955 a limited number of these sets, in their original editions, were attractively bound in a single-volume edition.
    There are four contemporary accounts of rides taken over this historic stage route during its two and one-half years of operation, beginning September 16, 1858, and continuing regularly thereafter until the Civil War compelled its aban-

donment in March of 1861. Originally, the route was intended to extend through the San Gorgonio Pass into San Bernardino. Lack of adequate watering facilities forced the adoption of the route along Carrizo Creek, through Vallecito, and past Warner's Ranch. The Lang book reprints all four contemporary accounts—the W. L. Ormsby of the *New York Herald*, pp. 13-102; the J. M. Farwell of the *Alta California*, pp. 111-128; the G. Bailey official report to the Postmaster General, pp. 105-108; the William Tallack, English traveler, pp. 129-163. Of these, only Ormsby traveled from East to West; the other three were eastward bound.

Ormsby was the sole passenger on this initial East to West trip, the stage pulling out from St. Louis September 16, 1858. The journey was made to San Francisco in about one hour short of 24 days. Pp. 89-94 detail the crossing of the Southern California desert, and include brief but vivid descriptions of Carrizo Creek, Palm Springs, Vallecito, and Warner's Ranch. In the Farwell account, pp. 112-113, there is mention of Temecula, Warner's, San Felipe, Vallecito, and Indian Wells. Bailey's short report to the Postmaster General includes a brief desert reference on p. 106. It is in the Englishman Tallack's narrative, however, that most readers find their sustained interest. Tallack, making his journey in the summer of 1860, directed his account—"The Longest Stage Ride in the World"—to the *Leisure Hour*, in London, during the year 1865. Pp. 140-142 consider that segment of the route extending across Warner's Pass and the Colorado Desert.

The San Francisco to Memphis volume (1858-1861) contains articles from the *San Francisco Daily Evening Bulletin;* Pumpelly's "A Journey by Stage-Coach to Arizona;" H. D. Barrow's "A Two Thousand Mile Stage Ride;" letter from an outgoing overland stage passenger—J. P. Mitchell; and others. Desert references are included as, for instance, pp. 17, 25-26, 62.

LAUDERMILK, J. D.

Pisgah—The Slumbering Midget. 1942. October issue of *Westways*. Illus.

Pisgah Crater lies about seventeen miles east of Newberry Station on Highway 66. Laudermilk estimates the eruption of Pisgah as being sometime between 300 and 5,000 years ago. (A reasonably *safe* guess, I should say.)

LAW, GEORGE

Trailing the Old Butterfield Stage. 1927. February issue of *Touring Topics*. Illus.

In this article, the author traces the routes of the two historic old stage lines. It is unfortunate he confuses the entirely separate Bradshaw Stage route with the Butterfield line. Similarly, one may question his reference to digging out ore in the Potholes. It's a capable article nevertheless.

LAWRENCE, ELEANOR

Horse Thieves on the Spanish Trail. 1931. January issue of *Touring Topics*. Illus.

"Daring and ruthless were 'Los Chaguanosos' who plied their thrilling trade on the caravan route from New Mexico to California before American occupation." This item tells of a colorful phase of early California history. Claiming a part in the narrative are such notorious characters as Pegleg Smith and the Indian Chief Walkara.

On the Old Spanish Trail. 1930. November issue of *Touring Topics.* Illus.

This article, its factual content enlivened with sustained interest, discusses "the caravan trade between Santa Fe, New Mexico and Los Angeles during the first half of the nineteenth century." Organized parties of from 75 to 200 Mexican horsemen, besides women, children, servants and slaves, formed trading caravans for the purpose of exchanging woolen goods (serapes and blankets) for horses and mules. The Mexican trading caravan would leave Abiquiu, in New Mexico, some-time in October, arriving at Los Angeles in about two and a half months. Here the members of the caravan would scatter from San Diego to San Francisco to barter off their goods, leaving Los Angeles sometime the following April. The caravans had their inception around 1831; continued until the gold rush days of 1849.

Peg-Leg Smith: His Story. 1932. October issue of *Touring Topics.* Illus.

It remains for Eleanor Lawrence to enlighten us with one of the most sensible and basically authentic accounts available concerning the life and exploits of that almost legendary character with the peg leg, and with the aura of a fabulous mine hovering persistently about him. Actually—and even aside from his notorious peg leg and ephemeral mine—Smith is one of the imperishable characters of the old west.

LAWTON, HARRY

Cahuilla Indians of Southern California. (See listing under Bean, Lowell J.)

Willie Boy—A Desert Manhunt. 1960. Balboa Island, California: Paisano Press. Words "First Printing January 1960" appear on title page. XII plus 224 pp. 25 photographs. Book and dust jacket designed and decorated by Don Perceval. End paper maps. 6 x 8¾.

Mr. Lawton tells the story of Willie Boy, the Indian youth who, some 60 years ago, murdered his girl friend's father (in Banning, California), kidnapped the girl and started on his wild escape jaunt over the High Desert country. Along the way he found it expedient to murder his sweetheart because she impeded his progress. Later, he shot and seriously wounded a member of the posse that was attempting to hunt him down. When his pursuers finally caught up with him they discovered —much to their relief—that he had already taken his own life. Mr. Lawton draws a vivid and exciting picture of this early High Desert manhunt.

LAYNE, J. GREGG

Western Wayfaring: Routes of Exploration and Trade in the American Southwest. 1954. Los Angeles: Automobile Club of Southern California. Designed by Ward Ritchie. Introduction by Phil Townsend Hanna. Maps by Lowell Butler. V, 63 pp. 28 route descriptions, each illustrated by a half-page map. 8¾ x 11⅛. Limited to 1500 copies. A few copies were specially issued for members of the Zamorano Club.

Among the trail routes discussed are those of DeAnza, El Camino Real, Jed Smith, Pattie, Young, Ogden, Walker, Bartleson-Bidwell, Frémont, Kearny, the Mormon Battalion, Manly, and the Butterfield Overland Mail. A good book and a useful one; a necessary tool that should be conveniently placed for quick reference in every library.

LEADABRAND, RUSS

It can never be said of Russ Leadabrand that all the rich cream of information assembled in his Guidebooks and Byway Series has been skimmed from the man-to-desert research of others. For Mr. Leadabrand is a member of that dedicated fraternity of desert lovers who are not afraid to get out of their cars, get off the pavement, and get trail dust on their boots. He is prodigal to the quaint, old-fashioned concept that the true historian should establish contact with history where history was made and—hopefully—from those who helped make it; not exclusively from library books where it has already been gathered by those brave souls who *were* courageous enough to go out in search of it.

Leadabrand must *see* and *feel* and *breathe* the desert he writes about. He rubs elbows with it, communes with it, shares understanding with it. And this is why, when we sit at his richly laden desert spread, we eat food fresh-baked from the oven; not warmed-up left-overs from another's hard-earned substance.

Desert Magazine Articles. From among the Leadabrand desert articles appearing in *Desert* Magazine I have selected the following for mention in this Bibliography:

> *Boom and Bust At Leadfield.* January 1957. An account of C. C. Julian's swindle city in Death Valley.
>
> *Burro Sanctuary On the Mojave.* December 1957. The story of the formation of the desert burro sanctuary.
>
> *Day In Greenwater Canyon.* October 1955. Describes a field trip to Greenwater Canyon in Death Valley.
>
> *Long Eared Problem Child of the Desert.* June 1956. This is Mr. Leadabrand's first article relating to the plight of the wild burro.

Exploring California Byways. (*Westways* articles.)

It was in early 1959 that Russ Leadabrand launched his timely plan of preparing a series of monthly articles which he chose to caption—*Let's Explore a Byway.* In June of that same year *Westways* began publishing them. Hopefully, Mr. Leadabrand and the magazine contemplated a year's duration for the series. Now, over *ten years* later, the series continues to gather interest with each successive article.

From the issues of the past years I have selected for listing in this Bibliography the following *Byway* articles that contain desert material:

> *Along the Border.* May 1964. (The byway leading from San Diego to Jacumba, including Tecate and the Campo area.)
>
> *Anza-Borrego.* November 1962.

Bakersfield To Boron. April 1962.

Dale Mining District. December 1966.

Devil's Punch Bowl. February 1964. (The Antelope Valley area.)

High Desert. March 1961. (The Morongo and Yucca Valleys, Joshua Tree, Twentynine Palms, and the Joshua Tree National Monument.)

Into Wild Palm Canyons. March 1964. (The palm oases from Thousand Palms out to Biskra.)

Joshua Tree National Monument. February 1966.

Kelso Valley, Jawbone Canyon. February 1967.

New Road Into Borrego. January 1965.

New Road Into Death Valley. April 1963. (Route from Big Pine via Eureka Valley.)

Palms To Pines Highway. April 1965. (Includes Palm Desert area.)

Panamint Valley. February 1962. (Area from Trona to Panamint Springs, including Wildrose Canyon and Panamint City.)

Randsburg. March 1966.

Salton Sea. February 1961. (Includes Yuma.)

San Bernardino Museum Country. April 1964. (Discusses archaeological sites of the Museum, including work along the Mojave River.)

Exploring California Byways. (The book.) (1967.) Los Angeles. The Ward Ritchie Press. 168 pp. Over 50 photographs. 16 maps. Index. Bibliography. Wrappers. 5¼ x 7.

This convenient, pocket-size book reprints—with indicated revisions—sixteen of the *Byway* articles appearing in *Westways* during the early life of the series. These explore California from King's Canyon to the Mexican border. There is considerable desert material, particularly No. I—Along the Butterfield Trail; No. 15—Through the Rand Mining District; No. 16—Into Southern Inyo County.

Guidebook To the Mojave Desert of California. A. (1966.) Los Angeles. The Ward Ritchie Press. 180 pp. Index. Bibliography. Wrappers. 5¼ x 7.

This book goes to the source and inception of every Mojave Desert trail and town and historic incident. To refer to it as another desert guide is to apply a restrictive dimension to its broad scope and to its basic concept. It qualifies as one of our most competent and useful books on the Mojave Desert area.

In general, the book relates to that portion of the Mojave sprawling from the Tehachapis to the restored ghost town of Calico. Included in this broad sweep of desert land is the Owens Valley, the High Desert region, and the Joshua Tree National Monument. Proper attention is given Antelope Valley with its Palmdale, Lancaster, Rosamond, Edwards Air Force Base, and Mojave. The ghost of Llano del Rio is quite thoroughly imbued with vitality; and Barstow, Calico, Death Valley, Hesperia, Apple Valley, Lucerne Valley and the Dale Mining District all receive generous mention.

Guidebook to the San Bernardino Mountains of California, A. (1964). Los Angeles. The Ward Ritchie Press. 118 pp. 32 illus. Double page map of area. Index. Bibliography. Wrappers. 5¼ x 7.

Interspersed with its mountain trail-guiding is a wealth of desert material, particularly on the fringe areas. At least one entire side of these mountains rises out of the desert and is closely related to it. This area is given emphasis in Chapters 7, 8 and 18.

Guidebook to the San Gabriel Mountains of California, A. (1963.) Los Angeles: The Ward Ritchie Press. 104 pp. 26 illus. Double-page map of area. Index. 5¼ x 7. Wrappers.

This is the first of the Leadabrand Guidebook series. As with the others, the first edition soon became exhausted and reprints followed. In 1964 the present item was revised, the revision showing 120 pp., 28 illus., bibliography and index. There is plenty of desert in this attractive volume. In fact, there is a little desert in about everything Russ Leadabrand writes. The desert won his close affection several years ago and he cannot seem to escape mention of it. (And may he never try.) The route suggested in Chapter 11 is guaranteed to give the traveler a feel of the desert, and the same comment applies to Chapters 14, 15 and 19.

Guidebook to the Southern Sierra Nevada, A; Including Sequoia National Forest. (1968.) Los Angeles: The Ward Ritchie Press. VIII plus 184 pp. 56 illus. 7 regional maps. Bibliography. Index. 5¼ x 7. Wrappers.

This most recent Leadabrand mountain guidebook, like those that precede it, dips freely into the Southern California desert areas. Ch. XIX (pp. 137-142) takes the reader out over the desert north of the town of Mojave, finally turning west up Jawbone Canyon. Ch. XXI (pp. 153-156) continues north of Mojave to Freeman's Junction where it turns northwest up the Walker Pass route.

The Southern Sierra guidebook is a worthy companion volume to its distinguished predecessors.

Guidebook to the Sunset Ranges of Southern California, A. (1965.) Los Angeles: The Ward Ritchie Press. 148 pp. 49 illus. Double-page map of area, also a single-page map. Bibliography. Index. 5¼ x 7. Wrappers.

This exceptionally well written guidebook is replete with desert lore. Technically, it is sometimes a matter of opinion as to just how much of these land elevations qualify as mountain, and how much qualify as desert. In other words, if a mountain range rises up from the desert, is it still desert? Does mere elevation determine the difference? Does the presence of trees transform a desert upheaval into a mountain? Just where is the precise line of demarcation? The answer, of course, is purely conjectural. All I know for sure is that when Mr. Leadabrand writes of the Banning to Idyllwild Highway, the Pines to Palms Highway, the Palm Springs Aerial Tramway, and the Julian Country, he is getting his feet in the sand and is breathing clean, fresh, desert air.

Here is fair sample of the Leadabrand style: "Then walk the land . . . Know the trees by their shape, their scent, their drop of leaves. Become familiar with the comings and goings of small birds and small animals. Learn the sounds: a falling acorn, the racket of the squirrel and jay, the call of the hawk out hunting. Observe the working of the wind; the pattern of the clouds and the pattern of cloud shadows. It will take time, but after a day and another day, after a week, a season, you will find yourself at home in this mountain kingdom. You will have learned the smaller secrets; and the high hills, familiar now, will seem a bright and friendly land."

Mines of the Mojave. 1963. October issue of Westways. 7 photos.

This article is not included in the *Byway* series. It provides a quick run-down of the early mining operations in the Mojave Desert. Mentioned are the Lost Gunsight, Borax on Searles Lake, Cerro Gordo, Panamint City, Darwin, Greenwater, Leadfield, Calico, Randsburg and others.

Photographer of the Desert. 1964. *Westerners, The* (Los Angeles Corral) *Brand Book* No. 11. 10 pp. 1 illus. Line drawing by Don Perceval. Map.

Mr. Leadabrand, Editor of *Westerners' Brand Book* No. 11, writes this article to accompany the portfolio of Burton Frasher's desert area photographs. According to Leadabrand, Frasher first visited Death Valley in the winter of 1920. In that early day of few roads—and these in poor condition—Frasher drove his Model T Ford, and other "cars of the day," into such lonely, isolated regions as Rhyolite, Titus Canyon, Scotty's Sand Spring, the Keane Wonder Mine, Chloride City; and mostly he used a 1914 National Geographic map to guide him. Frasher was with Chalfant while the latter was writing his *Death Valley, the Facts,* and several of his photographs help illustrate it. The W. P. A. book—*Death Valley, A Guide*—noted for its outstanding photographs—utilizes a number of the Frasher pictures. These are but two of many well-known desert books in which Frasher photographs appear.

LEE, BOURKE

Death Valley—Death Valley Prospectors—Death Valley Scotty—Lost in Death Valley. 1929. August 10, September 7 and 14 issues of *Saturday Evening Post.* 1930. November 29, December 6 issues of *Saturday Evening Post.*

The foregoing articles were later included in Bourke Lee's published volumes—*Death Valley* and *Death Valley Men.*

Death Valley. 1930. New York: Macmillan Company. 210 pp. Pls. 6¾ x 9⅝.

In separate chapters the author discusses Death Valley's Geology, Sun and Scenery, Early Inhabitants, Paiute Lore, Lost Emigrants, Mines and Mining, Plants and Animals. All the old-time characters—Manly and his party, Doty and his Jayhawkers, the Briers, Shorty Harris, Death Valley Scotty—these live and breathe again as flesh and blood heroes in Lee's spirited account of Death Valley. Into the decaying ruins of old ghost cities in the Panamints we wander with breathless awe. Suddenly these crumbling walls become intact; there is sound of many voices; music blares stridently from within the swinging doors of the old dance halls. The glamorous cities of the Panamints erupt once more with the riotous, carefree life of many years gone by.

Death Valley Men. 1932. New York: Macmillan Company. 319 pp. End paper maps. 6½ x 9.

Pp. 1-80 relate to Death Valley Scotty. Among other noteworthy desert characters referred to are Dad Fairbanks, Pete Auguerreberry, Le Moigne, Cocoran, Adrian Egbert of Cave Springs, and John Searles. Mention is made of the old-time desert towns of Shoshone, Baker, Keeler, Darwin, Mojave, Panamint, Trona, Ballarat, Skidoo, Rhyolite, Johannesburg and Atolia. Pp. 218-221 describe the then-intact Mono Rail in Layton Canyon.

LEE, MIKE E. (Compiled by)

Short Stories on Burro Schmidt's Famous Tunnel. N.d. 10 pp. Wrappers. Two editions were run.

Of marginal interest only, but surely an odd little item. Mike Lee's contribution to desert literature should commend itself to the curious-minded.

LEE, W. STORRS

Great California Deserts, The. (1963.) New York: G. P. Putnam's Sons. 306 pp. Map. Line drawings. 6 x 8¾.

Of a piece with such desert writers as Bourke Lee, Coolidge, Corle, Putnam, Hollen and Ainsworth—but not to be classified with such dedicated desert specialists as Long, Chalfant, Weight, Murbarger, Leadabrand and Henderson—the author turns in an entertaining book with scattered, fragmented references to de Anza, Death Valley Scotty, Frémont, Cerro Gordo, Panamint City, Vasquez, Butterfield, 20-mule borax wagons, Wozencraft, Randsburg, Mulholland, Anza-Borrego, David Griffith, Twentynine Palms, Hoover Dam, Coachella Valley, and an infinite number and variety of others.

LEONARD, ORVILLE H.

Land Where the Sunsets Go, The. Sketches of the American Desert. 1917. Boston: Sherman, French & Company. 212 pp. 5¼ x 7¾.

The Leonard book, written when our deserts were regarded as something to be abhorred and avoided, consists of sketches in both prose and poetry, all descriptive of desert scenery, desert characters, and desert interludes. The author's style is unique in its sheer beauty of expression. His description of the desert prospector, for example, is illustrative of the book's charm: "Where is he going? He knows not, quite; but desert miners in frequent gossips have told of districts here and there where he has never been, and in his dreams he sees a glowing prospect they've passed by. It matters not where his feet may lead him, so it be to a land that's new, for ever his mind sees a golden promise in the country he has not seen. There's a misty cloud on the mountain ridge over which a new trail dips, in the shape of a beckoning finger, and his spirit obeys the call."

Oddly enough, this little item has escaped popular appeal; yet it pulsates with the breath of the desert, and smacks of Mary Austin and John Van Dyke. It merits resurrection from oblivion, and a cherished spot in every desert library. And, in this pronouncement, let no man "say me nay."

LESLEY, LEWIS B. (Edited by)

Uncle Sam's Camels. 1929. Cambridge: Harvard University Press. 298 pp. 3 illus. Biblio. Fldg. map. 7 x 9⅞.

Included in this book is the *Journal* of May Humphreys Stacey (pp. 19-116) and the *Report* of Edward Fitzgerald Beale (pp. 137-281). Both the Stacey *Journal* and the Beale *Report* follow the progress of the camel caravan only as far west as the Colorado River. A further section of the book discusses the organization of the "Camel Brigade" under the direction of Mr. Jefferson Davis, then Secretary of War (1857-1858). Another section tells of the dispersion of the camels after they had served their usefulness in this abortive effort to establish a mode of transcontinental freight service.

West from the Colorado, and into California, the camel train (28 of the original 75 or 80 transported to this country) traversed a portion of the great Mojave Desert, finally arriving at Fort Tejon. For the purpose of creating diversion, two of the animals were detached from the main herd and taken over Cajon Pass into the sleepy little pueblo of Los Angeles. Here they remained for two days, after which interval they rejoined the herd at Tejon.

For some reason, or perhaps many reasons, the camel experiment was destined to failure even before the animals arrived in America. Yet the venture itself was not so poorly conceived as the end result would indicate. The camels repeatedly demonstrated their capacity to out-pack, out-distance, and out-smart the stupidly-stubborn mules. Perhaps they proved not so tractable as the mules, although this condition was largely attributable to a total absence of understanding on the part of the inexperienced drivers. Certainly the pebbly desert brought torture to hoofs conditioned to endure travel only upon the soft sands of the Sahara. Often the ungainly brutes created havoc among the mules and horses—frightening them completely out of control. But over and beyond this, the *personal* element exerted conspicuous influence. Mule skinners hated the camels before they ever saw them; hated them, first, because they were camels; second, because they were not mules. Mules were the only animals the mule-skinners understood. When they applied this unilateral knowledge to their attempted management of the camels, these old-world creatures violently resented it—and were not in the least reluctant to express this resentment in a manner that greatly irritated their would-be masters. The ensuing complications contributed no perceptible impetus to the promotion of effective transportation. The results were tragic; deplorable. The awkward, irascible beasts from the tranquil land of the Nile and its adjacent desert areas could not readily assimilate the customs and manners of this foreign land into the pattern of their age-old concepts and traditions. For them the barriers were too pronounced. They found it utterly impossible to orient themselves to the American way of life.

The subsequent history of this fantastic camel debacle is characterized by an unconscionable incidence of cruel abuses perpetrated upon these unfortunate animals by a people who never did understand them and resolutely opposed their presence. It is well, perhaps, that surprisingly few know of the obscure—but romantic—camel episode and its pathetic aftermath. The story is not a pleasing one, nor does it reflect favorably upon the temper of our pioneer history.

Singular and awe-inspiring are the weird tales that emerge from out the heart of desert land; tales of phantom camel herds and ghostly caravans. The original camels, or their descendants, or their spirit counterparts—as fancy dictates—continue to roam the vast, secluded stretches of our western deserts. At any rate, this is the story that comes to us, fresh from remote and desolate canyons deep in the seclusion of desert solitudes. We are told that sometimes, in the lonely hours of night, the nomadic herd is seen again, dimly visible in the eerie light of a feeble moon. Or when wild storms rage menacingly over the wasteland; when thunder crashes violently upon the desert calm, and lightnings flash their spectral glow across the troubled heavens, then—on occasion—we may glimpse the fugitive camel train, drifting forlornly toward the distant horizon on its bewildering pilgrimage to Mecca.

LEUBA, EDMOND

Bandits, Borax, and Bears: A Trip To Searles Lake In 1874. Translated from the French of Edmond Leuba by Allen L. Chickering. 1938. June issue of the *California Historical Society Quarterly.* 19 pp. 2 photographs.

In March of 1874, Leuba went out upon the Mojave Desert to examine certain borax beds. Leuba's greatest concern, while going through San Fernando Pass and as far out on the Mojave as the road leading through Walker's Pass, was that he might run into the notorious bandit Tiburcio Vasquez. His apprehension appeared well founded. When he arrived at the stage stop at Coyote Holes he was informed that Vasquez had struck the station and robbed freight trains and stages there only the day before. (For a detailed account of the Vasquez raid at Coyote Holes, see Greenwood, Robert—*California Outlaw*; Edwards, E. I.—*Freeman's: a Stage Stop on the Mojave.*)

There is constructive material in this item on the borax activities at Searles Lake, then owned and operated by the Searles brothers—Dennis and John. Included is what may well be the first printed account of the celebrated fight between John Searles and a grizzly.

Of even greater significance, the Leuba article may be the first published account of borax activities on Searles Lake. I have no knowledge of an earlier one. Leuba and Mr. Chickering indicate that the Searles boys had taken up property on the lake in 1874, the year Leuba visited them.

Many had regarded John R. Spears' *Illustrated Sketches of Death Valley* (1892) as our earliest detailed account of Searles Lake and the borax activity there. Also, it was generally assumed his photographs of Searles Lake, Death Valley and contiguous desert areas were the first ever taken of this then comparatively unknown region. The very early photograph appearing in this issue of the *California Historical Society Quarterly* is captioned "Searles Dwelling At Borax Works, Searles Lake, 1880."

LEWIS, W. S. et al.

Camels In Western America. (See listing under Gray, A. A.)

LINGENFELTER, RICHARD E. and DWYER, RICHARD A.

'Nonpareil' Press of T. S. Harris, The. 1957. Los Angeles: Glen Dawson. Limited to 250 copies. 60 pp. 2 illus. Also a facsimile copy of Vol. I, No. I of the *Panamint News.* 5¼ x 7½.

This is the story of T. S. Harris and his experience in Panamint as editor of the notable old mining town newspaper—*The Panamint News.*

LINGENFELTER, RICHARD E. (Edited by)

Cement Hunters, The. (See listing under Wright, James W. A.)

Desert Steamers, The. 1962. October issue of *Journal of the West.* 12 pp. 3 illus. Map.

Mr. Lingenfelter writes an interesting account of the days when steamers plied the waters of Owens Lake. There were two of them: the first to be launched and the last to disappear was the historic *Bessie Brady*; the other was christened the *Mollie Stevens.* The first, and more important of the two—the *Bessie Brady*—was launched in August of 1872; destroyed by fire on May 11, 1882.

The steamers were assigned various duties, but their chief purpose was to take the bullion ingots at Swansea dock that had been freighted down from the Cerro Gordo mines. The bullion was shipped across the lake and unloaded at the Cartago wharf. Unfortunately, as Mr. Lingenfelter explains, the water transportation proved *too* efficient. The freighters could not always haul the bullion south from Cartago fast enough to prevent an accumulation of it on the wharf.

LLOYD, ELWOOD

Enchanted Sands. 1939. Los Angeles: Arthur H. Steake. 61 pp. 4¾ x 8. Boards.

Mr. Lloyd offers this account of early Palm Springs and includes mention of the origin of its name. The reader will find it to be a delightful item, faithfully observant of the facts attending Palm Springs' beginnings. Included, also, is his exquisitely beautiful sketch on the artist Carl Eytel—"And of Such Is the Spirit of the Desert." Incidentally, Dr. Edmund Jaeger reprints Lloyd's tribute to Carl Eytel in his *Desert Magazine* article—*Art in a Desert Cabin.* (See listing in this Bibliography.)

LOEW, DR. OSCAR

(See listing under Wheeler, Lt. George M.)

LOFINCK, SEWELL "POP"

From Coso To Carricart. 1966. *Westerners, The* (Los Angeles Corral) *Brand Book* No. 12. 13 pp. 12 remarkably fine photographs.

This is one of the relatively few accounts to be written of Old Coso, seven miles (seven *hard* miles) southwest of the town of Darwin, and of the Hearst Modoc mine. Sharing comparable interest is the author's comment on the Minnietta

Mine, Cole's Flat, the Coso Hot Springs, Etcharren Valley, and Millspaugh. For over twenty years, by jeep and in a helicopter, "Pop" Lofinck patrolled this territory (so Editor George Koenig of *Brand Book* 12 tells us) "with a six-shooter on his hip . . . his beat covers a fascinating out-of-bounds land of sites and scenes that few have seen and of which even less has been written. Long before they were sealed off as the China Lake Naval Ordnance Test Station, most of the Coso Camps were forgotten history."

Mojave Desert Ramblings. 1966. China Lake, California: Maturango Museum. 160 pp. 51 photographs. Decorative wrappers.

To have known "Pop" Lofinck is a refreshing experience, seasoned with the tang of adventure. In his writing and in his conversation he exudes an almost unbelievable versatility, both in the scope of his general knowledge and in his peculiar ability to express that knowledge. "Pop" *knows* the desert. He should. He has studied it, and the life that endures on it, for more years than I would venture telling. Mostly, he knows *people*. He has a tremendous capacity for observation. Many of us see, or hear; and the thought-process stops just there. There is no propelling, forward motion; no coordinating thought process between sensory intake and interpretive mental response. Sewell Lofinck follows through and immediately interprets what he sees, hears, touches, tastes.

Out on the Naval Weapons Center at China Lake he is known as the "Desert Philosopher." For 15 years he "was given sole responsibility for the entire north range" of the immense 1000 square mile installation in the northwest corner of the Mojave Desert. He was "The Law of the Wild Horse Mesa." In 1962 Sewell Lofinck figured it was time to call it a day. But the Commanding Officer of NOTS had other ideas. "Pop" was transferred to the Public Information Office, and his new assignment was to write a column for the Station's weekly *Rocketeer*. The column and its substance were to be all his. And so, after four years, the Navy— and the thousands of *Rocketeer* readers—insisted that the best of his columns be preserved for all time in book form. The Board of Trustees of the Maturango Museum printed them because, as Publication Director C. E. Van Hagan so nicely expresses it: "Over the years Pop's army of readers has grown to include such strange bedfellows as Admirals and prospectors, physicists and cowpokes, engineers and desert rats; and because . . . much of what he has to say is worth remembering."

Sewell Lofinck's philosophy is a viable, pragmatic philosophy. It doesn't preach; it doesn't temporize; it doesn't equivocate. It comes straight from the shoulder and hits quick and hard like the jolt of a powerful stimulant. It kicks one back on his feet and implants the urge to get off the cushion and start walking again.

The Lofinck column often goes deep. It sometimes has the Emersonian touch, and smacks of an Ingersoll, or an Elbert Hubbard. Like this literary gem clipped from one of his recent columns:

"Although the only thing permanent in the universe is perpetual change, man has always wanted to capture the passing moment with drawings, paintings, sculpture, words, and now photography; to halt what is transitory and make the thought endure long beyond the passing day; to stop time, so to speak, and thus secure what is vanishing. Man's hope is to leave a record of the fleeting moment."

LONG, DR. MARGARET

Shadow of the Arrow, The. 1941. Caldwell, Idaho: Caxton Printers. 310 pp. 5 maps. 6⅜ x 9¼. Reprinted in 1950, with 354 pp., 25 pls., 5 maps, and with the inclusion of the Louis Nusbaumer *Diary* (pp. 294-299) and a discussion of the Bigler *Journal* (pp. 300-304).

Dr. Long has put together a carefully-written and authentic account of Death Valley, coupled with intelligent exploratory findings of the physical routes traversed by the emigrants of 1849—from Salt Lake, across Nevada, and thence to the Coast. The Doctor's book has not sustained itself by a parasitic nourishment upon the research of others. Here is a vigorous, first-hand contribution to Death Valley literature; one of the best, in my opinion, that has ever been made available. I would rate it among the first half-dozen Death Valley items of paramount importance.

Pp. 15-30, in a section entitled "Prologue," tell of an early automobile trip into Death Valley (1921) by the author. Pp. 33-73 cover the reliable story of Death Valley—its ghost towns, geological features, borax, zoology, botany, springs, Scotty's Castle, Ubehebe Crater, canyons, roads, mountains, lost mines and missing men.

The author is visibly influenced by the Brier narratives; even extends Mrs. Brier tentative credit for bestowing upon this desolate land its somber designation. Which, even though I do not agree, I cheerfully tolerate—and even acclaim—because she does it so beautifully.

Included in the revised edition are the "Log" of Sheldon Young; the Mrs. Edward Burrell *Letter* of Dec. 15, 1894; the Henry G. Hanks' paper in the *San Francisco Bulletin* of Feb. 10, 1869; the J. W. Brier *Letter* of July 26, 1884, in the *Inyo Independent;* extracts from the *Journal* of Addison Pratt; the *San Francisco Call* article of Dec. 25, 1898, written by Mrs. Brier; the *Interview with Captain John B. Colton* by Grant Wallace; and an article entitled "The Gunsight Mine," appearing in the *Inyo Independent* of Oct. 4, 1884.

LORTON, WILLIAM B. (Edited by John B. Goodman III)

Over the Salt Lake Trail In the Fall of '49. 1957. Privately printed in Los Angeles for the membership of the Zamorano Club as a keepsake from John B. Goodman, III and Gordon J. Holmquist. Edition limited to 150 copies. 18 unnumbered pp. 1 illus. No. 3 of the Scraps of California Series. 6⅛ x 7¾.

Mr. Goodman supplies the six-page introduction to this important "scrap" of Californiana. The core of the book is the five-page letter of William B. Lorton, here printed in book form for the first time. Lorton wrote his letter in Los Angeles on January 30, 1850, after crossing the Mojave Desert to Los Angeles via Cajon Pass. His letter gives us our only known reference containing the names of the entire personnel of that Death Valley group of 1849, designated by the author of this Bibliography as "The Party of Nine or Eleven" (Edwards, E. I.—*The Valley Whose Name Is Death;* 1940).

Incidentally, Mr. Goodman's classic introduction is, in itself, a significant contribution to Death Valley literature.

LOVELACE, LELAND

Lost Mines and Hidden Treasure. 1956. San Antonio: The Naylor Company. VII, 252 pp. 6 x 8½. Pp. 20-47, 192-198, and 250-252 relate to California desert regions.

Ch. 3 "Breyfogle's Lost Ledge," includes an erroneous account of Death Valley's early history. In the writing of it, the author apparently relies upon the early narrative of J. Ross Browne (1866 and 1869), long since regarded as being at variance with the factual background of Death Valley's romantic history. The Browne version, though, may well be tolerated, if for no other reason than it represents one of the earliest printed references to Death Valley. Browne had no source to draw upon save word-of-mouth gossip. It was not until many years later—in the early 1890's—that Death Valley's history received its first *authentic* relation.

This criticism, it must be stressed, is of minor significance when we consider the book as a whole. I rate *Lost Mines and Hidden Treasure* as one of the very best items in its category. Moreover, it is a book rich in Indian legend and desert lore. Every single yarn in this excellent collection stimulates an irresistible urge to grab pick and shovel, load the old burro, and venture forth on the eternal quest for hidden riches.

Donald Powell, in his *An Arizona Gathering*, informs that "Leland Lovelace is the pseudonym of Mrs. J. Lee Loveless."

LUMMIS, CHARLES F.

Mesa, Cañon and Pueblo. (1925.) New York: The Century Co. 517 pp. 5¾ x 8½.

This publication may be classed among the best of Lummis. Its content is given over mainly to New Mexico and Arizona; but Chapters 4 and 5—"Our Own Sahara" and "Death Valley" (pp. 50-79) relate to California deserts. It is unfortunate Dr. Lummis did not leave us at least one book devoted entirely to some California interest.

The Death Valley reference in Lummis is inexcusably inaccurate. The author assumes almost a belligerent disposition toward William Lewis Manly and makes no effort to temper his disregard for much that Manly said and did. This is particularly noticeable in his studied effort to discredit Manly's version of how Death Valley received its name. In assuming this position, Lummis was no doubt actuated by his friendship for Rev. Brier, the militant and irascible old preacher of Death Valley emigrant fame who entertained such a derisive attitude toward Manly. In fact, the Brier influence is both discernible and controlling in almost everything Lummis had to say about Death Valley.

It is worthy of mention that the author's description of the horrors attendant upon thirst is exceptionally well done.

Some Strange Corners of Our Country. 1892. New York: The Century Co. 270 pp. Illus. 5⅝ x 7¾.

Ch. 3—"The American Sahara," and pp. 28-42—"Death Valley and Colorado Desert" supply the author's reference to our desert lands. The Death Valley narrative in this book is colored by the Brier influence to an extent comparable to that appearing in his *Mesa, Cañon and Pueblo*.

LYLE, LT. D. A.

(See listing under Wheeler, Lt. George M.—*Preliminary Report Concerning Explorations and Surveys*.)

MacMULLEN, JERRY

Paddle-Wheel Days in California. (1944.) Stanford: Stanford University Press. XIV, 157 pp. 21 pls. 7 x 10¼. End paper designs.

The book supplies a well-written narrative of steam river and bay craft in California. Ch. XIII, "Deep Beneath Lake Mead" (pp. 97-106) may properly be included among our desert listings. If Mr. MacMullen dared include Colorado River navigation in his chronicle of California river steamers, then I dare include it among our California desert listings. Here are accounts of the steamers *Uncle Sam*, a side-wheeler; the *Cocopah* (No. 2); the *Colorado* (No. 1 and 2) the *Mohave* (No. 1 and No. 2); the *Gila*; the *Explorer*; the *Esmeralda*; and the *Nina Tilden*. One of these boats, the *General Jessup*, is reputed to have gone up the Colorado as far as the present site of Hoover Dam. Later, the *Searchlight* and the steel-hulled *St. Vallier* were launched. *Paddle-Wheel Days*, and—for desert lovers—the Colorado River chapter in particular, is a strengthening addition to any library.

MAGRUDER, GENEVIEVE KRATKA

Upper San Joaquin Valley, The: 1772-1870. 1950. Bakersfield: Kern County Historical Society. 84 pp. 6¼ x 9¼. 8 illus. 3 maps.

The author extends credit to Pedro Fages and *not* Father Garces for being the first to explore and describe the Upper San Joaquin Valley—"In the course of his expedition of 1772 he (Fages) made the first recorded journey through Cajon Pass, the first exploration of the Mojave Desert and of Antelope Valley, the first visit to Hughes Lake and Pine Valley, and the first march over Tejon Pass—" Mention is also made of the early American explorers into the valley—Jedediah Strong Smith, Ewing Young, Joseph R. Walker, Peter Lebec, John Charles Frémont, Kit Carson, and Edward Fitzgerald Beale. Two chapters are assigned to a study of Mexican Land Grants and one chapter is reserved for a concise description of Fort Tejon—an excellent one, by the way. A short bibliography accompanies the text.

MAJORS, ALEXANDER

Seventy Years On the Frontier. 1893. Chicago: Rand, McNally & Co. 325 pp. 5½ x 7¾. Reprinted in 1950. At least two reprints have appeared to date.

Pp. 150-156 present one of the very early accounts of Death Valley, appearing even before Manly's classic narrative. Not altogether accurate, however, is the author's interesting chapter on the Jayhawkers. Pp. 115-118 tell of the daring exploit of Carson and Beale in bringing help to the hard-pressed forces of General Kearny at San Pasqual.

MALONEY, ALICE B.

Richard Campbell Party of 1827, The. 1939. San Francisco: December issue of *California Historical Society Quarterly*, Vol. XVIII, No. 4. Pp. 347-354.

The author states, in her prefatory remarks, that "this paper is the result of a search for information regarding the source of the story, proofs of the journey, if any exist, and details of the life of Richard Campbell himself." Occasional mention may be found in isolated accounts (Bancroft, M. Morineau, Jedediah Smith, Carlos Carrillo, and Jacob Fowler) of a party of Americans in California during this early period (1827 and thereabouts) of our history. Most significant, perhaps, is the report of Lt. James H. Simpson in his *Journal of a Military Reconnaissance From Santa Fe, New Mexico, to the Navajo Country, etc.* (1849.) In this report, published in 1852, Simpson states "Mr. Richard Campbell, of Santa Fe, since my return, has informed me that, in 1827, with a party of thirty-five men and a number of pack animals, he traveled from New Mexico to San Diego by way of Zuni and the valley of the Rio de Zuni, and found no difficulty throughout the whole distance. He further states, there is no question that a good wagon-route furnishing the proper quantum of wood, water and grass can be found in this direction, both to San Diego and the Pueblo de Los Angeles."

Thus, from the resurgence of such vaguely-worded references, do we conclude that a tenable basis exists for the supposition that such a party did, in fact, make its unheralded expedition into California via the Southern route, far in advance of Kearny and Cooke.

MANLY, WILLIAM LEWIS

Death Valley in '49. Important Chapter of California Pioneer History. The Autobiography of a Pioneer, Detailing His Life From a Humble Home in the Green Mountains to the Gold Mines of California; and Particularly Reciting the Sufferings of the Band of Men, Women and Children Who Gave Death Valley Its Name. 1894. San Jose: Pacific Tree & Vine Co. 498 pp. 8 x 5½. Done in yellow cloth. Portrait of author as frontispiece. 3 full-page cuts, as follows: (1) opp. p. 202, "Leaving Death Valley—The Manly Party on the March After Leaving Their Wagons;" (2) opp. p. 218, "The Oxen Get Frisky;" (3) opp. p. 234, "Pulling the Oxen Down the Precipice."

The bulk of the first edition is reputed to have been stored in a basement, thus accounting for the water stains on so many of the Manly firsts. A small quantity were given to George Wharton James, thereby escaping the damp reception afforded the other copies. The James package contained eleven books in mint condition although, oddly enough, several had faulty pagination.

Three subsequent editions of the Manly have thus far been published: (1) Lakeside Classics—Vol. 25 (abridged) 1927; 307 pp; 4½ x 7. (2) Wallace Hebberd Edition (Santa Barbara); foreword by John Steven McGroarty; (1929); 524 pp.;

5¾ x 8¼. This edition contains the unfortunate typographical error on p. 488 that has occasioned so much confusion among Death Valley students—the substitution of the word "Dale" for "Wade." (3) Centennial Edition (Borden Publishing Company) 1949; 524 pp.; 33 pls.; folding map of Death Valley. This Bibliographer claims credit for finally discovering the solution to the problem of the enigmatical "family of Henry Dale," after the mystery had baffled such authorities as Wheat, Caughey, Ellenbecker, Long, and others. He made the discovery one evening, quite by accident, as he futilely endeavored to locate this particular passage in the Manly first.

Manly's *Death Valley* is included in the Zamorano 80—and it is eminently qualified for this distinction. Although we are inclined to associate the book, in its entirety, with the Death Valley episode, it is significant that only a relatively small portion of it (about two-fifths) is thus applicable. Not before the last page or two of the eighth chapter does the Death Valley story get under way. Chs. 9, 10, 11 and 13 relate specifically to the desert narrative; ch. 12 presents Dr. McMahon's story; ch. 14 is given over to Alexander Erkson's "statement" (see listing in this Bibliography); chs. 15, 16 and 17 record Manly's mining experiences in California *after* the Death Valley trek. (Reference is made to the review of Manly's book by Dr. Lummis in the February 1897, issue of *The Land of Sunshine*. This is reprinted in Edwards, E. I.—*Desert Harvest*.)

No other book that has ever been written about Death Valley can even remotely approach the Manly in historic importance. It is unlikely that one ever will. Manly's book unfolds the basic and authentic account of the Death Valley episode; its author is one of the acknowledged heroes of this vital chapter in our frontier movement. The book is *source* material. Not only is Manly historically sound, but the tenor of his narrative guarantees a quickening of the reader's interest with each successive page. Although by no means a brilliant student, Manly has a native capacity for translating routine activity into rousing adventure; and the reader is made to share vicariously every thrilling incident participated in by those sturdy argonauts of 1849. So energetically does Manly describe his thrilling experiences that the interest of the reader persists throughout the entire volume. The student of Death Valley literature, even its casual reader, will do well to fraternize with his Manly before proceeding to any other item on Death Valley. Not only will it give him perspective in his initial approach to the subject; it will afford premise for a surer interpretation of those inter-related events and emotional patterns associated with the Death Valley incident.

(Edited by Woodward, Arthur) *Jayhawkers' Oath and Other Sketches, The.* 1949. Los Angeles: Warren F. Lewis. XII. 168 pp. Illus. 6¼ x 9¼. Fldg. map. End paper designs. Photographs of Manly, Asabel Bennett, and Martha Ann Bennett.

Mr. Woodward has reprinted from *The Pioneer*, a weekly (later a monthly) newspaper published at San Jose, California, from 1877 to 1904, about fifty short articles written by William Lewis Manly, the hero of the historically-famous Death Valley episode of 1849.

Part 2 of the book applies to lost mines of Death Valley. In this section is included a letter from John B. Colton, another of the Death Valley pioneers of 1849. Part 3 relates to life in the California mines. Part 4 gives a pioneer miscellany. Part 5 reprints the Mrs. Edward Burrell letter, relative to the experiences of the Wade family on their exodus from Death Valley in 1849.

Mr. Woodward's book gratifies a long-recognized desire among students of this desert to have available in book form these important source accounts of Death Valley's dramatic history.

MANNING, JACOLYN

Law in Death Valley, The. A Drama of the Desert. 1931. Pasadena. 61 pp. 5⅛ x 7½. Wrappers.

The book contains four plays, two of them relating to Death Valley.

MARCUS, MSgt. STEVEN

Twentynine Palms. 1954. March issue of *Leatherneck* (magazine of the Marines). Illus.

This article gives the reader some idea of the extent of the huge Marine Base constructed at Twentynine Palms, out in the High Desert country, with "the Corps' largest unrestricted firing range for artillery, anti-aircraft and guided missiles. Its 600,000 acres could easily contain all of Camp Pendleton and Camp Lejeune, with Quantico thrown in for good measure."

MARCY, E. L.

Resurrection of Death Valley. 1966. Maywood, California: W. R. Beaumont. 47 pp. Many photographs. Line drawings. Maps. Wrappers.

Anything can happen in a book. The plan of *resurrecting* Death Valley supplies an anomalous approach to our subject of deserts. As though the Glen Canyon project were not sufficient in itself to arouse the ire of every dedicated desert lover, then Marcy's reservoir-oriented plan of flooding Death Valley should suffice to fill our cup of sorrow to overflowing. The author's plan contemplates a three-fold attack upon our beloved desert citadel: "a receptive drainage water reservoir two miles wide and eight miles long; a fresh water reservoir south of this, to capture Amargosa River water; and, finally, the hundred-mile expanse of Death Valley to the north, which would be irrigated by waste water reclaimed from the primary reservoir." It's just that simple. One other feature is included: "a 20-minute transportation system from Los Angeles to Death Valley." This of course. By all means.

The idea is not new. A chimerical plan, in many respects analogous to the Marcy concept, evolved in the fertile brains of two other engineers—James and Stretch—nearly a hundred years ago. Only their idea seemed a bit more feasible—at least in the telling of it. They proposed "turning the waters of the Gulf of California into the Colorado Desert and Death Valley." (See listing in this Bibliography.) *That* figures. Sounds much simpler than "converting Death Valley into a large water reclaiming facility. . . ." Meanwhile, we can only hope Mr. Marcy will reconsider, and not deny us of yet another of our fast-disappearing desert areas.

MARCY, CAPT. RANDOLPH B. (Journal of)

Marcy and the Gold Seekers. (See listing under Foreman, Grant.)

*Prairie Traveler, The: A Handbook for Overland Expeditions with Maps, Illustra-
tions, and Itineraries of the Principal Routes Between the Mississippi and the
Pacific.* 1859. New York: Harper & Brothers. XIII, 15-340 pp. Fldg. map. 30 pages
of line drawings. 4⅛ x 6½. Published by authority of the War Department. A
London edition, edited by Richard F. Burton, appeared in 1863. The book has been
reprinted.

Among the travel itineraries included in the book, No. VI covers the route
"From Great Salt Lake City to Los Angeles and San Francisco, California," via
Resting Springs, Salt Springs, Bitter Springs, Mohave River, "Cahoon Pass," giving
mileages (pp. 277-78). Itinerary No. XV covers the route "From Fort Yuma to
San Diego (pp. 292-93) via 'Carizo Creek', Vallecito, and Warner's Ranch." Pp.
308-14 detail Lt. Whipple's route from Albuquerque to San Pedro, including
desert passage from the Colorado River over the Mojave; pp. 315-17 cover his route
from Fort Yuma to Benicia, past Pilot Knob, Algodones, Cook's Wells, Alamo
Mocho, Deep Well, and San Gorgonio Pass.

Collectors take a justifiable pride in the possession of this delightful book, particularly (by first edition buffs) in its first state. There was a time when the book
was held in high esteem as a travel guide. It no longer enjoys this distinction, of
course, as the conditions that obtained when the little *Traveler* was first written
have long ceased to exist. But the basic charm of the book, and its appealing
quaintness, have taken on added luster over the years.

MARQUIS, H. H.

Chemicals from a Desert Dry Lake. 1942. June issue of *Desert.* Illus. Map.

The area referred to is the Dale Dry Lake, just east of Twentynine Palms. Little
has been written of this locality which at one time figured conspicuously in its
relation to the history of our High Desert country.

MARTIN, DOUGLAS D.

Yuma Crossing. 1954. Albuquerque: University of New Mexico Press. IX, 243 pp.
Map. 6¼ x 9¼.

Although of an apocryphal relationship to the Southern California deserts, such
books as *Yuma Crossing*, Edwin Corle's *The Gila*, and Edward S. Wallace's *The
Great Reconnaissance* tend to set the stage for the compelling drama that unfolds
as the actors move out upon the relentless desert. It was here at the Yuma crossing
—some ten or twelve miles below the point where the Gila joined with the Colorado
—that the plunge into our treacherous desert area received its initial impetus. It
was here that final preparations were accomplished; here that belts were tightened
for the strenuous ordeal that flung down its uncompromising challenge to the
courageous argonauts of 1849.

Mr. Martin gives a resumé of the more notable of these historic crossings—from the first recorded expedition of Captain Hernando de Alarcon to the coming of the railroad. Among the great characters in the history of our southwest pioneer movement, Martin includes Melchior Diaz, Don Juan de Onate, Padres Kino and Garces, Captain Juan Bautista de Anza, Kit Carson, the Patties, Kearny and his Army of the West, Cooke and the Mormon Battalion, Lt. Cave Couts, Charles Edward Pancoast—the Quaker, Col. Collier, and young Bob Eccleston of the Frémont Association. There is much to be found in this book that is newly-related; much that the student of California desert history wants to know—*must* know if he covets a sure understanding of those indomitable forces that made inevitable this great westward surge of humanity over the Yuma crossing and into the California deserts.

The book, together with Corle's *The Gila* and Wallace's *The Great Reconnaissance*, comprise the notable triumvirate of publications devoted to the region roundabout the junction of the Colorado and Gila Rivers.

MARTIN, MABELLE EPPARD (Edited by)

From Texas to California in 1849: Diary of C. C. Cox. (See listing under Cox, Cornelius C.)

MARTINEAU, JAMES H.

Tragedy of the Desert, A. 1910. Published in *Improvement Era*. Vol. 31, No. 9. July, 1928. This is a monthly publication of the Young Men's Improvement Assn. of the Church of Jesus Christ of Latter Day Saints.

The Martineau item has at best only a tenuous claim to reliability. It was published seven years after Martineau's death and eighteen years after it was first written. It was prepared from memory fifty-two years after the story was told to him by another who had experienced the events he described some nine years prior to the time he related them to Martineau. Now if this explanation doesn't make sense, then what hope exists for the article itself?

Despite its irregularities and inconsistencies, the story—as Martineau relates it —cannot be dismissed as entirely fatuous. There is too much of unquestioned accuracy in it to justify our regarding it lightly. Only an actual participant could have known—as far back as 1858—many of the detailed experiences related by the enigmatic "Mr. Bennett." In 1858 no books, and few—if any—newspaper accounts, could have come into the narrator's possession to supply him with firsthand knowledge concerning these experiences. Only direct participation could have produced such an intimate understanding of them.

Who *was* this mysterious "Mr. Bennett?" Was he the true Asabel Bennett of the authentic Manly-Bennett-Arcane group of 1849 Death Valley fame? I think he was. As a matter of fact—and quite indirectly—Manly himself substantiates this belief.

My opinion, in this instance, has altered considerably from that expressed in *Desert Voices* (Los Angeles: Westernlore Press; 1958). A more intensive study of the Martineau article, and perhaps a more knowledgeable evaluation of it, have conclusively identified the abstruse "Mr. Bennett" as the real Asabel Bennett of the original Death Valley party. In the preparation of the comment in *Desert*

Voices I was not entirely familiar with all the facts—including the Manly reference; or, perhaps more accurately, I did not intelligently utilize all the facts with which I was familiar.

For a detailed discussion of this challenging article see Edwards, E. I.—*The Mystery of Death Valley's Lost Wagon Train.*

MASON, WM. H. and BEAN, LOWELL J. (Edited by)

Romero Expedition, The. (See listing under Bean, Lowell J.)

MAXSON, JOHN H.

Death Valley—Origin and Scenery. 1963. Bishop, California: Chalfant Press. 59 pp. Maps. Line drawings. Many photographs. Wrappers.

The booklet presents a semi-technical geological discussion of Death Valley.

McCAIN, A. D.

Rattlesnake Recipes. (See listing under Hutchinson, Ted.)

McCLURE, JIM

California Landmarks, A Photographic Guide to the State's Historic Spots. (1948.) Stanford, California: Stanford University Press. XVI, 149 pp. End paper maps. 7 x 10.

The book contains 143 remarkably fine photographs and sectional maps. Geographically, the material is sectionalized into the following areas: (1) Southern Coast, (2) Mid Coast, (3) Mother Lode, (4) Scattered Historic. Desert interest centers in Section 4 in the photographs and brief comments on the Mono Lake area and Bodie. Pp. 135-146 provide the descriptive information regarding each landmark.

McDANIEL, BRUCE W.

California Desert Haunts. (1926.) Bureau of Research and Service. 16 pp. (inc. covers). Wrappers. 3¼ x 6¼.

This is a booklet designed to advertise the desert regions of Southern California.

Dune and Desert Folk. (1926.) Swetland. 31 pp. 7 x 10¼.

This is a book of prose sketches, descriptive of desert trees and shrubs.

McKEE, RUTH ELEANOR

Christopher Strange. 1941. Doubleday, Doran & Co. The words "First Edition" appear under copyright notice.

Part VII of this novel—The Promised Land 1882-89 (pp. 589-658)—relates to early Palm Springs.

McKENNEY, J. WILSON

Gold Builds a Road. 1937. December issue of *Desert.* Illus.

McKenney's article is one of the best available on the Bradshaw Stage Line.

Originally it had been hoped that the Butterfield Overland Stage Line would extend through the Indio-San Gorgonio Pass-San Bernardino route. This hope was negatived, however, by adverse reports concerning the availability of water. As a consequence, the Butterfield line followed a route through Carrizo, Vallecito and Warner's; and it operated over this route from 1858 to 1861, when the Civil War forced its close. The line was later revived for a time, but definitely abandoned as impracticable in 1867. The resourceful Bill Bradshaw proved that a feasible route *could* be opened from San Bernardino through San Gorgonio Pass, Agua Caliente (Palm Springs), Dos Palmas, Canyon Springs, Tabaseca Tanks, Chuckawalla Well, Mule Spring, over the Colorado River on Bradshaw's Ferry, and thence to La Paz. The old road can presently be located, and remains of some of the original stations are still visible. The route was used for the operation of stage and freight lines from around 1862 until 1877, when the Southern Pacific completed placement of its tracks from Los Angeles to Yuma.

Heat and Hardrock Not Terrifying to These Desert Invaders. 1938. January issue of *Desert.* Illus.

This article records the experiences of surveyors who mapped the 242-mile-route of the Colorado River Aqueduct across the Mojave and Colorado deserts.

On the Trail of Pegleg Smith's Lost Gold. 1957. Palm Desert, California: Desert Press, Inc. 50 pp. 19 illus. Wrappers.

This is a refreshingly different version of the ubiquitous Pegleg and his elusive mine. Mr. McKenney endeavors to correlate several of the more reliable versions into the semblance of a sensible interpretation of Pegleg's rather dubious claim to having found gold. More important than the lost mine study are Mr. McKenney's descriptive passages relating to the Colorado Desert.

There are Two Deserts. (See listing under Henderson, Randall.)

McNICHOLS, CHARLES L.

Crazy Weather. 1944. New York: The Macmillan Company. 195 pp. 5½ x 8. A second edition has appeared.

A novel of Indian life, *Crazy Weather* lays its plot mainly in the Mojave Desert and the Colorado River Valley.

MEADOWS, DON

Historic Place Names In Orange County. 1966. Balboa Island, California: Paisano Press. Words "first edition" appear. 141 pp. Numerous photographic illus. End paper maps. 6½ x 9½.

Although not directly related to our Southern California deserts, the book merits inclusion in this Bibliography because of the historical significance attaching to place name descriptions of areas in the southeastern portion of Orange County. Place names are numbered and listed alphabetically, with derivations supplied and map location references given.

Juan Flores and the Manillas. 1963. *Westerners, The* (Los Angeles Corral). *Brand Book* No. 10. 20 pp. 6 photographs. Maps.

The Editorial capsule preceding this article in *Brand Book* No. 10 reads: "Not only is this article by historian Don Meadows one of compelling interest; it is flavorably seasoned with essential bits of early California history. Much has been written into it that has not, heretofore, been reduced to writing. Portions of the factual material contained represent data available only to the author. Without his revelation of them, they would unquestionably have been lost to students of the baroque Flores incident. We regard Mr. Meadows' authentic paper as an important historical accounting."

The article relates the murder of Sheriff Barton of Los Angeles County, and the ultimate capture of the bandit gang in Santiago Canyon. The leader, Juan Flores, was finally apprehended in the region of Santa Susana Pass; was executed in Los Angeles.

MEANS, THOMAS H.

Death Valley. 1932. February issue of *Sierra Club Bulletin*. Illus.

This is an authoritative item on Death Valley, and one presenting useful geographical data.

MELLEN, HERMAN F.

Reminiscences of Old Calico. 1952. June, September, and December issues of *Historical Society of Southern California Quarterly;* also the *Calico Print* of May 1951, and March 1953.

In this article the author describes his experiences in the old mining town of Calico during its infancy years from 1852 to 1885.

MENDENHALL, WALTER C.

Colorado Desert, The. 1909. August issue of *The National Geographic*. Vol. XX. Pp. 681-701. 16 illus.

This early item is carefully written, and provides general information of the Colorado Desert area.

Ground Waters of the Indio Region, With a Sketch of the Colorado Desert, U.S.G.S. Water Supply Paper 225. 1909. Washington. Government Printing Office. 56 pp. 17 pls. 2 detached fldg. maps in end pocket.

This item relates to the exploration and development of the Colorado Desert—its geography, geology, water resources and reclamation.

Some Desert Watering Places in Southeastern California and Southwestern Nevada. 1909. Washington. U.S.G.S. Water-Supply Paper 224. Detached pocket map of desert region. 98 pp. 6 pls. 5⅞ x 9⅛. Wrappers.

Of the four principal Water-Supply Papers on California areas—Mendenhall, Waring, Brown, and Thompson—Mendenhall is the oldest, and by the space of several years. 323 springs are located and described, all numbered to correspond with location numbers appearing on the large map of the area covered. Included (pp.

5-30) is the author's discussion of the desert's physical features, its climate, water supply, hints on desert traveling, irrigation and artesian waters, and the main routes of travel in that day—Frémont's Trail, Old Spanish Trail, Mohave-Keeler Route, Death Valley Routes, Bullfrog Routes, Searchlight Route, Amboy-Dale Route, Mecca-Dale Route, Victorville Route, and the Banning-Dale Route.

Of special interest to lovers of the High Desert country roundabout Twentynine Palms, Yucca and Morongo Valleys, and Joshua Tree, is this account's early description of the area; the earliest—in fact—of any printed on-the-scene description I have yet discovered, save the one by George Wharton James in his *Wonders of the Colorado Desert* (1906).

MERRILL, FREDERICK J.

Mines and Mineral Resources of Imperial and San Diego Counties. 1914. San Francisco: California State Mining Bureau. 113 pp. Illus.

Historically and geologically there is some desert interest in this early report. Mineral deposits and mining activities in the desert areas of Julian, Dulzura, and elsewhere are discussed. Most important, desert-wise, is the section on "Desert Springs and Wells" (pp. 90-92). Here may be found interesting early data on Clark Well, Borrego Spring, Seventeen Palms Springs, Vallecito Springs, Hanna Well, Agua Caliente Springs, Mountain Palm Springs, Palm Springs (San Diego Co.), Mason Ranch, Carrizo Station, Mountain Springs, and Jacumba Springs. In the section on Imperial County the mining operations in the Cargo Muchachos, Tumco, Picacho, and Coyote Mountain are mentioned. Under the Imperial County section on Desert Springs and Wells are listed Soda Springs, Fish Springs, Frinks Springs, McCain Springs, Harper (Mesquite) Well, Kane Spring, Coyote Well, Yuba Springs and Sunset Springs.

MERRILL, ORIN S.

Mysterious Scott, the Monte Cristo of Death Valley, and Tracks of a Tenderfoot. (1906.) Chicago: Orin S. Merrill. 210 pp. 5¼ x 7½. Wrappers. Illustrated with early photographs of Death Valley and supplemented with a mining review of Southern Nevada.

In the back of the book are advertisements inserted by the now ghost towns and obsolete enterprises of Nevada's spectacular mining era. Interspersed throughout the narrative are stories of the "Mysterious Scott," our own inimitable Death Valley Scotty.

Most valuable of all, in Orin Merrill's book, are the chapters relating to his midsummer's trip through Death Valley. It is in these dramatic pages that we glimpse an intimate description of this most formidable region as it appeared before civilization spread over it the network of pavements and directional signs. We gain a retrospective view of a primitive land that relentlessly fought off its invaders with weapons that, for age upon age, had been forged in the tremendous crucible of God.

In his robust fashion, Merrill writes of the Valley whose intense heat burned into the very eyes of a desert prospector; of water supplies scheduled to hold over only until the next water hole was reached—and the water hole found to be dry; of corpses discovered with half-filled canteens beside them—the water being too hot to sustain life; of desert men with dry canteens, clinging desperately to their burros, trusting blindly to the unerring instinct of these faithful desert comrades to lead them to water; of ground so slimy and mushy that, in spots, it seemed to have no bottom; of prospectors who, instead of occupying their time looking for minerals, would feverishly devote their energies and perhaps their very lives to a frantic hunt for water; of thirst-tortured men stripped stark naked and running blindly, afterward falling on the sand and vigorously digging—like wild animals—in their futile search for water.

MILLER, ALDEN H. and STEBBINS, ROBERT C.

Lives of Desert Animals In Joshua Tree National Monument. 1964. Berkeley: University of California Press. 452 pp. Numerous photographic plates, several in color. 7¼ x 10½.

Sections relate to Birds (pp. 49-174), Mammals (pp. 275-349), Amphibians (pp. 350-361), and Reptiles (pp. 362-433). This is the definitive treatise on the subject, as it relates to the Joshua Tree National Monument.

MILLER, GEORGE

Trip to Death Valley. 1919. *Historical Society of Southern California Annual Publications.* Vol. XI, Part 2. Pp. 56-64.

This historically-important article describes the experience of George Miller's Death Valley trip—starting April 12, 1869—with W. H. Rhodes (Wm. B. Rood, or Rude), Paul Van Curen, and Eugene Landor, in search of the Lost Gun-Sight Mine. Rood was one of the original emigrants of 1849 who crossed Death Valley.

MILLER, H. C.

Mono's Slumbering Craters. 1930. February issue of *Touring Topics.* Illus.

This article presents detailed information concerning the volcanic cones of Eastern California, in Mono Valley. "The Mono Craters—a beautiful, slightly crescent-shaped range of twenty distinguishable volcanic cones—command the attention of everyone who enters desolate Mono Valley."

MILLER, RONALD DEAN

Mines of the High Desert. 1965. Glendale, California: La Siesta Press. 63 pp. 22 illus. Maps. Wrappers.

A capable account of the early mining activities near Twentynine Palms—the Dale, Supply, Brooklyn, Lost Horse, Gold Park, "Lost Spanish," Iron Chief, Iron Age, and others. The book does not confine itself to a rigid discussion of mines and mining, but dips entertainingly into the early days of freighting along the Banning-Dale road "with stops at the Old Adobe at Twentynine Palms and Warren's

Ranch (Morongo) and Well (Yucca Valley)." Another chapter that takes the reader back into early High Desert history is the one telling of the McHaney Gang.

The Virginia Dale's Two Forgotten Towns. 1957. April issue of *Desert.* Illus.

Illustrated by two photographs and a map, this article tells something of the history and present condition of three Dales—Old Dale, New Dale and the Virginia Dale Mine. The three are located in the Dale Mining District some 20 miles east of Twentynine Palms. Little actual history is known of this abandoned mining area, once the all-important industrial center of the entire High Desert country.

MILLER, WILLIAM J.

California Through the Ages. The Geologic Story of a Great State. 1957. Los Angeles: Westernlore Press. 264 pp. 108 illus. 5¾ x 8⅜.

This is one of our foremost publications having to do with the geological study of California. Pp. 113-115, 172-199, and 224-250 concern the Mojave and the Colorado desert areas.

MILLIGAN, CLARENCE P.

Death Valley and Scotty. 1942. Los Angeles: The Ward Ritchie Press. 194 pp. 5¾ x 8.

Author Milligan brings his readers an esoteric approach to the subject of Death Valley and its legendary character—Mr. Walter Scott. Perhaps the most pungent criticism to be urged against Death Valley literature is that a preponderance of it follows the tenor of an identical pattern. (In this connection it is suggested the following well-known writers be compared—Lee, Coolidge, Glasscock, Caruthers, Putnam). William Lewis Manly stands alone; so, likewise, do Spears, Wheat, Ellenbecker, Long, Chalfant, and Belden. And, after his own fashion, so does Clarence Milligan. He follows no pattern; resolutely beats his own pathway; is at all times unpredictable.

There must be noted, in passing, a reference to Asabel Bennett of Death Valley's Manly-Bennett party as the "Rev. Bennett." Feature old Asa as a wearer of the cloth! There were two or three Reverends in that ill-fated Death Valley expedition —including the garrulous Brier. But of this salient fact we may be certain—Asabel Bennett was not one of them.

Readers will encounter sporadic references to Frémont and Carson having been in Death Valley. They were not there; at least we know of no convincing evidence pointing to their presence in this desolate region. (See listings under Bonsall, Stephen—*Edward Fitzgerald Beale, a Pioneer in the Path of Empire;* Browne, J. Ross—*Adventures In the Apache Country.*) We find mention of Mrs. Arcane living to be 100 years of age. This may be, although Milligan gives us our first information of it. Did the author, perchance, refer to Mrs. Brier? Something is said in the book regarding one "Drayton"—a typographical error, no doubt, for "Dayton."

MITCHELL, JACK

Jack Mitchell, Caveman. 1964. Torrance, California: Ida Bailey, Cynthia Timberlake and Alberta Bailey. 164 pp. 16 illus. Maps. Wrappers.

This is the late Jack Mitchell's own account of his and Mrs. Mitchell's twenty years of pioneering experience at the Mitchell Caverns, twenty-two miles northwest of the town of Essex, California, in the Mojave Desert. His fascinating narrative has been carefully edited by his daughters, Cynthia Timberlake and Alberta Bailey.

Mr. Mitchell states that, during his twenty years at the caverns, he personally escorted more than forty thousand tourists on sight-seeing tours. Included in this number were scientists, photographers, writers, and instructors bringing out students on field study trips. Jack Mitchell and his wife occupied their pioneering years constructively. A twenty-two mile stretch of road was completed from Essex to the caverns; nine thousand feet of pipeline with supplying water tunnels and three reservoirs were a part of their extensive development program. Stone terraces were constructed, soil was hauled in, fifty fruit and shade trees were planted, trails were built to the caves and improvements made inside the caverns.

Most significant is the described effect of his desert living upon Mr. Mitchell's own life. He informs that he was a disbeliever when he came out upon the desert. During his life there he came to know, and believe in, the greatness of God. As so many others have discovered, the desert made it possible to recognize the presence of God and to communicate with Him.

The two adjoining caves, known as the Mitchell Caverns, now operated as a state park, are not—so Mr. William R. Halliday informs us in his excellent *Adventure Is Underground*—particularly large as caverns go, but contain "massive columns and draperies."

MITCHELL, JOHN D.

Lost Mines & Buried Treasures Along the Old Frontier. (1953.) Palm Desert, California: Desert Magazine Press. 240 pp. 6¼ x 9¼. Front end-paper map showing tentative location of the lost mines and buried treasure.

Desert material includes Pegleg's Black Nuggets, Lost Ledge of the Sheephole Mountains, Lost Golden Eagle Mine, Death Valley Gold, Black Gold, Lost Arch Placer Diggin's, Cave of the Golden Sands. In total there are 51 chapters, each vibrant with exciting accounts of elusive treasure. I think this latter book reflects everything the author's first book—*Lost Mines of the Great Southwest*—contains, and considerably more, both in its descriptive material and also the manner in which this material is presented. An interesting side light relates to the publisher's inclusion—through error—of "Tim Cody's Lost Ledge." This story was, in fact, written by Harold O. Weight, and was not supposed to be included in Mitchell's book. The error was eventually called to the publisher's attention by Mr. Weight and a gummed sticker, properly identifying the story, was pasted above the half-chapter heading; not, however, until some 400 copies of the 3,000 published copies had been distributed.

Lost Mines of the Great Southwest, Including Stories of Hidden Treasures. 1933. Phoenix: Rose & Allison. 174 pp. 8 pls. 5½ x 7⅞.

This is a privately printed book, and a scarce one. Its included chapters are short, factual, and not particularly interesting. In my opinion this book is just not on the same level with the author's later and more impressively narrated publication—*Lost Mines & Buried Treasure Along the Old Frontier*. Even so, it's a good and valuable book to have in one's library. Few libraries can claim this distinction.

MITCHELL, ROGER

Exploring Joshua Tree. 1964. Glendale, California: La Siesta Press. 36 pp. 8 photographs. Line drawings. Maps. Wrappers.

The book gives a quick summation of the Monument's history, its natural history, animals, plant life, climate and geology. Pp. 22-23 provide a three-route road guide to the area. Whenever my exploratory instincts take me into secluded areas of the Joshua Tree National Monument—and this occurs often—I carry the Mitchell book with me. In fact, I carry it in my camera case; and this is the *only* book to which I have accorded this honor. And I may say, in passing, that I find it almost as indispensable as my photographic equipment.

However, my conscience (my desert conscience, that is) would never cease to heckle me should I fail to resist one or two unfortunate comments by this capable author. In writing of the desert city of Twentynine Palms he refers to it as "a sleepy little desert community." It isn't; not even "on five days a week," as the author affirms. Nor can I *ever* forgive my author friend for informing his readers that "for nine years past, the town's existence largely depended on the nearby Marine Corps Training Center." For the information of Mr. Mitchell, and his readers and mine, let me hasten to assure that Twentynine Palms' "existence" and its very encouraging growth were adequately demonstrated over the many years prior to the coming of the Marine Base; and I have a notion its *continued* "existence" is assured *in spite of* the Marine Base. At no time during its past forty years or more has the problem of "existence" ever intruded into the delightful desert community of Twentynine Palms.

I could also comment upon the very questionable assertion that "the so-called jack rabbit homesteaders . . . boosted the economic growth of the high desert community." Or the equally dubious assertion that Joshua trees were "so named by the early Mormon settlers in Utah, because it reminded them of Joshua lifting his arms to heaven." (Whoever, Mormon or otherwise, ever saw Joshua lift his arms to heaven?)

MOHAHVE HISTORICAL SOCIETY

Mohahve (Vols. 1, 2, 3). Vol. 1, issued by the Victor Valley College in 1963 in a limited edition of 500 copies. XII plus 97 pp. 8½ x 11.

The first paragraph of the Preface reads:

> "This first edition of *Mohahve* is a collection of term reports compiled by the first Local Historical Research Class of Victor Valley College. These papers are submitted as resource material to be used by those interested in Local History. The actual offset plate masters were prepared by the student submitting the paper. No attempt was made to keep a fixed form or format in the preparation of these masters."

The entire production came under the direction of Lawrence C. Davenport,

Ed.D. The peculiar (and exasperating) spelling of the word "Mojave" derives from Frémont (this figures) in entering the name of the river on his map (1844) as "the Mohahve river."

The book consists mainly of a series of 44 interviews with early pioneer families in that sector of the Mojave Desert in and around Victorville. "To expedite the making of offset plates, it was decided to print the work in two volumes bound together." Thus, in describing Mohahve Vols. 1, 2 and 3, we are confronted by something of an anomaly in recording Vol. I as Vol. I and Vol. II, when—in reality—Vol. 2 is a volume separate and distinct from Vol. II in Vol. I. Hopefully, this somewhat confusing explanation may clarify our bibliographical problem, even though it doesn't make good sense. We can perhaps equate Vol. II of Vol. I with an understandable hypothesis by referring to it hereafter as *Part* 2 of Vol. I. Subsequent reference to Vol 2 will refer to a separate book in the Mohahve series; *not* to Part 2 of Vol. I.

Certainly Part 2 of Vol. I contains local history of primary importance. Here may be found articles on Apple Valley, Camp Cady, development of water resources, early history of the Victor District, the story of that little-known magazine—"The Kingdom of the Sun" (how collectors yearn for even one issue of it), telephones, Dead Man's Point, Oro Grande mining, pioneer churches, railroads, lodges, schools. Over 300 photographic reproductions of early scenes and early settlers illuminate the text.

In gathering and assembling material for Vol. I, the students were brought into direct confrontation with the vital, practical aspects of historical research. While acquiring their own educational objectives, they were performing a definite community service. They were capturing source material while those sources were still available. This commendable accentuation of a personal, physical contact with original sources, in lieu of pirating information garnered by another's effort, merits sincere admiration—both for the students and for the faculty members who inspired and directed the work.

Mohahve Vol. 2, scarce in its original state (it has been reprinted), was produced directly by the Mohahve Historical Society in 1964 in an edition limited to only 150 copies. (Copyright date is 1965 and the title page, which may prove misleading, states "Second Issue." Presumably, these words relate to the series and not to a re-issue of *Mohahve* No. 2.) At any rate, I have been given to understand that my copy—as described—is *Mohahve* No. 2 in its first state. The book contains 39 mimeographed pages; illustrative maps; 16 early photographic prints *pasted* in. This second volume is in uniform size with Vol. I. The several research papers included were compiled by members of the Mohahve Historical Society.

Of special historical interest are the articles on "A Military Reconnaissance of the Wagon Road from San Pedro to the Colorado River in 1858-59," "The John Brown Toll Road Through Cajon Pass," the Carden and the Penn interviews.

Mohahve Vol. 3, issued in 1966, contains XIII plus 151 pp., approximately 150 photographic reproductions, is uniformly sized with Vols. 1 and 2. A large folding map of the Old Trails is attached to the back cover. The content is divided among four parts: Origin, spelling and meaning of the name "Mohahve," Early Settlers,

Historical Sketches, and Field Trips. The section on Field Trips reflects considerable historic value. Of particular interest are the excellent articles authored by Gladys Steorts. Attention should be directed to one misstatement of historical fact which the authors may wish to correct in subsequent revisions of their book. On page 106 reference is made to the monument denoting the place "where the first wagon train of Mormon Pioneers came through the pass, enroute to the San Bernardino Valley in 1851." The "first wagon train of Mormon Pioneers came through the pass" in the late fall of 1849, under the leadership of Jefferson Hunt. There were seven wagons—their occupants all Mormons—remaining with him from an original 107, the others having defected in an attempt to accomplish a more direct westerly route to the goldfields of California. (Some 27 wagons among this defecting group became trapped in what is now known as Death Valley.) Incidentally, referring to the book's foot-note citation, Mr. Beattie does *not* say the 1851 train was the first wagon train of Mormon pioneers to cross Cajon Pass into San Bernardino. Not to my knowledge, certainly; and, if he does, he is in error.

MOODY, RALPH

Old Trails West, The. (1963). New York: Thomas Y. Crowell Company. XIV plus 318 pp. Maps. Illus. End paper trail maps. 6¼ x 9¼.

Considered are the Gila Trail, El Camino Real, Old Spanish Trail, Santa Fe Trail, Big Medicine Trail, Oregon Trail, and the California Trail. Of immediate Southern California desert interest are the Gila and Old Spanish Trails. The Gila Trail (pp. 12-122) crossed the Colorado River near the present site of Yuma, dipped south into old Mexico to circumvent the Algodones sand dunes, re-entered California approximately where Calexico is now located, crossed the difficult desert route to Carrizo Creek, followed up the sandy washes of Carrizo Corridor past Vallecito, Box Canyon, and on to Warner's Ranch. Over this trail passed Kearny and the Army of the West, Cooke and the Mormon Battalion, the hordes of California gold seekers, the Butterfield stages.

The Old Spanish Trail dropped southwest from Salt Lake, crossed the Mojave Desert, climbed over Cajon Pass and into Los Angeles via San Bernardino. The route was subsequently referred to as The Mormon Road (or Trail).

MOORE, BILL

Mojave Desert Cut-off. 1954. March issue of *Westways.* Illus.

This article explains the advantages that flow from the 100-mile cut-off road from Amboy, on Highway 66, through Twentynine Palms and on to Interstate 10.

MOREAU, W. T.

Death Valley—Land of Strange Contrasts. 1933. February issue of *National Motorist.*

This article tells about Death Valley and the ghost cities of Greenwater and Rhyolite (Nevada).

MORGAN, DALE L.

Jedediah Smith and the Opening of the West. (1953). Indianapolis: Bobbs-Merrill. 458 pp. 20 illus. 6¼ x 8¾.

"Jedediah Smith was the first to go from Missouri overland to California, first to cross the length of Utah and Nevada, first to travel by land up through California and Oregon, first to cross the Sierra Nevada. This is a biography that measures up to its subject." (From Glen Dawson.)

Note: Dale Morgan and Carl I. Wheat collaborated to produce for the California Historical Society, in 1954, the elaborate Smith item entitled *Jedediah Smith and His Maps of the American West.*

MORHARDT, 'AIM

Western Men and Desert Gold. (See listing under Early, Lee.)

MORRIS, HENRY CURTIS

Desert Gold and Total Prospecting. 1955. Washington: Privately published. 60 pp. 20 illus. 7 x 10¼.

This is a book of general desert interest, much of it relating to the Nevada desert area. Pp. 19-22 tell of Death Valley Scotty. The author gives an early-day account of desert localities, but fails to record much basic informational material relating to incidents and activities that must surely have occupied his attention while he was there. (See also, *Mining West at Turn of Century*, 1962, by same author.)

MORRISON, LORRIN L.

Warner—The Man and the Ranch. 1962. Los Angeles: Lorrin L. Morrison. 87 pp. 25 photographic reproductions; maps; illustrations. Wrappers.

In his Preface Mr. Morrison explains that his book purposely omits mention "of the complicated transactions . . . of titles of the ranch, the Hot Springs and the surrounding area. . . . The history of the man and the ranch is what we have been advised is wanted."

Students of Colorado Desert history cannot escape recognition of the impact exerted by Warner and his famous ranch upon the lives of literally thousands of people who crossed the desert on foot, on mule or horse back, in wagons, or as passengers on the Butterfield overland stages. To a considerable extent they exercised a compulsive influence upon the political and economic development of our State. They profoundly affected our transportation frontiers, gave impetus to our agricultural potential, stimulated industry, contributed to a better social understanding among divergent groups, buttressed military operations.

The Morrison book assembles pertinent information relating to Warner and his ranch in a fast-moving sequence of men and events. The researched material is well documented by direct quotations from Warner's own *Reminiscences*, telling of his early trapping experiences with Ewing Young (they first crossed the Colorado Desert in the fall of 1831); by extracts from the *Diary* of W. H. Emory; by an account of the historic Pauma Massacre, from Millard F. Hudson's article in the *Historical Society of Southern California Annual* of 1906; and by several extracts from Warner's own newspaper, the *Southern Vineyard*. Two additional chapters are included, one detailing the operation of the Butterfield Stages; the other supplying a résumé of the Civil War activities in California. In both these historic events the Ranch of Warner played an important role and performed conspicuous service.

MORROW, HONORE

Beyond the Blue Sierra. 1932. New York: William Morrow & Co. 341 pp. 5½ x 8¼.
This is an historical novel, well written, of the De Anza expedition.

MORTON, C. V.

Botany. (See listing under Coville, F. V.)

MOTT, ORRA ANNA

History of Imperial Valley, The. 1922. Berkeley: Univ. of Calif. 145 pp. (From "California Local History. A Centennial Bibliography.")

MOWRY, SYLVESTER

Report On His March In 1855 From Salt Lake City To Fort Tejon (Edited by Bailey, L. R.). 1965. Pp. 329-346 in the Winter issue of *Arizona and the West*.
Mowry, with a detachment "consisting of raw dragoon recruits" left Salt Lake for Fort Tejon, California, in July of 1855. They followed the Spanish Trail route over the Mojave Desert, past Stump Springs, Resting Springs, the Pure Water Spring on the Amargosa, Bitter Springs, and over Cajon Pass to San Bernardino. The Cajon Pass crossing was necessitated by a shortage of supplies, making it necessary for the final leg of their march to Fort Tejon to be made via Los Angeles. The march from Salt Lake to the Tejon required fifty-four days, thirty-seven of which were occupied in actual trail marching.

MUNK, J. A.

Southwest Sketches. 1920. New York: G. P. Putnam's Sons. 311 pp. 133 pls. 6¼ x 9¼.
The book is almost exclusively of Arizona. However, chs. 10, 11 and 12 (pp. 275-311) are of California interest, with chs. 10 and 11 having a direct bearing upon our local deserts. Ch. 10—"Big Irrigation Projects"—is confined to the Salton Sea area; ch. 11—"Southwest Climate"—has reference to climatic conditions in the Colorado Desert.

MUNZ, PHILIP A.

California Desert Wildflowers. 1962. Berkeley: University of California Press. 122 pp. 96 color photographs. 172 line drawings. 2 maps. Wrappers.
This is one of those indispensible desert reference books—the kind one carries in

his car or in his pocket every time he goes out on the desert. A sensible desert-book lover will, of necessity, equip himself with two copies—one for his library, another for his work copy.

Elsewhere in this Bibliography I have emphasized the advantage of *color* in any book on flowers, or cacti, or birds. Some of us are color-conscious, and must rely upon it in attempting identification. The 96 color plates are of inestimable assistance to novices like myself. Time upon time I have proven its efficacy in the field. Moreover, it does not inhibit my already limited botanical knowledge by recourse to a jargon of meaningless words and technical phrases. It articulates in infinite detail a minute description of every wildflower listed; and the author's diction is understandable to the lay reader.

MURBARGER, NELL

Ghosts of the Glory Trail. 1956. Palm Desert, California: Desert Magazine Press. XI, 291 pp. 55 photographic illustrations. 8 maps. 6¼ x 9¼. Reprinted by Westernlore Press.

I was forced to draw upon exiguous California desert material (pp. 274-277 only) in the effort to justify the inclusion of this book in our Bibliography. Even so, if Nell Murbarger had not once mentioned a California desert area, I would yet have devised pretext for her book's listing in our present volume.

Ghosts of the Glory Trail is a magnificent contribution to desert literature, and it comes superbly written. In my knowledge there is no other book that describes so adequately and yet so charmingly the subject of desert ghost towns. The author chooses Nevada and Utah as her locale; the California reference is in the nature of a descriptive "Ghosttown Directory" to some seventeen of our State's ghost towns. The introductory chapter, "Ghost Country," is a classic in desert literature. In the reading of it one is privileged to participate vicariously with Miss Murbarger in glimpsing the Shekinah glory of her ghost town trail.

In 1958, Miss Murbarger's book—"Sovereigns of the Sage"—came off the press. This book, as its title page informs us, presents "true stories of people and places in the great sage brush kingdom of the Western United States." A remarkable book, this; but to Nevada goes the privilege of supplying the locale.

Ghost Towns of Inyo, The. 1964. *Westerners, The* (Los Angeles Corral) *Brand Book* No. 11. 18 pp. Line drawing by Don Perceval. 4 photographs (one-excessively rare—of the long vanished ghost town of Lookout).

This article, by that incomparable authority on ghost towns (*Ghosts of the Glory Trail, Sovereigns of the Sage, Ghosts of the Adobe Walls*), employs her usual captivating style in this article appearing in Editor Russ Leadabrand's desert *Brand Book*. Included are the ghost towns—past or still lingering—of San Carlos, Bend City, Chrysopolis, Owensville, Ida, Kearsarge City, Cerro Gordo, Panamint City, Ballarat, Lookout, Greenwater, Leadfield, Skidoo, Tramway, and—of course—"the sorry little ghost" of Manzanar, utilized as a War Relocation Center for Japanese residents of California.

MURNANE, LEONARD F.

101 Adventures of Panamint Pete. N.d. Randsburg: Randsburg Times. 102 pp. 5½ x 7⅝. Words "First Edition" appear on title page.

These short sketches will afford interesting reading; and that, I presume, is their avowed purpose.

MURPHY, THOMAS D.

On Sunset Highways. 1915. Boston: The Page Co. 380 pp. Fldg. road map of California. 16 colored pls. and 40 duogravures.

Ch. 7, pp. 133-158, furnishes an account of the Imperial Valley and the San Diego back country that will prove worth-while reading. And remember, as you read, that the book was written in 1915; not in 1969.

MURRAY, TOM G.

Death Valley Scotty. 1961. 36 pp. Unnumbered. Decorative (photographs) wrappers. 9 x 12.

This is a book of photographs—over 30 of them—telling much of the story of the inimitable Scotty. A beautiful book, and one certain to enhance a Death Valley collection.

MYRICK, DAVID F.

Railroads of Nevada and Eastern California (Vols. 1 and 2). 1962-63. Berkeley: Howell-North Books. Vol. 1 considers the Northern Roads; Vol. 2 the Southern. Fldg. pocket map of railroads in Vol. 1. XVI plus 453 pp. in Vol. 1; XIII plus 480 pp. in Vol. 2. A proliferation of photographs—hundreds of them—in each volume. Each vol. 8¾ x 11¼.

This superb work is a classic in the literature of our western deserts. Primarily, it is the definitive account of western railroads—43 of them in Northern Nevada, 26 in Southern Nevada. Several of these roads penetrated our Southern California deserts. These include the Carson & Colorado, extending south from Benton to Keeler along the east side of Owens Valley; and the Nevada and California, continuing to Mojave from Owenyo. Pages 166-209, Vol. 1, are abundant in their mention of Mojave Desert material. In Vol. 1 there is reference to the Bodie & Benton Railway, extending from Bodie to Mono Mills, skirting a portion of the east side of Mono Lake (pp. 298-313). Of some interest is Mr. Myrick's mention of the enigmatic Owens River Valley Electric that was supposed to have covered the 4-mile rail gap between Bishop and Laws (pp. 313-315).

Vol. 2 is even more prolific in its contribution to Southern California desert history. Nor should we deny passing mention to the western desert portion of bordering Nevada, whose rail communication presents an historic appeal on a par with that of our California desert roads. Of particular interest in this connection are the Las Vegas and Tonopah, Bullfrog-Goldfield, Lida Valley, Tonopah and Tidewater, Tecopa and Greenwater. Ubehebe and Greenwater connote a California appeal because of their Death Valley association. This is also true of the Death Valley Railroad (pp. 608-621). Even more directly applicable to our Southern California deserts are the well-written chapters on the Atlantic & Pacific Railroad, the Randsburg Railway, the Trona Railway, the historic Monorail (Epsom Salts Railroad), the Calico Railroad, the Borate & Daggett Railroad, the Ludlow and Southern Railway, and the Amboy-Saltus. Pages 762-840 supply a definitive history of these roads.

Valuable as are these books in their relation to the railroad operations in Nevada and California, their usefulness as authoritative reference sources embraces a much broader scope. Wherever these rails were laid, there also could be found the towns and villages of yesterday. The inevitable sequence of events followed a familiar pattern. First the discoveries of gold or silver or copper; then the mushrooming of mining towns, with their urgent need for a railroad. Disintegration followed an almost identical pattern: failure of the mines, an eroding of towns, the ultimate abandonment of the rail lines.

Fortunately, not all the mines closed down—at least not before other sustaining industries moved in. Some of the early towns continued to flourish and even develop into sizeable cities. A few railroads continued to operate. All too often, however, the failure of one was the failure of all three—the mines, the towns, and the railroads.

Although incidental to his central theme, Mr. Myrick does not neglect the accentuation of this early regional history of Nevada and California. His books hold an irresistible appeal to the student of desert lore as well as those whose interest is centered exclusively in the history of railroads.

The Myrick books house a remarkable collection of photographs—scarce and early photographs of long-vanished trains and towns and mining operations.

NADEAU, REMI A.

City Makers. 1948. Garden City, New York: Doubleday & Company, Inc. XIII, 270 pp. 5½ x 6¼. End-paper maps. Words "First Edition" appear under copyright notice. Reprinted in 1965.

This book may be regarded as one of the best accounts concerning the development of Los Angeles from a dreamy little Mexican Pueblo to the nation's third largest city. Frequent desert references appear, particularly, in ch. 3—"Birth of the Inyo Trade" (pp. 31-43); ch. 8—"Battle of Cerro Gordo" (pp. 104-120); ch. 10—"The Bandidos" (pp. 139-158); and ch. 11—"Silver In the Panamints" (pp. 159-173). Among the noteworthy sections in this book are those relating to the Chinese Massacre, the advent of the Southern Pacific, the birth of San Fernando, and the exceptionally fine account of Vasquez and Chavez. The 1965 reprint is strengthened by the inclusion of numerous interesting photographs.

Ghost Towns and Mining Camps of California. (1965). Los Angeles: The Ward Ritchie Press. 278 pp.; end paper photographs. 6⅜ x 9¼.

Much of the material in this book appeared in the author's *Ghost Towns.* Nadeau failed to up-date his "Points of Interest" summation at the conclusion of each chapter. The end result is misleading. Many of the old ghost towns—as they exist today—are not as he describes them in his new book. He should have inserted dates to identify his descriptions. A good item, notwithstanding. Numerous early photographs contribute definite value to it. Pp. 221-269 relate to our Southern California desert area.

Ghost Towns of California. (1954.) Los Angeles: *Fortnight Magazine.* 68 pp., 8½ x 11. Wrappers.

Pp. 47-68 supply material on the Kern River Camps, Cerro Gordo, Panamint, Mammoth, Bodie, Calico, Julian, Randsburg and Death Valley.

King of the Desert Freighters. 1964. *Westerners, The* (Los Angeles Corral) *Brand Book* No. 11. 26 pp. Line drawing by Don Perceval. 7 photographs.

In this article Nadeau relates the story and recounts the experiences of his great, great grandfather (Remi Nadeau) who "from 1869 to early 1882, . . . was the leading wagon freighter of Southern California, and dominated the cargo traffic to the desert mining camps of Eastern California."

Water Seekers, The. 1950. Garden City, New York: Doubleday & Company, Inc. 309 pp. 2-page map. 6 end-paper photographs. 5⅝ x 8⅜. Words "First Edition" appear under copyright notice.

The book is sectionalized under two major divisions, Part 1 covering the Owens Valley aqueduct episode; Part 2 the Colorado River break in 1905-06, and the ultimate construction of the Hoover Dam together with the accomplishment of the huge reclamation project in Imperial Valley. Pp. 115-124, in Part 1, present a graphic account of the tragic San Francisquito Dam disaster. Nadeau's book encourages reading, not alone for purposes of research, but also because of the lingering pleasure that derives from it. One cannot read the book without experiencing fine entertainment; one cannot emerge *from* that reading without having achieved a surer understanding of the subject to which the author has so successfully applied his effort.

NEIHARDT, JOHN G.

Splendid Wayfaring, The. 1920. New York: The Macmillan Company. 290 pp. 24 pls. 5¼ x 7¾.

This is one of that distinguished quartet of books relating to the exploits of Jedediah Smith, the other three being Dale's account of the *Ashley-Smith Explorations,* the Sullivan item—*Travels of Jedediah Smith,* and Morgan's *Jedediah Smith and the Opening of the West. Splendid Wayfaring* is the most readable of the four; however, it touches only briefly upon the Mojave Desert crossing. Of further interest is the Sullivan book—*Jedediah Smith, Trader & Trailbreaker.*

NEWHALL, NANCY (Story); ADAMS, ANSEL (Photos); KIRK, RUTH (Guide); HAMLIN, EDITH (Maps)

Death Valley. 1954. San Francisco: 5 Associates, Inc. 56 pp. 9 x 12. End-paper maps of Death Valley.

Of first importance are the remarkably fine photographs by Ansel Adams. There are 34 of these, mostly full-page, 10 of them in color. The 9-page descriptive and historical text by Nancy Newhall is about as accurate and well-written as any I have read. The Guide section, by Ruth Kirk, supplies desert travel advice, describes points of interest, discusses flora and fauna. Most of this material appeared first in the October 1953 issue of *Arizona Highways*.

NIBLEY, PRESTON

Pioneer Stories. 1940. Salt Lake: Deseret New Press. The 4th printing shows 328 pp. 5½ x 7⅞.

The chapter entitled—"Indian Revenge and A Brother's Devotion," by Anthony W. Ivins, pp. 181-191 reprints the article by the same name appearing in *Improvement Era* for May 1916, Vol. XIX, No. 7. (See listing in this Bibliography under Ivins, Anthony W.)

NORDHOFF, F. W.

Fruit of the Earth. (1955.) New York: Vantage Press. 159 pp. 5⅝ x 8¾.

This is a book of short sketches, beautifully done, of desert and mountain areas. The author is a brother of Charles B. Nordhoff, co-author of the Bounty trilogy; son of Walter Nordhoff, author of *Journey of the Flame*; grandson of Charles Nordhoff, writer on early California. Contained in this book are his delightful little desert sketches—Desert Water Holes, Desert Oddity, Death Valley Oddity, Death Valley Ghost, The Desert, Desert Interlude, Desert Vacation, Prospector's Luck and Palm Springs—1912.

NORRIS, FRANK

McTeague, A Story of San Francisco. 1899. Doubleday & McClure Co. 442 pp. 5 x 6¼. A Zamorano 80 item. There have been many reprint editions of this work.

This book, a novel, ably depicts early San Francisco and—as though motivated by some Fabian influence—determines to conclude its plot in a macabre Death Valley setting. Why this melodramatic touch to an otherwise powerful novel, I have been unable to determine. Certainly this derelict ending lends no adornment to the plot—either cultural or historical.

Merely as divertive comment, I may add that the offensive (?) wording on p. 106 was considerably modified in later issues—even of the first edition.

NOYES, ALFRED

Beyond the Desert. (1920.) New York: Frederick A. Stokes. 85 pp. 5¼ x 7⅝.
This is a short, interesting story; its plot laid in Death Valley.

NUSBAUMER, LOUIS

Diary. (See listing under Bruff, J. Goldsborough—*Gold-Rush;* also, under Long, Dr. Margaret—*The Shadow of the Arrow*, Revised Ed.; and Koenig, George—*Valley of Salt*—*Memories of Wine*.)

Nusbaumer was one of the Death Valley pioneers of 1849, and his recently published *Diary* imparts historical information of the utmost importance.

OBERTEUFFER, ORA L.

This Is My Desert Song. 1939. March issue of *Desert.* Illus.

Life at Trona, the town on Searles Dry Lake (the "Salt Lake" of the Jayhawkers), is ably commented upon by the author who—for many years—was a resident of the place. The Trona of today is far different from the quiet, peaceful little company-owned village Mrs. Oberteuffer writes about.

O'DELL, SCOTT

Country of the Sun. Southern California: An Informal History and Guide. (1957.) New York: Thomas Y. Crowell Company. VIII, 310 pp. Decorative end papers. 5½ x 8¼.

The author successfully manages to weave many of Southern California's conspicuous historical incidents and people into his narrative. In the doing of it he employs a unique arrangement. He endeavors to sectionalize his account under the nine southern counties. Almost every county—and particularly Inyo, San Bernardino, Riverside, Imperial and San Diego—produces its quota of desert history: the Death Valley Party, the Mormon Battalion, Kearny and San Pasqual, and the notable desert crossings.

At the conclusion of each chapter the author lists "Places To Go," "Fiestas, Festivals, and Events," and "Books To Read." This final category could better have been omitted entirely, as it suggests a pitifully restricted reference that is not actually reflected by the text. Perhaps most of the few books he lists are worth noting (I say "perhaps"), but certainly many of the better ones are *not* listed. This is unfortunate. As an example, at the conclusion of his Orange County chapter he states, "There are lots of Monographs, but only one book of interest. . . ." etc. It is suggested Mr. O'Dell try Terry Stephenson, or J. E. Pleasants, or Don Meadows, as illustrative of some of the really fine literature available on Orange County. Also, he might dip into Father Crespi's diary for some truly virgin material. Desertwise, Mr. O'Dell omits reference to Manly, James, the Jaeger books, Van Dyke, Glasscock, Lee, Long, Belden, Weight, Coolidge, Henderson, Krutch, Wilson, Wynn, and numerous others whose books represent a vital contribution to the areas covered.

ODENS, PETER

Drama In the Sun (Tales From the Imperial Valley). 1965. Calexico, California. 64 pp. Line drawings. 16 photographs. Wrappers.

Chapters tell of the Cargo Muchacho Mines, the Mormon Battalion, the Carrizo Corridor, a series of sketches "taken from an article written by Elizabeth Harris" in the publication *The Valley Imperial* (see listing in this Bibliography), and other desert tales.

Outlaws, Heroes and Jokers of the Old Southwest. 1964. Yuma, Arizona: Southwest Printers. Pages unnumbered; 28 illus. Wrappers.

This is an entertaining little book, with its desert setting in the states of California, Nevada and Arizona. The brief California interest centers around Rice,

Blythe, Randsburg, and Temecula Valley. The short stories are just that—stories; disconnected, of no informative value, but possessing the faculty for good entertainment. The photographs are perhaps the most important feature of the book.

OERTLE, V. LEE

Salton Sea Shoreline Guide. 1964. Palm Desert, California: Desert-Southwest Publishing Co. 48 pp. 49 photographs. Map. Wrappers.

This thorough Guide should prove most helpful to one visiting the Salton Sea area, particularly for the first time. The Guide lists motels, camp grounds, trailer parks, marinas, water skiing areas, villages, miscellaneous informative data.

OLIN, GEORGE

Animals of the Southwest Deserts. 1954. Globe, Arizona: Southwestern Monuments Association. Popular Series, No. 8. Gila Pueblo. 112 pp. 6 x 9. Wrappers.

Mr. Olin's book is a reliable guide to desert animals, discussing—in order given—the range, habitat, and description of each. There are some 42 sectional headings, each section being illustrated by a sketch of the particular animal described. The illustrations are by Jerry C. Cannon.

OLIPHANT, J. ORIN (Edited by)

On the Arkansas Route To California. (See listing under Green, Robt. B.)

OLIVER, HARRY

Desert Rat Scrap Book. 1946. (And continuing.)

This originally-conceived five-page newspaper is the "only newspaper in America you can open in the wind;" and it sold for 10 cents—"only one measly thin dime." And, I may add, *well worth it.*

Desert Rough Cuts. A Haywire History of the Borego Desert. (1938). Los Angeles: The Ward Ritchie Press. 64 pp. 6½ x 9⅝.

"Pictures are by the author. Many of them woodcuts." Here is humor, *desert* humor, by that notorious perpetrator of desert tales—the Sage of Good Fort Oliver.

99 Days In the Desert with Sandy Walker. N.d. (1943?) Corona, California: Green Lantern Print Shop. 42 pp. End map. Wrappers.

This little book offers a compilation of articles from the author's newspaper column—"Desert Briefs."

Old Mirage Salesman, The. (1952.) Palm Springs: The Printery. 111 pp. 5¾ x 8¾. First printing 2000 copies; autographed edition.

The book is compiled by Oliver's daughters, Amy and Mary, from their father's newspaper—*The Desert Rat Scrap Book.* "Pictures are the work of the Old Mirage Salesman, many of them woodcuts." Says the title page, "A whimsical desert digest of refreshing nonsense heralding the life of the Southwest's foremost story-telling Desert Rat, Harry Oliver: Editor, Humorist, Historian, Publicist, Pioneer, Photographer, Prospector, Showman, Builder, Hermit and Secessionist."

O'NEAL, LULU RASMUSSEN

Peculiar Piece of Desert, A—The Story of California's Morongo Basin. 1957. Los Angeles: Westernlore Press. 208 pp. 17 photographs. End paper maps. 5½ x 8¼. Edition limited to 450 copies.

The value of a desert book is largely determined—first, by the importance that attaches to its subject matter; second, by the scope and significance of the source material it includes. *A Peculiar Piece of Desert* is our one definitive treatise on the increasingly popular High Desert country embracing the area in—and adjacent to —the Morongo and Yucca Valleys, Twentynine Palms, and the Joshua Tree National Monument. The material in this item is intelligently assembled, carefully documented, and entertainingly presented. Moreover, in the reading of it, there can intrude not the slightest doubt of its authenticity.

Mrs. O'Neal has done for the High Desert country precisely what Spears did for Death Valley, what James and Chase accomplished for the Colorado Desert, what Mrs. Wynn succeeded in doing for the Randsburg District and a portion of the Mojave. The extent of her research is prodigious. She goes back twenty-five thousand years in her relation of the area's development, brilliantly depicting the part the Indians played in this desert's fascinating history; she supplies a minute and detailed description of its individual communities and points of interest— Morongo, Yucca Valley, Joshua Tree, Twentynine Palms, the Dale mines, the Monument—even including the more important side trips from its central areas. Coupled with all this pertinent data, the book presents a scholarly discussion of the desert's geological features, its flora, fauna, and related subjects. Because of its content and the extremely small number of copies printed, this book—long out of print—is much sought after. A reprint is urgently needed. Fortunate indeed is the library that houses one of these valuable books.

ORMSBY, WATERMAN L.

Butterfield Overland Mail, The. 1952. San Marino: Huntington Library. 179 pp. End paper maps. Edited by Lyle H. Wright and Josephine M. Bynum. The book has been reprinted.

Ormsby was the "only through passenger on the first *westbound* stage." Pp. 89-130 describe the route across the desert from Tucson to San Francisco. Pp. 104-113 contain specific California material. The date—September and October 1858.

There are three other contemporary narratives portraying the journey from San Francisco to St. Louis; but this book does not include them. Ormsby gives us the only east to west narrative over the 2700-mile route. (See listing under Lang, Walter B.)

OVERHOLT, ALMA

Death Valley's Road to Nowhere. 1930. July issue of *World's Work.* Illus.

This is a knowledgeable account of the construction, by H. W. Eichbaum, of an early toll road into Death Valley.

PACIFIC COAST BORAX COMPANY

High Spots of "Death Valley Days." 1939. 65 pp. Wrappers. Photograph of the "Old Ranger."

This interesting little item—Vol. I No. I—contains six stories, ostensibly produced as plays for the radio script "Death Valley Days." Included are: Pearl of Great Price; Codfish McPherson; Three Little Hills of Gold; Rusty and the Lone Sheep; The Winged Mail; The Bell of San Gabriel. To satisfy the curious-minded as to exactly what a Radio Script looks like, one is actually produced in this book— "The Desert Baby" date—May 19, 1939; time—9:30 P.M.

20-Mule Team, The—and a Sketch of Its Famous Driver: Borax Bill. N.d. 16 pp. (Unnumbered). 2 photographs—1 of Borax Bill, the other (double page) of a 20-mule team. Wrappers.

This item (probably published during the early 1900s) is impressively written and supplies carefully assembled information concerning the 20-mule Borax Teams, with particular attention to the mules, the wagons, the jerk-line, and the driver.

PACIFIC RAILROAD SURVEYS

Reports of Explorations and Surveys To Ascertain the Most Practicable and Economical Route For a Railroad From the Mississippi River To the Pacific Ocean. 1856-57. Washington: Beverly Tucker, Printer. Senate Ex. Doc. No. 78, 33. Congress 2nd Session. 9½ x 11⅞.

The unwieldy title, as here shown, will explain why this massive and voluminous series of reports are commonly referred to as "The Pacific Railroad Surveys." There are, paradoxically, twelve *volumes* in the set, but actually thirteen *books*. The two parts of Vol. XII are so extensive that a thirteenth book was added to house part two. The entire *Report* is addressed to Mr. Jefferson Davis, then Secretary of War. Among these thirteen books are three that relate in substantial part to our Southern California desert areas—Vols. III, V, and VII; and by far the most important of the three, desertwise, is Vol. V.

Vol. V: Lt. R. S. Williamson was in charge of the survey described in Vol. V. This covered the territory west of the lower Colorado to the Pacific Ocean. Associated with Williamson was the twenty-eight-year-old scientist—Dr. William Phipps Blake—destined to be among the most important, and perhaps *the* most important, member of the entire survey team. With the possible exception of Lt. Whipple (Vol. III), Dr. Blake is the man who left us the most detailed, and unquestionably the most interesting, record of the entire survey. Vol. V has much to tell concerning Tejon Pass, the Great Basin, Mojave River, San Fernando Pass, the Cajon, San Gorgonio Pass, Warner's Pass, the Carrizo Corridor, Warner's Valley, Camp Yuma, and the Colorado Desert generally. In Vol. V are 26 colored lithographs, including the very early one of Los Angeles. Elsewhere it is noted that Williamson's group was the first surveying party to prove that the Salton Sea is below tide-level.

Vol. III: Of California desert interest are chapters 14, 15 and 16 (pp. 112-136), all relating to the Mojave Desert. These are a part of the Lt. Whipple report; but Dr. Blake also adds to this interest by his comments on the geology of the region.

Vol. VII: Two members of the survey group make important contributions to this book—Dr. Thomas Antisell in his Geological Report of the Mojave River Valley and of the district from San Diego to Fort Yuma; Chas. H. Poole on the route from San Diego to Ft. Yuma. (See listings under Antisell, Thomas; Blake, W. P.; Poole, Charles H.; Whipple, A. W.; Williamson, R. S.)

PAINE, RALPH D.

Greater America, The. 1907. N.Y.: Outing Publishing Company. 327 pp. 52 illus. 5¾ x 8½.

This is a book of interesting sketches of relatively unimportant incidents occurring in widely scattered localities throughout our western states. Ch. 18—"Where Ranch and City Meet," pp. 244-262, supplies material on early Los Angeles and particularly Lucky Baldwin's Santa Anita Ranch. Chs. 19 and 20—"The Gold Camps of the Desert," pp. 263-285, and "On the Road To Bullfrog," pp. 286-297, provide intimate descriptions of events in the early Nevada gold towns—Goldfield, Tonopah, and Bullfrog. Ch. 21—"The Men of the Untamed Desert," pp. 298-320, takes the reader all the way into Death Valley. Some early and entertaining experiences are narrated concerning this desert and its most famous character—Death Valley Scotty. Like so many of our travel writers, the author gives us a plethora of irrelevant incidents; occasionally neglects important material concerning places and events which he must surely have observed in that early day.

PALMER, T. S.

Chronology of the Death Valley Region in California, 1849-1949. An Index of the Events, Persons and Publications Connected With Its History. 1952. Washington: Byron S. Adams, Printer. 25 pp. 6 x 8¾. Wrappers.

This items stands alone in its field, and supplies a type of information and reference that is indispensable to any well-balanced collection of desert material. The work consists, first, of a three-page introduction; second, the Chronology itself, occupying eight pages of the text and classifying chronologically an approximate 200 significant events relating to Death Valley; third, a subject classification of Death Valley reference material (pp. 13-16); and, fourth, an alphabetical topic index (pp. 17-25) listing, by name and date, nearly 300 persons and events identified with Death Valley history. The late Dr. Palmer, one of the country's leading authorities on Death Valley, was a member of the Death Valley Expedition in 1891; revisited it in 1938, after a lapse of 47 years. Dr. Palmer mentions 1863 as the year the name "Death Valley" first appeared in published book form (Hittell's *Resources of California.)*

Place Names of the Death Valley Region in California and Nevada. 1948. 80 pp. 6 x 9. Wrappers.

Dr. Palmer, one of the members of the original Death Valley Expedition of

1891, edits a book that ranks high on the list of basic items having to do with Death Valley. It is reported that only 200 of these books were printed, of which number 50 copies were offered for sale.

PALMER, GEN. WM. J.

Report of Surveys Across the Continent in 1867-'68 on the Thirty-fifth and Thirty-second Parallels for a Route Extending the Kansas Pacific Railway to the Pacific Ocean at San Francisco and San Diego. 1869. Philadelphia: W. B. Schelheimer (Printer). 250 pp. 2 large fldg. maps of the route surveys. 6 x 9.

Mojave Desert mention—pp. 38-40, 49, 102-05, 145-47; 174-75, 244 and 246; Morongo and High Desert mention—pp. 43-44; 48, 51, 68-69, 81-82, 88-89, 105, 116, 133, 152-53, 164, 245, 248. P. 242 lists population of Indian tribes over the United States as of April 1867. Included are tables of elevation, distance, and grades on pp. 244-250. Pp. 196-236 contain reports by Dr. C. C. Parry, Geologist and Naturalist for the Survey. Gen. Palmer's *Report* describes the surveyed territory with reference to its timber, coal, water, climate, and its agricultural, mineral and manufacturing resources. In Dr. Parry's account, reference is made (pp. 232-236) to the probable passage of the Grand Canyon by James White—thus adding fuel to the controversial subject of who was the first man to travel the full length of the Grand Canyon. The James White *Narrative* is printed in full. Mr. Francis P. Farquhar, in his Bibliography of books of the Colorado River and the Grand Canyon (Glen Dawson—1953), mentions that the name "Grand Canyon" probably makes its first appearance on the Palmer map.

Under Gen. Palmer's supervision, 100 men—besides the military escort, teamsters, and so on—participated in this important railway survey that opened vast areas of the West to the public knowledge. For the present-day reader this *Report* assumes considerable significance, and for reasons not contemplated by its author. Insofar as I have been able to determine, it constitutes the first *printed* account of the High Desert region where now flourish the attractive communities of Twentynine Palms, Joshua Tree, Yucca Valley, and Morongo Village. It must be noted that the Washington Survey notes of 1855 and the Green Survey notes of 1856 were not reduced to printed form. (Pp. 4, 39-40, 46, 47, 131, 145, 174-75.)

In his description of the territory covered by the Survey, Gen. Palmer clearly identifies Bristol Dry Lake (Perry Basin), Amboy Crater (Perry Crater), and Pisgah Crater (p. 39-40). Says Palmer, in further describing his route, "A reconnoissance was made by myself from the Crater, in Perry Basin, about 80 miles west of the Colorado crossing southwestward to San Bernardino. . . . The outlet from Perry Basin is by 'San Diego Pass', a smooth pass of long and uniform grade, whose entrance is 10 miles nearly due southwest, from the Crater . . . the line runs west and south, through 'Lucky Gap', for 17 miles to the summit of the Bullion Range. . . . Thence it descends 10 miles by a uniform slope to the Morongo Basin."

His so-called "San Diego Pass" is not the Pass (Sheephole Pass) presently utilized by the highway extending from Twentynine Palms to Amboy, but is—in all probability—the old Bagdad Pass route. If so, then Palmer would have come out in the vicinity of present-day Twentynine Palms. He assigns no name, other than

"Morongo Basin," to this now popular desert area; neither does he make direct mention of the Oasis of Mara, which he must surely have seen and perhaps visited, although I choose to believe he inferentially alludes to it (p. 105). The old Chuck Warren Ranch (Covington) location in the Morongo Valley is clearly identified in his *Report*. So, likewise, are Morongo Pass and Morongo Canyon, to which he specifically refers by name.

Another noteworthy feature distinguishes this important item. Death Valley receives copious mention throughout the text (p. 32, 34, 47, 131, 228) with a nonchalant disregard for the fact that the *Report* is one of the very earliest book references to this desert area and one of the first to designate it by name—Death Valley.

My personal copy of the Palmer book is rather unusual. It is bound in three-quarters maroon leather; bears the handwritten signature and notation of "Wm. J. Palmer—Glen Eyrie library 1902." Two personal letters from Fr. W. Cragen addressed to the General are pasted in.

PALOMARES, DON JOSE FRANCISCO

Memoirs. 1955. Los Angeles: Glen Dawson. 205 copies printed and bound by George Yamada. Drawings by Janice Pettee. End sheet maps from Emory's *Notes of a Military Reconnoissance* (1848). Full-page color pl. of Los Angeles in 1857. 8 unnumbered and 69 numbered pp. 5 x 7½.

The *Memoirs* were translated from the manuscript in the Bancroft Library by Thomas Workman Temple II. Palomares was born in Santa Barbara in 1808. His account is of peculiar historic appeal when we consider that it reflects, in its recounting of incidents and in its description of life in those early days, the viewpoint of a native Californian. Pertinent to the subject of our desert Bibliography is the author's version of the Battle of San Pasqual, between Kearny's Dragoons and Pico's Californians. Presumably, Palomares was a participant in this battle. Several narratives are left us by those engaged on the American side; here, then, is a lively account by a member of the native opposition force.

The author embellishes his narrative by the inclusion of passages dealing with the treatment accorded Indian horse thieves; with the method of training native cattle to lead obstreperous herd animals; of campaigns against the Americanos; and of the American burial of their dead on "El Morrow" (Dead Man's Island). The book is most attractively done; and its content—while gruesome in parts— guarantees sustained reading interest.

PANCOAST, CHARLES EDWARD (Edited by Hannum, Anna P.)

Quaker Forty-niner, A. 1930. Philadelphia: University of Pennsylvania Press. XV, 402 pp. 14 illus. 6 x 9¼. End paper maps. The book has been reprinted.

The Pancoast book is one of the best of our overland diaries. Although specific mention of the Colorado Desert crossing is brief (pp. 258-267), the entire narrative is directly associated with the great overland trek of 1849. Pancoast ventures into the exigencies of his journey with an approach that is at once enthusiastic and sympathetic. He meets all types and manners of people—from Abraham Lincoln to renegade squatters and degenerate Indians. In the course of his nine months' journey from Fort Leavenworth to the mines he saw it all and was, himself, a conspicuous part of it all. Says Mr. John Bach McMaster, in his expressive Foreword—"Narratives such as this of Mr. Pancoast, records of the first men on the spot, are source material for the social history of our country. It is from such as these that we come to know just what happened at the very beginning." Of all the many narratives written of that memorable overland surge during those epochal years of 1849 and 1850, the Pancoast stands alone in the distinctive character of its point of view, and in the energetic manner employed by the author in depicting people and events.

PARCHER, MARIE LOUISE and WILL C.

Dry Ditches. 1934. Bishop, California: by "The Parchers." 41 pp. Line drawings by B. G. Purdy. Foreword by W. A. Chalfant. 5⅜ x 8⅛.

The book, as its title suggests, was written after Los Angeles completed the aqueduct that caused much of the beautiful Owens Valley to revert to the barrenness of desolation. Bill Chalfant was implicit in his resentment against Los Angeles—"an ambitious city." In his *The Story of Inyo*, Chalfant writes: "Neither the completion of the aqueduct, the passage of time, nor the benefits, along with injuries, that have come to Owens Valley give reason for changing the statement that the diversion of Owens River water from appurtenant lands to be used on tracts two hundred miles distant, in a different water shed, was won through perversion of the intent of the Reclamation Act. In phrasing more accurately descriptive than elegant, 'the government held Owens Valley while Los Angeles skinned it.' "

In the revised edition of this same book, Chalfant expresses even more poignantly the rather pitiful predicament of the Owens Valley people: "This was the home of their hearts; the land and people they understood and loved. The mere payment of so much per acre or so much per lot, and of the cost of the boards and nails and paint in their dwellings, did not compensate for what they surrendered."

It was in this setting that Mr. and Mrs. Parcher wrote their tragically appealing book. It is a literary gem, "written"—as Chalfant words it in his Foreword, "from the heart."

PARKER, HORACE

Anza Borrego Desert Guide Book. 1957. Palm Desert, California: Desert Magazine Press. 2 fldg. maps by Jack P. Welch. 108 pp. 60 illus. 6¼ x 9¼. 500 copies, numbered, in a special collectors' edition. Revised in 1963.

This attractive book, done in stiff, colorful boards with white plastic spiral, is one of the most attractive and conveniently arranged guide books ever to come off the press. The photographs are of extraordinary value, particularly because of their historical importance. Of special interest is the chapter "San Felipe-Vallecito," pp. 59-69. Here is a guide book that is distinctive in its style, attractive in its format, valuable for its photographs, and unique in its accomplished purpose of bringing the reader something entirely different—and altogether pleasing—in the way of guide books.

The recognized merit of the first edition, oddly enough, is definitely surpassed by the revision which can make claim to 31 more pages (and every page is a rewarding experience in *this* book), 28 more photographs, and an extended scope of subject coverage. Among the areas covered are the Anza-Borrego Desert, Coyote Canyon, Borrego Sink, Truckhaven Trail, Superstition Hills, Grapevine Canyon, San Felipe-Vallecito, Ocotillo, Bow Willow, Indians, Background History, Safety Hints, Accommodations and Travel Logs.

First Sixty Years of Guenthers Murrieta Hot Springs, The. 1961. Balboa Island, California: Paisano Press. 36 pp. Replete with photographic reproductions, mainly of the Guenthers and their inviting establishment. Decorative pictorial wrappers.

Dr. Parker has done a commendable job in his arrangement of photographs and descriptive comment. The booklet is a beautiful souvenir, not only of this lovely desert resort, but of the skill and enthusiasm of the family that created and maintained it. From the year 1797, when the first known white man visited the hot springs, the important events of historic interest are traced, by date, to 1902, when Fritz Guenther purchased Murrieta Hot Springs. From that year forward its development under the one family ownership and management is narrated and illustrated.

Historian's Search For Sackett's Lost Wells, An. 1964. *Westerners, The* (Los Angeles Corral) *Brand Book* No. 11. 8 pp. Line drawing by Don Perceval. Bibliography.

Dr. Parker, leading authority on the Anza-Borrego desert area, relates the background history of Sackett's Well and of his futile search to re-locate it. He gives some very sensible reasons why it may well be difficult to locate the actual wells, even though one were standing directly over them.

This article details a most remarkable piece of desert exploration. For thrills and adventure, coupled with modern research methods and intelligent know-how, I have not read of a more exciting hunt—not even for buried treasure—than Horace Parker's search for the lost Sackett. And locating what must surely be the precise area is not sufficient to placate this implacable desert explorer. "I think we'll find it," he writes, in concluding his article. I think so, too; and I hope I'm there with him when he does.

Historic Valley of Temecula, The: the Early Indians of Temecula. 1965. Balboa Island: Paisano Press. 34 pp. Illus. by Leverne Parker. Wrappers.

This attractive publication is the first in a series designated *Paisano Press Libritos*—or "little books"—each relating to a phase, or epoch, or particular subject having a bearing upon "the historic valley of Temecula." Logically, this first *Librito* tells of the early Indians of Temecula. With his characteristic thoroughness and enthusiasm, Dr. Parker has brought out an historically important document concerning a subject about which little has been written.

Historic Valley of Temecula, The: The Treaty of Temecula. 1967. Balboa Island, California: Paisano Press. 26 pp. 8 illus. Map. Reproduction of Treaty. Wrappers.

This publication is Librito No. Two of *The Historic Valley of Temecula*, companion in size and style to Librito No. One, covering the subject of Indians. The present item considers the unratified Treaty of Temecula drawn in 1852 between the Indians and the United States Government. Around this little-known incident, Dr. Parker constructs a narrative of singular historic appeal.

Temecula Massacre, The. 1963. *Westerners, The* (Los Angeles Corral) *Brand Book* No. 10. 17 pp. 4 photos.

The Editorial Capsule, introducing this notable desert item, reads: "Who ever heard of the Temecula Massacre? Our well-informed author tells us it was 'the bloodiest battle of the Mexican War in California'. The Temecula Massacre arose as an aftermath of the Pauma Massacre which, in turn, had its inception in the Battle of San Pascual. The historic significance of these three inter-related events supplies the nucleus of this study. Dr. Parker, author and historian, is our most knowledgeable source on the Anza-Borrego country; and he is intimately familiar with the region round about Temecula."

PARKER, RONALD B.

Recent Volcanism At Amboy Crater San Bernardino County California. 1963. San Francisco: California Division of Mines and Geology. Special Report 76. 21 pp. 13 photographs. Line drawings. Fldg. map of Amboy Crater in cover pocket.

A semi-technical description of Amboy Crater on Highway 66 in the Mojave Desert.

PARSONS, GEORGE W.

Thousand Mile Desert Trip and Story of the "Desert Sign Post," A. 1918. October n.p. 16 pp. 13 pls. 6¾ x 9½. Wrappers.

The author was instrumental in the posting of directional signs in Death Valley. This account, published in 1918 but referring to a 1901-02 expedition into Death Valley, is not altogether accurate in its detail, although sufficiently reliable in its overall narration. The photographic reproductions are of especial interest. (See Ryan, Claude F.—*Story of the "Desert Sign Post."*)

PATENCIO, CHIEF FRANCISCO (as told to Boynton, Margaret)

Stories and Legends of the Palm Springs Indians. 1943. Los Angeles: Times-Mirror. 132 pp. 5½ x 8.

This book is composed of sketches and legends of the Indians living in and around Palm Springs.

PATTERSON, ALLAN

Life At Greenwater. 1953. January issue of Harold and Lucile Weight's *Calico Print* magazine. 4 pp. 6 photographs.

The author was in the short-lived mining town of Greenwater during its heyday—but not as a miner. Mr. Patterson, a mining school graduate, was active as a surveyor and assayer in several of the Nevada boom towns. The reproduction of early Greenwater photographs stimulates added interest in the article.

PATTERSON, TOM

Riverman, Desertman. (See listing under Dekins, Camiel.)

PAXTON, JUNE LeMERT

Desert Peace and Other Poems. 1946. Corona, California: Green Lantern Print Shop. 70 pp. 4 pls. 4¾ x 7½. Reprinted in *Desert Moods* (1962).

Here are verses by the desert poet and philosopher of Yucca Valley, California. Although not formidable in quality or style, these poems may well be tolerated by the most discriminating reader. They come laden with the clean, fresh air of the desert; and they are certain to arouse no frictional response.

Drifts From the Desert. 1946. Yucca Valley, California: *The Desert Spotlight.* (October 1946 through the August 1948 issue.) Illus.

This listing is in the nature of a *Desert Spotlight* serial contribution, comprising two or three pages monthly, and telling of life in the High Desert country at Yucca Valley and surrounding areas. Charmingly and graciously Mrs. Paxton writes of the desert in which she has lived for so many years. Her articles are important—first, for their descriptive material; second, for their fine wholesome philosophy. Few writers there are who create quite the same feeling of close perceptive intimacy with the desert and its peculiar characteristics. To read Mrs. Paxton's articles is almost the equivalent of a personal visit in her desert home. (Note: A similar contribution by Mrs. Paxton appeared in *Ghost Town News* during the life of that publication at Knott's Berry Place.)

My Life On the Mojave. 1957. N.Y.: Vantage Press. 168 pp. 2 desert pls. 5½ x 8¼. The words "First Edition" appear over the copyright notice.

Mrs. Paxton's book is not a history of the desert. It tells little or nothing of the early pioneers, the historic landmarks, the initial effort that transmuted this lovely desert paradise from a dreaded, unknown wasteland into what is perhaps the most beautiful and climatically beneficial of all our California desert areas. The book is, as it purports to be, a saga of the author's long and colorful life in the High Desert country, along the road that leads to Twentynine Palms. The style of her writing is conversational; and, like her conversation, the substance of her writing is enriched by the fine, wholesome philosophy of the desert that has sustained her over the many eventful years of her personal contact with it. Her experiences, far out upon this quiet land, and the philosophic insulation the desert has provided against loneliness of mind and illness of body, are charmingly and intelligently presented on the pages of her book.

Perhaps no other book more effectually awakens, or stimulates, such an irresistable urge to go out upon the desert—and *live* there, and thrill to its indescribable beauty, and absorb something of its peace and contentment.

PEARSON, G. C. (Edited by Goodman, Jessie H.)

Overland in 1849. 1961. Los Angeles. Introduction and notes by John Bartlett Goodman III. 55 pp. Line drawings by Mr. Goodman. Fldg. map. 6¼ x 8¼.

This publication makes available the first reprinting of a portion of the Pearson letters from the file of the *San Jose Pioneer*. (In 1961 LeRoy and Ann Hafen reprinted "installment number 4"—corresponding to the Goodmans' chapter "The Salt Lake Trail"—in their *Supplement To the Journals of Forty-Niners*. See listing in this Bibliography.) Pearson, perhaps loosely associated with the so-called Gruwell-Derr Company, left Salt Lake a few days in advance of the Jefferson Hunt Party in the late fall of 1849.

Pearson's route took him over the Mojave Desert past Archilette, or Hernandez Springs (Resting Springs), the Amargosa River, Agua de Tomas (Bitter Springs), over the Cajon Pass and into the San Bernardino Valley. Pages 31-46 (The Salt Lake Trail) cover that portion of the book relating to the California deserts. Mr. and Mrs. Goodman designate this book as No. 6 in their series "Scraps of California."

PEATTIE, DONALD CULROSS

Desert Palm, The. 1952. March-April issue of *Pacific Discovery*. Illus. Later this article was included in a book by the author.

This article enters into a discussion of the Washingtonia specimens in California. Six photographs by the Weights and Don Ellis accompany the text.

The author is sadly confused in his historical accounting and in certain of his personal deductions. He speaks of Emory having "brought, in 1846, General Kearny's Army of the West safely across the terrible wastes of the then-unknown desert." Now I am glad to concede the greatness of Lieut. Col. Emory; but I refuse to ascribe to him the magnitude of greatness suggested by Mr. Peattie. Just to keep the record straight, General Kearny brought his *own* Army across—*including* Lieut. Col. Emory. Again, our author friend tells us the Army of General Kearny "saw from the Little San Bernardinos the towering, barren rock wall of the San Jacintos, and as they crawled across the Coachella Valley toward the mouth of Carrizo Creek Canyon, at a spot then called the Ojo Grande Spring, they descried a shady grove." Now this is a neat trick if one can do it; but one can't. And, finally, try as I may, I cannot accept Mr. Peattie's assertion that the palms Emory saw at Ojo Grande Spring are now "no less than Palm Springs, one of the glossiest pleasure resorts in the world." One wonders—first, that Mr. Peattie would write such nonsense; second, that *Pacific Discovery* would print it.

Road of a Naturalist, The. 1941. Boston: Houghton Mifflin Company. 315 pp. 6¼ x 9¼.

The first three chapters—"To the Mojave," "Survival On the Desert," and "Death Valley, Christmas, 1849"—all relate to the California deserts, and occupy the first fifty pages of the book. Of importance is Peattie's information relative to the Joshua tree (pp. 22-23). The chapter on Death Valley is beautifully done, and the story of the emigrants is told in a credible manner.

PEET, MARY ROCKWOOD

San Pasqual—A Crack In the Hills. 1949. Culver City, California: The Highland Press. 227 pp. 14 pls. End paper maps. 5½ x 8½.

This is the story, well told, of the San Pasqual Valley from early Indian days, through its pioneer history, and to the present time. While the entire region is closely associated with desert interest, the chapters with primary desert appeal are No. 4—"The Battle of San Pasqual" (pp. 39-50), No. 30—"San Pasqual Battlefield Monument" (pp. 215-218), and No. 8—"Indian Reservation" (pp. 57-62).

PEIRSON, ERMA

Kern's Desert. 1956. Bakersfield: Kern County Historical Association, this being their 18th annual publication. VIII, 68 pp. 20 illus. End paper maps of vicinity covered by text. 6¼ x 9¼. I am informed that only 188 copies of the first edition were published. At any rate, the supply was almost immediately exhausted. A second printing appeared early in 1957; a third in 1964.

Kern's Desert records the beginnings and much of the subsequent history of such towns and regions as Mojave, Indian Wells Valley, Red Rock Canyon, Brown, Willow Springs, Boron, Goler Canyon, the Yellow Aster and Randsburg, Johannesburg, Red Mountain, Atolia, Inyokern, Ridgecrest, China Lake, Muroc Lake and the Edwards Air Force Base, Rosamond, Garlock and Goldtown. The many interesting early photographs serve to enliven the text.

Desert lovers have long awaited this book. This Bibliography laments the paucity of literature relating to the great Mojave Desert. With the exception of Death Valley, and of the Old Spanish Trail route stretching from Cajon Pass to Nevada, little or nothing of descriptive value has been written of this vast desert area—save Marcia Wynn's excellent *Desert Bonanza* and occasional magazine releases. *Kern's Desert* supplies a recognized need, and supplies it well. It is a notable contribution to desert literature.

A new book by Erma Peirson—*The Mojave River and Its Valley*—is scheduled for release within the near future.

PERKINS, EDNA BRUSH

White Heart of Mojave, The. (1922). New York: Boni and Liveright. 229 pp. 8 pls. End paper map. 6 x 8⅞.

Two middle-age ladies—the author and a friend—entered Death Valley before modern highways and directional signs had stripped this sterile land of many of its terrors. *The White Heart of Mojave* is now well on its way toward becoming a scarce desert item; and the fact that the binders did a rather faulty job only tends to quicken its ultimate scarcity.

The author writes charmingly, indulging now and then in a vagrant description of some personal incident or experience. Often in describing a thing she permits it to remain detached from the very essence that justified its description in the first place. In other words, the reader is impelled to believe that her descriptions are not always integrated with the thing she describes. He emerges from his reading with the conviction that he has someway failed to enrich his knowledge of the central theme itself.

The author, in her excursive ramblings, appears primarily concerned with the relatively trivial experiences and impressions of her own group, and does not choose to confine her effort to an intimate study of the desert. There is so much she *could* have told us, back in 1922; so much, indeed, that I should like now to read in her book. Yet I search in vain for an early account of Death Valley's intriguing history, of its flora and fauna, its inhabitants, its geology, its borax industry, its mining activities. Hopefully, I seek a more detailed description of the several ghost towns as they appeared in 1922; and I search for mention, however meager, of the incomparable Scotty. What I get mostly is irrelevant camp gossip and vapid descriptions of hurried excursions over the desert.

Irrespective of its failure to stimulate any considerable interest on the part of its readers with respect to Death Valley, the book commends itself—first, because it supplies an early account of the desert; second, because what the author has written is *well* written and bravely conceived. Every collector of desert material should fortify his collection with a copy of the *White Heart*.

An interesting sidelight stems from the author's description of her visit to the abandoned ghost town of Skidoo, and of a singular incident that occurred there. Says Mrs. Perkins: "The place (Skidoo) was littered with paper-covered books and old magazines. In one house we found a pile of copies of a work entitled 'Mysterious Scotty (sic), or the Monte Christo of Death Valley.' Needless to say we stole one, which became a treasure to be brought out in the idle hours of the camp fire." With copies of Merrill's book presently fetching exorbitant prices, if and when they can be located, the author would perhaps have found sufficient justification in appropriating a goodly number of these books, particularly since it is elsewhere reliably reported that the copies remaining in this desert shack were later destroyed by rain.

Dr. Margaret Long, in her notable book on Death Valley—*The Shadow of the Arrow*—pays generous tribute to Mrs. Perkins. Says the Doctor—"The Perkins' charming little poems in prose catch the elusive spirit of the desert and portray admirably the sense of its mystery and power."

PERKINS, GEORGE E.

Pioneers of the Western Desert: Romance and Tragedy Along the Old Spanish or Mormon Trail and Historical Events of the Great West. (1947). Los Angeles: Wetzel Publishing Company, Inc. 103 pp. 13 pls. 5¾ x 8¼.

The main portion of the text extends from p. 11 to p. 64; the remaining pages are reserved for desert poems. The pioneer routes traced are mainly those extending through Nevada. Pp. 44-49, "Chas. Coulson Rich-Flake-Canon and Bigler Expedition Across Southern Nevada in 1849," tie in with the historic Sand Walking caravan from which emanated the defecting Death Valley groups.

PETERSON, FRED W., M.D.

Desert Pioneer Doctor and Experiences in Obstetrics. 1947. Calexico Chronicle. 85 pp. 11 pls. 5¾ x 8¾.

This is the story of one doctor's life, experience, and temperament—as he persisted in his "high calling" in the Imperial Valley. The first section contains 130 pp.; the section on obstetrics 85 pp. The book supplies much interesting material on the Indians and early pioneer life.

PETTIT, EDWIN

Portion of Biography. 1954. (See listing under Hafen—*Journals of Forty-Niners,* and Van Dyke, Walter—*Account.*)

This portion, extracted by Hafen from the *Biography of Edwin Pettit* (Salt Lake, 1912)—together with the accounts of Van Dyke, Seeley, and Hogan—relates to the Pomeroy Wagon Train expedition over the Old Spanish Trail route across Cajon Pass to San Bernardino in 1849. The Pomeroy group followed in the wake of the Hunt wagon train out from Salt Lake to San Bernardino in the fall of 1849.

PICKWELL, GAYLE

Desert Life. 1936. February. California State Department of Education. Science Guide for Elementary Schools. Vol. 2, No. 7. 43 pp. 17 desert pls. 1 col. frontispiece. 1 map. 6 x 9. Wrappers.

This item contains a curriculum unit of the desert; also, a 5-page bibliography of desert material.

Deserts. (1939.) New York: Whittlesey House. 174 pp. 9⅜ x 11⅞.

This book's chief asset is its excellent photographic plates. The text discusses deserts in general, their mountains, winds, rains, surfaces, plants, animals, and problems.

PIERCE, GEORGE FOSTER

Parson's Progress To California. 1939. June-September issues of the *Historical Society of Southern California Quarterly.* Edited by G. G. Smith.

Rev. Pierce, his wife and family came overland to California in 1859 as passengers on the Butterfield Stage. The narrative is taken from Bishop Pierce's biography, published in 1888. Pp. 71-74 take the preacher across our California deserts via the Southern route. Unfortunately, the Reverend was more of a sermonizer than narrator. He could have given us an important description of this early desert crossing. But he didn't. He just—preached.

PIPKIN, GEORGE, et al.

Ballarat. (See listing under Hubbard, Paul B.)

POLLACK, PAUL W.

California Holiday (formerly *California Magazine*). 1954. Summer Ed. Vol. 2, No. 4—June-July-August.

The cited issue of the magazine runs articles on Colton, Redlands, Fontana, Victorville, Apple Valley, Yucaipa, San Bernardino, Barstow, Needles, and Calico. Its outstanding feature is its excellent photographic illustrations—18 of them full page, 26 half page, 6 in color.

POOLE, CHARLES H.

Report Upon the Route From San Diego to Fort Yuma, via San Diego River, Warner's Pass, and San Felipe Cañon. 1857. Washington, D. C. Vol. VII of *Pacific Railroad Surveys.*

Poole, Chief Engineer for the expedition, submitted his report under Appendix B of Vol. VII. Pp. 20-25 cover the route along the wagon road via Warner's Ranch, Warner's Pass, San Felipe Valley, thence to the Colorado River. The report was written sometime between 1853-1856. (See listing under *Pacific Railroad Surveys.*)

POURADE, RICHARD F.

Mr. Pourade, "Editor Emeritus, *The San Diego Union*," has authored a series of books of uniform size and format, with San Diego as their focal point of interest. Beginning with the early Spanish explorers, and continuing the historical narrative to the present time, the books may be listed chronologically as follows:

     1960—The Explorers
     1961—Time of the Bells
     1963—The Silver Dons
     1964—The Glory Years
     1965—Gold In the Sun
     1966—Ancient Hunters of the Far West

The 1966 book varies somewhat from the first five, which measure 8¾ x 11¼; contain from two to three hundred pages each; display, in total, literally hundreds of photographic illustrations and maps—many of them in full color. The series was commissioned by James S. Copley, chairman of the corporation—The Copley Press, Inc.; published by the *Union Tribune* Publishing Company.

The scope of historical coverage in this series is of staggering proportions, and the volumes are unusually attractive. The scholarly (and pleasantly *readable*) text contains a wealth of information that is not restricted to San Diego but encompasses the entire southern and southwestern portions of the State. Two of the books—*The Glory Years* and *Gold In the Sun*—do not directly bear upon our desert areas. The other three, listed here in alphabetical order, merit separate discussion.

Explorers, The.

The two final chapters describe the trek across the formidable Colorado Desert of "the first of the great land explorers who were to open up the American West"— Juan Bautista de Anza. Anza made two attempts; and in the second (1775-76) he successfully forged a route over the desert with colonists for settlement in California. After crossing the Colorado River they turned south, into what is now Old Mexico, to circumvent the treacherous Algodones Sand Dunes. Crossing north into the United States at a point near the present Calexico, they pushed north and northwest past San Sebastian (Harper's Well) across San Felipe Creek into Borrego Valley, thence through Coyote Canyon and the Cahuilla Valley and on to their destination. Their route took them over the San Carlos Pass at an approximate elevation of 1900 feet. In general, this is the same route followed by later groups—Kearny and the Army of the West, the Mormon Battalion, the 1848-50 Gold Seekers, and—later—the Butterfield stages, except these latter groups continued over the desert to Carrizo Creek and on up the Carrizo Corridor past Vallecito, through Box Canyon, and into San Felipe Valley and Warner's Ranch.

Silver Dons, The.

Among the many distinguishing features that elevate the beautiful Pourade books into their well-deserved Aristocracy of Literary Merit, and one most likely to be overlooked by the engrossed reader, is the author's colorful book and chapter titles. The present volume affords pleasing illustration of this. Chapter headings, quite generally, follow this same trend: The Lash of Greed, Winds of Change, The Burning Trail. The "Burning Trail" obviously pertains to the hot, sandy wastes and searing winds of the Colorado Desert route.

The Silver Dons is one of our great California desert books. It is dependable because of its historical accuracy, enjoyable because of the refinement in its literary style, educational because of its broad spectrum of desert coverage. In the area of this coverage may be found comprehensive accounts of early trail blazers—Smith, Pattie, Carson, Armijo, Young, Warner and others; the Battle of San Pasqual, the march of the Mormon Battalion, the Gold Seekers, the Garra Revolt, the Railroad Surveys, the Jackass Mail, the Butterfield Overland Stages, the early Ranchos, the Boundary Surveys, the coming of the Rails, and California's participation in the Civil War.

This book, in keeping with the others, contains nearly a hundred illustrations, including several in full color.

Time of the Bells.

Here, again, is an instance of what one may term "an inspired title." *Time of the Bells.* Of course this refers to the Mission Period; but, what a colorful and expressive designation of it! There is scattered desert material throughout this fine book, particularly in Chapter Five—"Opening the Land."

(Edited by) *Ancient Hunters of the Far West.* (See listing under Rogers, Malcolm J.)

(Text by) *Colorful Butterfield Overland Stage, The.* (See listing under Reed, Marjorie.)

POWELL, H. M. T.

Santa Fe Trail to California, The. 1849-1852. The Journal and Drawings of H. M. T. Powell. 1931. San Francisco: The Book Club of California. Printed by Grabhorn. Edition limited to 300 copies. Bound in tan cloth with natural niger back. Edited, with a Foreword, by Douglas S. Watson. 16 full-page drawings (Los Angeles, San Diego, Santa Barbara, Tumacacori, San Xavier del Bac, de Flores, and the Missions of San Diego, San Luis Rey, San Juan Capistrano, San Buenaventura, Santa Barbara, Santa Ynez, San Luis Obispo, San Miguel, San Juan Bautista, Santa Clara); also 2 fldg. maps, being facsimiles of Emory's famous map with Powell's route indicated thereon. 10 unnumbered pages followed by pp. 1-272. 10 x 14.

Powell, a member of the so-called Illinois Company consisting of 11 men, 3 of whom died of cholera en route, began his overland journey April 3, 1849. On October 30 of the same year Powell first stepped foot on California soil, after crossing the Colorado River—in common with several thousand other emigrants—near the mouth of the Gila. The Southern California desert trek occupied about one month, the group following—in general—the Kearny-Cooke trail, arriving in San Diego December 3, 1849. (Pp. 162-186 of the Journal.)

Besides being perhaps the supreme artistic achievement among all the Grabhorn Press releases (not forgetting the Whitman, Mandeville, Esope, and the first Bibliography) this book is—as the printers express it—"an American classic for all time." The Grabhorns give us our first and only printing, to date, from the original journal account found written in an old leather-bound note book from which several previously used pages had been torn. Powell's drawing of Los Angeles (March 17, 1850) is one of the earliest ever attempted, antedating the lithographic reproduction in Vol. V of the *Pacific Railroad Surveys* by some two or three years. (The Hutton drawing is earlier, even, than the Powell.)

Powell possessed a well-defined artistic ability, and his drawings are expressive of it. However, his artistic talent is demonstrated not alone by his sketches, but reflects itself in his brilliant journalistic style. For sheer interest, consistently sustained, and for rich flavor in expression, no other diarist excels him; perhaps none is his equal. His is assuredly one of the great overland journals of all time, and is beyond doubt a classic in its field. He is the Washington Irving of the gold rush era.

No collection of overland narratives should omit the Powell. The book, fortunately or unfortunately, is scarce in the extreme. Writing in 1947, the author of the present Bibliography has this to say concerning Powell's work: "Of all my Grabhorns, I consider the *Santa Fe Trail to California*, by Powell, to be the most important. It's worth $200 of any man's cash—provided he can find it (book *and* cash, that is). There were only 300 copies, published in 1931. It's a beautiful thing; contains among the earliest drawings of California." The book is worth considerably more than $200 now.

POWELL, LAWRENCE CLARK

Southwestern Century, A. 1958. Van Nuys, California: J. E. Reynolds. Limited to 500 copies. Typography by Carl Hertzog; illustrations by Tom Lea; binding by Ward Ritchie. (A formidable combination.) 6½ x 10.

This is "a Bibliography of One Hundred Books of Non-Fiction about the Southwest." A quick run-down of the one hundred included items indicates that fifteen contain Southern California desert material and have been entered in this Bibliography.

Elsewhere—I believe it was in *Desert Harvest* (1962)—I quoted from Dr. Powell's *A Southwestern Century* and added the comment that it was "my *favorite* bibliography, by long odds." I continue to abide by this appraisal. Having said this, further comment would appear superfluous—except to stress the fact that I came by this judgment carefully and earnestly, having arrived at my choice after more than a passing acquaintance with a personal library collection in excess of a hundred bibliographical items.

POWERS, PROF.

Death Valley, Land of Mystery; Millions in Sight; Suggestions to Prospectors. 1919. Los Angeles: Efficiency Printing & Publishing Company. 11 pp. 5⅜ x 7⅜. Illus. Wrappers.

This item is of no importance, insofar as new material on Death Valley is concerned; but it's a queer little publication at that. And an early one.

POWERS, STEPHEN

Afoot and Alone; a Walk From Sea to Sea by the Southern Route. Adventures and Observations in Southern California, New Mexico, Arizona, Texas, etc. 1872. Hartford: Columbian Book Co. 327 pp. A Zamorano 80 item. (Cowan P. 181.)

Chs. 18 and 19 (pp. 236-263) give a rambling and incoherent account of that portion of the author's journey extending over the Colorado Desert.

POWNALL, JOSEPH (Edited by Cleland, Robert Glass)

From Louisiana to Mariposa. 1849 for the manuscript; 1949 for the book. *Rushing For Gold,* in which it it appears. The *Pacific Historical Review* also prints the Diary in their February 1949, issue.

Pownall's account of his actual desert crossing from Yuma to Warner's Ranch occupies only a few lines, and contributes little or nothing of interest in its relation to our California desert literature.

PRATT, ADDISON

Diary. 1954. Pp. 66-112 in LeRoy and Ann Hafen's *Journals of Forty-Niners.*

The Pratt *Diary,* as recorded by the Hafens, begins October 2, 1849; extends through December 22, 1849. Extracts from this *Diary* (entries showing from October 9 through December 22, 1849) also appear in Dr. Margaret Long's *The Shadow of the Arrow.* Pratt relates the story of the journey of the seven wagons (all Mormon) in the historic Sand Walking Company who remained with Captain Jefferson Hunt, proceeding along the Old Spanish Trail over the Cajon Pass into San Bernardino. It was from the Sand Walking Company that the Death Valley groups seceded to travel their disastrous cut-off route.

PRATT, HELEN

Mystery of "Giant Rock." 1947. September issue of *The Desert Spotlight.* Illus.

Frank Critzer, suspected of being a German agent during World War II, lived in his rock cave at Giant Rock near Yucca Valley. When officers came to investigate, Critzer touched off a home-made bomb, destroying himself and wounding some of the deputies. (See listing under Jones, Harlow—*Mysterious Giant Rock.*)

PRATT, ORVILLE C.

Journal. 1954. Pp. 341-359 in LeRoy and Ann Hafen's *Old Spanish Trail.*

The Pratt *Journal,* as recorded by the Hafens, begins August 27, 1848, extends through October 25, 1848. Says Hafen—"The only journal with daily entries for a complete trip over the Old Spanish Trail came recently to the knowledge of historians. . . . Orville C. Pratt, a young lawyer, bound for California and Oregon, made the trip and kept the daily record."

PRATT, PARLEY PARKER

Diary of 1851. 1935. March and June issues of *California Historical Society Quarterly* (Vol. 14, Nos. 1 and 2—"A Mormon Mission to California in 1851.")

The March issue of the Quarterly presents some material in keeping with our desert interest. Pratt traveled over the Old Spanish Trail, and records—in his Diary —a brief description of Bitter Springs and other important points along this early route to Los Angeles.

PRESTON, JACK and ROBINSON, MRS. EDWARD G.

Desert Battalion, The. 1944. Hollywood: Murray & Gee, Inc. 98 pp. Cartoon illus. 5⅜ x 7½. Wrappers.

The Desert Battalion of 600 girls made over 105 weekly trips to remote areas in their entertainment of the men of Patton's army out on the desert. They covered 350,000 miles by bus, and entertained about 250,000 men.

PREUSS, CHARLES (Translated and edited by Gudde, E. G. and E. K.)

Exploring With Frémont. 1958. Norman: University of Oklahoma Press. XXIX, 162 pp. 6⅜ x 9⅜. 16 illus. Map of Frémont's expeditions.

A valuable book this, with the private diaries of Charles Preuss nicely translated into English. Preuss was cartographer for Frémont's first, second, and fourth expeditions. His estimate of Frémont is, to say the least, most original and refreshing. No one interested in the ubiquitous Frémont should fail to read this book and ponder over the author's appraisal of this controversial figure. Preuss has a highly developed perceptive quality, despite its melancholy shadings. For desert lovers, pages 124 to 129 will yield excellent material on the early crossing of the Mojave.

PRIESTLEY, HERBERT INGRAM (Translated and edited by)

Colorado River Campaign 1781-1782; Diary of Pedro Fages. 1913. May issue of the University of California Publications of the *Academy of Pacific Coast History.* Vol. 3, No. 2. 101 pp. (See listing under Fages, Pedro.)

There is little of basic California desert material contained that has not been amplified by later and more intensive travel observations over the area. This fact, however, does not detract from the importance that attaches to the Fages Diary as being one of our very earliest narratives of the region.

Franciscan Explorations in California. (Edited by Fisher, Lillian E.) 1946. Glendale: The Arthur H. Clark Company. 189 pp. 2 maps. 5 headbolts. 6½ x 9⅝.

This enlightening brief of the exploratory and colonizing effort of the Franciscans stems from an unfinished manuscript by Dr. Priestley, edited by Lillian Estelle Fisher. The manuscript outlines each separate Spanish exploration, with a listing of the names bestowed upon towns, rivers, mountains and places of interest; also with a quick summation of the founding of the missions. The reader is given a comprehensive résumé of: The First Journey to Monterey; East Bay Penetration; The Procession of Missions; Anza's Trail Blazing; Bay Shore Explorations; The Exploration of Inland Valleys; and the Exploration of the River Valleys. Desert material obviously reflects itself in the accounts of Garces and Anza in their several desert crossings. Pp. 46-56 supply passages of desert interest.

PRIESTLEY, J. B.

Midnight on the Desert. 1937. New York: Harper & Brothers. 310 pp. 6 x 8¾. Words "First Edition" appear under copyright notice. The book has gone into several reprint editions.

A reference to the Mojave Desert in the vicinity of Victorville is to be found on pp. 71-89; but it is doubtful if Southern California desert lovers will nourish any higher sense of appreciation for the words of the Englishman than he entertained for our California deserts. Says Priestley—"I remember, however, that we found the Mohave Desert disappointing, much inferior to its Arizona neighbor at that season." And again—"I do not think I found this section of the Mohave downright frightening, but I never made friends with it." Surely this inimical regard for the great Mojave will prove more than the desert can bear.

The Death Valley reference on pp. 266-270 is quite well done, despite the penalty our academic guest imposes in forcing us to accept his comments along with inordinately large doses of "Ouspensky." The Englishman seemingly has a penchant for "Ouspensky." Many of us do not.

PUMPELLY, RAPHAEL

Pumpelly's Arizona. 1965. Tucson: The Palo Verde Press. 141 pp. 4 line engravings, 4 halftone plates. 3 maps. Edited by Andrew Wallace. Preface by Will Rogers, Jr. 6¼ x 9¼.

This attractive book is "an excerpt from *Across America and Asia* by Raphael Pumpelly, comprising those chapters which concern the Southwest." The scarce original, even when located, was usually—of necessity—priced at a figure that would negate the desire of many American collectors to acquire it. The reason being, of course, that the average American is not sufficiently interested in Pumpelly's travels in Asia to pay an exorbitant price for the questionable privilege of reading about them.

In this new book we have an early, basic item on Western Americana. We also have a short but rewarding account of the Colorado Desert crossing (pp. 110-114). It may be noted that this same passage occupies pages 64-66 in the 1871 edition of the Pumpelly.

The Introduction and intelligent editing of Andrew Wallace lend further distinction to this important book.

PUTNAM, GEORGE PALMER

Death Valley and Its Country. (1946.) Duell, Sloan and Pearce. 231 pp. 5¾ x 8¼. End paper maps. Reprint editions have followed the original.

This is an account of the Death Valley region by a well-known writer who lived in the Valley and studied it first hand.

Death Valley Handbook. (1947.) Duell, Sloan and Pearce. 84 pp. 5½ x 8¼. End paper maps.

This item supplies—"detailed records of the Valley's climate, with a list of its plants and flowers, best known birds and animals, an outline of its history, and data helpful to rock collectors."

Hickory Shirt, A Novel of Death Valley 100 Years Ago. 1949. New York: Duell, Sloan and Pearce. 252 pp.

In this book the Manly account is fictionized. The Death Valley story moves swiftly and holds interest.

PYLE, ERNIE

Ernie Pyle's Southwest. 1965. Palm Desert, California. Desert—Southwest, Inc. 107 pp. Illus. by Bob Bales. Trail-Notes by Ed Ainsworth. 7¼ x 10¼.

The sketches are all desert—Arizona, New Mexico, Nevada, Utah and California. Those directly relating to our California deserts are: Death Valley, pp. 60-61, 79-80; Barstow, pp. 75-78; Palm Springs, pp. 90-103.

Ernie Pyle, born in 1900, became a well known columnist for the Scripps-Howard newspapers in World War II, winning the Pulitzer Prize for his dispatches in 1944. He met death in the war with Japan on the small South Pacific island of IeShima on April 18, 1945.

(See also *Home Country*, 1947, by same author.)

QUIETT, GLENN CHESNEY

Pay Dirt. 1936. D. Appleton-Century Co. 506 pp. Illus. 6¼ x 9⅛. Reprinted.

The book presents an interesting résumé of the golden trek and reflects, with colorful precision, the glamorous atmosphere of the gold fields. Pp. 405-426 supply material bearing upon our California desert mining activities. Included in this section are the Kern River operations, the founding of Mojave by the Southern Pacific in 1876 and its regional gold discoveries in 1896, the beginnings of Goler in 1893, the opening of the Yellow Aster mine at Randsburg, the settlement of Johannesburg in 1897 through the promotional efforts of Chauncy M. Depew and his associates, the spectacular discovery of the Silver Queen on Soledad Mountain in 1933 by George Holmes (the mine later sold for $3,170,000), and the 1865 drama of the Cerro Gordo Mines which produced $17,000,000 in silver, lead and zinc. Panamint, Darwin, Ballarat, Greenwater and the Keane Wonder Mine are all included within the scope of the author's review. Finally (pp. 419-426), we find a sensibly-worded account of Death Valley Scotty.

Christmas Journey Into the Desert. 1959. Downey, California: Elena Quinn. 61 pp. Pen and ink sketches by Johannes Laven. 5¾ x 8½. In 1960 an orientation map of The Anza Trail was printed as a supplement to the book. This folds into a cover pocket in copies of the second edition (1960).

"A narrative concerning the colonists of the Anza Expedition who crossed the deserts of the American Southwest, during the Christmas season of 1775, in a journey from the Northern Provinces of Mexico to San Francisco Bay, for the purpose of Founding a city by that great Inland Sea." The story is based on Dr. Bolton's translation of the diaries of de Anza and Font. Emphasis is placed upon the desert birth of a child to one of the women in the expedition.

A beautiful story, told with charming simplicity and compassionate understanding. Always, in a collection of books, there are a few special favorites set apart from all the others. *Christmas Journey Into the Desert* is one of these. Sharing comparable mention with Mr. Quinn's delightful narrative is the exquisite craftsmanship of Elena Quinn, the publisher.

Mesa Grande Country. 1962. Downey, California: Elena Quinn. 90 pp. 46 photographic reproductions. Map. 7¼ x 10¼.

The talented and artistic Quinns have produced, in *Mesa Grande Country*, a book rivaling in beauty and concept their early *Christmas Journey Into the Desert*. Mr. Quinn defines this concept as being, in effect, "some observations about the quiet life and times on a high plateau in the San Diego back country." His orientation map shows the area roundabout to encompass the famous Warner Ranch with its historic old homestead, the hot springs, and Lake Henshaw. Along this area, and south to Santa Ysabel, Highway 79 snakes its scenic course. Just south of Lake Henshaw—and at no great distance west of the Highway—is the Mesa Grande. Close by and partially surrounding it is the famous domain of Warner, the Borrego Desert, and the Carrizo Corridor country.

"This," Mr. Quinn eloquently observes, "is a country of earth and sky where the long view of life is responsive to unhurried contemplation."

There is much in the book about the Indians and Indian life and customs in this section. From the Edward H. Davis collection of Indian photographs have been reproduced 22 illustrative photographs. Elena Quinn has published 21 present-day photographs from her album.

As in *Christmas Journey*, the creative artistry of Elena Quinn has contributed significantly to the beauty and quality of this fine book.

RAMSEY, ROBERT E.

Romance of the Desert, The. 1924. New York: James F. Newcomb & Company. 36 pp. Pen and ink drawings. Book is privately printed by the Pneumatic Scale Corp. Ltd. of Norfolk Downs, Mass. 4½ x 6⅞.

A queer little item, this; evidently an advertising venture glorifying Borax and "Borax Bill." "Borax Bill" would appear to be a generalization, inclusive of *all* the 20-mule team drivers. Let's look in on a typical passage:

"So vast the dimensions and so sparse the animal life that this thunderous silence appals one most when broken by the disconcerting scratching of a crawling lizard among the bleaching bones at your feet. In front of it all stands the desert's ghastly semaphore, the thorny arms of the giant cahuara waving to the wayfarer its significant warning that he is now in Nature's Inferno—the Death Valley of California."

If "bleaching bones" and "the giant cahuara" can't sell borax, there appears but little hope for it.

RANSOM, JAY ELLIS

Arizona Gem Trails and the Colorado Desert of California. 1955. Portland, Oregon: Mineralogist Publishing Company. 96 pp. 27 pls. 6 x 9¼. Wrappers.

"A field guide, for the gem hunter, the mineral collector, the uranium hunter." So says the author, in what we may consider to be another of those masterpieces of understatement. For the book is more than a guide book. This, of course; but essentially it is history, and geography, and geology, and the story of lost mines.

RAUP, H. F.

San Bernardino, California: Settlement and Growth of a Pass-Site City. 1940. Berkeley: University of California Press. Vol. 8, No. 1 of Publications in Geography. 52 pp. 1 fldg. map. 5 diagrams. 9 pls. 6¾ x 10⅜. Wrappers.

The item relates in part to desert areas adjacent to San Bernardino, particularly the Cajon Pass and the San Gorgonio Pass.

REED, LESTER

Old Time Cattlemen and Other Pioneers of the Anza Borrego Area. 1963. Palm Desert, California: Desert Printers, Inc. 147 pp. Double-page map of area. 61 early photographs. Line drawings. Pictorial wrappers. Spiral binding.

On two occasions the Reed book emerges upon the periphery of historical importance. The author includes extracts—and his own personal comment—relating to a diary prepared by John Taylor, a member of a sizable wagon train party crossing the Colorado Desert to Carrizo Creek, thence over the sandy washes of the Carrizo Corridor past Vallecito, on through Box Canyon, and along the San Felipe Valley to Warner's Ranch. The train was enroute from Comanche County, Texas, to California. Many of its members were deserters from the Confederate army. That which imparts historic significance to this diary is the fact that it would appear to be a day-by-day account of one of the last overland parties to travel the 85-year-old Colorado Desert route to California. Mr. Reed mentions they arrived at Carrizo Creek on the evening of October 12, 1864, and on October 25 passed through Warner's Ranch.

It must be borne in mind that the Pacific Railroad Surveys of the late 1850s demonstrated the feasibility of the Imperial-Coachella Valley route through San Gorgonio Pass to San Bernardino. Their data was made available to the public by Lt. Williamson's published report of 1856 (Vol. V of the *Pacific Railroad Surveys*). By 1861, at the commencement of the Civil War, the Butterfield stages were discontinued; and by the mid-fifties the impact of the Gold-Rush emigrants had largely subsided. I know of no other diary or journal record reflecting the movements of a wagon train party over the old route subsequently to the early 1850s. The old trail from Carrizo Creek to Warner's had dropped into almost total oblivion. It had served its purpose, and the world promptly forgot it. Those who still found occasion to travel it left little or no written record of their experiences. This late travel diary of John Taylor is, in effect, a roll-back of the curtain of obscurity that shrouds this route from the late 1850s to comparatively recent times. It permits an intimate glimpse into an era concerning which so very little is known. How unfortunate that Mr. Reed did not publish this historical document in its entirety in lieu of selecting only random extracts from it!

The second notable contribution of this book to Western history is the author's relation of an 1886 cattle drive of about 2000 steers from a ranch 40 miles southeast of Tucson to Warner's Ranch. Elsewhere in this Bibliography I have called attention to the paucity of source accounts relating to desert cattle drives. Our cattle drovers were never so articulate—on paper, surely—as were the soldiers, the Mormons and the Gold Seekers. I could locate but one published account (Bell's "Log" of an 1854 cattle drive) for inclusion in this Bibliography, plus mention of another diary still in manuscript form. Yet it is reasonably certain that Texas cattlemen drove large herds over the desert to the California markets during the 1850s and the 1860s. Although occurring at a much later date, the author's vivid portrayal depicts trail conditions and places that, in 1886, were essentially identical to those prevailing in 1854.

One chapter, at least in my opinion, is outstanding in Mr. Reed's desert book. Reference is to Chapter 6—"Desert Cattle Drive In 1910"—in which the author takes his readers on a conducted tour from Warner's Ranch, through San Felipe and Blair valleys, down narrow Box Canyon and the steep slope of Mason Hill into Mason Valley, Vallecito and the Carrizo Corridor. He mentions an evening meal being served at the historic Palm Springs Oasis, midway in the Corridor. From Carrizo Creek the drive plunged into a portion of the rugged desert region until it reached its feeding ground destination in Imperial Valley. It is in this chapter that we find the author's skillfully handled narrative of the incident of his horse being bitten by a rattler. This is a superb piece of desert writing; so outstanding, in fact, that it merits a separate printing.

Old-Timers of Southeastern California. 1967. Redlands, California: Citrograph Printing Co. 294 pp. Over 150 photographs. Line drawings. Pictorial wrappers. Spiral binding.

As indicated by its title, the book deals mainly with old-time desert characters. The book does not concern itself so much with incidents and places as with people. There is some material on Cerro Gordo and the Owens Valley area.

REED, MARJORIE (Text by Pourade, Richard F.)

Colorful Butterfield Overland Stage, The. (1966.) Palm Desert, California: Best-West Publications. The deluxe edition contains 21 pp. in addition to three unnumbered introductory pages. End paper maps of the route of the Butterfield stages. Deluxe edition limited to 100 copies. 11¼ x 8½.

The book contains reproductions in color of 20 of Miss Reed's beautiful paintings of scenes along that portion of the route of the Butterfield Trail extending from San Francisco to Yuma. Of special interest to desert lovers are the paintings captioned: Holdup In Frémont Pass, Warner's Pass, Warner's Ranch, San Felipe Valley, Box Canyon and—above all—Vallecito. The descriptive text by Mr. Pourade clarifies the locale of the several paintings and adds a peculiar charm to the book.

REID, JOHN C.

Reid's Tramp; or, a Journal of the Incidents of Ten Months' Travel Through Texas, New Mexico, Arizona, Sonora and California, etc. 1858. Selma, Alabama. 237 pp. (Cowan P. 188; Wagner-Camp No. 307.)

Concerning this item Cowan states: "Uncommon, and but little known. John C. Reid started his tramp in 1856 with the Mesilla Valley Co. The ultimate purpose was to explore the Gadsden Purchase." Wagner-Camp mentions a reprint in Austin, Texas; 1935.

RENSCH, HERO EUGENE

Fages' Crossing of the Cuyamacs. 1955. September issue of *California Historical Quarterly*.

The author discusses principally that portion of Fages' *Diary* relating to the route over the short-cut Indian trail across the Cuyamaca Mountains from Vallecito to San Diego.

Woods' Shorter Mountain Trail To San Diego. 1957. June issue of *California Historical Quarterly*.

In his Report of 1858, Isaiah Churchill Woods, superintendent of the first mail route established by the Government (June 22, 1857), writes a series of entries— Sept. 8 through Oct. 27—covering his journeys from Fort Yuma, through Alamo Mocho, Carrizo Creek, and Vallecito. From Vallecito he turned off the regular route past Warner's Ranch and Santa Ysabel, taking "the shorter mountain trail" into San Diego.

In one of the best-written articles of its kind, Mr. Rensch devotes attention to tracing the route of this "shorter mountain trail." Of major historical importance, and mentioned time and again in the journals and diaries of the early travelers, this obscure route and the references appertaining to it have never been developed. Mr. Rensch has supplied material approaching a suitable conclusion to this intriguing hiatus in the study of variant overland routes across the Southern California desert regions and adjoining mountains.

RICE, GEORGE GRAHAM

My Adventures With Your Money. (1913). Boston: The Gorham Press. 363 pp. 5⅛ x 7⅝.

The chapter entitled "The Greenwater Fiasco," pp. 133-143, is important in its relation to desert material; also chs. 2, 5, 6, and 7 are closely integrated with the

Greenwater section in their discussion of the old mining camps of Goldfield, Rawhide, Tonopah, Bullfrog, and others. The author treats mainly the financial aspects of these several ventures. Graham—his actual name was Jacob S. Herzig—was quite a character in his time. His shady stock manipulations brought him before the law on several occasions. Even so, his knowledge of Greenwater and the nearby Nevada mining towns was an intimate one.

RICE, WILLIAM B. (Edited by Caughey, J. W.)

Los Angeles Star, The: 1851-1864. 1947. Berkeley: University of California Press. XVI, 315 pp. 5⅝ x 8⅝.
This is the story of "the beginnings of journalism in Southern California." It is in the Appendix (No. 1) that we find an item of historical importance bearing upon desert material. Extracts from a Journal maintained by one "P. : : : : : : C.," a member of the Reese Brothers' caravan, are printed under the caption "Early Freighting on the Salt Lake—San Bernardino Trail." The article originally appeared in the *Star* on Feb. 18, 1854. (See listing under Anonymous—*Early Freighting On the Salt Lake-San Bernardino Trail.*)

RICH, CHARLES C.

Diary. 1954. Pp. 181-192 in LeRoy and Ann Hafen's *Journals of Forty-Niners.*
The Rich *Diary*, as recorded by the Hafens, begins October 8, 1849; extends through January 15, 1850. (Refer to listing under Evans, John Henry—*Charles Coulson Rich, Pioneer Builder;* also Bigler, Henry W.—*Extracts From the Journal of.*) Rich was with those who worked their way down Mt. Misery into Beaver Dam Canyon.

RICHARDS, IRMAGARDE

Desert Treasure. (See listing under Heffernan, Helen.)

RINEHART, ROBERT E.

Death Valley Borax Beds. 1909. October issue of *Overland Monthly.* Illus.
Rinehart gives the reader a sensible and unpretentious account of the borax industry.

Naming of Death Valley. 1908. August 16 issue of the *Illustrated Weekly Magazine*, appearing in the Los Angeles *Times*.
(Refer to comments appearing under James, George Wharton—*Heroes of California;* also to Edwards, E. I.—*The Mystery of Death Valley's Lost Wagon Train.*)

RIPLEY, VERNETTE SNYDER

San Fernando Pass, The, and the Traffic That Went Over It. 1947—March and September—December issues, and 1948—March and June issues of the *Historical Society of Southern California Quarterly*. Produced in 4 parts. 120 pp. 10 photographs. Maps.
Should a controversy arise concerning the San Fernando Pass locale—whether

it be mountain or desert—I'll concede the point either way. In the meantime I wish to place this thoroughly-researched article in our Bibliography. To me, at least, the Pass has always felt "deserty." The Pass, generally referred to as "San Fernando Pass," but also known as "Newhall Pass," "Frémont Pass," and "Beale Pass," is located only a stone's throw off the Newhall-Saugus highway, a few miles beyond San Fernando. The article, although thoroughly researched, is mainly a continuation of excerpts—one after another in rapid succession—from accounts appearing in newspapers and magazines describing the Pass. The reader will likely discover it far more difficult to find his way through this wearisome maze of quotations than to forge his way over the Pass itself. The urgent need is for a general summation of these multitudinous accounts in narrative form, with the quotations set aside either in notes or in an appendix.

ROBERTS, BRIGHAM H.

Mormon Battalion, The: Its History and Achievements. 1919. Salt Lake: Desert News. 96 pp. 5¼ x 7½. Fldg. map of Cooke's route. Wrappers. Some hard bound.

The author details the march of the Battalion from Fort Leavenworth to San Diego. Ch. 6—"The March of the Battalion From the Colorado to the Pacific Ocean" (pp. 45-53)—relates specifically to the march across California. This chapter also contains Cooke's Bulletin of January 30, 1847. Chs. 7 and 8 are of some importance with respect to their portrayal of the Battalion's subsequent activities in California, after completing their historic trek across the continent. The author refers copiously to Cooke's *Journal* and to Tyler's account.

ROBERTS, OLIVER (more properly Oliver Roberts de la Fontaine)
(Compiled by Walter, Wm. W.)

Great Understander, The. True Story of the Last of the Wells Fargo Shotgun Express Messengers. (1931). Aurora, Ill.: William W. Walter. 315 pp. 5¼ x 7¾.

The punctuation in this peculiar item is atrocious and intolerable, the commas being as plentiful as the sands of the desert—and as indiscriminately placed. Toward its conclusion the book degenerates into an inordinate dissertation upon the merits of some abstruse religious philosophy. The author was born in 1857; presumably came to California as a very young man. The book records that he walked from the town of Mojave on across the desert, "one hundred and five miles," to Darwin garbed in "a Prince Albert coat, a derby hat, high heeled boots, white shirt and collar, and a summer overcoat." It is at this juncture that our "true life story" becomes impregnated with elements of the bizarre and fantastic. The author tells how the hot sun puts "fight and life" into sidewinders. (Actually, it will kill them within 10 minutes.) He avers that these same lively little sidewinders are "far more poisonous and dangerous than the ordinary, big rattler." (It has been my observation that the "ordinary, big rattler" is no piker, either.) He speaks of lizards jumping two feet off the ground to catch flies. (Doubtless the lizards were more agile in those days.) Finally, one is inclined to question the farcical assertion that two coyotes will "sneak up behind and take a nip out of the calves of the legs." (It is suggested the "nip" was elsewhere taken; and not necessarily by the rapacious coyotes.)

On pp. 103-119 may be found an account of the Indians burning one of their number at the stake, in a secret ceremony avowedly witnessed by the author. If this gruesome account be true, and not merely a figment of the writer's aberrant imagination, then it is ostensibly of some historical consequence. In view of all that has gone before, however, the entire episode takes on an equivocal meaning.

After being ruthlessly chased over the desert by a huge rattlesnake, the author came to Death Valley. And then things really began to happen. "I had not gone far when my foot struck something very light and round, and it rolled away. This startled and aroused me, somewhat, and upon looking I found that I was fairly surrounded with the bones and skulls of both men and beasts. The thing which had rolled when my foot struck it was the bleached skull of a human being." He goes on to inform us that "nearly four hundred emigrants had perished here about twenty-seven years before, for the want of water." (Actually, history records the death of but one emigrant within Death Valley in 1849.) Finally, he proceeds to blame the Mormons for this entire catastrophic debacle. In his "true" narrative he asserts that he even examined the remains of the wagons. (Refer to Edwards, E. I.—*The Mystery of Death Valley's Lost Wagon Train* for a detailed assessment of this incident.)

Well, perhaps he did. Although of an anomalous character, and given to extreme exaggeration, the book possesses at least the semblance of a factual basis. The author's descriptions of localities and incidents are too accurate (in part, at least), and much too vivid, to be entirely fatuous. Even though his claim to truthful assertions often appears a bit tenuous, the book still is worth reading and—to the collector at least—worth owning. From first to last it is vibrant with excitement and high adventure. And although we may not readily correlate his account of these adventures with our own knowledge of places and conditions, we will *read* the the book—once we start it—and we'll enjoy it. And no doubt, from the reading of it, we shall acquire information of the desert in that early day which is not elsewhere available.

In his *Tales of the Pioneers* (pp. 98-109), and also in his *Gold, Guns & Ghost Towns* (pp. 143-153), W. A. Chalfant reviews Oliver's book by re-telling several of the incidents and experiences related by the author. He mentions (as does the author in his book) that Oliver studied assaying and mining engineering, and in 1887 was appointed Assistant Adjutant General of Nevada. Says Chalfant— "When he died, on April 30, 1920, he was in charge of a mining property in Western California. He had become a Mason and a Shriner; and, more important, he had become sincerely religious. During his residence in San Francisco he had married. The wife of Richard Jose, noted singer, was his step-daughter."

In the October 1899, issue of *Wide World Magazine*, pp. 20-24, there appears an article by an Oliver Roberts entitled "What I Found In the Mine."

ROBERTSON, WILLARD

Oasis. (1944.) New York: J. B. Lippincott Company. 220 pp. 5¾ x 8¼. The book has been reprinted.

This is a novel, with its locale someplace in a California desert—*your favorite desert*, if you will. I recommend Mr. Robertson's *Oasis*—without hesitation—as being a top-rated novel of the desert. The fine descriptive powers of the author, together with his wholesome philosophy, lend character to the book. Moreover, it's a fascinating yarn he has to tell, and he tells it exceedingly well. I am willing—and eager—to go all the way out in praise of this fine book.

ROBINSON, MRS. EDWARD G.

Desert Battalion, The. (See listing under Preston, Jack.)

ROBINSON, MARSHALL

Sketches In Prose and Rhyme. 1888. Carson City: Daily Index Print. 5⅞ x 8⅛. "Part First—Rhyme," consists of 80 pp. of poems; "Part Second," shows 32 pp.

The prose section invites our attention in view of the early date of the journey described by the author on pp. 1-17 under the caption "A Trip in Southern California in '79." One's interest is stimulated by the locale of this particular journey—the Inyo mines; Hawley's Station on the Mohave; Garlic Spring; Cave Spring; McLean's Ranch; the Gladstone Gold and Silver Mining Company's locations in the Mojave at the "Vulture, Blue Belle, Shiloh, Richmond and Empire, the Lookout, Hidden Treasure, and Surplus;" and—finally—Death Valley. On pp. 13-17, under the sub-title "Romance of Real Life In Death Valley," the author mentions in a superficial manner the experiences of his group in this desert. Little or nothing however, is given us by way of accurate description of the valley itself. Pp. 25-32 are perhaps more important. Here, under the caption "A Sight-Seer on the C. & C.," our author takes us over the Carson and Colorado Railroad from Carson to Keeler, on the east side of Owens Lake.

ROBINSON, W. W.

People vs. Lugo. 1962. Los Angeles: Dawson's Book Shop. 46 pp. Limited to 300 copies. 6⅜ x 9½.

This celebrated case opens upon a murder in Cajon Pass, continues through the Los Angeles courts, ends in the San Bernardino valley. An interesting tale of Los Angeles justice in the early 1850s.

Story of Kern County. 1961. Los Angeles. Title Insurance and Trust Co. 64 pp. 32 photographs. Double-page map of Kern County. Wrappers.

Desert references include Fort Tejon (pp. 21-23), the Mojave desert areas of Rosamond, Muroc, Edwards Air Force Base, China Lake and N. O. T. S., Ridgecrest, Inyokern, and Boron (pp. 48-50).

Story of Riverside County, The. 1957. Los Angeles: Title Insurance and Trust Co. Wrappers.

Included is the account of Pedro Fages' visits, the Anza expeditions, the Pacific Railroad Survey through San Gorgonio Pass, the Butterfield Stages, Palm Springs, and the Coachella Desert.

Story of San Bernardino County, The. 1958. San Bernardino: Pioneer Title Insurance Co. 79 pp. 31 photographs. Map of San Bernardino County. Wrappers.

Considerable space is given to the early Spanish explorations in the area. Mention is made of Jedediah Smith's visits, the Walkara horse-stealing raids, the Death Valley party, Mormon colonists, the Bradshaw road extending from Los Angeles to the Colorado River, Borax and the Searles Lake activity, gold and silver mining in and around Randsburg and the Calico and Providence mountains, the Victor Valley area, and the Apple Valley development.

ROCKWOOD, CHARLES ROBINSON and HEFFERNAN, DR. W. T.

Born of the Desert (by Rockwood); *Personal Recollections of the Early History of Imperial Valley* (by Heffernan). 1930. Calexico, California: Calexico Chronicle. Wrappers.

Rockwood's story of the reclamation of the Imperial Valley was first published in a special edition of the Calexico *Chronicle*, in 1909. This article was reprinted, with few deletions, in Otis B. Tout's *The First Thirty Years* (1931).

ROGERS, BILL

Camera Shots of Ghost Cities. (See listing under Comfort, H. G.)

ROGERS, JOHN

Account. From Merced *Star* of April 26, 1894. (See listing under Belden, L. Burr—*Death Valley Heroine.*)

John Rogers was Manly's scouting partner, and shared equal honors in their heroic effort to save the families of Bennett and Arcane by rescuing them from the terrors of the Long Camp on the floor of Death Valley. Manly wrote his book—*Death Valley in '49;* the magnanimous, but less articulate, John Rogers gives us this contemporaneous account. (Refer to Edwards, E. I.—*Death Valley's Neglected Hero.*)

ROGERS, MALCOLM J.

Ancient Hunters of the Far West. 1966. San Diego: The Union-Tribune Publishing Company. Sponsored by James S. Copley, chairman of the Copley Press, Inc. Edited by Richard F. Pourade. Produced in cooperation with the San Diego Museum of Man. Contributors—H. M. Wormington, E. L. Davis, Clarke W. Brott. 208 pp. 8⅝ x 11¼.

The titles assigned to the five "Parts" of the book will perhaps best explain its content: "A Journey Into Man's Past" (discovering the San Dieguito People); "The Ancient Hunters—Who Were They?"; "When Did Man Come To North America?"; "How Did They Live and How Long Ago?"; "How Stones Became Tools and Weapons."

The book contains some sixteen full or half-page colored photographic plates of desert scenes, in addition to several tinted or colored maps, diagrams, and black and white photographic plates. Among desert areas included in this fascinating study are the Panamint Valley, that portion of the Mojave north of Ludlow and east of the Cady Mountains, the Picacho Hills country on the California side of the Colorado, the Colorado Desert in eastern Imperial County, the Anza-Borrego Desert, southeast Inyo County, Mojave Desert south of the Mesquite Hills (south of Baker and North of Ludlow), Pilot Knob or Black Mesa near Ogilby, the Carrizo Wash and following the edge of the Fish Creek Mountains, off Highway 78 in San Diego County and seven miles from Borrego Springs just west of Ocotillo Wells, and the raked gravel "pictographs" north of Blythe.

ROLLINS, JAMES H.

Recollection. 1954. Pp. 261-268 of LeRoy and Ann Hafen's *Journals of Forty-Niners.*

Rollins—with Bigler, Rich, Farrar, and Cannon—was a member of the contingent that separated from the original Sand Walking Company of 1849, and packed down Mt. Misery into Beaver Dam Canyon. The Rollins autobiographical sketch was dictated in 1898.

ROLT-WHEELER, FRANCIS

Boy With the U. S. Survey, The. (1909.) Boston: Lathrop, Lee & Shepherd Co. 381 pp. 37 pls. 5¾ x 8. Photographs taken by the U. S. Geol. Survey.

A novel, based upon factual data. Ch. 8, "The Land Where It Never Rains" (pp. 149-171), refers to Death Valley.

ROMER, MARGARET

History of Calexico, A. 1922. *Southern California Historical Society Annual Publications.* (Vol. XII, Part II). A reprint edition of this item contains 45 pp., 5 pls., fldg. map of Imperial and Coachella Valleys; 6 x 9¼; wrappers.

This item embraces far more than a mere descriptive narrative of early Calexico. It recites the story of the Valley as it existed in ancient times, and tells of the successive inroads of the powerful Colorado into this desert basin, its waters extending even to the approaches of San Gorgonio Pass. Then, centuries later, there emerged those stalwart pioneers of the reclamation project—Wozencraft, Rockwood, Ferguson, Heffernan, Heber, Chaffey, Hoffman, and others. The chapter on "The Floods, 1905-1906" presents one of our best comprehensive accounts of the Colorado River break and the resultant formation of the Salton Sea. Similarly, the dramatic closing of these breaks by the Southern Pacific Company is competently related. Unquestionably, this is one of the outstanding Southern California desert items.

ROMERO, CAPT. DON JOSE

Expeditions. (See listing under Bean, Lowell, J.)

ROPP, ROY M.

Cabot Yerxa—Adventurer. 1941. November issue of *Western Trailer Life.*

The article describes Yerxa's relation to the Colorado and Mojave Deserts.

Yerxa homesteaded 11 miles northwest of Palm Springs in 1913, in what is now known as Desert Hot Springs. His remarkable Indian Pueblo attracts thousands of curious, interested visitors.

ROSE, L. J.

Massacre on the Colorado. 1859. *Missouri Republican* of November 29.

This letter is reprinted in Robert Glass Cleland's *The Cattle On a Thousand Hills* (1941) under Appendix IV, pp. 306-315. Rose was one of the group of emigrants who, in the latter part of August 1858, were attacked by the Mojave Indians. At the Colorado River the Indians launched their concerted attack and killed several of the white men. Out of nearly 400 head of cattle only 17 were saved; of 37 horses, only 10 remained. The remnant of the party returned to Albuquerque. Mr. John Udell was a member of this group, and he—too—writes of their experiences. Four companies of infantry, under Lt. Col. Hoffman, were later dispatched on a punitive expedition against the Mojaves.

Mr. Rose later became prominent in the development of the San Gabriel Valley. His ranch lay east of the City of San Marino, and was known as Sunny Slope. Rose was an uncle of Attorney Henry W. O'Melveny. (See listing under Cleland, Robert Glass—*Cattle On a Thousand Hills;* also under Udell, John—*Journal.*)

ROSENER, ANN

Story of the Pacific Coast Borax Co. (See listing under Woodman, Ruth C.)

ROWNTREE, LESTER

Ronnie and Don. 1953. New York: The Viking Press. 160 pp.

This book is a juvenile, narrating the experiences of two boys on the Mojave. It is of definite educational value; and an effort has been made to check the data on desert flora and fauna with reliable sources.

RUDKIN, CHARLES N. (Translated and edited by)

Voyage On the Colorado—1878, A. (See listing under Berton, Francis.)

RUGELEY, HELEN J. H.

From the Mississippi To the Pacific: An Englishman In the Mormon Battalion. (See listing under Whitworth, Robert W.)

RUSSELL, CARL PARCHER

Bodie That Was, The. 1929. November issue of *Touring Topics.*

This is an early and dependable article on the famous old mining camp of Bodie. Notable illustrations, 16 of them, accompany the text.

RUSSELL, MAUDE CARRICO

Old Indian Burial Grounds. 1947. January issue of *The Desert Spotlight.* Illus.

In Sec. 33, Twp. 1N, R 9E, San Bernardino County, one acre is officially designated as Indian burial ground. This article, by the one perhaps best fitted to write on early Twentynine Palms history, describes the Indians who lived here in 1909-1910; their habits, their customs, and their ancient burial place.

Old Trails to Twentynine Palms. 1946. December issue of *The Desert Spotlight.* Illus.

Miss Russell, an authority on the High Desert country comprising the present towns of Morongo, Yucca Valley, Joshua Tree and Twentynine Palms, first visited this area in May of 1910. Her article is given added interest by the inclusion of two early prints—one of the caravan taken near the present site of Whitewater; the other of Warren's Well as it appeared at that early day in the history of this desert.

Yesterdays of Twentynine Palms. 1947-1948. *The Desert Spotlight.* These articles ran serially, appearing in the October, November and December issues of 1947; in the January, February, April, June, July, and August issues of 1948. Illus.

Historically, the Maude Carrico Russell articles are among the most important to be published by this short-lived magazine. The author, now passed on, was intimately familiar with the High Desert country, embracing Morongo and Yucca Valleys, Joshua Tree, and Twentynine Palms. Her articles in the immediate series relate mainly to the Indians who formerly occupied this area. The August 1948, article covers "The Infancy of the Twentynine Palms School System." Early photographic plates enhance the series. Included, also, is Miss Russell's version of the sordid Willie Boy tragedy.

RUSSELL, RICHARD JOEL

Land Forms of San Gorgonio Pass, Southern California. 1932. Berkeley: University of California Publications in Geography. 121 pp. 35 pls. 7 diagrams. 3 loose charts in front of book relating to temperature and precipitation. 1 fldg. map. 7¼ x 10¾.

The San Gorgonio Pass and surrounding desert areas are considered in this paper.

RUST, H. N.

Desert Sea, The. 1891. October issue of *The California Illustrated Magazine.* No. I, Vol. I.) 10 pp. 3 illus. Map.

An early article on the Salton Sea describing the February 1891 overflow of the Colorado River into the Salton basin.

On the Mojave Desert. 1899. February issue of the *Land of Sunshine.* Pp. 125-126.

This is an early account of Amboy Crater, located five miles east of Bagdad and plainly visible from Highway 66.

RYAN, CLAUDE F.

Story of the "Desert Sign Post." 1926. *American Quarterly* of October 1.

The item reprints, with slight omissions, the paper by Parsons entitled—*A Thousand Mile Desert Trip.* (See listing in this Bibliography.)

SALISBURY, ALICE

Desert Treasure. (See listing under Heffernan, Helen.)

SAMPSON, FRED V.

Desert Adventure. 1947. September issue of *The Desert Spotlight,* and continuing serially through August of 1948. Illus.

Says the author, and I think he says it magnificently, "There is but one real way to know the desert and that is to go to it and become a part of it, to be absorbed by it completely." In just such an attitude did Mr. Sampson approach his intimate study of the wild life of the desert.

SAN BERNARDINO COUNTY MUSEUM

Agua Mansa. 1961. Summer issue of the Museum Quarterly.

Several authorities contributed to this interesting 34-page booklet:

L. Burr Belden—the Introduction
Grace Shepard Newman—"Agua Mansa" (a poem)
Gerald A. Smith—Agua Mansa, Home of Pre-historic Indians
Clark Harding Jones—Agua Mansa. Settled by Those Who Spoke Spanish
Marie Wood—Augua Mansa Today

SARTOR, E. LOUISE

I Remember Bodie. 1952. December issue of *Desert.* Illus.

The author records her memories of old Bodie at the turn of the century.

SAUNDERS, CHARLES FRANCIS

Lowest, Hottest, Dryest Spot in America. 1919. December issue of *Travel.* Illus.

This is an early article on Death Valley, introducing no new material, but possessing those attributes common to all Mr. Saunders' writings—sincerity, exactness, beauty.

Southern Sierras of California, The. 1923. Boston: Houghton Mifflin Company. XIII, 367 pp. 32 pls. Publ. date on title page. 5½ x 8¼.

An estimable book, enlivened by a sustained desert interest. If those imposing mountains—San Jacinto and San Gorgonio—rising precipitously from the desert can be associated with our central theme, then pp. 136-174 should be noted. Chapters on "The Cajon," "Temecula," "Jewel on Palomar's Breast," and "Roundabout to Pala" are packed with desert interest. Particularly applicable is the appealing chapter on "The Lost Pass of San Carlos."

Under the Sky in California. 1913. New York: Robert M. McBride Co. 299 pp. Photographs. 5¾ x 8⅜.

Pp. 1-48 comprise the section of this book having to do with the deserts of California. Chapter titles of this section include—"The Mohave," "The Colorado Deserts of California," "In Palm Canyon," "Spring Flowers of the Desert."

Western Wild Flowers. 1933. Garden City, New York: Doubleday, Doran & Co., Inc. XIV, 320 pp. 57 pls. 6¼ x 9¼. Words "First Edition" appear under copyright notice.

Frequent reference is made throughout the text to desert flowers and shrubs. In particular, Ch. 5 on the Joshua Tree (pp. 46-53), and Ch. 31 on "Desert Notables and Oddities" (pp. 292-304), have material of interest.

With the Flowers and Trees in California. 1914. New York: McBride, Nast & Co. 286 pp. 4 colored illus. 28 half-tones. 5¾ x 8½.

There are numerous desert references in this volume, especially in Ch. 4—"Tree Hunting on a California Desert," (pp. 66-88).

SAYRE, JAMES A.

Bonanza In Borax, A. 1964. July issue of *Journal of the West.* Pp. 277-290.

In this intelligently documented study, Mr. Sayre has put together the definitive record of John Searles and his borax activities at Searles Lake on the Mojave Desert, together with the later development of the great borax industry at this same location. In his comprehensive account of the Searles Lake activities, even though he cannot avoid the occasional use of statistics, his perceptive analysis at all times remains delightfully non-technical.

Happily, there is an intruding factor that contributes most importantly to my own high estimate of this article. Although prepared in a Graduate Seminar in California History, Mr. Sayre is a former employee of the American Potash and Chemical Corporation at Trona, on Searles Lake. He actually *worked* there for eight years. What an effective concomitant to successful research! Particularly if one attempts a study of the chemical processes at Trona. I know. I, too, worked there—once upon a time.

SCARFOGLIO, ANTONIO

Round the World In a Motor Car. 1909. London: Grant Richards. 368 pp. 70 illus. 6 x 9.

The author writes of an auto tour (imaginary or otherwise) through portions of America, Asia and Europe. The book indicates an ambivalent regard for America—not only with respect to our land, but also to our people. The Italian, it would appear, both loved and loathed our country; was both complimentary and contemptuous of the men and women he met here.

Of immediate interest is his empirical account of the drive from Ogden, Utah, to Los Angeles, over the Mojave Desert. He reports this trip as having been taken in the month of March. Goldfield is mentioned; also Tonopah, Troy and Rawhide. Little of value is to be found, however, as the author leaves us only a skeletal picture of these fabulous old Nevada mining towns of a day long dead.

Slightly more detail is devoted to Greenwater. Scarfoglio arrived here—so he tells us—some six or eight months after the town's collapse.

At this point, our intrusive visitor flings a captious barb at America. "Greenwater," says Scarfoglio, "concludes the analysis of the American town. We have seen the germination at Ely; the flowering at Goldfield; the rotting away at Greenwater. Thus, depicted on the desert in three great strokes, is the whole of American psychology. The story of the soul of the people is always written on the walls of its homes, and a people which has no homes and which does not live in them is certainly a people which has no soul."

Next, our impassioned guest from Italy passes through Death Valley, and he does so in two short and nonsensical paragraphs. Blithely he hies himself over the intervening desert country to San Bernardino, and thence to Los Angeles where he spews out his noble Roman contempt for "the brutal and violent invasion of a man badly dressed, chewing tobacco, and with dirty finger nails"—a *reporter*, of all people, from "the greatest newspaper in Los Angeles." So first it's our morals, next it's our clothing, then our tobacco, and finally our dirty finger nails.

One may well be inclined to question if Horatius ever actually motored across the Mojave. In any event, we need attach but little importance to this early account of our deserts, be it factual or spurious.

SCHILLING, FRANK

Imperial Valley and Its Approaches, The. 1952. *Westerners, The* (Los Angeles Corral) *Brand Book* No. 4.

Mr. Schilling's capable article on the Imperial Valley and its contiguous areas appears on pp. 59-80 of the *Brand Book* for 1950. 4 pls. illustrate this portion of the book. The author sectionalizes his article as follows: Spanish Explorers; American Trappers; Scouts and Adventurers; the Widney Sea; Water Comes to the Desert; Disaster Comes to the Valley. There is much on Alarcon, de Anza, Cooke and his Mormon Battalion, Wozencraft, Widney, the "Great Break" in the Colorado River and the resulting flood.

SCHMID, DOROTHY CLARK

Pioneering In Dulzura. 1963. San Diego: Robert R. Knapp. Words "First Edition" appear under copyright notice. VIII plus 159 pp. 29 photographs. End paper maps. 5¾ x 8½.

There are those who scoff at local history, and contend that it is futile to attempt to equate it with the *broader* concept of history—a concept academically referred to as the "Frontier Hypothesis," the darling of some professional historians. For such as these, I doubt if the Dulzura book will hold appeal. For the rest of us it should prove delightful reading. Personally, I have not really *seen* Dulzura—physically, that is. But, after reading Dorothy Schmid's book, I plan to go there and stay there long enough to meet some of the really wonderful people she tells about, and see some of the exciting scenery she describes.

SCHWACOFER, LEONARD

Out of the Golden West, Vol. I. Tales From the Desert. (1943.) Anaheim, California: Mother Colony Press. 55 pp. 10 pls. Fldg. map. 5 x 6½. Numerous sketches. Wrappers.

A group of stories are reliably presented in this booklet, among them: The Phantom Ship, The Great Stone Face, Testudo the Desert Turtle, Don Coyote, Historic Vallecito, The Camel Brigade, An Empire Below the Sea. *Tales From the Desert* makes for good reading.

West o' the Colorado. 1934. Hemet, California: *Hemet News.* 3½ x 5½. Wrappers.
  The book consists of a number of prose sketches of the desert.

SCOTT, FERRIS H.

Palm Springs Area Year Book. 1952. Santa Ana, California: Duke Printing Service. 74 pp. 8½ x 11. Wrappers.
  A good item on Palm Springs and vicinity. The photographic plates, many of them showing early scenes in Palm Springs, contribute to the value of the book. Some 40 of these plates are in color. An attractive two-page resort-recreation map is included.
  Additionally, sections include accounts of the Palm Springs Indians, Wild Flowers, Water, Date Palms, and the Salton Sea. Here is a fascinating book, with its material well-assembled and beautifully displayed.

SEELEY, DAVIS

Sketch. 1954. (See listing under Hafen, LeRoy and Ann—*Journals of Forty-Niners,* and Van Dyke, Walter—*Account.*)
  This extract, together with the accounts of Van Dyke, Hogan and Pettit, refers to the Pomeroy Wagon Train's expedition over the Old Spanish Trail route across Cajon Pass to San Bernardino in 1849.

SERVEN, JAMES E.

Guns of Death Valley. 1959. *Westerners, The* (Los Angeles Corral) *Brand Book* No. 8. 14 pp. 7 illus.
  In this article Mr. Serven becomes gun-oriented and relates phases and incidents of Death Valley and several of the contiguous ghost town areas involving the use of guns. This is an original approach, certainly; and an entertaining one. Deserving of mention is the fact that Mr. Serven knows his Death Valley history, and does not choose to subvert its factual accuracy to achieve dramatic effect.

Ill-Fated '49er Wagon Train. 1960. The *Historical Society of Southern California Quarterly.* 12 pp. Double page route map.
  This is a condensed, factual tracing of the routes of the several contingents that comprised the Jefferson Hunt Wagon Train that left Salt Lake for Los Angeles in the late fall of 1849. Among the defecting groups from the Hunt Train was one destined to gain fame as the Death Valley party of 1849-50.

SETTLE, GLEN A. (Compiled and edited by)

Bears—Borax and Gold. (1965). Kern-Antelope Historical Society, Inc. 52 pp. 16 early desert photographs. Art work by John Burgess. Wrappers.

The title is reminiscent of the Chickering article on Leuba's *Bandits, Borax and Bears.* The book is a compilation of four articles:

> John Searles—A California Bear Hunter
> Dennis Searles—Diary of a Desert Journey
> Mel Sanford—Desert Prospectors
> Martin Engel—Lost Mines I Did Not Find.

The John Searles article first appeared in 1892, in John Randolph Spears' *Illustrated Sketches of Death Valley* (see listing in this Bibliography); credit is given Paul Hubbard for supplying the *Dennis Searles' Diary of his trip to Searles Lake in 1890;* Mel Sanford's early mining experiences in and near Ballarat, and Martin Engel's timely observations about the lost mines he never could find, add their quota of good desert material.

Here Roamed the Antelope. 1963. Kern-Antelope Historical Society, Inc. 64 pp. 16 early photographs. Art work by John Burgess. Wrappers.

Compiled in this collection are:

1. *Reminiscences* of John D. Covington who came to Antelope Valley in 1869; lived there throughout most of his long life. Of some interest is Mr. Covington's reference to Tiburcio Vasquez, including his robbery at Coyote Holes. (See listing under Edwards, E. I.—*Freeman's: A Stage Stop On the Mojave.*)

2. *The Hart of Antelope Valley* is the product of students of English and Rhetoric in the Antelope Valley Union High School. The finished product is something in which the participating students, their faculty advisors, and the community of Antelope Valley may know a definite pride.

3. *History and Letters* of E. M. Hamilton. This section comprises one letter (April 3, 1913) addressed to Miss Minta Thomason.

4. *Antelope Valley At the Turn of the Century* by Clarence J. Gerblick relates interesting early history of Willow Springs, Rosamond, and Ezra Hamilton.

5. Mr. Settle, the compiler of all these early historical articles, prepares the final section of the book—*A Chronological Review of Dates Important In Antelope Valley History.* In it he lists 39 date-groupings of events. This chronology first appeared in his booklet *Tropico,* in 1959.

Tropico: Red Hill With a Glamorous History of Gold. 1959. Pages unnumbered. 7 photographs. Wrappers.

This is the story of Ezra Hamilton and his historic Willow Springs strike in 1896. Of some interest to old-timers in this area is Mr. Settle's reference to the two-story hotel constructed in Rosamond by Mr. Hamilton. This is the building reputed to have contained a quantity of high grade gold quartz in its walls. Incidentally, the top story had to be removed after the Kern County earthquake in 1952. Mr. Settle's Chronology of 39 date-groups—included in his 1963 *Here Roamed the Antelope*—first appeared in this 1959 *Tropico*. It extends from 1772 to 1948.

SHANNON, THOMAS

Account. From *San Jose Daily Mercury* of Nov. 16, 1903. (See listing under Belden, L. Burr—*Death Valley Heroine.*)

Shannon was one of the Jayhawker group of the 1849 Death Valley pioneers. His *Account* sheds further understanding upon the Death Valley episode.

SHEDD, JOHN CUTLER

Desert Lore. 1931. Los Angeles: Press of Jesse Ray Miller. 41 pp. 6½ x 9½. Soft bound.

This little-known item consists of 16 poems and 22 full-page sepia photographs of the desert. The author acknowledges his indebtedness to Willard Selwyn Wood and Spencer R. Atkinson for these remarkably fine photographs.

SHELTON, CHARLES E.

Photo Album of Yesterday's Southwest. Palm Desert, California: Desert Magazine, Inc. 191 pp. 192 photographs. 12½ x 9¼.

A collection of early photographs, some of them of considerable historic value; many of them not—particularly those of unknown individuals. Unfortunately for our California deserts, most of the pictures are of people and places in Arizona and Nevada. Only a dozen or so relate to California.

SHIELDS, E. F.

Coachella Valley Desert Trails and the Romance and Sex Life of the Date. (1952.) 40 pp. 38 pls. 5¾ x 8¾. Wrappers.

This neat little brochure contains articles on date culture in Coachella Valley, on Twentynine Palms and the Joshua Tree National Monument, Palm Springs, Palm Desert, Indian Wells, Thousand Palm Canyon, and the Salton Sea Area. One rarely encounters an advertising medium that delivers such pronounced historical interest as may be found in the Shields' item.

SHINN, G. HAZEN

Shoshonean Days. 1941. Glendale: The Arthur H. Clark Company: Privately printed in an edition of 250 copies. 183 pp. 6½ x 9½.

During the years 1885-1889, the author lived among the Indians of Southern California. This illuminating account records his recollections of this five-year period. Mr. Shinn provides a competent portrayal of Indian life, character and legend. Historical data, unique because of their intimate nature, are interwoven in the narrative which concerns the region in and around San Bernardino, the San Gorgonio Pass, Palm Springs, Morongo Valley, and Warner's Ranch. The Morongo family figures prominently throughout the book.

California Scrap-Book, The. 1869. San Francisco: H. H. Bancroft & Co. 704 pp.

A 400-word article, captioned "Death Valley," is included among the numerous articles selected by Shuck for his 700-page *Scrap-Book*. He credits his anonymous article to the *S. F. Golden City* of June 28, 1868. The unknown author follows a familiar pattern so common to many of our earlier writers on Death Valley. There is the usual imaginative and distorted account of perishing men, women and animals; of "children, crying for water, (who) died at their mothers' breasts, and with swollen tongues and burning vitals, the mothers followed." The writer did maneuver to permit two of the party to escape; but he has it that "eighty-seven persons, with hundreds of animals, perished in this fearful place."

Were this all, the article could well have been omitted from this Bibliography. There appears one sentence, however, that immediately arrests attention: "Mr. Spears says that when he visited it (Death Valley) last winter, after the lapse of eighteen years, he found the wagons still complete, the iron works and the tires bright, and the shriveled skeletons lying in many places side by side."

Could this "Mr. Spears" refer to John Randolph Spears, author of *Illustrated Sketches of Death Valley*, produced in 1892? If so, then we are confronted with something of an anomaly; for John Randolph Spears stresses the fact, in his authoritative book on Death Valley, that this desert's history is "found only in tradition. *As I gathered it,* here it is." (The italics are mine.) And in his introductory preface to *Illustrated Sketches*, John Randolph Spears makes it clear that his *first* visit to Death Valley was either late in 1891 or early in 1892. Yet the "Mr. Spears" in the Shuck *Scrap-Book* is supposed to have visited this desert in 1867, or 25 years earlier than John Randolph Spears visited it for the first time.

It is possible, of course, for more than one man by the name of Spears to have visited Death Valley. Possible; but improbable in this instance. At any rate, curious. This "Mr. Spears" of the *S. F. Golden City* item was apparently assumed to be well known, else the publication would have identified him by first name or initial, if not by qualifying comment. Was he an explorer, a prospector, a writer? If, in fact, he was an early Death Valley writer, then where are his writings? Or, if he was a well-known and knowledgeable authority on Death Valley, then surely there would be some written record of him. If so, then where *is* this record?

All of which is perhaps of small concern to the average Death Valley reader. But to the student of Death Valley history it poses a choice curiosity piece. 1868 is an early date in the known life of Death Valley; the first recorded *printed* appearance of this name was in 1863. So, if not John Randolph Spears, then who was this inscrutable "Mr. Spears" of the early 1868 *Golden City* article? (For a detailed assessment of the early groups entering Death Valley, see Edwards—*The Mystery of Death Valley's Lost Wagon Train.*

SHUMWAY, NINA PAUL

Patriarch of Palm Springs. 1949. July issue of *Desert*. Illus.

This article relates the story of Dr. Welwood Murray and early Palm Springs.

Mrs. Shumway gives her readers an understanding account of Dr. Murray, the pioneer settler of Palm Springs.

Your Desert and Mine. 1960. Los Angeles: Westernlore Press. Introduction by Harold O. Weight. XV plus 322 pp. 13 illus. 5¾ x 8⅜.

This is the story of the date industry in the Coachella Valley; also of the founding of Palm Springs (Riverside County). Included is what appears to be the true background account of old Fig Tree John, the Indian, and the nicely portrayed character of the respected desert artist—Carl Eytel. Naturally, we are favored with yet another account of the ubiquitous Indian savage—Willie Boy. (There should be some repressive act or influence that would discourage further inclusion of this degenerate killer in our otherwise refreshing desert literature.) Willie Boy wasn't even an *imaginative* killer—if there is such a thing as an imaginative killer. The best he could do was murder a defenseless old man and an equally defenseless young girl. Neither the killer nor his captors even *simulated* imagination. Willie had already killed himself by the time his pursuers found him. As long as he remained alive he eluded them. It required no spectacular feat to track down a dead man.

Mrs. Shumway's chapters—"Off for the Waterhole Country," "Gold Strike," and "Headed Home" (pp. 226-244) are of classic proportions in the field of desert literature. In them she narrates an early trip through what is now the Joshua Tree National Monument, on into the area bordering the old Bradshaw Road.

SITGREAVES, CAPTAIN L.

Report of an Expedition Down the Zuni and Colorado Rivers. 1854. Washington: Senate Printer. 33 D Congress 1st Session. Senate. 198 pp., plus 79 full-page plates of Landscapes, Mammals, Birds, Reptiles, Fishes, and Plants. 6 x 9¼.

Included is a 19-page Report by Sitgreaves, followed by tables of distances, geographical positions and meteorological observations; an 8-page Report on the natural history of the country passed over, by S. W. Woodhouse, M.D., the surgeon and naturalist to the expedition; sections on zoology, reptiles, fishes, botany, and a medical report by Dr. Woodhouse.

It is in the January 25, 1853, Report by Dr. S. W. Woodhouse (p. 40) that we find interesting material relating to the Colorado Desert and, more specifically, the Carrizo Corridor with mention of Vallecito, San Felipe and Santa Isabelle. Here, also, is one of the relatively few references to the historic Palm Springs Oasis in the Carrizo Corridor: "On this creek there has been a grove of large palms, a few of which now remain."

SLOCUM, DR. SAMUEL M.

Life Saving In Death Valley. 1910. August issue of *Touring Topics.*

An early account of a victim of thirst in Death Valley. The article, as related by Dr. Slocum, verges on the melodramatic; but his prudent recommendation for the installation of directional signs guiding the traveler to water in that early day was no doubt partially responsible for their subsequent installation.

SMITH, GERALD A.

Early Man On the California Desert. 1964. *Westerners, The* (Los Angeles Corral). *Brand Book* No. 11. 15 pp. 2 photographs. Line drawings by Don Perceval.

An exceptionally fine archaeological study of the very early inhabitants of our California Deserts.

(With KNIGHT and HAENSZEL.) *Historic Chronology of San Bernardino and Riverside Counties.* (See listing under Haenszel, A.)

SMITH, GERALD A. et al.

Indian Picture Writing of San Bernardino and Riverside Counties. 1961 (Spring). San Bernardino: County Museum Association. 36 pp. 12 photographic illus. Pen drawings. Wrappers.

This is a discussion of the location, appearance and meaning of the pictographs in San Bernardino and Riverside Counties. Included is some attempt at interpretation of such famous markings as the Hemet Maze Stone, the Anza pictures in Nance Canyon at the lower end of Cahuilla valley, the giant figures on the Colorado Desert 30 miles north of Blythe, and others of comparable interest.

SMITH, G. G. (Edited by)

Parson's Progress To California. (See listing under Pierce, Geo. Frederick.)

SMITH, GRANT H.

Bodie: The Last of the Old-Time Mining Camps. 1925. March issue of *California Historical Society Quarterly*, Vol. IV, No. 1. Pp. 64-80.

This item gives clear definition to the famous old mining camp of Bodie.

SNELL, GEORGE

And If Man Triumph. 1938. Caldwell, Idaho: Caxton Printers. 215 pp. End paper maps. 5⅞ x 8½.

The author endeavors to fictionize the actual experiences of the Manly-Bennett Death Valley party of 1849. The result is a fresh and spirited novel, the fictional characters assuming both the names and the roles of the real-life characters developed in Manly's *Death Valley in '49.*

It is unfortunate that the author imputed such a dubious character to Mr. Lew West and to Mrs. J. B. Arcane, both actual pioneers in the Death Valley trek. And Mr. Snell's inference of a secret love affair between the estimable wife of Mr. Arcane and Manly's heroic scouting partner, John Rogers, is utterly reprehensible.

Any manipulation of facts in an ambitious effort to accomplish literary expediency is, after its fashion, a type of incipient fabrication that may result in irreparable harm, particularly when disparagement of character is involved. If the inherent facts attendant upon some memorable achievement do not—in themselves—indicate sufficient dramatic appeal, it would appear advisable for the aspiring author to choose some other theme for the exercise of his talent.

SNYDER, ANDREW

True Story of the Vasquez Murders. 1949. September issue of the *Historical Society of Southern California Quarterly*.

Mr. Snyder was in the general mercantile and horse business in the fall of 1872 at a place called Tres Pinos (later named Paicines), then in Monterey County (later in San Benito County). Vasquez and his men struck the store in the evening, robbed it of $430 and about a thousand dollars in merchandise. Also, they took with them eleven horses, using them to pack off the stolen merchandise. Others coming to the store that evening were bound, some were killed; but the lives of Snyder and his wife were spared.

SOUTH, MARSHALL

Healing Waters at Agua Caliente. 1947. July issue of *Desert*. Illus.

Marshall South gives us an exhaustive account of San Diego County's "Agua Caliente" located 3½ miles beyond Vallecitos. Considerable emphasis is placed upon the health-restorative properties of the springs.

"Lost Ship" of the Vanished Sea, The. 1947. February issue of *The Desert Spotlight*.

This is another of the many yarns—and an unusually good one it is—of the mythical "Lost Ship of the Desert."

SPEARS, JOHN RANDOLPH

Illustrated Sketches of Death Valley and Other Borax Deserts of the Pacific Coast. 1892. New York: Rand, McNally & Company. 226 pp. 57 pls. 1 map. 5¼ x 7½. Appears in both cloth and yellow wrappers. Several variants occur in the pages of advertisements.

Spears favors his readers with an intimate word-picture of Death Valley as it appeared in 1891. It will be noted that his book precedes the Manly by two years. *Illustrated Sketches* is noted for its early photographs in almost the same degree as for its textual content. It is conceivable that these may be the first pictures ever published—perhaps ever taken—of the Death Valley region. Maximum importance attaches to them.

It is in *Illustrated Sketches* that we first read of Aaron Winters and his historic discovery of borax deep in the heart of Death Valley; and of his now-classic exclamation to the delicate wife Rosie—"She burns green! We're rich, by ——." Although reluctant to admit it, and disclaiming all intent to disparage the author, some of us cannot wholly rationalize certain factors involved in his presentation of this fabulous discovery, particularly those having reference to the source of supply and the specific functioning of the chemicals involved in perfecting the borax test. We cannot altogether escape the mawkish impression that even our reliable Spears tended to over-dramatize both the circumstances and the technique attendant upon this historic event.

From this entertaining account we learn something of the desert's history—although all that we learn is not entirely accurate. In the course of our reading we encounter the "White Arabs" and the "Desert Tramps;" we are regaled with the stirring narrative, perhaps for the first time told in print, of John W. Searles and his borax mining enterprise on the Searles Dry Lake where now is located the huge plant of the American Potash & Chemical Corporation of Trona. (But see listing under Leuba, Edmond.) Spears also includes a description of the early freight wagons used in the 20-mule team borax outfits—those ten sturdy old wagons that were in constant use without a single breakdown during the five years the Works were in operation. Significantly, even after standing exposed to the rigors of Death Valley weather for *fifty years*, two of these ancient wagons were sufficiently preserved to participate in the San Francisco Bay Bridge celebration.

Many books and articles written of the Mojave Desert and its glamorous Valley of Death—and particularly among those written prior to 1930—are of an ephemeral nature, arousing only a passing interest in the country they attempt to describe. Spears' *Illustrated Sketches*, on the other hand, is a book equally as distinguished as it is distinctive; and its substance guarantees as perpetual the sustained interest that pulsates throughout every chapter. It is as adequate and as dependable a commentary on Death Valley and the Mojave Desert today as it was in that day—years ago—when Spears wrote it. It is Death Valley's number two book; and it will probably continue to remain so. Certainly no desert collection even merits the name without a copy of the Spears.

Miners Homes In the Mojave Desert. 1894. March issue of *The Chautauquan.* 5 pp. 7 illus.

The reader must be date-conscious to grasp the relative importance of this very readable piece of desert writing. 1894 was a long time ago for Death Valley literature. Manly came out with his *Death Valley in '49*—the incomparable, top-rated account of this desert—during 1894; Spears himself had written the second-rated account only two years previously (*Illustrated Sketches of Death Valley*). This present little-known article relates certain aspects of desert living in that early day which—to my knowledge—are not elsewhere touched upon by any source writer. It must be remembered that Spears was *there*. He personally visited most of the homes he wrote about. His descriptions are not speculative. The early mining camps—that is, the *homes* in these early mining camps—are described in minute detail. "To every district," writes Spears, "there is a camp and in some several—the gatherings of miners, merchants, teamsters, and mechanics, with gamblers and other leeches, about the mines the prospectors found. . . . The homes to be seen in these camps are almost invariably spoken of as shanties. They are usually houses built with walls of inch boards nailed vertically to the flimsiest of frames, with roofs of similar boards or of tin or of corrugated iron. Sometimes the cracks in the walls are battened and sometimes not. Sometimes there is a floor of boards and sometimes the sand of the mesa serves the purpose. . . . Though incapable of fending off the blazing heat of summer or of keeping out the biting cold of winter these houses are not usually the homes of ignorance or even of squalor." Spears writes of Belleville, Candeleria, Daggett, Mojave, Calico, Marietta, Ash Meadows; of such characters as Aaron Winters and his wife Rosie, of John Searles, Tom Purcell, and Cub Lee.

The illustrations are reproductions of early photographs—one taken of a typical miner's shanty, others of the ghost of Marietta, the ranch at Death Valley (before the days of the date palms), Calico, and an unnamed silver mining camp.

Through Death Valley. 1893. February issue of *California Illustrated Magazine.*

In the compass of a few brief pages, Spears gives comprehensive coverage to the full scope of his subject. As in *Illustrated Sketches,* the work is distinguished by a refinement of composition that should commend itself to the most exacting reader. The several text illustrations include three early photographs.

Attention is given to the subject of freighting and to descriptions of the huge borax wagons; also to the origin and development of the Greenland (now Furnace Creek) Ranch on the floor of Death Valley. He concludes his article with the following appraisal of Death Valley which constitutes one of the best word-pictures, and also one of the first published accounts by an eye-observer, of this fabulous wasteland: "To most tourists Death Valley presents a complete picture of desolation. The mountains are rugged and devoid of verdure; the lowland is a salty waste, where only the mesquite, thorny and gnarled, and the sage brush of the color of ashes thrive. Even these have a constant struggle for life with the searing sand-storms. As to the fauna of the country, one finds the gauntest of coyotes and the leanest of wild cats; the lizard and the rattlesnake, each with horns; the centipede and the tarantula. In the wailings of its mammals, the terrors of its reptiles, and the suffocation and oppression of its atmosphere, Death Valley is in the season a veritable type of the fabled sheol. Its dangers have never been, nor can scarcely be adequately described. And yet because of its magnificent geological pictures of the wonderful powers of nature, because of its resources in salt and minerals, because of its anthropological studies of the region round about, and because of the novel experiences which the tourist will surely have, there are few places that will better repay him for his time and trouble."

Spears was a reporter on the New York *Sun.* He came into Death Valley around 1892, mainly to report upon the borax industry. Historian Harold O. Weight, one of the most knowledgeable of all our desert writers, appropriately refers to Spears as "Death Valley's first trained reporter."

SPELL, HAZEL M.

Twentynine Palms Story, The. 1953. (November.) Revised in 1954 with 40 pp. Line drawings. 5⅞ x 8⅓. Wrappers. Mimeographed. (The first ed. contains 26 pp. and measures 6¼ x 8½. Wrappers. Mimeographed.) A third revision was published in 1959.

This is the basic historical account of Twentynine Palms, written by one of the town's pioneers. So friendly and intimate is the style employed that the reader feels himself a part of that which he reads. The narrative is accurately sketched, and the sources may be regarded as authentic. Of special importance are those portions of the book relating to early settlers in the region, to activities of the prospectors, and to the mines and the mining era generally.

STACEY, MAY HUMPHREYS (Journal)

Uncle Sam's Camels. 1929. (See listing under Lesley, Lewis B.)

Stacey accompanied the "Camel Caravan," and his *Journal* ably covers its movements as far west as the Colorado.

STANDAGE, HENRY

Journal. 1928. (See listing under Golder, Frank Alfred—*March of the Mormon Battalion from Council Bluffs to California, The.*)

Standage was a private in Company E of Cooke's Mormon Battalion.

STANDARD OIL COMPANY

Across Death Valley in a Ford Car. (1926.) *Standard Oil Bulletin.* Illus.

This is an advertising medium, extolling the virtues of the New Zeroline "F" for Model T Fords, and citing the feat of an old Model T in successfully crossing Death Valley.

STEBBINS, R. C.

Lives of Desert Animals In Joshua Tree National Monument. (See listing under Miller, A. H.)

STEERE, COLLIS H.

Imperial and Coachella Valleys. (1952.) Stanford: Stanford University Press. 90 pp. 60 pls. 2 maps. 5⅛ x 8⅞. Wrappers.

This illustrated guide book to the Imperial and Coachella Valleys supplies a wealth of information—some of it accurate; some of it not so accurate. In particular is this true of the first edition which was shortly superseded by a second edition (1953), correcting many (but not all) of the errors showing in the first.

STEPHENS, FRANK

California Mammals. 1906. San Diego, California: The West Coast Publishing Company. 351 pp. Illus. Fldg. map. 7 x 10¼. West Coast Nature Series.

An exhaustive treatise, with special attention extended to a description of the characteristics of the smaller desert animals. According to the author—"No general work concerning the mammals of this State has been published since 1857 when Baird's Vol. VIII of the Pacific Railroad Reports was issued." (Note that Mr. Stephens made this comment in 1906.)

STEPHENS, L. DOW

Life Sketches of a Jayhawker of '49. 1916. 68 pp. 6¼ x 9½. Wrappers. Photographs of 21 of the original Jayhawkers (including three members of the Brier family and W. L. Manly).

This important book is source material. It is particularly valuable in tracing the movements of the 1849 pioneers prior to their entrance into Death Valley, and also their movements subsequently to leaving it. As relates specifically to Death

Valley, the book is of no value whatsoever. Stephens confuses even the geographical location of the Valley. To be sure, he was only 22 when he passed through this desert, and he did not write his book until some 66 years later. Fundamentally, however, the cause for his distortion of the basic facts is not altogether attributal to age nor yet to reliance upon a faulty memory. Mr. Stephens frankly believed that Death Valley was the region round about Searles Lake where, in fact, the Jayhawkers *really* suffered, and *actually* experienced death. He is implicit in his reference to the Searles Lake area as Death Valley; when he vaguely refers to the *true* Death Valley where they burned their wagons, he has no name for it. To him, to *all* Jayhawkers (and this includes the Brier family), it was just one of many desolate valleys; not so deadly, not so ominous, not so forbidding as the wearisome deserts that came after it—Panamint, Searles Lake, and Mojave. The Jayhawkers had not really begun to experience hardships in Death Valley, except those occasioned by abandoning their wagons. They had food, and water, and strength. Their stay in the Valley was relatively short—only one week. It was the Manly-Bennett-Arcane party—fathers, mothers, children—who came to *know* Death Valley. They *lived* in it, *suffered* in it, all but *died* in it for five long, terrifying weeks. They could *never* forget it; and, because of them, the world shall forever remember it.

Page 40 of the narrative of this famous old Death Valley character tells of an early visit to Warner's Ranch. On page 50 he mentions crossing the Colorado Desert to La Paz. And finally, on page 52, he describes a return trip over the Colorado Desert, camping at "Dos Palmos." This would indicate that these last two trips were over the Bradshaw Trail.

STEWART, RAMONA

Desert Town. 1945. (Serialized version in *Collier's.*) The first book printing was in 1946. Reprints have followed.

Desert Town is a novel, with plot laid in the Mojave Desert. It is thought the author used Barstow as her locale. Her descriptions of the desert appear impeccable; but why so talented an author would choose to develop so revolting (in my opinion) a theme, is beyond comprehension.

STILES, ED (As told to Johnston, Philip)

Saga of the Twenty Mule Team. 1939. December issue of *Westways.* Illus.

Stiles makes claim to the honor of driving the first of the historic three-wagon trains that played so colorful a part in the great borax-mining renaissance of Death Valley. Again we are mindful of the importance attaching to all such *source* accounts of our deserts' incidents and epochs.

STOCK, CHESTER

Mohave's Petrified Forest. 1936. December issue of *Westways.* Illus.

The author writes of the petrified forest in upper Last Chance Gulch. Says the author—"Some of the trees stand rooted where they grew ages ago. The most abundant tree is the locust and with it occurs a palm. Oak, pine and cedar have also been identified." It will be noted this article was written over 30 years ago. Don't expect too much today.

When Titans Roamed Prehistoric Death Valley. 1936. March issue of *Westways.* Illus.

The article describes the accidental discovery of the lower jaw and several teeth of the skull of a titanothere, and the resultant "finds" depicting life in Death Valley as it was millions of years ago. The "titanothere," Stock tells us, are "distant cousins of the rhinoceros."

STORMS, W. H. and FAIRBANKS, HAROLD W.

Old Mines of Southern California: Desert, Mountain, Coastal Areas. 1965. Toyah-vale, Texas: Frontier Book Co. 96 pp. Wrappers.

The book supplies a semi-technical description of specific mines and mining areas, particularly in the San Diego, Orange and San Bernardino Counties. There are interesting descriptions of the Carrizo Corridor and the Calico-Salton Sea district. (Reprint of 1893 Report of State Mineralogist.)

STOVER, JACOB Y.

Narrative. (See listings under Caughey, John Walton—*Southwest From Salt Lake In 1849 and the Jacob Y. Stover Narrative;* Hafen, LeRoy and Ann— *Journals of Forty-Niners,* pp. 274-291).

Stover was one of the group (from the Sand Walking Co.) who packed down Mt. Misery into the Beaver Dam Wash.

STRETCH, R. H.

U. S. Government Bulletin. (See listing under James, T. E.)

STROBRIDGE, IDAH MEACHAM

In Miners' Mirage Land. 1904. Los Angeles: Baumgardt Publishing Company. 6 copies were hand-bound in full morocco, 24 copies in ¾ green morocco, and the remainder of 1,000 copies were done in heavy paper. The binding was fashioned by the author at her Artemisia Bindery. 130 pp. 6½ x 8½.

This is the first of the notable trio of Strobridge books and, probably, the best of the lot. It consists of desert sketches—essays and stories. The author's style reminds one of Mary Austin; but this resemblance we can well abide. The book offers delightful reading; merits a conspicuous position in any desert collection. The other Strobridge books—*The Loom of the Desert* (1907), and *The Land of Purple Shadows* (1909)—do not contain any essential reference to the desert.

STUART, GORDON

When the Sands of the Desert Grew Gold. 1961. Pacific Palisades, California: Gordon Stuart. 204 pp. 17 photographs. Spiral binding. 6 x 8½.

The author is writing about Imperial Valley "before Salton Sea was born" and also in its later years. "This is not a history of Imperial Valley," he tells us; "it is a picture . . . of life as it was lived by the people in the first chapter."

Readers will admire this book—the *spirit* of it, its *concept*, its revelation, its rugged *realism*. "There are many errors in this book (Mr. Stuart printed it himself; says it required over two years to do it), found after printing. I will not point them out; thus depriving you of the joy of finding them." If errors exist, I am sure they are not culpable errors; and I—for one—would not "point them out" even though I should happen to run headlong into them. There are far too many historical gems in this book to be concerned about an occasional typographical error.

The author takes us back to the year 1904, the day he arrived in Imperial Valley. The fun starts here. And the book *is* fun to read. But it is more. It gives one a solid look into the infancy of Imperial Valley by one who was there and helped make it. There is considerable to be found in this entertaining book of Harold Bell Wright, W. F. Holt—the founder of Holtville, the valley towns—some that have survived to the present and others long non-existent, the history of early roads over the Algodones sand dunes.

STUART, HOMER A. and RUTH L.

Desert Spotlight, The. 1946. (April) to 1948 (August). Yucca Valley, California: Desert Spotlight Publishing Co.

The Desert Spotlight is a magazine devoted principally to the High Desert country of Morongo and Yucca Valleys, Joshua Tree, and Twentynine Palms. In all, there were published 26 monthly, including occasional bi-monthly issues. Each issue averages from 16 to 20 pages, and the magazine measures approximately 9 x 11½. All issues are generously illustrated with photographic reproductions that serve to vitalize the textual content of the articles.

Representative writings from twelve authors have been selected for inclusion in this Bibliography: Anonymous, Bagley, Ewings, Ford, Fox, Godwin, Jones, H., Jones, S., Paxton, Pratt, Russell, South.

The Desert Spotlight captured, while yet there was time and opportunity, a collection of historically important desert fact and lore. It marks the initial attempt to assemble source information on the High Desert region. Sporadic efforts have recurrently been exerted, and notable articles have appeared in various publications. But here is a magazine dedicated, in its near entirety, to the collection and the preservation of historical material on an area destined to become one of the outstanding desert retreats in California. Located at an elevation ranging from 1900 to 3600 feet, skirted on the south by the spectacular Joshua Tree National Monument and on a portion of its northern boundary by the huge Marine Base, this region is a desert area separate unto itself. The Mojave claims it; the Colorado includes it. Actually, it belongs to neither; being a third and distinct desert entity standing buffer between its two huge neighbors.

Few there are—or ever were—whom we may consider qualified to speak of the early history of this desert. Of these few, who still remained when *The Desert Spotlight* flourished, Maude Carrico Russell is among the foremost. She, too, has since passed on; but much of her knowledge of this period has been reduced to writing on the pages of *Spotlight*, and thus preserved for all time to come. Maude

A. Fox also contributed several articles on pioneer people and events. Harlow Jones, Stanley Jones, Jean Fridley, Helen Bagley, June LeMert Paxton, Ed Malone, Howard Clark, F. V. Sampson, Belle E. Ewing, Nell Murbarger, Marshall South—all these and many others are among the list of *Spotlight's* distinguished contributors. It succeeded in salvaging historical material that otherwise may have been irrevocably lost. Fortunate is the desert collection that can lay claim to a complete 26-issue run of this unusual publication.

STURTEVANT, PAT and GEORGE

New Gateway to Death Valley. 1949. November issue of *Desert*. Illus.

This article unfolds the advantages of a new road opening into Death Valley National Monument from Trona, on Searles Lake, through Wildrose Canyon. The new route makes accessible a few of the old ghost towns and historic land marks in the Panamint Mountains and the Panamint Valley. There is generous comment on Panamint City in the Sturtevant article.

SULLIVAN, MAURICE S.

Travels of Jedediah Smith, The. 1934. Santa Ana: Fine Arts Press. 195 pp. 6½ x 9¾. Fldg. map.

Portions of the text tell of Smith's journey across the Mojave to the San Gabriel Mission in 1826. This book contains Smith's own Journal and the Diary of Alexander McLeod. (Sullivan also produced *Jedediah Smith, Trader & Trail Breaker*.)

When Indians Brought the First Mail Into California. 1934. April issue of *Westways*. Illus.

The article recalls an unique mail service conducted by the Indians from Tucson to San Gabriel via the Salton Sea, Palm Springs, San Gorgonio Pass and the original San Bernardino (several miles southeast of the present site). This occurred in the early 1820's.

SUTHERLAND, MASON

Californians Escape to the Desert. 1957. November issue of *National Geographic*. Pp. 675-724. Numerous photographs; most of them in color.

The photographs commend this article; the text is more citizen-illuminating than historically helpful. There is an especially good black and white photograph of sections of the old plank road over the Algodones sand dunes; artist Johnny Hilton bursts forth in colored splendor, as do "Calico Fred" Noller and Harry Oliver. Anything that brings innocent happiness to an individual I, in turn, am eager to acclaim; but the Geographic's intransigent resolve to glorify individuals at the expense of our beautiful desert scenery is a trait I deplore. In substantially all the colored illustrations in this article the otherwise lovely desert scenery is subordinated to a group of horseback riders, "Caddy Wagons" carrying "a happy foursome," a "salesman" endeavoring to peddle a sandy subdivision parcel, a group of picnickers, the author and friends emulating professional bowlers with "odd concretions in Yuha Wash," and—naturally—the inevitable bathing beauties (unfortunately, bikinis had not come into vogue when this article was written).

SUTTON, ANN and MYRON

Life Of the Desert. (1966.) New York: McGraw Hill Book Company. Published in cooperation with The World Book Encyclopedia. 232 pp. Numerous photographic plates, many of them in color. 7½ x 10¼.

The outstanding feature of this book is displayed in its photographic plates. These make possible a visual presentation of the desert's animal life. A few purely scenic plates are included. The instructive portion of the text may be found in the Appendix (pp. 201-226.)

SWEENEY, LT. THOMAS W. (Edited by Woodward, Arthur)

Journal of: 1849-1853. 1956. Los Angeles: Westernlore Press. 278 pp. 9 illus. Ed. limited to 450 copies. 5½ x 8⅜.

In this historical journal is our earliest and perhaps most graphic account of Fort Yuma. Frequent text references to the Colorado Desert crossing are found throughout the book (see pp. 49-51, 114-118, 137-142, 149-150). Dr. Woodward infuses added interest into the *Journal* text by the inclusion of some 56 pages of Bibliographical Notes. (See, in particular, pp. 217-224, 227-228, 232-237.)

SYKES, GODFREY

Colorado Delta, The. 1937. Carnegie Institute of Washington. American Geographical Society, Special Publication No. 19. VII, 193 pp. Fldg. map. 74 illus.

Frequent references are made to the Southern California desert region, among the more important being those mentioned in Ch. 8—"The Imperial Valley" (pp. 108-123). Here are sectional sub-headings such as—Discovery of Salton Sink as Depression Below Sea Level—1853; Projects for the Economic Developing of the Basin—1859-1900; Establishment of Irrigation System and Beginning of Settlement—1901-1903; Complete Break-Through of the River and Diversion to Salton Sink—1905; Attempts to Close the Breach, with Final Success in 1907; Topography of Imperial Valley and Related Area; The All-American Canal. Pp. 68-76 also contain material of importance with reference to the Salton Sea.

Pp. 177-188 list a detailed and exhaustive bibliography of the Salton Sea region. Personally, I regard the Bibliography as the most important feature of this very important book.

TALLACK, WILLIAM

California Overland Express, The. The Longest Stage-Ride in the World. 1935. Los Angeles: The *Historical Society of Southern California.* Special Publication No. I. 85 pp. 6¼ x 9½. (Wagner-Camp No. 425.)

Carl I. Wheat writes the introduction; J. Gregg Layne assembles a check list of published material on The Butterfield Overland Mail. Reference to the route as it extended eastward over the Colorado Desert in 1858 may be found on pp. 34-35 and 70-71. This account appeared originally in *"The Leisure Hour,"* London, 1865. It is also reprinted in Walter B. Lang's *The First Overland Mail; Butterfield Trail.* Tallack, the Englishman, narrates his trip from San Francisco to St. Louis. Three contemporary accounts also describe trips over this early historic stage route; but these are not included in this item. (See listing under Lang, Water B.—*First Overland Mail, The.*)

TAYLOR, CHARLES A.

Story of Scotty and His Great Western Drama. 1906. New York: J. S. Ogilvie Publ. Co. 114 pp. of text. 4 pls. 14 full pp. of advertisements. Illus. Wrappers. 4⅞ x 7¼. The title on the title page reads—"The Story of 'Scotty' (Walter Scott), King of the Desert Mine."

This book, early and scarce and melodramatic, is merely a glorified promotion scheme for the Santa Fe, and a crude publicity stunt for a play the author contemplated producing. It is one of those much-sought-after "oddities" in Death Valley literature.

TERRELL, JOHN UPTON

War On the Colorado River. 1964. *Westerners, The* (Los Angeles Corral) *Brand Book* No. 11. 12 pp. Line drawings by Don Perceval.

No bibliography of our Southwest desert area would be entirely complete without some reference to the prolonged Colorado River water dispute among the several States affected. Terrell's article supplies a good summation of it.

THOMPSON, DAVID G.

Mohave Desert Region, California; A Geographic, Geologic, and Hydrologic Reconnaissance. 1929. Washington: U.S.G.S. Water Supply Paper 578. XI, 759 pp. 34 pls. 7 detached maps in end-pocket. 47 pls. and sketch maps. 5¾ x 9. Wrappers.

"The Mohave Desert region, in southeastern California, is a part of the so-called 'Great American Desert', a vast region that covers nearly one-sixth of the area of the United States."

See, also, D. G. Thompson's *Routes to Desert Watering Places in the Mohave Desert Region, California,* consisting principally of descriptions, travel suggestions, road logs. U.S.G.S. Water Supply Paper 490-B. 1921. 269 pp. 2 fldg. maps. 5 detached fldg. maps in end-pocket. 15 pls. 5⅞ x 9⅛. Wrappers.

Part I of this voluminous report deals with general features, including a discussion of the region's geography, history, settlements, population, transportation, mineral resources, agriculture and stock raising, flora and fauna, soils, climate, drainage, geology, structure, and ground water. The discussion of Death Valley, for example, (pp. 14-16, inc.) is unusually accurate and exceptionally well done. The historical narrative of Part II provides a description of the following valleys—Indian Wells, Coso, Rose, Searles, Salt Wells, Panamint, Pilot Knob, Leach, Avawatz, Granite, Fremont, Golden, Superior, Goldstone, Bicycle, Langford, Red Pass, Harper, Coyote, Antelope, Mohave River Basin, Kelso, Soda Lake, Silver Lake, Amargosa, Pahrump, Mesquite, Ivanpah, Roach, Las Vegas, Sutor, Lucerne, Fry, Johnson, Bessemer, Means, Ames, Surprise, Lavic, Broadwell, Bristol-Lanfair Basin, Ward, Rice, and the Colorado River Basin. The section on Morongo, Warren, Copper Mountain, Twentynine Palms, and Dale Valleys is by Mr. John S. Brown. (See listing in this Bibliography.)

THRALL, WILL H.

Haunts and Hide-Outs of Tiburcio Vasquez. 1948. June issue of the *Historical Society of Southern California Quarterly.* 16 pp. 5 photographs.

Mr. Thrall comments that the bandit career of Joaquin Murietta lasted only three and one half years; that of Vasquez and his band twenty-three years, the last three of these being occupied almost entirely in Southern California.

The Thrall article goes into some depth exploring the history of Vasquez and his operations. It tells of the Tres Pinos raid, the holdup of the Owens Valley Stages at the Coyote Holes Stage Station (Freeman's), the capture at Greek George's place. (Note: In 1947, third and fourth quarters of the *Southern California Historical Society Quarterly*, an article on Tiburcio Vasquez appears, authored by Ernest R. May.)

TODD, CHARLES BURR

Battles of San Pasqual—A Study, The. 1925. Pomona: Progress Publishing Company. 23 pp. 2 pls. 4½ x 6. Wrappers.

This little brochure, seldom encountered, presents a competent summation of the historic battle of San Pasqual. The author quotes, first, from General Kearny's report of the battle which, he tells us, was "obtained by courtesy of the Secretary of War, and which is not given in any volume accessible to the general public within our knowledge." The Kearny report is dated at San Diego, Dec. 13, 1846, and is addressed to Adjutant General Jones. (Refer to pp. 10-15 of the brochure.) Actually, General Kearny's report is printed in Bartlett's *Personal Narrative* (pp. 113-115, Vol. 2; 1854); also in Coy's *Battle of San Pasqual*, published in 1921. The author includes the State Historical Commission account, based largely upon the journal of Lt. Emory (pp. 15-20). The concluding portion relates to the San Pasqual Valley generally.

TOUT, OTIS BURGESS

First Thirty Years, The—Being An Account of the Principal Events in the History of Imperial County, Southern California, U.S.A. (1931.) San Diego. 429 pp. Illus. Maps. Bibl. Pp. 9-12. 8¼ x 11.

The book is compiled mainly from items appearing in the files of early newspapers, and classified chronologically under the several towns in Imperial Valley. The text is profusely illustrated with more than 250 photographs of scenes and individuals. Among some of the historic events described (far too briefly, unfortunately) are Kearny's Expedition, Pacific Railway Surveys, Closing the Big Break in the Colorado, Hoover Dam, the Plank Road over the Algodones Sand Dunes.

TRAVIS, PAUL W.

Wind Machine in the Pass, The. 1956. February issue of *Westways*. Illus.

Mr. Travis writes of Dew Oliver's Electric Power Generator, erected in 1926, just north of the present highway between the Palm Springs turn-off and Whitewater, on Interstate 10. This gadget was a 10-ton wind turbine erected on a circular track for the purpose of increasing wind pressure, the idea being to generate power over Southern California. The wind funnel is said to have stood until 1942 when it was dismantled for scrap metal. The remains of this unsuccessful experiment are still visible from the highway. (A short article regarding this same fantastic creation appears in the Los Angeles Westerners' Corral—*The Branding Iron*, for September 1955, by Harry C. James.)

TRIGG, MURIEL VAN TUYL

Twentynine Palms. 1945. March, April and May issues of *Atlantic Monthly*.

When the depression was at its height, Mr. and Mrs. Trigg left Pasadena for the beautiful desert at Twentynine Palms. Here they constructed their own adobe home—"Singing Sands." Mrs. Trigg tells just how they accomplished all this. She tells, also, something of the character of this peaceful desert, and of the influence it had upon their lives.

TUCKER, MARY

Books of the Southwest: A General Bibliography. N.d. (1937?) J. J. Augustin. 105 pp. 4⅝ x 7⅜. Wrappers.

This book classifies, under 25 subject headings, a number of the books written about our Southwest country.

TURNER, GEORGE

Narrow Gauge Nostalgia. 1965. Harbor City, California: J-H Publications. Words "First Printing, December, 1965" appear under copyright notice. 160 pp. Numerous photographs. 8¾ x 11¼.

California desert mention may be found in the Bodie and Benton Railway (Section I), pages 9-26; the Carson and Colorado Railroad Album (Section 3), pages 38-60; and the Plaster City Narrow Gauge Railroad (Section 8), pages 139-159. The principal appeal of this book is largely confined to its photographs. Most of these, being of trains or railroad equipment, will receive favorable response from railroad buffs.

Slim Rails Through the Sand. 1963. Long Beach: Johnston & Howe. 104 pp. End paper map. Numerous photographs. 8¾ x 11¼.

Although primarily a book for rail fans, the desert enthusiast will find much to capture his interest, both in the photographs and in the brief comment accompanying them. This is the book that tells of the Carson and Colorado Railroad, at one time extending from Mound House, southwest of Dayton, Nevada, and running southwest to skirt the eastern side of Walker Lake, past Mina, Belleville—with a spur to Candeleria, finally dropping south into California near Benton and extending past Laws (near Bishop), and on to Owenyo and Keeler. The photographs—particularly those of Candeleria (Nevada), Keeler, and Cerro Gordo—are of historic interest.

TURNER, HENRY SMITH (Edited by Clarke, Dwight L.)

Original Journals. (1966). Norman: University of Oklahoma Press. 173 pp. 8 illus. Map. 6¼ x 9¼.

Turner served with Kearny in the conquest of New Mexico and California in 1846-47. On November 25, 1846, the Company forded the Colorado and started their march over the barren desert "destitute of everything but sand, of which there was much to impede our progress." On November 28 they arrived at "Karissa" (Carrizo) Creek; on December 2 they passed through Box Canyon, arriving at Warner's the following day.

Turner appears so obsessed with thought of possible conflict with the "Mexicans," and so consumed with abject loneliness for his wife, that he has little inclination to occupy his time describing the country through which he travels.

TWAIN, MARK (SAMUEL L. CLEMENS)

Roughing It In California. 1953. Kentfield, California: The L-D Allen Press. 90 pp. 6¾ x 10¼. Limited to 200 copies.

The original *Roughing It* was, of course, published long before 1953; 1872 to be exact. This attractive fine-press item is chosen, in lieu of the entire book, because it isolates the California material from the original work which relates principally to another state. The section of immediate desert interest is "Roughing It At Mono Lake" (pp. 23-36).

TYLER, SGT. DANIEL

Concise History of the Mormon Battalion in the Mexican War, 1846-1847. 1881 (or 1882). (Salt Lake City.) 376 pp. List of Survivors at end of book is dated March 1882. 6⅛ x 9. A Zamorano 80 item. (Cowan P. 234.) Reprinted in 1964 by the Rio Grande Press.

"*The Concise History of the Mormon Battalion* is a book more important for content than style, although some of the accounts of the sufferings of the half-trained Mormon volunteers as they starved and thirsted on the Southwestern deserts are effective in their simplicity. The author, Sgt. Tyler, marched with the Battalion from Council Bluffs to San Diego. If for no other reason than that it is the only attempt at a complete picture of the march written by a participant and from the Mormon viewpoint, Tyler's book would be invaluable. . . . Read with judgment, the *Concise History* is a splendid eye-witness account of one of the great chapters in Southwestern history—the breaking of the first wagon road from Santa Fe, New Mexico, to San Diego, California." (From Harold Weight's review in *Calico Print.*)

The passage relating to the desert crossing is brief. All of Ch. 25 (pp. 242-246) is devoted to it; also pp. 246-251 of Ch. 26. The introductory chapter occupies nearly one-third of the book, and is given over to a resumé of the history of the Mormon Church. The ten pages relating to the desert crossing offer little of value except to detail the sufferings of the men of the Battalion; and, in this respect, the Standage diary appears more vivid. Ch. 28 gives an account of the Battle of San Pasqual.

Even as early as 1904, Ingersoll—in his *Century Annals of San Bernardino County*—refers to this book as being "exceedingly rare."

UDELL, JOHN

Journal Kept During a Trip Across the Plains Containing An Account of The Massacre of a Portion of His Party by the Mojave Indians. 1946. Los Angeles: N. A. Kovach. Reprint of Udell's Journal. XVII, 87 pp. 5¼ x 8¾. It is stated there is but one known original of the rare first edition; Kovach believes there are eight.

Of importance, in this Journal, is Udell's account of the tragic experience befalling the emigrant party of which he was a member. In the latter part of August 1858, after repeated molesting by the Mojave Indian hordes, the caravan was finally attacked in force and suffered the loss of eight of its number, with thirteen wounded—some quite severely. Nearly all the cattle were killed or stolen, and only eight or ten of the horses remained. There was no alternative but to turn back from the Colorado River, where this final attack had occurred, and abandon—for a time—the westward journey.

In June of 1859, Udell finally made it to Los Angeles. He mentions some of their camping places after crossing the Colorado (pp. 76-78): Clear Lake, Pah Utah Creek, Rock Spring, Moral (sic) Springs, Soda Springs and Lake, the Sink of the Mojave River. (See listing under Rose, L. J.—*Massacre On the Colorado.*)

ULLMAN, WILLIAM A. (As told by Bailey, Vernon)

Into Death Valley 50 Years Ago. (See listing under Bailey, Vernon.)

VAILE, FRED

Burro Prospector. 1963. *Westerners, The* (Los Angeles Corral) *Brand Book* No. 10.

The Editor of *Brand Book* No. 10 writes, in his Editorial Capsule: "The late Fred Vaile, respected Westerner of the Los Angeles Corral, writes this article just as he would tell it to us in person. In a rambling, conversational style, Fred takes us over the trails with him; and at all stages of his narrative he holds us in complete captivation. This man was one of the West's best informed prospectors, his experience taking him into Death Valley, the Dale Mines, and other mining areas on the Mojave. The discerning reader will garner more than just passing entertainment from this saga of an era and an image that have all but vanished from our land."

VAN DYKE, JUDGE DIX (As told to Johnston, Philip)

Law On the Desert. 1937. November issue of *Westways*. Illus.

This is an account of incidents and experiences in the life of the late Judge Dix Van Dyke—the grand old man of Daggett. Here, as in so many of the *Touring Topics'* and *Westways'* articles, history has been captured and made available for all future generations—while yet there was time. In *Law On the Desert*, Johnston has brought us source material direct from the lips of the man responsible, above all others, for the creation of the atmosphere surrounding these epoch-making events.

Old Times In Daggett. 1943. February issue of *Westways*. Illus.

This is source history, by Daggett's leading citizen—the late Dix Van Dyke.

VAN DYKE, JOHN C.

Desert, The. 1901. New York: Charles Scribner's Sons. XIX, 233 pp. 5 x 7⅜. Numerous reprints have appeared.

This is the well-known classic of the desert; "a poem in prose." The book speaks of desert regions in general; of the Mojave and Colorado in particular. It is beautifully written, as the following penetrant description of the desert will indicate: "What tongue shall tell the majesty of it, the eternal strength of it, the poetry of its wide-spread chaos, the sublimity of its lonely desolation! And who shall paint the splendor of its light; and from the rising up of the sun to the going down of the moon over the iron mountains, the glory of its wondrous coloring."

VAN DYKE, WALTER

Account. 1954. (See listing under Hafen, LeRoy and Ann—*Journals of Forty-Niners,* pp. 300-305; also, under Coy, Owen C.—*The Great Trek.*)

Van Dyke narrates the experiences of the Pomeroy Co., a party of about 50 wagons traveling along the Old Spanish Trail behind the Sand Walking Company, having left Salt Lake on Nov. 3, 1849. Four accounts of the Pomeroy Wagon Train are published by the Hafens—(1) Portion of the Edwin Petit *Biography;* (2) David Seeley *Sketch;* (3) Extract from Goudy Hogan *Journal;* (4) The Walter Van Dyke *Account.*

Overland to Los Angeles by the Salt Lake Route in 1849. 1894. *Historical Society of Southern California Annual Publications.*

Van Dyke, a member of the Pomeroy Co. narrates the experiences of his party's expedition from Salt Lake (Nov. 3, 1849), along the Old Spanish Trail to Los Angeles.

VAN NOSTRAND, JEANNE SKINNER

Audubon's Ill-Fated Western Journey. 1942-1943. December and March issues of *California Historical Society Quarterly.* Vol. XXI. Pp. 289-310.

This article quotes from a diary kept by Jacob Henry Bachman, a member of Audubon's company. It assists in establishing reasons for the disasters attending Audubon on his overland journey to California in 1849. Heretofore there were no known available records throwing light upon this particular chapter in the great overland movement of 1849. (See listing under Bachman, Jacob Henry.)

VEATCH, DR. JOHN A.

Discovery of Borax in California. (See listing under Browne, J. Ross—*Report Upon the Mineral Resources, etc.*)

Report of Dr. John A. Veatch to the Borax Company of California. 1857. San Francisco: Whitton, Towne & Co. 16 pp. (Cowan P. 237.)

Says Cowan, "Dr. Veatch asserted that he was the first to discover borax in California. This is the earliest report upon the subject." Portions of the Veatch letter to the Borax Company are reprinted in the California Division of Mines publication—*Minerals of California.*

VER PLANCK, WILLIAM E. (with a chapter on Salt in
California Indian Culture by Heizer, Robert F.)

Salt In California. 1958. San Francisco. *Division of Mines* Bulletin 175. 168 pp.
2 fldg. pocket maps. Numerous pls. and diagrams. 8¾ x 11¼. Bibliographies
accompany several of the chapters. Pp. 121-164 given over to statistical tables.
Edition limited to 3000 copies.

The book supplies an approach to California desert literature that is unique in
view of the fact that no other publication, to my knowledge, presents desert history
in its relation to the salt industry. Pp. 15-37, 73-79, 115-119 discuss the salt industry in the following desert areas—Dale Lake, Danby Lake, Cadiz Lake, Bristol
Lake, Koehn Lake, Saline Valley, Death Valley, Soda Lake, Searles Lake, and other
points where salt reserves may be found.

In keeping with the character of releases by the Division of Mines, this book
contains material of major importance. Here is an exhaustive account of one of
the minor industries of our State that is vital to the welfare of all its people.

From the introductory paragraph to the chapter on the history of the salt industry, we read as follows: "The salt industry of California may be said to have
started in 1856 when a small quantity of natural salt was placed on the market."
And again, in a further section: "The salt deposits of the Salton Sea were known
and described as early as 1848 and were worked on a small scale."

It is elsewhere reported that in, or about, 1815 the first of several salt expeditions
from the pueblo of Los Angeles traveled in "creaking old carretas with their massive wooden wheels" to the present Salton Sea area—then but a vast sink in the
Colorado Desert. And the spot chosen was approximately that established many
years later by the Liverpool Salt Works. It is further stated that salt works were
established in the early 1830s at a place known as the Salinas, within the limits of
the present city of Redondo Beach. The salt works, after the American occupation, were apparently run for a time on a cooperative basis; but in 1853 the mercantile firm of Johnson and Allanson, in Los Angeles, purchased the works.

It is unfortunate these fascinating historical data relating to the "jornada para
sal," and subsequent early activities in the salt industry, were omitted from Mr.
Ver Planck's otherwise definitive treatise. (See listing under Guinn, J. M.—*Las
Salinas.*)

VICTOR VALLEY COLLEGE

Mohahve (Vol. I). (See listing under Mohahve Historical Society.)

VOTH, HAZEL HUNT and BENTON, JOHN C.

Death Valley National Monument—A Bibliography. 1941. U.S. Dept. of Int. Nat'l.
Park Service. 26 pp. 8 x 10½. Wrappers.

This little soft-bound booklet is a short subject bibliography of Death Valley
material. Assistance for the preparation of this work was provided by the Works
Progress Administration and Civilian Conservation Corps. Contents are grouped
under (a) General, (b) Geology and Selected Sciences, (c) Flora and Fauna.

VROMAN, HARRY

Lost Horse and Found Gold. 1953. November issue of *Calico Print.* 3 pp. 4 photographs.

Prospector Johnny Lang lost his horse. In searching for it he sat down on a ledge of rock to remove a stone from his shoe. The ledge of rock showed the dull yellow gleam of gold. And thus did the Lost Horse Mine come into existence. This article gives a good description of it.

WAITMAN, LEONARD

Horse Soldier Forts of the Mojave Desert. 1968. Vol. XV, No. 3 of the San Bernardino County Museum Association. Foreword by Gerald A. Smith, 56 mimeographed pages.

Discussed are the early Mojave Desert forts of Camp Rock Springs, Fort Marl Springs, Soda Lake Redoubt, and Camp Cady, with the principal portion of the booklet devoted to Camp Cady.

WALKER, ARDIS MANLY

Death Valley & Manly, Symbols of Destiny. 1962. Palm Desert: Desert Magazine, Inc. Published by Death Valley '49ers Inc. Publ. No. 8. 43 pp. The Manly Map. Wrappers.

This is the Death Valley story, or rather that portion of it, involving William Lewis Manly.

Francisco Garces: Pioneer Padre of Kern. 1946. *Kern County Historical Society.* 99 pp. 7 full-page illustrations and jacket design by Joan Cullimore. 6⅛ x 9⅛. Limited to 500 copies.

"The charming, tragic story of the lone padre of the deserts." Readers will find this to be a delightful item; well-written and without any confusion of historical facts. The illustrations by Joan Cullimore enhance the text. A library that posseses one of these 500 copies is fortunate.

Freeman Junction. 1961. San Bernardino: Inland Printing and Engraving Co. 16 pp. 3 illus. As an introduction, Mr. Walker quotes briefly from *The Valley of Dry Bones,* by Robert Glass Cleland. Wrappers.

The booklet contains some account of the early individuals and groups crossing over Walker Pass.

Kern River Valley Centennial Vignettes. 1966. Glendale, California: La Siesta Press. 70 pp. 19 line drawings by Francis L. Smart. Map. Wrappers.

This is a well written, historically important treatment of towns, mines and people along the Kern. Included, and outstanding, among the "Vignettes" are: Keysville, Havilah, Havilah's Old China House, Summer Ranch, Andy Brown's Old Mill, and Last House. In appraising a book, one of my infallible tests of quality is whether a verse or a paragraph or a chapter, descriptive of some person or place, kindles an insatiable urge to go *visit* that person or that place. The "vignettes" I have mentioned do just that. Although no longer to be seen, the "Last House," in my opinion, is far and away the best thing in the book. It is of classic proportions.

The line drawings are exquisitely done. Drawings, vignettes and the publisher's craftsmanship, fashion this little book into a completely desirable item for any bookshelf.

Manly Map and the Manly Story, The. 1954. Published by the Death Valley 49ers, Inc. Publication No. 2; and printed and distributed by the Desert Magazine Press, Palm Desert, California. 24 pp. 5½ x 8½. Wrappers. Reproduction of the interesting and novel Manly map.

The book tells how the author located the rare Manly map, and continues with the story of Manly's participation in the memorable Death Valley episode.

Sierra Prologue. 1938. Bakersfield, California. 23 pp. Wrappers.

From a number of addresses delivered before the Kern County Historical Society, Mr. Walker selected portions for his popular booklet *Sierra Prologue.* Included are chapters on Keyesville, Havilah, and Bakersfield, together with accounts of early settlers, mines, Indians, and industries.

WALKER, FRANKLIN

Literary History of Southern California. 1950. Berkeley: University of California Press. 282 pp.

Reference is made in this book to desert writers and desert literature. (See pp. 180-226.)

WALLACE, ANDREW (Edited by)

Pumpelly's Arizona. (See listing under Pumpelly, Raphael.)

WALLACE, EDWARD S.

Great Reconnaissance, The. (1955). Boston: Little, Brown & Co. XII. 288 pp. 24 illus. 5¾ x 8⅝. Words "First Edition" appear under copyright notice.

Quoting from the dust wrapper review—"This is the story of the men who explored, surveyed, and charted the new American boundary with Mexico after 1848; the scouts and pioneers who opened up the vast unknown country; the engineers who blazed the trails across desert and mountain for roads and railroads to the Pacific; the scientists who studied the new regions; the artists who illustrated them."

The relationship of this work to the subject of our California deserts is tantamount to that of an introduction to a book, of a synopsis to a chapter, of a syllabus to a course of study. *The Great Reconnaissance* effectually shapes the pattern for an intelligent understanding of the vital forces set in motion during those epochal years of 1848 to 1861, when our nation faced its crucial interim between the close of one war and the opening of another. Our new boundary with Mexico had to be surveyed, and all the vast area encompassed by it had to be intelligently explored. And the great westward surge, all the while, gained momentum—on over the relentless desert region of California to the Pacific, and thence northward to empire.

And so it is, in Mr. Wallace's book, that we meet those notable actors in this historic drama—Kearny, Emory, Carson, Cooke, Bartlett, Whipple, Couts, Ives, Frémont, Carvalho, Old Bill Williams, and others sharing comparable fame. All the associated incidents of this colorful period are ushered in, even to the inclusion of such isolated segments of the movement as the Mormon War, the "Great Western," and the dramatic camel episode. These, and a generous assemblage of other events, are closely integrated into the central theme of the narrative.

One would expect a subject of this nature and magnitude to be highly technical and involved. Perhaps it is; but Mr. Wallace's *presentation* of it is neither technical nor involved. I consider his book one of the most entertaining historical narratives I have ever read. He achieves the distinction of coordinating factual data and absorbing narration with impeccable precision. A great book, this; a monumental historic accounting. It supplies a definite need, long recognized, in the literature of our westward migration.

The Great Reconnaissance, together with Martin's *Yuma Crossing* and Corle's *The Gila*, afford us our choice triumvirate of great books whose substance is responsive to the historical appeal of the region round about the confluence of the Colorado and Gila Rivers.

Recently a book came off the press, authored by an aspiring young "professional historian" who writes: "A pioneer work on the Corps in the West is Edward S. Wallace, *The Great Reconnaissance*, which catches the flavor of the time but is not intended to be scholarly . . ." To all of which this Bibliographer hastens to add: "Well thank God for that!"

WALLACE, WILLIAM SWILLING

Antoine Robidoux 1794-1860. A Biography of a Western Venturer. 1953. Los Angeles: Glen Dawson. X, 59 pp. 1 lithograph (frontispiece). 5⅛ x 7½. End paper maps. Limited to 450 copies. (Grant Dahlstrom at the Castle Press, Pasadena.)

Ch. 5 (pp. 34-39) relates to Robidoux's activities while engaged as an interpreter with General Kearny in his California campaign. In this chapter we are given some account of the Army of the West and the Battle of San Pasqual.

WARING, GERALD A.

Springs of California. 1915. Washington: Dept. of Int. U.S.G.S. Water Supply Paper 338. 410 pp. 3 end-pocket maps. 14 pls. and sketch maps. 5⅞ x 9. Wrappers.

The paper submits a special study of the springs in California, "particularly those which yield mineral waters and which are utilized to a greater or less extent by the State and by tourists as recreation and health resorts." An early, scarce, important desert item.

WARNER, J. J.; HAYES, BENJ.; WIDNEY, J. P.

Historical Sketch of Los Angeles County. 1936. Los Angeles: O. W. Smith. A reprint of the 1876 original. 159 pp. 3 photographs. 6 x 9¼.

Pages 41-51 re-print the Journal of Dr. John S. Griffen, published for the first time in the first edition of this item. (See listing of the reprint of this *Journal* under Griffen, John S., M.D.—*A Doctor Comes to California* in the *California Historical Society Quarterly*, 1943.)

On page 89 is some mention of Rev. J. W. Brier having preached the first Methodist sermon to be delivered in Los Angeles (June 1850). Major Horace Bell quotes this Brier account, five years later (1881) in his *Reminiscences of a Ranger*. On page 116 there is an interesting paragraph on John Goller (or Galler)—blacksmith and wagon-maker—he of Death Valley fame.

WASSON, JOS.

Bodie and Esmeralda. 1878 (May). San Francisco: Spaulding Barto Co. 80 pp. 2 fldg. diagrams of Bodie and Aurora. 4 illus. 4½ x 2⅛. Has been reprinted.

The title of this interesting little pamphlet is expanded to read: "An Account of the Revival of Affairs in Two Singularly Interesting and Important Mining Districts, Including Something of their Past History, and the Gist of the Reports of Profs. Benj. Silliman and Wm. P. Blake, the late J. Ross Browne, and State Mineralogists R. H. Stretch and H. R. Whitehill—Also, Detailed Description of Mines Most Developed, Tunnels, Mills, etc.—Also, General Resources of Mono and Esmeralda Counties—With Maps and Illustrations."

WATERS, FRANK

Colorado, The. (1946.) New York: Rinehart and Company. XII, 400 pp. Illus. One of the "Rivers of America" series.

Ch. 5, "The Desert" (pp. 83-102) makes reference to the Mojave and Colorado Deserts of California. The chapter on "Imperial Valley" (pp. 295-324) discusses the reclamation project in Southern California.

WAUER, ROLAND H.

Badwater—Self-Guiding Auto Tour. 1962. Death Valley: Death Valley Natural History Association. 25 pp. 20 illus. Wrappers.

The *Guide* picks up directional mileage from Furnace Creek Ranch to such points of interest as Golden Canyon, Mushroom Rock, Devil's Golf Course, Natural Bridge Canyon, and Badwater. A map of the route covered is urgently needed.

WEAVER, RAY

Old Pauline Weaver. 1965. March issue of *The Branding Iron*, quarterly publication of the Los Angeles Corral of *The Westerners*.

This account, written by Pauline Weaver's grand nephew, gives one of our best summations of Weaver's life and activities. His article is implemented by a few additional notes, assembled by Arthur Woodward.

WEBER, F. HAROLD, JR.

Silver Mining In Old Calico. 1966-67. Contained in three issues of *Mineral Information Service*—May 1966, January 1967, February 1967.

The author states that prospecting for silver in the Calico Mountains was definitely under way in 1880-81, although actual discoveries may have been made around 1875. The article names and discusses many of the famous mines in the area: Silver King, Cuba, Garfield, Sue, Snowbird, Waterman, Waterloo, and others. Mining activities were practically discontinued in 1896. The total value of produced silver in the Calico district is estimated at around 13 to 20 million. There is good indication that the supply of mineral is far from being exhausted. The article devotes itself quite extensively to a detailed geologic study of the area.

WEEKS, GEORGE F.

California Copy. 1928. Washington: Washington College Press. 346 pp. 16 pls. 5⅝ x 8⅞

The author, at 76 years of age, recalls events and personal experiences that occurred during his colorful career as newspaper editor.

The first 106 pp. recount the author's experiences in or near the Colorado Desert. An entire chapter (pp. 272-282) is utilized to describe a series of singular events occurring at Palm Springs during this early period of its history. Photographs of the desert oasis, as it appeared in 1887, accompany the text. Ch. 24 (pp. 231-238) is rich in material relating to the Indians of the Colorado Desert. Pp. 219-229 discuss mining activities near Death Valley, and tell of "the mine which one man found and lost and which made another man an unexpected millionaire and a Governor." Pp. 229-230 mention the Lost Gunsight Mine.

WEIGHT, HAROLD and LUCILE

Whenever I think of deserts (which is most of the time) I think of Harold and Lucile Weight. For many years they have known close communion—physical, mental, spiritual—with our Southwest desert areas. The Weights do not acquire their knowledge of the desert by dredging the worked-over tailings of another's research. They walk out into it, study it, commune with it, penetrate its secrets. They are not afraid to leave the pavement and get dust on their boots. As a result, originality is a concomitant of their writing. Originality—and sound, basic knowledge.

Fortunately, the Weights have the talent and the capacity to translate their knowledge into enduring literature. Both Harold and Lucile are trained and experienced in the art of writing history in a manner that enables all who read to understand and enjoy.

Back in 1950 the Weights acquired ownership of the historic old newspaper—*The Calico Print*. During 1950-51-52 they brought out 17 issues of the *Print* in tabloid newspaper form. Beginning with the issue of June 1952, and bi-monthly thereafter, the *Print* became a sizeable magazine with an attractive format. Nine issues only were made available, the concluding number appearing in November

1953. Subsequently the author-historians have "concentrated upon publication of occasional books and booklets."

In my collection of desert material no book is more genuinely treasured than the two-volume, hard-bound set of *Calico Print*—one volume containing the tabloids, the other the nine magazines. Regrettably, for purposes of this Bibliography, many of the articles relate to the Nevada deserts and thus not eligible for inclusion.

Calico Print (the magazine) *Tales and Trails of the Desert West*. 1952 (June, August-September, October-November); 1953 (January, March, May, July, September, November). Each of the nine issues runs from 35 to 43 pages, the magazine measures 6 x 9.

In the nine-issue run of *Calico Print*, in its magazine format, a so-called "Folio" section is included in several of the issues. Of special interest among these Folios is the one devoted to an exhaustive study of Wm. B. Rood, of Death Valley pioneer fame. This appeared in the Aug.-Sept. issue of 1952. Of a piece with the Rood account is the Folio on Belmont, Nevada (Oct.-Nov., 1952); Greenwater, California (January 1953); The Great Survey (March 1953); and the Lost Ship of the Desert (November 1953). In addition to articles authored by the Weights, there are contributions from other distinguished writers—Adelaide Arnold, L. Burr Belden, Ed Rochester, Edmund C. Jaeger, Jerry Laudermilk, Arthur Woodward, Senator Charles Brown, Allen Patterson, Ruth Kirk, and others. Photographic reproductions, distributed generously throughout the magazines, enhance their textual content.

Among the authors whose articles are listed herein are Arnold, Belden, Norman, Patterson, Vroman and Weight.

Forgotten Road To Gold. 1963. *Westerners, The* (Los Angeles Corral) *Brand Book* No. 10. 24 pp. 8 photographs. Map.

The Editor of *Brand Book* No. 10, in his Editorial Capsule, writes: "Much has been written and told of the Butterfield Stage Line. Few know of this other, and perhaps equally romantic, pathway of travel across the Colorado Desert. Bradshaw attempted the rather obvious route that Butterfield rejected. His wagons rumbled through the San Gorgonio Pass and across the desert to Ehrenburg. In this narrative the well known Western authors have salvaged a vital fragment of California history, and have secured it for all time to come." Fondly do I recall the times I have *jeeped* with the Weights over the secluded sandy wastes of the historic old Bradshaw Road, past Dos Palmas Oasis and along the Salt Creek Wash to the old stage station sites of Canyon Springs, Tabaseca Tanks, Chuckawalla Wells, Mule Springs, and on toward the Colorado River.

Rhyolite: The Ghost City of Golden Dreams. (1953.) Twentynine Palms, California: The Calico Press. Published in a regular and a deluxe edition. 32 pp. 16 pls. 5½ x 8⅜. Wrappers. Printed by Hubbard Printing, Ridgecrest, California. The words "First Printing, February, 1953" appear under copyright notice. Has gone into reprint editions. Revised in 1959 and again in 1966.

This item, one of the Weights' special publications, concerns the old ghost towns of Rhyolite and its surrounding desert area in Nevada and California. The Weights

—Harold and Lucile—can write; and that which they write may be considered precisely and factually correct. Moreover, they write beautifully. I know of no finer descriptive passage relating to our deserts than the following, which has been extracted from their *Rhyolite*:

"Against the dark Bullfrog Hills, the ruins of Rhyolite—bone-white in the light of the early sun—seem fantastically out of place and time. The very permanence of these stone and concrete walls is an offense against reality. For Rhyolite is a city that should never have been, and its ruins are the ghosts of a dream.

"Other camps have been born in the frenzy of a mining boom, have flourished briefly and died. But most of these other short-lived ones were largely wood and canvas and burlap and adobe, and their remnants have blended quietly into the desert again.

"Not so Rhyolite—built of concrete, brick and stone to be the metropolis of southern Nevada. Banks, churches, opera house, big concrete school never used to even half capacity, the finest railroad passenger station in the state, ice plant, electric light and power, telephone exchange, water systems, newspapers—Rhyolite had all these before a single mine was proven by depth, or was a profitable producer."

It must be noted that, while Rhyolite is actually in Nevada, its proximity to California—both physically and historically—warrants its inclusion in this California desert Bibliography.

WEIGHT, HAROLD O.

California's First Gold—At the Potholes. 1952. *Westerners, The* (Los Angeles Corral) *Brand Book* No. 4. Pp. 17-22. 7 pls.

This is Weight's account of "The Potholes"—that once-great placer camp on the California side of the Colorado River ten miles northeast of Yuma. Here, in 1781, Spanish colonists from Sonora made the first discovery of gold in California, over 65 years before Marshall made his initial strike on the American River.

Greenwater, The Ghost That Went Away. 1953. January issue of *Calico Print.*

Greenwater, the copper camp, with a one-time population of over a thousand eager souls has completely disappeared from the eastern slope of the Funerals, just over the ridge from Death Valley. Twenty-five miles to the southeast is the town of Shoshone, and here the buildings from Greenwater were moved when the latter gave up the ghost. Weight very casually inquires: "Which place, then, is most truly the ghost of Greenwater?" This query, however, does not deter him from turning in one of the best accounts available of this short-lived mining town.

Grey Jewels of Bagdad. 1949. November issue of *Desert.* Illus.

Although this article would appear to be intended for rockhounds, it is given listing because of its excellent description of the Bagdad area and the Amboy Crater. A notable supplement to this and all Weight articles are the exceptional photographs illustrating the text.

Hunting Rocks in the Calicos. 1948. January issue of *Desert.* Illus. Map.

This is an account—both descriptive and historical—of the country surrounding the old ghost mining town of Calico. The article is slanted toward the activities of Larry and Lucille Coke in their intensive study of the history of the region.

Kit Carson at Bitter Springs. 1952. January issue of *Westways*. Illus.

An excellent account this, of the now-abandoned Bitter Springs camp near Baker, California, once a stopping point along the Old Mormon or Salt Lake Trail. The story of the adventure of Kit Carson and Alexander Godey in recovering some stolen horses from a near-by Indian camp is retold in this article.

Lost Gold of Havilah. 1957. February issue of *Westways*.

This is one of Mr. Weight's shorter magazine articles; but a distinguishing characteristic of all his writing is his demonstrated ability to write perceptively, and with an acute alertness for historical accuracy. He vitalizes every paragraph with carefully researched source material, and his readers soon become aware that they can approach his writing with an assurance of its factual soundness. This short article on Havilah, as its title suggests, is slanted toward the town's early mining activities.

Lost Gold of the Great Dunes. 1955. October issue of *Desert*. Illus.

This article is included because of its excellent description of the Algodones Sand Dunes along the eastern edge of Imperial Valley and extending southeastward to the Mexican border. Says the author—"Those tawny mountains—the Sahara of America—were the ghost-sands of a vanished inland sea and of a forgotten extension of the Gulf of California." These dunes, according to Weight, are "from two to more than six miles wide and more than 40 long. Individual all-sand mountains rise more than 300 feet above mesa level." The author reminds us that Kearny and Cooke were forced to detour around these dunes; and so, likewise, did the gold-seekers of 1849. The Butterfield Stage lines and the first Colorado River canals were forced below the border to evade the treacherous sand. From 1916 to 1926 the clumsy old plank road served as a bridgeway for traffic, pending the completion of the highway.

Lost Mines of Death Valley. (1953.) Twentynine Palms, California: The Calico Press. Printed by Hubbard Printing, Ridgecrest, California. 72 pp. 17 pls. 1 map (by Norton Allen). Cover photo designs. 5¾ x 8¾. Wrappers. Words "First Edition" appear under copyright notice. Revised and enlarged in 1961. 80 pp.

The book has to do mainly with accounts of the Lost Breyfogle Mine. In Mr. Weight's own words, this is "the first authentic history of Breyfogle's gold." Additional stories of Death Valley treasure are included: John Galler's Nuggets, Alvord and the Wire Gold of the Panamints, Charley Wilson's Blue Ledge of the Ballarat Trail, and the Buried Treasure of the Jayhawkers.

Lost Ship of the Desert. 1953. November issue of *Calico Print*.

Many have written of the fabled "Lost Ship of the Desert," but none more realistically than Harold Weight. In the *Calico Print* "Folio" section for volume 9 of his magazine he has authored the lead article and has implemented it with a proliferation of stories, legends, notes, and interviews—all bearing upon the Lost Ship. Paul Wilhelm contributes a capable article, and so does Burr Belden. Others who have pooled their knowledge concerning the fantastic possibility of a one-time ship becoming sand-locked on an ancient desert sea are J. A. Guthrie, the *San*

Bernardino Guardian, Ed Stevens, Adelaide Arnold, and O. J. Fisk. So great was the demand for this material that the Weights—Harold and Lucile—prepared separately bound copies of the "Folio" section in 1959 as a publication of their *Calico Press*. These, in turn, have gone into several editions.

Summer Visit To the Panamints, A. 1960. July issue of *Desert*.

The article supplies the historical background of many of the old-time Panamint mining camps and other places of interest: Ballarat, Panamint City, Wildrose Springs, Skidoo, Charcoal Kilns, Mahogany Flats, Telescope Peak, Auguerreberry Camp and Harrisburg Flats, Emigrant Springs and, finally, Death Valley.

They Blazed the Desert Trail. 1948. Desert Cavalcade of Imperial Valley. Publ. by Desert Magazine Press, El Centro, California (now at Palm Desert, California).

This is a comprehensive account of the early crossings of the Colorado Desert in Southern California. If the reader desires a thumb-nail sketch of this desert's history, he will find it accurately and conveniently prepared for him in this four-page article. Ushered onto the vast Colorado Desert stage are such colorful actors as de Anza, Pedro Font, Kearny and his Army of the West, Cooke and the Mormon Battalion, the Gold-Seekers, the Jackass Mail and the Butterfield Overland Stages.

Twenty Mule Team Days In Death Valley. 1955. Twentynine Palms: The Calico Press. 44 pp. 33 photographic illus., including the outside cover pls. End paper map. Wrappers. $5\frac{3}{8}$ x $8\frac{3}{8}$. No. 3 of Weight's Southwest Panorama Series. A portion of the copies are in a deluxe edition, and contain a reprint (the first, by the way) of the Death Valley portion of the Henry G. Hanks' item—*Borax Deposits of California and Nevada*—from the Third Annual Report of the State Mineralogist of California (1883). The copies without the report contain 36 pp. Has gone into several reprints.

Here, at last, is the all-inclusive saga of the 20-Mule-Teams of Death Valley's colorful borax episode. Mr. Weight has utilized every available avenue of research in collecting and assembling his data for this romantic chapter in Death Valley's historic lore.

WEIGHT, LUCILE

Chia. 1957. January-February issue of *Pacific Discovery*. Illus.

It is doubtful if Lucile Weight has authored a more informative article than this; certainly not one more beautifully written. Nor, in my opinion, has another —particularly on the subject of Chia, the "magic food from America's past." If the reader demands beauty of expression—here is a fine sample of it: "If a spirit haunts these stones as I use them here by another desert oasis, I know it is a good spirit—a survival in time of the prayers of an Indian woman for her brave's good journey. And when I follow lonely trails across black desert mesas, sometimes it seems the mirage-quivered air half reveals shadowy forms ahead . . . there they go, a band of lithe and sun brown men, to trade with river tribes or to outwit the wild bighorn sheep—and each with his little skin pouch of chia, safeguard for the hungry miles."

Lost Mission of the Colorado. 1950. October issue of *Westways*. Illus.

This article touches upon a phase of California history about which very little is known. The Weights—Lucile and Harold—must be credited for pioneer effort in supplying much original data on this area. The instant article establishes the location of the lost Mission San Pablo y San Pedro de Bicuñer, the Mission upon whose altar Pedro Fages placed the bodies of the four Franciscan missionaries—Father Francisco Garces, Juan Diaz, Juan Antonio Barraneche and Jose Matias Moreno—who were martyred four months prior to Fages' arrival. The Weights located the site of this early Mission about eight miles *up* the Colorado River and one mile south of Laguna Dam. This finding contradicts Bancroft, Engelhardt, Coues and Bolton, who have fixed the site of Bicuñer near Pilot Knob, 20 miles *down* the river from its true location near the present Laguna Dam.

Rock Titans and Giant Lillies. 1951. October issue of *Westways*. Illus.

The author outlines, descriptively, a scenic tour from Indio through Thousand Palms, Desert Hot Springs, Devil's Garden, Morongo Valley, Yucca Valley, Joshua Tree, Twentynine Palms, and the Joshua Tree National Monument.

In passing, it should be noted that this issue of *Westways* is replete with inviting itineraries—Heald's "Roaming the Sun Country," Tollinger's "Back Roads of the Mojave," Orland's "Trails Through Death Valley," West's "Pines, Palms and Pleasure," McKenney's "The Imperial Way to San Diego," and others.

WELLES, PHILIP

Meet the Southwest Deserts. 1960. Globe, Arizona: Dale Stuart King. Photography by Marvin H. Frost, Sr. 82 pp. 63 illus. Index.

Notable in this valuable reference tool are its photographic plates. The desert areas discussed are the Great Basin Desert in Utah and Nevada, the Mojave Desert in Southern California and the southwest portion of Nevada, the Sonoran Desert in Southern California (Colorado Desert) and northwestern Mexico, and the Chihuahuan Desert in northern Mexico. Desert plants, cacti, mammals, ungulates, meat-eating animals, rodents, bats, birds, lizards, amphibians and insects—all these are readably described and discussed. A most helpful desert book, and one the desert traveler should always have quickly available in his car.

WELLES, RALPH and FLORENCE

Bighorn of Death Valley, The. 1961. U. S. Government Printing Office. XV plus 242 pp. 78 photographs. Maps. Wrappers.

This exhaustive treatise would appear to cover all the essential facts concerning the Bighorn. One aspect of this study interested me profoundly—how may we account for the decrease in the bighorn population? In 1961 the number of Bighorn was estimated at between 600 and 900. The authors have quite conclusively eliminated the possibility of excessive predation, and the threat of the wild burro; all other causes, in fact, but the one suggested by their apt conclusion: "Only unchecked human encroachment appears actually to threaten the future status of the Bighorn."

WENTWORTH, MAY

Fairy Tales From Gold Lands. 1867. New York: Roman & Company. 234 pp. 4½ x 7.

Ch. 10 is entitled "Death Valley" (pp. 204-234). It is a fairy tale with its nebulous setting in Death Valley—in Death Valley, that is, as the author fantastically conceives it. If the term "Death Valley" bears reference to the Death Valley as we know it today, then this book gives us one of our earliest printed mentions of it.

WERNER, JANE—and the STAFF OF THE WALT DISNEY STUDIO

Based on the film narration by James Algar, Winston Hibler, and Ted Sears. *Living Desert: A True-Life Adventure.* (1954.) New York: Simon and Schuster. 124 pp. 90 col. pls. Black and white drawings. 6¼ x 9.

The text of this attractive book follows the film narration and is illustrated by one of the largest collections of color plates ever to be assembled in any single item of desert literature.

WERNER, LOUISE

We Climbed Coxcomb Peak. 1953. May issue of *Desert.* Illus.

The article describes the Sierra Club's climb to the highest point in the Coxcombs. Coxcomb Mountain is due east of Twentynine Palms. There is no mistaking its identity; the name derives from the serrated edges of its summit.

WESTERNERS' BRAND BOOKS—LOS ANGELES CORRAL

The Los Angeles Corral of Westerners issued the first of its series of Brand Books in 1948. Subsequent issues appeared in 1949, 1950, 1952, 1953, 1956, 1957, 1959, 1961, 1963, 1964, and 1966, thus making twelve in all. The first ten books are of uniform size, each measuring 8¼ x 10¼. Brand Book No. 11 measures 6½ x 9½; No. 12 measures 7¼ x 10¼. The first ten were designed and published by the Homer H. Boelter Lithography, No. 11 by The Ward Ritchie Press, No. 12 was designed by Arthur H. Clark, Jr., and George Koenig, and printed by the Stephens Printing Company (the Edward S. Curtis section by the Homer H. Boelter Lithography).

Editors of these several books are: No. 1—H. E. Britzman, No. 2—Paul Galleher, No. 3—Homer H. Boelter, No. 4—Paul Bailey, No. 5—Bert Olson, No. 6—Arthur H. Clark, Jr., No. 7—W. W. Robinson, No. 8—Don Meadows, No. 9—Henry H. Clifford, No. 10—E. I. Edwards, No. 11—Russ Leadabrand, No. 12—George Koenig.

Contributing artists to the series are Martin Johnson, John B. Goodman, Don Perceval, Clarence Ellsworth, Holling C. Holling. Photographic contributions are by Lonnie Hull, Clyde Reavis, and others.

Special folio sections include the Russell Bronze Reproductions (No. 3), Don Perceval's "Names On Cows" (No. 4), California In Lithographs (No. 7), a Charles Russell Sketch Book (No. 7), a Maynard Dixon Sketch Book (No. 8), a Frontier Sketch Book by Joseph B. Girard (No. 9), an Adam Clark Vroman Collection (No. 9), Pioneer Gold Coinage (No. 9), Clarence Ellsworth Paintings (No.

10), Desert Photographs of Burton Frasher (No. 11), Edward S. Curtis Indian Photographs (No. 12), Gold Rush Church Photographs (No. 12).

The following articles, having to do with our Southern California deserts, are listed in this Bibliography:

Bailey, Paul—Slavers in the Mojave
Bailey, Richard C.—Red Rock Canyon
Belden, L. Burr—Forgotten Army Forts of the Mojave
Cleland, Robt. G.—Exile On the Colorado
Cody, Iron Eyes—"Little White Chieftain," Clarence Ellsworth
Conkling, Roscoe P.—Butterfield Overland Mail in California
Edwards, E. I.—Death Valley's Neglected Hero
          —Mystery of Death Valley's Lost Wagon Train
Frasher, Burton—Portfolio of Desert Area Photographs
Henderson, Randall—Desert Was Our Beat
Leadabrand, Russ—Photographer of the Desert: Burton Frasher
Lofink, Sewell—From Coso To Carricot
Meadows, Don—Juan Flores and the Manillas
Murbarger, Nell—Ghost Towns of Inyo
Nadeau, Remi—King of the Desert Freighters
Parker, Dr. Horace—Historian's Search for Sackett's Lost Wells
          —Temecula Massacre
Schilling, Frank—Imperial Valley and Its Approaches
Serven, Jas. E.—Guns of Death Valley
Smith, Gerald A.—Early Man In the California Desert
Terrell, John Upton—War On the Colorado River
Vaile, Fred—Burro Prospector
Weight, Harold O.—California's First Gold: At the Potholes
Weight, Harold and Lucile—Forgotten Road to Gold
Wheelock, Walt—Following Frémont's Fifth Expedition
Woodward, Arthur—Garra Revolt
Wright, Wm. Lawton—Warner's Ranch Butterfield Station Puzzle
   (See listing under Edwards, E. I.—*Twelve Great Books.*)

WESTON, CHARIS and EDWARD

California and the West. 1940. New York: Duell, Sloan and Pearce. 127 pp. 96 pls. 10½ x 11½.

Roughly one half the book is given over to the subject of deserts. The photographic illustrations are of first importance.

WHEAT, CARL I.

Books of the Gold Rush. 1949. San Francisco: The Colt Press. Pages unnumbered. Printed by Grabhorn in a limited edition of 500 copies. Five title page reproductions. A chronological index is provided. 241 books relating to the Gold Country are listed with brief descriptive comment. 6¾ x 10¼.

Of the 241 books listed in the Wheat item, 17 display sufficient desert interest to indicate inclusion in this desert Bibliography.

Forty-Niners in Death Valley, The. 1939 (December). The *Historical Society of Southern California Quarterly.* Vol. XXI, No. 4. Pp. 102-117. 6½ x 9¼.

A tentative census of the Death Valley parties is offered by Mr. Wheat in this distinctive contribution to Death Valley literature.

Pioneer Visitors to Death Valley After the Forty-Niners. 1939. Reprinted from the *California Historical Society Quarterly,* Vol. XVIII, No. 3. September 1939. 22 pp. 2 pls. 6½ x 9¼.

This item contains material on various early-day groups that entered Death Valley subsequently to the emigrants of 1849. Among these several groups, Wheat mentions the E. Darwin French Expeditions of 1850 and 1860, the Mormon Expedition, the San Bernardino Meridian Survey, the George Expedition, Manly's Second and Third Visits, the McCormack Party, the Boundary Survey Party, the Blasdel Expedition, and the Miller-"Rhodes" Party.

Trailing the Forty-Niners Through Death Valley. 1939. San Francisco: Taylor & Taylor. Reprinted from the *Sierra Club Bulletin.* Vol. XXIV, No. 3, of June, 1939. 36 pp. 4 pls. 2 page maps. 1 fldg. map. 6½ x 9¼.

This foundational work on Death Valley attempts to trace the geographical routes followed by the several groups of emigrants on their exodus from Death Valley in the winter of 1849-50. The author's extensive research into source material, coupled with his close familiarity with the region itself, eminently qualify him to write intelligently upon this intriguing phase of Death Valley study.

WHEELER, LT. GEORGE M.

Annual Report Upon the Geographical Surveys West of the One Hundredth Meridian, in California, Nevada, Utah, Wyoming, New Mexico, Arizona and Montana. Being Appendix JJ of the Annual Report of Engineers for 1876. 1876. Washington: Govt. Prtg. Office. VI, 355 pp. 9 fldg. maps and diagrams, numerous single-page diagrams. 5¾ x 9⅛. A separate folder, 6¼ x 9¼, containing 7 fldg. topographical atlas sheets, accompanies the volume.

Lt. Eric Bergland (pp. 109-125) discusses the feasibility of diverting the Colorado River for purposes of irrigation. Cajon Pass, Ivanpah, Soda Lake Spring, the Bradshaw Stage route, the Butterfield Stage route, Fort Yuma—all these, and others are graphically described. Dr. Oscar Loew supplies the major portion of the material submitted in this report, discussing meterological conditions of the Mojave Desert, the geological and mineralogical character of Southeastern California, alkaline lakes, thermal and mineral springs, brackish waters of Southern California, physical and agricultural features of Southern California with emphasis on the Mojave Desert, and the geographical distribution of vegetation in the Mojave Desert. Lt. R. Birnie submits a report on desert regions in and about Panamint and Death Valleys, Searles Lake, Coso, Darwin, Cerro Gordo, and Owens Lake. Other contributors are Lts. Marshall, Carpenter, Morrison, Whipple; also Henshaw

(Ornithology), Rothrock, Conkling, Marcou, Scudder, Le Conte, Yarrow, Gotschet, and others.

To the average lay reader, a Government publication is something of a literary abstraction that one may conceivably omit from his reading agenda. All too often this is true; but there are exceptions. The Wheeler item is one of these exceptions. It makes for *good* reading; *interesting* reading.

Preliminary Report Concerning Explorations and Surveys Principally In Nevada and Arizona. 1872. Washington: War Dept. 96 pp. Fldg. map. 9⅜ x 11⅞.

These explorations, occurring in 1871, touch upon California desert areas, particularly in and around Death Valley (pp. 15-17, 50-52, 63-64, 83-84). Astronomical aspects of the region are discussed together with the topographical, physico-geographical, meteorological, geological, natural historical, and mineralogical features. Considerable space is devoted to the Indians of the locality, to climate, mines, and agricultural possibilities. In California mention is made of regions in and about Deep Springs Valley, Fish Spring, Kearsarge, San Carlos, Lone Pine, Coso, Granite Mountain, Telescope Peak, Cottonwood Canyon, Death Valley, and Amargosa Valley. E. P. Austin, G. K. Gilbert, and Lt. D. A. Lyle contribute reports, the latter making reference to the mysterious disappearance of the guide Egan (pp. 83-84). Chalfant, in his *Story of Inyo* (pp. 220-224), discusses the Egan incident in some detail.

WHEELOCK, WALT

Desert Peaks Guide (Part I). 1964. Glendale, California: La Siesta Press. 40 pp. Illus. Maps.

A carefully compiled directory and guide to peaks in the Mono area, the White Range, Inyo Range, Coso and Argus Ranges.

Following Frémont's Fifth Expedition. 1966. *Westerners, The* (Los Angeles Corral) *Brand Book* No. 12. 15 pp. 4 photographs. Maps.

The Editor of *Brand Book* No. 12 comments as follows on this excellent Frémont article: "Few are more intimately familiar with the Sierra and desert ranges and trails than Walt Wheelock. Indefatigable researcher, mountain climber, writer, and publisher of the La Siesta Press, he is noted for his 'Desert Peaks Guide', and 'Ferries of the South' . . . to name but a few. It is from perhaps one of his finest books that the foregoing is shared on Frémont's little known Fifth Expedition in search of a Central Railroad Route to the Pacific."

Walker's Railroad Routes. (See listing under Adler, Pat.)

WHIPPLE, LT. A. W.

Pathfinder in the Southwest, A. (Edited by Foreman, Grant.)

Report of Lieutenant Whipple's Expedition from San Diego to the Colorado, 1849. 1851 (Feb. 1). Washington. 31st Cong. 2nd Session, Senate Ex. Doc. No. 19, 28 pp. 5½ x 9. Reprinted by Westernlore Press in 1961 under the title *The Whipple Report.* (Edited by Edwards, E. I.)

It was on this Expedition that Lt. Cave Couts was sent as military escort to Whipple. (See listing under Couts, Lt. Cave Johnson.) The Report contains a vocabulary of the Yuma Indians (pp. 23-28); also Dr. Parry's weather observations (pp. 19-22). Leaving San Diego on Sept. 11, 1849, the party arrived at the Colorado on October 2 of the same year.

One of the distinguishing features of the Whipple-Couts expedition is that it represented a group traveling from west to east; not, as in the instance of the Gold-Seekers, from east to west. Whipple writes one of the best of our overland narratives. Incidentally, his description of the little palm oasis between Vallecito and Carrizo is exceptionally well done.

WHIPPLE, LT. A. W.; IVES, LT. J. C.; et al.

Reports of Exploration for a Railway Route Near the Thirty-fifth Parallel of North Latitude, from the Mississippi River to the Pacific Ocean. 1856. Vol. III of the *Pacific Railroad Surveys*, 33rd Cong. 2nd Session, Senate Ex. Doc. No. 78.

The chapters captioned "Colorado River to Mormon Road" and "From the Mormon Road to the Pacific" detail the Mojave Desert crossing. The Whipple content of this book is reproduced in Grant Foreman's—*A Pathfinder in the Southwest* (1941). In this latter volume Foreman edits and annotates the itinerary of Lt. Whipple during his explorations for a railway route from Fort Smith to Los Angeles in the years 1853-54.

Lt. David P. Stanley, Quartermaster of Whipple's party, is reported to have prepared a diary of the expedition—*Diary of a March From Fort Smith, Arkansas, to San Diego, California: 1853.* Multigraphed format. 37 pp. Only a few copies are said to have been issued. (See listing under *Pacific Railroad Surveys.*)

WHITWORTH, ROBERT W.

From the Mississippi To the Pacific: An Englishman In the Mormon Battalion. 1965. Summer issue of *Arizona and the West.* (Pp. 127-160). Illus. Map. Edited by David B. Gracy II and Rugeley, Helen J. H.

Whitworth was "one of the two young Englishmen traveling with the Mormon Battalion (who) kept a diary of his experiences." His companion was Wm. Biddome. It is reported that the 4½ x 7¼ inch booklet "was rescued from a gutter beside the Gunter Hotel in San Antonio during a flood in 1913 by Joseph J. Brown. . . ." The Editors' comment that ". . . it seems that Whitworth was not a Mormon when he enlisted, and that he was not converted during his year's association with the Battalion. . . . Nothing is known about Whitworth before his arrival in the United States, or after his discharge from the Mormon Battalion." It has always been supposed, perhaps solely on the basis of assumption, that only one enlisted member of the Battalion was a non-Mormon (John Allen). The Mormon Battalion member Standage, in his diary, remarks: "He (referring to Allen) did not belong to the Church . . . and never was a Mormon."

I do not question the Editors' sincerity in believing this to be, in fact, an authentic diary maintained by a Robert Whitworth. There is no question as to a

Robert Whitworth's connection with the Battalion. Standage lists a Wm. Whitworth as a private in Company E; also a Robert Whitworth as a private in Company C. The name—Wm. Biddome—appears as a private in Company E. I do not doubt Mr. Joseph Brown's veracity in claiming he fished out a muddy diary "from a gutter beside the Gunter Hotel in San Antonio during a flood in 1913."

However, at the incurred risk of being criticized for what may appear to be a divisive attitude on my part, I must express my own personal doubt concerning the authenticity of this muddy note book that purports to be a diary of a member of the Mormon Battalion. Even in Texas I question if such an incredulous incident could occur. At best its claim to authenticity is a tenuous one and, to me at least, is suspect. Here is a dramatic rescue of a diary that no one knew existed. It is found in a Texas gutter sixty-six years *after* the occurrence of the events it describes. The Editors could not at first be absolutely certain in their own minds that it was *written* by a Robert Whitworth. They state: "At the outset, the author of the diary was unknown to the editors. The only name mentioned other than those of the commanders was 'R. W. Whitworth,' which appeared on the side of a drawing of a soldier standing beside a cactus plant." Well now! Furthermore, *if* this were the rare, heretofore unheard-of diary of a non-Mormon English boy in the Battalion, its owners must have regarded it as extremely precious. Yet no apparent effort appears to have been made by anyone to recover this rare item that had been cherished and cared for during sixty-six long years.

There are too many reasonable possibilities available that just might effectually explain this phenomenon. The diary in the gutter could have been the aftermath of a prank, or a history class assignment, or a budding author's clutch at fame. Ostensibly the muddy little note book was not duly authenticated. The Editors give no indication that an effort was made to determine the age of the paper, to conduct a chemical analysis of the material used in the writing, to utilize the various facilities presently available to experts in ascertaining the age and authenticity of a document.

Oddly enough, the Whitworth *Diary* appears to be not the only document flushed out of its hiding place by water during the year 1913. (See listing under Jaeger, L. J. F.)

Before my incredulity develops into irrevocable intransigence, may I suggest that the diary contains little of interest and nothing of importance to our California deserts. The Colorado River was supposed to have been crossed on January 11, 1847. On the 16th the Battalion is reported to have arrived at Carrizo Creek. January 19 finds them plodding through Box Canyon, and on the 21st they made camp at Warner's Ranch.

WIDNEY, ERWIN

We Build a Railroad. 1931. March issue of *Touring Topics*. Illus.

As a young man, Mr. Widney worked with a Southern Pacific construction camp when this railroad extended its lines from Mojave north to the Owens River Valley in 1908. This is an unusually interesting article, and touches upon a phase of Mojave Desert history about which very little has been written.

WILHELM, PAUL

Vagabond House at 1000 Palms Oasis. 1941. April issue of *Desert.* Illus.

This is perhaps our basic account of the Thousand Palms Oasis. Of all men, Paul Wilhelm is best qualified to write about it. He has lived there.

WILLARD, STEPHEN H.

Desert of Palms, The. N.d., n.p. Wrappers. 6 pp., unnumbered. 4 full-page photographic illus. 6 x 9.

This little-known item is a descriptive gem, beautifully—even eloquently—written. Unfortunately, in telling of the desert's beauty, the author omits reference to its history. We may be reasonably sure the book was written after 1906 and probably well before 1917.

WILLETT, GEORGE

Birds of the Southern California Desert. 1951. Los Angeles County Museum. Illustrations by William D. Berry. 39 pp. Wrappers.

Forty-six different kinds of California desert birds are described and illustrated. Only one colored illustration is shown. The descriptions are sufficiently nontechnical to enable an amateur to distinguish without too much difficulty the different species.

WILLIAMS, ALBERT JR.

Lost Mines. 1893. September issue of *The Chautauquan.*

We must view this article in its true perspective. In 1893 very little had been written of mines and mining in Death Valley and the Mojave. And particularly the *lost* mines. Author Williams acknowledges indebtedness to several sources. From the *Mining Industry*, of Denver, he secures information concerning the Lost Breyfogle. From "a California paper" he quotes information of "an iron-stained quartz ledge in Death Valley." Again he draws on the *Mining Industry* for material on the Lost Gunsight. We learn nothing new; but any Death Valley literature released prior to 1900 must never be regarded lightly.

WILLIAMSON, LT. R. S.

Report of Explorations in California for Railroad Routes to Connect With the Routes Near the 35th and 32d Parallels of North Latitude. 1856. Vol. V of *Pacific Railroad Surveys.* (Reports dated 1853-1856.) Washington: Beverly Tucker, Printer. 9½ x 11⅞. 7 fldg. maps. 3 colored maps. 10 pls. on fossils and shells; 1 geology pl.; 28 botany pls.; 26 colored lithographs. (Cowan P. 168; Wagner-Camp No. 261-267.)

The book consists of four parts: Williamson's General Report, the Geological Report by Dr. W. P. Blake, the Botanical Report by E. Durand and T. C. Hilgard, the Zoological Report—Mammals by S. F. Baird, Birds by A. L. Heerman, Reptiles by Edward Hallowell, Fishes by Charles Girard. Additionally, there are three Appendices—Distances and Altitudes, Latitudes and Longitudes, Data for Profiles. The entire *Report* is addressed to Mr. Jefferson Davis, then Secretary of War. Southern California desert references may be found on pp. 30-43 in Part One; pp. 89-129,

174-176, 212-252 in Part Two. Williamson's group was the first surveying party to prove that the Salton Sink was below sea level. Of particular interest are the illustrations, lithographs, and plates. There are some 100 illustrations in black and white, and 26 lithographs in color. Chief in importance among these is the one of Los Angeles (Plate X, Part I) which ranks among the earliest views available of our present-day metropolis. Others deserving mention are Plates XI and XII— The Colorado Desert and Signal Mountain, and the Mission of San Diego. This important work supplies the first discovery account of the San Gorgonio Pass as an economic route of travel; also, our first authentic portrayal of the Colorado Desert.

To those devoted to the High Desert country—Morongo and Yucca Valleys, Joshua Tree, and Twentynine Palms, it will be of interest to know that in Vol V may be found one of the earliest printed references to this region.

WILSON, B. D.

Indians of Southern California in 1852, The. 1952. (See listing under Caughey, John Walton.)

Narrative. (See listing under Bynum, Lindley and Cleland, R. G.)

WILSON, FRANK

Last Western Manhunt, The. 1966. San Diego: Gerald O'Neal of *Acoma Books.* Pages unnumbered. Wrappers.

This (as one may surmise) is another Willie Boy item; but it has certain commendable features. Mr. O'Neal designed the book and hand-set the type. The result is a pleasingly attractive booklet in an edition limited to only 75 copies. Harry Lawton, our outstanding authority on Willie Boy, authors a three-page Introduction. The Sheriff Wilson report to the Supervisors of Riverside County is here published for the first time. The report occupies six pages of the booklet. A two-page bibliography is included, listing fourteen published works on this heroic (?)woman-killer of the High Desert.

WILSON, JOAN and EVANS, CAROLYN

Remembrances of the High Desert. (See listing under Evans, Carolyn.)

Yucca Valley. (See listing under Evans, Carolyn.)

WILSON, NEILL C.

Silver Stampede. The Career of Death Valley's Hell-camp, Old Panamint. 1937. New York: Macmillan Co. 319 pp. 25 pls. 6¼ x 8¾. End paper relief map. Words "First Printing" appear under copyright notice.

This desert item is packed full of absorbing interest combined with historical accuracy. Here is the authentic saga of old Panamint—the roaring "hell camp" of Death Valley. The book, however, makes for more than just entertaining reading. It has captured, while time would still permit, the story—not merely of one isolated mining camp—but of a tremendous epoch in our vast, national panorama. For one brief interlude the curtain to romance and glamour is lifted; the characters of an era long dead crowd boisterously upon the silent stage; the breath, the atmosphere and the dreams of a by-gone age pound vigorously along the quiet corridors of the desert. *Silver Stampede* is a great book—not alone for desert lovers, but for all who nourish high regard for our country's cherished traditions.

Telescope Peak from Death Valley. 1928. February issue of *Sierra Club Bulletin.*
    This article is descriptive of a climb from the floor of Death Valley to the summit of Telescope Peak. (See listing under Clyde, Norman—*High-Low.*)

WOLFF, DR. JOHN E.

Route of the Manly Party in 1849-1850—Leaving Death Valley for the Coast. N.d. (1931?) N.p. 29 pp. 13 pls. 6¼ x 9⅜.
    This is perhaps the first published attempt to trace the physical route of the Manly-Bennett Party, locating their exodus from Death Valley through Redlands Canyon. Some of our later writers disagree with Dr. Wolff as to the precise location of this route. By the same token there are others who agree with him. The book represents a worthy effort. It also represents a scarce and valuable item.

WOOD, HARVEY

Personal Recollections. 1955. Pasadena: Grant Dahlstrom at the Castle Press. XXIV, 27 pp. End paper maps—Mexico to California. 7 illus. 6½ x 9½. End papers tinted on a few of the copies.
    Wood prepared his *Recollections* in 1878. In 1896 the *Mountain Echo* Job Printing Office at Angels Camp, Calaveras County, printed 12 copies. Only two of those copies are known to exist today. This present reprint edition is limited to 200 copies, 100 of which are for members of the Zamorano Club; 100 available for sale. The introduction and notes are by John G. Goodman III. Wood, a member of the group of emigrants known as the Kit Carson Associates, came up through Mexico, traveled down the Gila, crossed the Colorado about the middle of June, 1849. The journey across the desert followed Cooke's route, and is detailed on pp. 15-17. (This book is No. 1 of the series—"Scraps of Californiana.")

WOOD, WILLARD S.

Bad Indian In the Morongo. 1935. April issue of *Westways.* Illus.
    This is perhaps the earliest of the authentic accounts of the Willie Boy tragedy occurring in the High Desert country back in 1909. Also it is one of the best.

WOODBURY, DAVID O.

Colorado Conquest, The. 1941. New York: Dodd, Mead and Company. XIV, 367 pp. 10 pls. 6 x 8¾. End paper maps.
    "The Epic Story of Imperial Valley, Boulder (now Hoover) Dam and the Taming of a Mad River." This item relates the Salton Sea story and discusses the vast Imperial reclamation project.

WOODFORD, A. O.

Red Rock Canyon. 1957. January-February issue of *Pacific Discovery.*

This short, factual article contains nine remarkably fine photographic plates by Blackmer Humphrey.

WOODHOUSE, DR. S. W.

Report of Sitgreaves Expedition. (See listing under Sitgreaves, Capt. L.)

WOODMAN, RUTH C. and ROSENER, ANN

Story of the Pacific Coast Borax Co. 1951. Pacific Coast Borax Co. 60 pp. Illus. 1 relief map. 7½ x 10.

This attractive brochure is typical of the outstanding craftsmanship of The Ward Ritchie Press. Among its chapter headings are such captions as Borax From the Earliest Times, The Discovery at Teel's Marsh, Death Valley, She Burns Green, The Twenty Mule Team, The Founding of the Pacific Coast Borax Company, The Calico Mine, Building of the Tonopah and Tidewater Railroad, The Lila C., The Death Valley Railroad, In the Funeral Mountains. The photographic illustrations are of considerable importance. The item rates high in its historical contribution to Death Valley literature.

WOODRUFF, ALDEN M.

Journal (From the Arkansas State Gazette of April 26, 1850). 1937. See listing under Bieber, Ralph P.—*Southern Trails to California in 1849* (pp. 283-322).

Woodruff, a member of the Little Rock Company, traveled the southwest trail to the gold fields. His route, generally, followed Col. Cooke's trail over the Colorado Desert.

WOODS, ISAIAH

Report. (See listing under Rensch, H. E.—*Woods' Shorter Mountain Trail To San Diego.*)

WOODS, S. D.

Lights and Shadows of Life on the Pacific Coast. 1910. Funk & Wagnalls Co. 474 pp. 5½ x 8⅛.

Desert material is reflected in: a. Ch. 17—Into the Desert (pp. 309-328); b. Ch. 18—Death Valley and Its Secrets (pp. 329-346); c. Ch. 20—Unique Characters of the Desert (pp. 369-384). Chs. 22 and 23 also contain desert mention.

The author's account of Death Valley's history, influenced by the Brier version, is grossly inaccurate. Yet, in the writing of it, he achieves the distinction of producing one of the most scholarly and profoundly beautiful descriptions ever penned of Death Valley. It may be likened to a sublime eulogy pronounced upon this sterile land, a type of eloquent beatitude upon the supernal majesty and awful desolation of this desert. *Lights and Shadows* is no ordinary book. The author is a brilliant scholar and his writing demonstrates this fact. So does his personal record.

It is to be remembered that this book was published in 1910; the trip into the Mojave Desert occurred in 1882.

One choice sentence from Woods' fascinating book should stimulate a concert of nostalgic longing among his delighted readers—"Life (in those days) was not large, but it was peaceful."

WOODWARD, ARTHUR

Camels and Surveyors In Death Valley. 1961. Palm Desert, California: Desert Printers Inc. Publication No. 7 of the Death Valley '49ers, Inc. 73 pp. 6 illus. Wrappers.

This book concerns the Nevada-California Border Survey of 1861. The "Eastern Boundary Sketches" are reprinted from the 1861 files of the Sacramento Daily Union. These "sketches" represent one of the important source documents relating to Death Valley history.

Garra Revolt of 1851, The. 1948. *Westerners, The* (Los Angeles Corral) *Brand Book* No. 1. 8 pp. 4 photographs.

Woodward indicates the Garra Revolt was precipitated by the levying of a tax by the officials of San Diego County. The tax assessments, relates the author, "were levied principally against the Luiseno, Diegueno and Cupeno tribes." Much of the initial fighting occurred at Warner's Ranch. Eventually the services of the Cahuilla—"a fierce and independent group of Indians"—were enlisted to fight the Garras (father and son) and their followers. ". . . the Cahuilla," says Woodward, "were known to be a fierce and independent group of Indians, led by one of the most able strongmen ever to appear among the desert tribes, Juan Antonio . . ." With the Cahuilla as allies against the Garras, the revolt came to an abrupt end.

Lances at San Pascual. 1948. *California Historical Society* Special Publication No. 22. 84 pp. 7⅛ x 10⅝.

The book discusses Kearny's war with the Californians in the south. The account contains early descriptions of the southwest desert country including Warner's Ranch, Carrizito Cañon, and the valley of San Pasqual. An attempt is made to correlate source accounts of the conflict between the Army of the West and the Californians.

Oasis at Vallecito. 1942. March issue of *Desert.* Illus.

This article is certain to impress the reader as an intelligent presentation of material relating to the romantic old stage station of Vallecito. Here in this green "Little Valley," back in 1781 or 1782, appeared the redoubtable Fages, perhaps the first European to visit the spot. Kearny and his dragoons of the Army of the West arrived here in 1846. The next year (January) came Lt. Col. Philip St. George Cooke and the Mormon Battalion. With them, also, came the wagons. Lt. Cave Couts camped here for several days in December of 1848. Then, within a few short months, there poured into this same "Little Valley" unending hordes of gold seekers. In 1851, or 1852, the original sod building was erected. In 1857 Vallecito became a station along the Butterfield Overland Stage Route. In 1934 and 1935, restoration of the old landmark was accomplished and the site donated to the City of San Diego.

WOODWARD, ARTHUR (Edited by)

Jayhawkers' Oath and Other Sketches, The. (See listing under Manly, Wm. L.)

Journal of Lt. Thomas W. Sweeny. (See listing under Sweeny, Lt. Thomas W.)

WOON, BASIL

Desert Stampede. 1948. November issue of *Westways*. Illus.

My only criticism of Mr. Woon is that he has not written oftener about our deserts. He does it so effectively. The instant item is typical. The author journeys over the Colorado Desert and—appropriately—the High Desert country in and around Twentynine Palms. His last paragraph I like: "We might as well face it. The desert lands have known gold rushes, but this is the greatest stampede of all . . . and where once they took the gold out, now they pour it in."

Incredible Land. (1933.) New York: Liveright Publishing Company XXVII, 374 pp. 5⅞ x 8⅜.

Mr. Woon displays a quality in his descriptions that is lost to most writers. Illustrative of this is his laconic comment to the effect that a traveler in Death Valley can see the world in its making and doubt that God is its maker. Death Valley and Mojave Desert material is found on pp. 237-263; Palm Springs reference is noted on pp. 150-155; and specific mention of Death Valley Scotty is given on pp. 246-254.

WRIGHT, HAROLD BELL

Winning of Barbara Worth, The. (1911.) Chicago: The Book Supply Company. 512 pp. Illus. 5½ x 7¾. Numerous reprints have followed the first edition.

This is the outstanding novel on the reclamation of the Imperial Valley. Margaret Romer, in her *History of Calexico*, points out that Wright was formerly a preacher in the Ozark country and that he suffered both from poor health and poor finances. His good friends, the W. F. Holts of Imperial Valley, urged him to come to California. This he did, starting the ranch known as the "Wright Place," located between El Centro and Holtville. Here he recouped both health and finances. Says Margaret Romer—"Out of appreciation, Mr. Wright wrote *The Winning of Barbara Worth*. He idealized his friend Mr. Holt in the character of Mr. Worth. Mr. Holt's daughter was made the heroine but was not actually found on the desert, as the story goes. The successful lover and the hero who closed the gap was Mr. H. T. Cory, while Mr. Rockwood was represented as the Seer. The novel is in no sense a history, although it follows, in a general way, the trend of events in the Valley." (Parenthetically, Margaret Romer possesses the happy faculty of writing excellent reviews.)

WRIGHT, JAMES W. A.

Cement Hunters, The. 1960. Los Angeles: Glen Dawson. Attractively designed and printed in an edition of only 200 copies, by J. Wilson McKenney's Wilmac Press. XI plus 52 pp. Edited by Richard E. Lingenfelter. 5½ x 8½.

Mr. Lingenfelter dates the first search for the "Lost Cement" in 1861; by 1879 the effort to locate the legendary "Lost Cement" resulted in the discovery of some actual lodes that eventually proved quite lucrative. In 1879, J. W. A. Wright visited Mammoth City and many of the new mining districts along the Sierra from Mono Lake to Bishop Creek. He collected material concerning the efforts of the Cement Hunters who followed the legendary lure of what was believed to be "reddish cement, richly bejeweled with nuggets of coarse gold." His findings were first published in serial form during November and December of 1879. Mr. Lingenfelter summarizes it nicely in the closing sentence of his enjoyable Preface: "Yet the Cement itself can never be found, for that is the way of 'lost mines' and that is what makes them lost."

WRIGHT, WILLIAM LAWTON

Warner's Ranch Butterfield Station Puzzle, The. 1961. *Westerners, The* (Los Angeles Corral) *Brand Book* No. 9. 28 pp. 4 photographs. Map.

A reprint of this article, limited to 300 copies and with an additional page Addendum, was issued by the late Mr. Wright to his friends. Inscribed in my copy are the words "A small token of our great friendship." It was, indeed, a great friendship we shared for one another; and it was a great bond of kindred historical interest we held in common for our southern California deserts and especially the desolate Carrizo Corridor that sprawled from Carrizo Creek past Vallecito toward Warner's Ranch.

"Bill" Wright is our absolute authority on the Warner Ranch area; and one of his greatest services was to correct a careless error that someone had committed in designating—by plaque—the Kimble-Wilson Store building as a Butterfield Station. This designation occurred in the year 1930. Mr. Wright proves, beyond the slightest doubt, that the old Warner Ranch House was itself the true Butterfield Station. In a magnificently forged chain of evidence—a masterpiece of irrefutable reasoning—Mr. Wright, in this brilliant article, re-writes an important chapter in western history.

WYNN, MARCIA RITTENHOUSE

Desert Bonanza: A Story of Early Randsburg, Mohave Desert Mining Camp. 1949. Culver City, California: M. W. Samelson. 263 pp. 5¾ x 8¾. 15 pls. 1 map (sketch). Words "First Edition" appear under copyright notice. Reprinted by The Arthur H. Clark Company in 1963.

While the author accentuates the historical background of the old mining camp of Randsburg, she does not neglect the great Mojave Desert that surrounds it. For here is no meager, apathetic account of this vast desert region. On the contrary, her descriptions are energized first—by an innate knowledge of the country she describes; second—by a native ability to transmit this knowledge in a delightfully-entertaining manner. *Desert Bonanza* has established itself as an item of considerable importance desert-wise. Not too much has been written of the Mojave Desert region, except—of course—with reference to Death Valley and the early emigrant trails into San Bernardino over the Cajon. It is reasonable to assume that *Desert Bonanza* may be regarded as the initial effort, of any consequence, to assemble important *primary* material relating to the huge area surrounding the famous old "Rand Camp" that had its beginning back in 1896.

Pioneer Family of Whiskey Flat. 1945. Los Angeles. XI plus 130 pp. 4 photographs. Words "First Edition" appear under copyright notice. 5½ x 8.

This is a pleasant story of life in Whiskey Flat (it was called Whiskey Flat before its name was changed to the more respectable, but much less colorful, Kernville). "This is not a story," writes Marcia Wynn, "of famous people or historical high lights. It is the chronicling of the every-day living and background of an industrious, middle-class American pioneer family, who, in their struggle to get a foothold in a new land, were armed only with pride and industry, plus a remarkable ingenuity in making the best possible use out of the raw materials at hand when shaping them to their simple needs."

Even so, the book is rich in its background historical interest. There is mention of Havilah—some 18 miles from Whiskey Flat, of "Lovely" Rogers and his discovery of the Big Blue ledge, of Keyesville and Quartzburg, of El Oso Viejo (J. A. Delameter) and his freighting from the railhead to Whiskey Flat; even the famous Vasquez is brought into the narrative.

When Ezra Hamilton Found Gold at Willow Springs. 1951. November issue of *Desert.* Illus.

This is the story of Hamilton's strike on the Mojave Desert and of the desert waterhole at Willow Springs.

YEAGER, DORR G.

Bob Flame in Death Valley. 1937. Dodd, Mead and Company. 238 pp. 5¾ x 8⅛. End paper map.

This is a novel, telling of a Ranger's experiences in Death Valley.

YOUNG, ERNEST

North American Excursions. 1947. London: Edward Arnold & Co. 302 pp. with 8 pp. index. Illus. and maps.

This is a book of vivid descriptions. Desert references are: Ch. 23—"Phoenix to Palm Springs" (pp. 258-263); Ch. 24—"The Desert Hills" (pp. 269-283); Ch. 25 —From the Desert to the Ocean" (pp. 284-292). Eleven photographic plates appear in the desert section of the book.

YOUNG, EVELYN R.

Ezra Hamilton and the Rich Red Hill. 1958. October issue of *Westways.* 6 photographs. Map.

The article concerns Willow Springs and Rosamond. There is some mention of one of Rosamond's first buildings—the Hamilton Hotel, the oasis at Willow Springs, and the Tropico Mine. The article is short, but the author imparts considerable historical information in the short space allotted.

YOUNG, OTIS E.

West of Philip St. George Cooke, The. 1809-1895. 1955. Glendale, California: The Arthur H. Clark Company. 393 pp. 10 illus. 1 fldg. map of Cooke's routes. 6¾ x 9¾. Being No. V of Clark's Western Frontiersman Series.

This is the complete historical and biographical account of the life and military activities of P. St. George Cooke, touching upon the Riley Expedition, Black Hawk's War, the Snively Affair, the Pawnee Village and South Pass Expeditions, the Conquest of Santa Fe, the Mormon Battalion, the Frémont-Kearny affair, the Apache and Sioux Campaigns, Bleeding Kansas, the Utah Expedition, and the Civil War. The California Desert reference is in the chapter on the Mormon Battalion, and specifically on pp. 219-223. Material is taken from such source references as Cooke's own writings, and those of Tyler, Standage, Bigler, and Roberts.

YOUNG, SHELDON

Log. (See listing under Long, Dr. Margaret—*The Shadow of the Arrow;* Hafen, LeRoy and Ann—*Journals of Forty-Niners;* and Edwards, E. I.—*Into an Alkali Valley.*)

Sheldon Young was one of the Death Valley pioneers of 1849. His *Log* gives us our first written description of Death Valley—this being a day by day account of the emigrants' sojourn in the "alkali valley" over the Christmas week of 1849.

ZAMORANO CLUB

Zamorano 80, The. 1945. Los Angeles. Printed by Grant Dahlstrom. 66 pp. 6¼ x 9¼. 500 copies.

The compilers, all knowledgeable book collectors, deny that their "selection includes the eighty most important books in the field of Californiana," explaining that "after all, importance is a relative matter." They define their selection as being "those books which we believe should be cornerstones of any real collection of Californiana."

I submit that when a book possesses "cornerstone" attainment it reflects about as much "importance" as a book can muster. Surely the selection of a "cornerstone" book is in every respect as much "a relative matter" as is the selection of a book based upon its "importance." With all deference to the distinguished gentlemen responsible for the selection of titles in *Zamorano 80,* there are a few of these listed books that I would not accommodate in *my* library; and I am reasonably certain there are other collectors who share this opinion with me. For if some of these eighty titles come under the category of "cornerstone books," then it would appear that the superstructure quality of a "real collection of Californiana" is itself suspect.

With few exceptions, bibliographies have not been included among the listings in this volume. There are at least two reasons for the inclusion of *The Zamorano 80.* First, the book exerted conspicuous influence among collectors to secure its eighty listings—most of them scarce, some of them almost impossible to come by.

Second, and more important to our immediate purpose, *The Zamorano 80* lists 16 items—one-fifth of its entire content—that are also to be found in this present Bibliography of desert material.

ZINK, ORION M.

Mystery Death in the Dunes. 1949. February issue of *Desert*. Illus. Map.

Says *Desert*—"Here is one of the most intriguing stories to be published by *Desert Magazine* in many years." It is a tale of the Algodones Sand Dunes between El Centro and Yuma, and it tells of the discovery of seven skeletons (in 1947), each with the remains of an early-model gun beside it. Significantly, there was no trace of animals. No positive record of the massacre has yet been revealed.

Part Two

SUPPLEMENTAL REFERENCE SECTION

A. CHECK-LIST OF BOOKS CONTAINING ONLY INCIDENTAL REFERENCE TO CALIFORNIA DESERT REGIONS

LISTED IN this section are those books whose desert reference is incidental to the central theme of the item itself and, in my judgment, not of a nature to contribute basic or useful information to our study of deserts.

It must be borne in mind that the value attaching to a desert reference is not determined by the extent of that reference. Brevity does not necessarily denote an absence of such value. A single chapter, even a page, may suffice to establish a book as one of our great pieces of desert literature—and this irrespective of the subject matter of the book itself. An instance in point is Manly's incomparable *Death Valley In '49*. In its relation to Death Valley literature it has no peer. Yet only two-fifths of the entire volume is devoted to Death Valley.

The bibliographer should carefully examine every book, if this be possible, to ascertain if it offers constructive material germane to his subject. Yet his judgment in this regard may be suspect and a wide divergence of opinion prevail among his readers as to the relative values assigned. Thus, in lieu of omitting a doubtful book entirely, I have chosen to include it under this general listing and with little or no descriptive comment. In so doing, I again claim sanctuary from whatever criticism follows as the result of unintentional omissions; reminding readers that no bibliographer ever has, or ever will, accomplish absolute finality in his high resolve to assemble all that has been written concerning his chosen subject.

ABRAMS, LEROY. *Deserts and Desert Flora of the West, The.* Pp. 168-176. ("Nature and Science on the Pacific Coast.")

ADAMS, E. H. *To and Fro in Southern California; With Sketches in Arizona and New Mexico.* 1887. P. 59; Ch. 20.

AINSWORTH, ED. *California 1951.* Pp. 185-200; 205-216. *California Jubilee.* 1948. Pp. 185-200; 205-216.

ANONYMOUS. *Historic Facts and Fancies—California.* N.d. Pp. 21-28. *Secret of Death Valley.* (Buffalo Bill Library) n.d. A novel.

ARTHUR, EDWARD. *Let's Go Prospecting.* 1954.

AUSTIN, MARY. *Lands of the Sun, The.* 1927. Pp. 169-193. (Mojave Desert.)

BAILEY, PAUL. *Claws of the Hawk, The*. 1966. Fictionized account of Wahker the Ute.

BAILEY, PAUL. *Walkara, "Hawk of the Mountains."* 1954. Pp. 21-45. (Pegleg Smith.)

BAKER, WILLARD F. *Boy Ranchers in Death Valley*. 1928. A novel. Juvenile.

BANNING, WILLIAM and GEORGE HUGH. *Six Horses*. 1930. Pp. 115-131. (Jackass Mail.")

BARKER, JOHN. *San Joaquin Vignettes*. 1955. Pp. 79-85.

BARNETT, LINCOLN (and Staff of Life Magazine). *World We Live In, The*. 1955. Pp. 176-196.

BARTLETT, RICHARD A. *Great Discovery of the American West*. 1962. Pp. 339-364.

BAXTER, E. M. *California Cactus*. 1935.

BEADLE, J. H. *Five Years In the Territories*. 1873. Pp. 150-152. (Death Valley.)

BECHDOLT, FREDERICK R.—*When the West Was Young*. 1922. Pp. 3-24. (Death Valley.)

BELL, WILLIAM A. *New Tracks In North America*. 1965 reprint (one volume) from 1870 original (2 volumes). Pp. 320-325. (Colorado Desert.)

BENSON, LYMAN and DARROW, ROBERT. *Manual of Southwestern Desert Trees and Shrubs, A*. 1944.

BISHOP, W. H. *Old Mexico and Her Lost Provinces*. 1883. Pp. 469-472.

BOUTELLE, MARTIN J. *On the American Sahara With Lou Westcott Beck and "Rufus."* 1913. 12 pp. Desert verse.

BRADLEY, GLENN D. *Winning the Southwest*. 1912. Pp. 13-38; 145-173.

BRIDGES, T. C. and TILTMAN, H. H. *More Heroes of Modern Adventure*. 1930. Pp. 32-42.

BRYANT, EDWIN. *What I Saw In California—Being the Journal of a Tour*. Years 1846-47. 1848. Ch. 34. (San Pasqual.)

BRYANT, HAROLD CHILD. *Outdoor Heritage*. 1929. Pp. 131-155.

BURDETT, CHARLES. *Life of Kit Carson; the Great Western Hunter and Guide*. 1862. Pp. 275-292.

BUTCHER, DEVEREUX. *Exploring Our National Parks and Monuments*. 1947. Pp. 153-155; 168-170. (Death Valley; Joshua Tree Natl. Monument.)

CABALLERIA, FR. JUAN. *History of San Bernardino Valley From the Padres to the Pioneers*. 1902. (Typographical error under Times-Mirror Press shows date as 1992.) Ch. XXI. Pp. 100-106.

CALLAHAN, ROBERT E. *Human Whirlpool*. 1946. Pp. 257-384. (Palm Springs.) A novel.

CAMPBELL, FRANK M. *Fantastic Plants of Our Western Deserts*. 1924. January issue of National Geographic.

CARR, HARRY. *West Is Still Wild, The*. 1932. Pp. 27-36; 235-251.

CLARKE, CLINTON C. *Pacific Crest Trailway, The*. 1945. Pp. 37-38.

CLELAND, ROBERT G. *California: The American Period*. 1922. Pp. 218-223; 239-243. *California Pageant: The Story of Four Centuries*. 1950. Pp. 38-47; 118-121.

CLINE, GLORIA GRIFFEN. *Exploring the Great Basin*. 1963. Pp. 33-40; 155-160. (Garces; Jed. Smith.)

CONE, MARY. *Two Years In California*. 1876. Pp. 53-55; 58-60.

COOLIDGE, DANE. *Horse-Ketchum*. 1930. A novel. *Lost Wagons*. 1932. A novel. *Shadow Mountain*. (1919.) A novel. *Snake-Bit Jones*. 1936. A novel. *Wunpost*. 1920. A novel.

CRITES, ARTHUR S. *Pioneer Days In Kern County*. 1951. Pp. 257-260.

CROFT, HELEN DOWNER. *Downs, the Rockies and Desert Gold, The*. 1961. Ch. 21 (Death Valley).

CROW, JOHN A. *California As a Place to Live*. 1953. Pp. 122-134.

DAKIN, SUSANNA BRYANT. *Rose, or Rose Thorn?* 1963. Pp. 1-11. (De Anza Expedition.)

DARTON, N. H. *Guide book of the Western United States*. 1933. Pp. 242-269.

DAWSON, NICHOLAS "CHEYENNE." *Narrative*. 1933. P. 68. (Colorado Desert.)

DEETH, SANDRA L. *Desert Dwellers*. 1930. 192 pp. Poems.

DE LANEY, PAUL. *Toll of the Sands, The*. 1919. A novel. (Death Valley.)

DE VOTO, BERNARD. *Year of Decision: 1846, The*. 1943. Pp. 359-387. (Colorado Desert.)

DRURY, AUBREY. *California, An Intimate Guide*. 1935. Pp. 128-148.

DUMKE, GLENN S. *Boom of the Eighties in Southern California*. 1944. Pp. 119-131; 188-189; 239.

EDWARDS, WM. and HARRADEN, BEATRICE. *Two Health Seekers in Southern California*. 1897. Pp. 81-89.

EICHMANN, GRACE SHULL and ROBBINS, NOLA. *Land of the Golden Poppy, The*. 1929. Pp. 51-56. (Death Valley.)

FEDERAL WRITERS PROJECT OF THE WORKS PROGRESS ADMINISTRATION. *California, A Guide To the Golden State*. 1939. Pp. 526-528; 539-546; 610-654. (Colorado and Mojave Deserts.)

FLOWER, JESSIE GRAHAM. *Grace Harlow's Riders on the Great American Desert*. 1921. A novel.

GIST, MARION and EVELYN. *Coachella Area Motor Tours*. 1951.

GOETZMANN, WILLIAM H. *Exploration and Empire*. 1966. Pp. 177, 365, 471-474. (Unfortunately the brief, two or three paragraphs relating to Death Valley are inaccurate in certain of their historical details.)

GRAY, ZANE. *Tales of Lonely Trails*. 1922. Pp. 373-394. *Tappan's Burro*. 1923. Short stories.

GRISSOM, IRENE WELCH. *Under Desert Skies*. 1938. Poems.

GROH, GEORGE W. *Gold Fever*. 1966. Pp. 133-140. (Death Valley.)

HAFEN, LEROY and ANN W.—*Diaries of William Henry Jackson, The*. 1959. Pp. 120-164. (Mojave Desert.)

HAFEN, LEROY. *Overland Mail, The*. 1926. Pp. 63-70; 109-115. (California Mail Routes.)

HALL, D. J. *Enchanted Sand*. 1933. 275 pp. (This item not personally examined. Reportedly, it deals mainly with Arizona. Pp. 250-253 are said to relate a desert crossing through Needles, Barstow and over Cajon Pass.)

HALL, SHARLOT M. *Cactus and Pine: Songs of the Southwest*. 1924. 251 pp. Poems.

HARRIS, ALBERT W. *Cruises of a Schooner, The*. 1911. Pp. 31-66.

HARRIS, DEAN. *By Path and Trail*. 1908. Pp. 219-225.

HASELTON, SCOTT E. *Cacti for the Amateur*. 1947.

HERTRICH, WILLIAM. *Palms and Cycads, Their Culture in Southern California*. 1951.

HIGGINS, C. A. *To California Over the Santa Fe Trail*. 1908. Pp. 90-94.

HOLLON, W. EUGENE. *Great American Desert, The*. 1966. (Death Valley.)

HUMPHREY, ZEPHINE. *Cactus Forest*. 1938. Ch. 12. *Green Mountains to Sierras*. 1936. Pp. 181-191.

HUNT, AURORA. *James Henry Carleton*. 1958. Pp. 202-217. (Warner's Ranch area; the California Column.)

HUNT, ROCKWELL D. *California's Stately Hall of Fame*. 1950. Pp. 265-270.

HUTCHINSON, ADGER. *Desert Land*. 1954. 24 pp. Poems.

KYNE, PETER B. *Three Godfathers, The*. 1952. Short story.

LAMPMAN, CLINTON PARKS. *Great Western Trail*. 1939. Pp. 261-268.

LANTIS, DAVID W. *California: Land of Contrast*. 1963. Pp. 34-54; 55-77 (Mojave and Colorado Deserts). Some material on Death Valley.

LAPHAM, MACY H. *Criss Cross Trails*. 1949. Written by a scientist in the Soil Survey. Pp. 74-79; 128-131; 201-205; 231-235. (Colorado and Mojave; Death Valley.)

LATTA, F. F. *San Joaquin Primeval: Uncle Jeff's Store*. 1929. This item has not been personally examined. It is said to contain material on Death Valley.

LAYNE, J. GREGG. *Annals of Los Angeles.* 1935. Pp. 78-82. (Outlaws, Camels, Butterfield.)

LEOPOLD, A. STODDARD (Edited by). *Desert, The.* Life Magazine's Nature Library. 1961. Deserts of the world, with some reference to the Mojave and other California desert areas.

LEWIS, OSCAR. *Autobiography of the West,* The. 1958. Pp. 42-47; 234-236; 243-252; 280-283. (Colorado and Mojave deserts.)

LUMMIS, C. F. *Tramp Across the Continent, A.* 1892. Chs. 18-19.

McDANIEL, BRUCE W. *Desert-Gods' Crucible, The.* 1926. Poems.

MacDOWELL, SYL. *We Live In a Trailer.* 1938. Pp. 198-209.

MACK, EFFIE MONA. *Nevada.* 1936. Pp. 20-21; 29; 136-139.

MANNING, REG. *Cartoon Guide of California.* 1939. *What Kinda Cactus Izzat?* 1941.

MARKHAM, EDWIN. *California the Wonderful.* 1944. Pp. 255-266.

MARTI, WERNER H. *Messenger of Destiny.* 1960. Relates to Lt. Archibald H. Gillespie and his California adventures in 1846-47.

MASON, WILLIAM and CARLING, JAMES. *Where Shall We Go? A Guide to the Desert.* 1939.

MILES, SANDE. *Three Pals on the Desert.* 1946. A juvenile novel. (Death Valley.)

MILLS, ENOS A. *Romance of Geology.* 1932. Pp. 228-245.

MORHARDT, J. E. *Death Valley Poems.* 1951. Contains 38 poems about Death Valley.

MORRIS, HENRY CURTIS. *Mining West At Turn of the Century.* 1962. Pp. 37-40. (Death Valley.)

MORRIS, MADGE. *Lure of the Desert and Other Poems, The.* 1917.

NATIONAL GEOGRAPHIC MAGAZINE. *New Rush to Golden California.* June 1954. Pp. 817-824.

NEWMARK, HARRIS. *Sixty Years In Southern California 1853-1913.* 1916. Pp. 169-170; 231-235; 386-388. (Colorado Desert; Cerro Gordo.)

NORTON, HENRY K. *Story of California, The.* 1913. Pp. 219-222.

OSTROTH, VERA E. *Colorful California.* 1952. Pp. 15-28; 37-42.

PEAVLER, H. G. *Rhymes of the Singing Sand.* 1938. Poems.

PETERS, COL. D. C. *Kit Carson's Life and Adventures.* 1874. Pp. 96-103.

PETINAK, DR. MARKO J. *Dates As Food.* 1939.

PICKWELL, GAYLE. *Amphibians and Reptiles of the Pacific States.* 1947.

POPENOE, PAUL B. *Date Growing In the Old World and the New.* 1913. P. 27.

POWELL, ALEXANDER E. *End of the Trail, The.* 1914. Pp. 172-178.

POWERS, WM. E. and LOGAN, R. F. *Transcontinental Excursion Guide Book*. 1952. Pp. 223-226.

PYLE, ERNIE. *Home Country*. 1947. Pp. 267-279. (Cave Springs; Scotty's Castle.)

REMY, JULES and BRENCHLEY, JULIUS. *Journey to Great Salt Lake City*. (2 vol.) 1861. Pp. 416-466.

RENSCH, HERO E. and ETHEL G. *Historic Spots In California: The Southern Counties*. 1932. (Also see the third edition—1966.)

ROBERTSON, FRANK C. and BETH KAY HARRIS. *Boom Towns of the Great Basin*. 1962. Pp. 286-294. (Bodie, California.)

ROBINSON, WALTER WALLACE. *Mohave Rhymes*. 1924. 60 pp. Poems.

RUSH, PHILIP S. *Historical Sketches of the Californias, Spanish and Mexican Periods*. 1953. Pp. 42-43; 82-84; 86-87.

RUTH, KENT. *Great Day In the West*. 1963. Pp. 34-35. (Ft. Tejon.)

SABIN, EDWIN LEGRAND. *Kit Carson Days 1809-1868. Adventures in the Path of Empire*. (2 vol.) 1935. (Index listing.) Pp. 50; 70; 104; 218; 370; 512; 376-382.

SCHAEFER, JACK. *Our Challenging Deserts*. 1958. July issue of *Holiday*.

SCHERER, JAMES A. B. *The Lion of the Vigilantes—William T. Coleman, and the Life of Old San Francisco*. 1939. Pp. 301-304. (Death Valley.)

SCHUMACHER, GENNY (Edited by). *Deepest Valley*. 1962. Pp. 17-28. (Owens Valley.)

STAHL, F. A. *Rolling Stones*. 1928. Pp. 161-167.

STONE, IRVING. *Men To Match My Mountains*. 1956. Pp. 139-143.

THOMAS, SEWELL. *Silhouettes of Charles S. Thomas*. 1959. Pp. 132-141. (Death Valley and Walter Scott.)

THOMPSON, RUTH. *Comrades of the Desert*. 1922. Stories.

THORNBER, J. J. and BONKER, FRANCES. *Fantastic Desert Clan, The*. 1932. *Sage of the Desert, The*. 1930.

TODD, REV. JOHN D. D. *Sunset Land, The; or, The Great Pacific Slope*. 1870. Pp. 31-32. (Death Valley.)

TRAVERS, JAMES W. *California: Romance of Clipper Ships and Gold Rush Days*. 1950. Pp. 197-201.

TRELAWNEY-ANSELL, E. C. *I Followed Gold*. 1939. Pp. 300-307. (Death Valley.)

TRUMAN, BEN C. *Occidental Sketches*. 1881. Pp. 181-203. (Vasquez.)

U. S. CIRCUIT COURT OF APPEALS. *Keane Wonder Mining Company vs. James Cunningham*. 1915.

VAN DYKE, JOHN C. *Open Spaces, The*. 1922. Pp. 78-101.

VESTAL, STANLEY. *Kit Carson*. 1928. Pp. 231-244.

VOSBERG, STELLA SHERWOOD. *Desert Fables.* 1934. 78 pp. Poems.

WHEELER, RUTH. *We Follow the Western Trail.* 1941. Pp. 78-89; 106-122.

WHITING, J. S. and R. J. *Forts of the State of California.* 1960. Pp. 21-22; 27; 61; 82-83; 89-90. (Forts Defiance, Fremont, Piute, Tejon, and Yuma.)

WILLARD, DANIEL E. *Adventures in Scenery.* 1942. Pp. 107-128.

WILSON, JOHN FLEMING. *Scouts of the Desert.* 1920. A novel.

WILSON, NEILL C. *Treasure Express. Epic Days of the Wells Fargo.* 1938. Pp. 270-274.

WILSON, RUFUS R. *Out of the West.* 1933. Pp. 128-130; 336-340.

WINTHER, O. O. et al. *Overland Mail Centennial: 1857-1957.* 1957. The portion applicable to our desert interest relates to the California route of the Butterfield Overland Mail.

WORTH, PAULINE WILSON. *Death Valley Slim.* 1909. Short stories.

B. PARTIAL RECORD OF JOURNALS, DIARIES, NARRATIVES, LETTERS, ACCOUNTS, REMINISCENCES, REPORTS, ETC. OF PIONEERS CROSSING THE COLORADO AND MOJAVE DESERTS

TWO PRINCIPAL OVERLAND ROUTES, each with its understandable variations, were available to the pioneers in their trek across our Southern California deserts to the coast. The more northerly of the two was known as the Old Spanish Trail or, as time passed, the Mormon Road. This route led southwest from Salt Lake across the Mojave Desert through what is now Parowan, New Castle, Mountain Meadows, Moapa, Las Vegas, Cottonwood Springs, Mountain Springs, Resting Spring, Tecopa, Salt Springs, Bitter Spring, Barstow, Victorville, and the Cajon Pass to San Bernardino and Los Angeles. The southerly route led directly over the Colorado Desert, from Yuma crossing, dropping immediately south into Mexico where it passed Cooke's Wells and Alamo Mocho, thence heading north into the present United States at the approximate site of Calexico; thence northwest through Indian Wells, Carrizo, Palm Springs (in the Carrizo Corridor), Vallecito, Warner's, and on into Los Angeles or San Diego.

SYMBOLS: C.—Colorado Desert; M.—Mojave Desert; C.M.—Both Deserts.

ALDRICH, LORENZO D. (Journal)—C.

(1) Dawson, Glen—*Journal of the Overland Route to California and the Gold Mines.*
Aldrich was one of the Gold Seekers who came via the Southern route in 1849.

ANONYMOUS—P. : : : : : : (Account)—M.

(1) *Los Angeles Star* of Feb. 18, 1854.
"Extracts from a Journal of a Trip from G. S. L. City Utah Territory to San Bernardino, Cal."
(2) *Pacific Historical Review, XI*—March, 1942.
(3) *The Los Angeles Star* (Rice; 1947).
"Early Freighting on the Salt Lake-San Bernardino Trail."
Descriptive of a trip made by the Reese Bros. Caravan during the winter of 1853-1854. Carvalho mentions passing this party on their return to Salt Lake.

ANONYMOUS ("The Traveler") (Journal)—C.

(1) Bieber, Ralph P. *Southern Trails to California.*
"The Traveler" crossed the Colorado Desert in 1849.

ANTISELL, T. (Articles)—C.M.

(1) Pacific Railroad Surveys, Vol. 7.
Antisell was with the Railway Surveys group. (1853-1855.)

ARMIJO, ANTONIO (Diary)—M.

(1) Hafen, LeRoy & Ann—*Old Spanish Trail*.
Armijo came over the Old Spanish Trail in 1829-1830, transporting goods from New Mexico to California.

ASHLEY, WM. HENRY (Narrative)—C.M.

(1) Dale, Harrison Clifford—*The Ashley-Smith Explorations and Discovery of a Central Route to the Pacific 1822-1829*.
Ashley accompanied Smith on certain of the latter's expeditions.

AUBREY, FRANCOIS XAVIER (Diary)—M.

(1) Bieber, Ralph P.—*Exploring Southwest Trails*.
Aubrey, with a party of 18 or 20 men—Americans and Mexicans—came through Cajon Pass, crossing the Mohave Desert in July 1853. They used pack animals only; no wagons.

AUDUBON, JOHN W. (Diary)—C.

(1) The Arthur H. Clark Company—*Audubon's Western Journal: 1849-1850*.
(2) Foreman, Grant—*Marcy and the Gold Seekers*.
(3) Bari, Valeska—*Course of Empire*.
Audubon traveled to the gold fields in 1849 via the Southwest route.

BABCOCK, LEONARD (Recollections)—M.

(1) Hafen, LeRoy and Ann—*Supplement to Journals of Forty-Niners*.
Babcock was among those who turned back from Mt. Misery in November of 1849 to follow Hunt's train into Los Angeles. Babcock's account, written many years after the events he tries to describe, is badly jumbled and confused.

BACHMAN, JACOB HENRY (Diary)—C.

(1) Van Nostrand, Jeanne Skinner—*Audubon's Ill-Fated Western Journey*. (*California Historical Society Quarterly*. Dec. 1942).
Bachman was one of Audubon's company (1849-1850), and supplies data that heretofore have escaped notice.

BAILEY, G. (Report)—C.M.

(1) Lang, Walter B.—*First Overland Mail*.
Bailey, a "Special Agent, etc.", prepared this brief report for the Postmaster General of his 1858 trip over the mail route of the Butterfield overland stage from San Francisco to St. Louis.

BANCROFT, H. H. (Guide)—C.

(1) *Guide to the Colorado Mines* (1863).
(2) *California Historical Society Quarterly* (March 1933).
This is Bancroft's scarce, descriptive Guide to the old Bradshaw Trail route over the Colorado Desert.

BANDEL, EUGENE (Letters and Journal)—C.M.

(1) Bieber, Ralph P.—*Frontier Life in the Army 1854-1861*.
Bandel, a young German soldier, was in one of the companies under Lt. Col. Hoffman sent out on a punitive expedition against the Mojave Indians in 1859.

BARTLETT, J. R. (Book)—C.
(1) Bartlett, J. R.–*Personal Narrative*. (2 vol.)
Bartlett explored regions affecting the Mexican Boundary survey. (1850-1853.)

BELL, JAMES G. (Diary)—C.
(1 & 2) *Southwestern Historical Quarterly* (Texas) 1932, and its reprint captioned—
"A Log of the Texas-California Cattle Trail, 1854." Edited by J. Evetts Haley.
Bell, at 22, was employed by John James to assist in driving the latter's herd of
cattle from San Antonio to Los Angeles, over the Colorado Desert.

BIGLER, HENRY W. (Journal)—C.M.
(1) Hafen, LeRoy and Ann—*Journals of Forty-Niners*.
(2) *Utah Historical Quarterly*—Vol. 5, Nos. 2, 3 and 4 (1932).
(3) *Overland Monthly*, September 1887.
Bigler was one of the group of 49'ers in the Sand Walking Co. who packed down
the gorge at Mt. Misery. Bigler was also a member of the Mormon Battalion; was
with Marshall at Coloma during the period of the great gold discovery.

BLAKE, W. P. (Articles)—C.
(1) *Pacific Railroad Surveys*, Vol. 5.
(2) MacDougal, D. T.—*The Salton Sea*.
(3) Cory, H. T.—*Imperial Valley and the Salton Sea*.
Blake was connected with the Railway Surveys group. (1853-1855.)

BLISS, ROBERT S. (Journal)—C.
(1) *Utah Historical Quarterly* Vol. 4, Nos. 3 and 4. July and October, 1931.
Bliss was a member of the Mormon Battalion. His Journal briefly describes their
desert crossing (pp. 83-85).

BRADY, PETER R. (Reminiscences)—C.
(1) Bailey, L. R.—*The A. B. Gray Report*.
Brady's *Reminiscences* relate to the A. B. Gray survey in 1853-1854 along the
32nd Parallel for the Texas Western Railroad.

BREWERTON, LT. GEO. V. (Description)—M.
(1) *Harper's New Monthly*, August 1853.
(2) Hafen, LeRoy and Ann—*Old Spanish Trail*.
(3) Brewerton, Geo. V.—*Overland with Kit Carson*.
An account of the ride with Kit Carson from Los Angeles eastward over the Old
Spanish Trail. (1848.)

BRIER, J. W., SR. (Article)—M.
(1) Heap, Gwinn Harris—*Central Route to the Pacific*.
(2) Belden, L. Burr—*Death Valley Heroine*.
Brier was one of the original forty-niners of Death Valley.

BRIER, MRS. J. W. (JULIET) (Articles)—M.
(1) *Carson City News* of June 8, 1913—"Last Account."
(2) Belden, L. Burr—*Death Valley Heroine*.
(3) *San Francisco Call* of Dec. 28, 1898—"Our Christmas Amid the Terrors of Death
Valley."
(4) Long, Dr. M.—*Shadow of the Arrow*.
Mrs. Brier was one of the original Death Valley pioneers of 1849.

BRIER, J. W., JR. (Articles)—M.
(1) *Out West Magazine*—March and April 1903—"The Death Valley Party of 1849."
(2) *Inyo Independent* of July 26, 1884—"True Story of the Perishing Emigrants."
(3) Beldon, L. Burr—*Death Valley Heroine.*
(4) Long, Dr. Margaret—*Shadow of the Arrow.*
   Brier, as a lad of six, crossed Death Valley in 1849.

BROWN, JUDGE H. S. (Account)—M.
(1) Hafen, LeRoy and Ann—*Supplement to Journals of Forty-Niners.* Brown was with
   a company of Packers, the first group to travel from Salt Lake to Los Angeles over
   the Mojave Desert in the fall of 1849.

BROWN, JAMES S. (Book)—C.M.
(1) Hafen, LeRoy and Ann—*Journals of Forty-Niners.*
(2) Brown, James S.—*Life of a Pioneer.* (1900.)
   Brown (like Addison Pratt) narrates the experiences of the seven wagons of the
   Sand Walking Co. that followed Hunt into San Bernardino. Brown was also a
   member of the Mormon Battalion; was with Marshall at Coloma during the
   period of the great gold discovery.

BROWNE, J. ROSS (Book)—C.
(1) Browne, J. R.—*Adventures In the Apache Country.*
   Browne traveled from California to Arizona in December of 1863.

BURRELL, MRS. EDWARD (Letter)—M.
(1) *San Jose Pioneer*—Dec. 15, 1894—"Across the Plains in 1849."
(2) Woodward, Arthur—*Jayhawkers' Oath.*
(3) Long, Dr. Margaret—*Shadow of the Arrow.*
   Letter contains data on the Henry Wade party, of the Death Valley pioneers of
   1849.

CANDEE, DR. JOEL (Diary)—C.
(1) Foreman, Grant—*Marcy and the Gold Seekers.*
   Dr. Candee was a member of the Knickerbocker Party, one of the groups of 1849
   emigrants to the gold fields via the Southwest route.

CANNON, GEO. Q. (Narrative)—M.
(1) Hafen, LeRoy and Ann—*Journals of Forty-Niners.*
(2) *Juvenile Instructor* (1869).
(3) Cannon, Geo. Q.—*A Trip To California.*
   Cannon, a member of the Sand Walking Co., was among those who packed down
   the gorge at Mt. Misery.

CARDINELL, CHARLES (Diary)—C.
(1) July, 1922 issue of the *California Historical Quarterly* under caption—"Adventures on the Plains."
(2) A 150-copy reprint from the *Quarterly.*
   Cardinell was a member of the Capt. Parker H. French Overland Expedition to
   California, and came to the gold fields via the Southern route in 1850.

CARSON, KIT (Autobiography)—C.M.
(1) Carson, Kit—*Autobiography.*
   Carson was with General Kearny in California in 1846, and participated in the
   Battle of San Pasqual. He also worked with Frémont.

CARVALHO, S. N. (Journal)—M.

(1) Carvalho, S. N.—*Incidents of Travel and Adventure in the Far West; with Col. Frémont's Last Expedition.* (1857.)

Carvalho was the artist with Frémont's fifth and last expedition, on its return. He gives us a detailed account of the trail from Las Vegas to San Bernardino, via Bitter Springs (about 20 air miles west of Baker), in 1854. He tells of meeting Pegleg Smith on this expedition. His is one of the few accounts detailing this California segment of the Old Spanish Trail; perhaps the only significant descriptive account of Frémont's Fifth Expedition.

CHAMBERLAIN, SAMUEL E. (Book)—C.

(1) Chamberlain, Samuel E.—*My Confession.*

Chamberlain, with two or three others, deserted the Glanton gang just before these desperadoes were killed by a band of Indians; crossed the Colorado Desert to the gold fields, apparently in the latter part of April and the early part of May in the year 1850.

CHAMBERLIN, WM. H. (Diary)—C.

(1) *New Mexico Historical Review,* January, April, July and October issues of 1945. Article captioned—"From Lewisburg to California in 1849." (Edited by Bloome, Lansing B.)

Chamberlin was one of the 1849 emigrants traveling the Southern route to the California gold fields.

CHEESMAN, DAVID W. (Edited by Foy, Mary E.) (Memoir)—M.

(1) *Historical Society of Southern California—Annual Publications* 1930, captioned—"By Ox-team From Salt Lake to Los Angeles: 1850."

Cheesman followed the Old Spanish Trail route from Salt Lake to Los Angeles in 1850.

CLARKE, A. B. (Journal)—C.

(1) Clarke, A. B.—*Travels In Mexico and California, etc.*

Clarke was with the Hampden Mining Co., numbering 46 men, who left New York by boat to Mexico. They arrived at the junction of the Colorado and Gila on June 20, 1849. On June 26 they started across the desert, arriving at Warner's on July 3.

COLLIER, JAMES (Adventures)—C.

(1) Foremn, Grant—*Adventures of James Collier, First Collector of the Port of San Francisco.*

Collier came to San Francisco in 1849 via the Southern trail.

COLTON, JOHN B. (Articles)—M.

(1) Woodward, A.—*Jayhawkers' Oath*—(containing "Death Valley Mines," originally in *San Jose Pioneer* of Dec. 15, 1895).

(2) Long, Dr. M.—*Shadow of the Arrow*—from *San Francisco Bulletin*—Feb. 4, 1903, entitled "Interview with Capt. John Colton."

Colton was a member of the Jayhawker Party of Death Valley fame.

COOKE, PHILIP ST. GEORGE (Journal)—C.

(1) Bieber, Ralph P.—*Exploring Southwest Trails.* (Reprinted from original.)

(2) Cooke's later expansion of his Journal into a book—*The Conquest of New Mexico and California.* Reprinted by Biobooks.

(3) Cooke's brief report in Emory's *Reconnoissance*. (House Ed.) (Reprinted in *Utah Historical Quarterly*. January, 1954.)
(4) *The Conquest of New Mexico and California*. Horn and Wallace reprint.
Cooke was the leader of the Mormon Battalion in 1846-1847.

COUTS, LT. CAVE J. (Diary)—C.
(1) Zamorano Club Publication—*From San Diego to the Colorado In 1849*.
(2) Foreman, Grant—*Marcy and the Gold Seekers*.
Couts' *Diary* records the 1849 journey from San Diego to the Colorado. Couts furnished military escort to Lt. Whipple's survey party at the mouth of the Gila.

—————— (Journal)—C.
(1) Couts, Lt. Cave J.—*Hepah, California!*
The *Journal* relates to Couts' journey from Monterey, Nuevo Leon, Mexico to Los Angeles in 1848-1849, under command of Major Lawrence P. Graham.

COX, CORNELIUS C. (Diary)—C.
(1) Coy, Owen C.—*The Great Trek*.
(2) Martin, Mabelle Eppard—"From Texas to California in 1859; Diary of C. C. Cox." *Southwest Historical Quarterly* Vol. XXIX—July 1925; Oct. 1925; Jan. 1926.
(3) Foreman, Grant—*Marcy and the Gold Seekers*.
Cox was one of the 1849 gold seekers who followed the Southwest trail.

CRESPI, FATHER JUAN (Diary)—M.
(1) Bolton, Dr. Herbert E.—*Crespi's Diary*.
Crespi accompanied Portola in 1769. He gives us our first written description of Los Angeles.

DAWSON, NICHOLAS "CHEYENNE" (Narrative)—C.
(1) Grabhorn Press—*Narrative of Nicholas "Cheyenne" Dawson*.
Only one short paragraph is devoted to the Colorado Desert crossing; but this paragraph is of considerable interest. Says Dawson—"When we reached it (meaning the California desert), we were relieved by finding a new road, which circled more to the south and passed some spots of grass where wells had been sunk by Americans, and water found." (1849.)

DERR, PETER (Experiences)—M.
(1) Hafen, LeRoy and Ann—*Journals of Forty-Niners*.
Note: The Gruwell-Derr group was "The first company to reach Los Angeles over the trail from Salt Lake City in the fall of 1849." This was a company made up of packers. "Available information about these men and their trip is scant. They passed the Hunt wagon train at Chickon Creek, Utah, on Oct. 8; the Record Book of Rancho del Chino notes their arrival on Oct. 27-29, 1849. These packers made fast time, enjoyed good health, but lost about thirty animals from the scarcity of water and grass." (Hafen.) There were 23—perhaps 50—wagons in the train.

DURIVAGE, JOHN E. (Letters and Journals)—C.
(1) Bieber, Ralph P.—*Southern Trails to California in 1849*.
(2) Foreman, Grant—*Marcy and the Gold Seekers*.
Durivage was one of the 1849 emigrants to California traveling via the Southwest trail.

ECCLESTON, ROBERT (Diary)—C.
(1) *Overland to California On the Southwest Trail.* 1849.
Eccleston traveled to the gold fields via the Southern trail. He was 19; was a member of the Frémont Association.

EGAN, HOWARD (Diary)—M.
(1) Hafen, LeRoy and Ann—*Journals of Forty-Niners.*
(2) Egan Estate publication—*Pioneering the West: 1846 to 1878.* (1917.)
Egan was in the party leaving Salt Lake shortly after the Pomeroy Wagon train, and who overtook and passed them on the Old Spanish Trail.

EMORY, COL. W. H. (Book)—C.
(1) Emory—*Notes of a Military Reconnoissance.*
(2) Emory—*United States and Mexican Boundary Surveys.*
Emory was with General Kearny and the Army of the West in 1846; later succeeded Bartlett as leader of the Boundary Survey.

ERKSON, ALEXANDER (Statement)—M.
(1) Manly, W. L. *Death Valley in '49.*
(2) Hafen, LeRoy and Ann—*Journals of Forty-Niners.*
Erkson was in the wagon party who turned back at Mt. Misery to rejoin Hunt on the Old Spanish Trail. Although they did not overtake Hunt, they followed his lead safely into San Bernardino. Our only important account of this largest faction of the Sand Walking Co. of 1849 (65 wagons).

ESTUDILLO, LT. JOSE MARIA (Diary)—C.
See Romero, Capt. Don Jose.

EVANS, GEO. W. B. (Diary)—C.M.
(1) Dumke, Glenn S.—*The Mexican Gold Trail.*
Evans traveled from Mexico north through Southern California in 1849. Interesting light is shed on one group of the Death Valley Party of 1849.

FAGES, PEDRO (Diary)—C.M.
(1) Priestly, H. I.—*Diary of Pedro Fages. The Colorado Campaign: 1781-1782.*
Fages was sent on a punitive expedition against the Yumas. Fages, supposedly, was the first white man to travel from the Colorado to San Diego.

FAIRCHILD, MAHLON DICKERSON (Reminiscences)—C.
(1) March 1933 issue of *California Historical Society Quarterly* Vol. XII, No. 1—"A Trip to the Colorado Mines in 1862."
Describing early Los Angeles (1862) and the trip to the Colorado mines through El Monte, Cucamonga, San Bernardino, San Timoteo, San Gorgonio Pass, Agua Caliente, Indian Villages and Martinez.

FARRER, WILLIAM (Diary)—M.
(1) Hafen, LeRoy and Ann—*Journals of Forty-Niners.*
Farrer was in one of the groups in the Sand Walking Co. who packed down the gorge at Mt. Misery. (1849.)

FARWELL, J. M. (Letter Reports)—C.M.
(1) Lang, Walter B.—*First Overland Mail.*
Farwell writes one of the leading contemporary accounts of rides taken over the Butterfield Stage Line during the two and one-half year period of its operation from September 1858 until March 1861.

FLINT, DR. THOMAS (Diary)—M.
(1) *Southern California Historical Society's Annual Publications* for 1923—*Diary of Thomas Flint*.
Flint crossed over the Old Spanish Trail during the months of November and December in 1853.

FONT, FATHER PEDRO (Diary)—C.
(1) Bolton, Dr. Herbert E.—*De Anza Expeditions*.
Font accompanied De Anza on the latter's second expedition in 1775-1776.

FRÉMONT, J. C. (Book)—M.
(1) Frémont—*Exploring Expedition to Oregon and North California*.
Contains the account of Frémont's crossing of the Mojave Desert from Tehachapi Pass to the Wasatch Mts. from April 15 to May 1, 1844.

GARCES, FATHER FRANCISCO (Diary)—C.M.
(1) Coues, Dr. Elliot—*On the Trail of a Spanish Pioneer: The Diary and Itinerary of Francisco Garces (Missionary Priest) in His Travels Through Sonora, Arizona, and California. 1775-1776.* (2 vols.)
(2) Galvin, John—*A Record of Travels In Arizona and California, 1775-1776.*
Garces accompanied De Anza on the latter's first expedition across the Colorado Desert and as far as the Mission San Gabriel. He again joined wth De Anza on the second expedition, but separated at Yuma, traveled along the Colorado to Mojave, thence across California to San Gabriel, thence by way of Tulare Valley back to Mojave.

GONZALEZ, RAFAEL (Account)—C.
(1) Bean and Mason—*The Romero Expeditions 1823-1826.*
Gonzalez was an enlisted man in the 1823-24 expedition from Santa Barbara to the Colorado River.

GRANGER, LEWIS (Letters)—M.
(1) Dawson, Glen—*Letters of Lewis Granger.*
(2) Hafen, LeRoy and Ann—*Supplement to Journals of Forty-Niners.*
Granger was among those who turned back from Mt. Misery in 1849 to follow the Hunt Wagon train into Los Angeles via Cajon Pass.

GRAY, A. B. (Report)—C.
(1) Bailey, L. R.—*The A. B. Gray Report.*
Gray conducted the survey of a route on the 32nd parallel for the Texas Western Railroad in 1854.

GREEN, ROBERT B. (Journal)—C.
(1) *On the Arkansas Route To California In 1849.* (Edited by Oliphant, J. Orin.)
Green was one of the 1849 emigrants traveling the Southern route to the California gold fields.

GRIFFIN, DR. JOHN S. (Diary)—C.
(1) *California Historical Society Quarterly*, Vol. XXI, Nos. 3 and 4, and Vol. XXII, No. 1.
(2) Society's reprint in book form—*A Doctor Comes to California.*
(3) J. J. Warner in *An Historical Sketch of Los Angeles County, California.*
Dr. Griffin served under General Kearny in the Army of the West at the Battle of San Pasqual in 1846.

GRUWELL, J. D. (Account)—M.
(1) Hafen, LeRoy and Ann—*Journals of Forty-Niners*.
See notes under Derr, Peter.

HAMELIN, JOSEPH P. JR. (Journal)—M.
(1) Hafen, LeRoy and Ann—*Supplement to Journals of Forty-Niners*.
Hamelin was a member of the Pomeroy Wagon Train leaving Salt Lake November 3, 1849, bound for Los Angeles over the Old Spanish Trail.

HARRIS, BENJAMIN BUTLER (Reminiscence)—C.
(1) Harris, Benj. B.—*The Gila Trail*.
Harris "formed one of a horseback party, each with at least one pack mule, that left Panola County, Texas, on March 25, 1849" for the gold fields of California. They began their trek over the Southern route, after crossing the Colorado River on August 17.

HARRIS, LEWIS BIRDSELL (Letters)—C.
(1) Hunt, Aurora—*Overland By Boat in 1849*. (September 1949 issue of the *Historical Society of Southern California Quarterly*.)
Harris crossed the Colorado River October 11, 1849, and followed the Southern route over the Colorado Desert.

HAYES, JUDGE BENJAMIN (Diary)—C.
(1) *Pioneer Notes From Diary of . . .*
(2) Hill, Joseph J.—*History of Warner's Ranch and Its Environs*.
Hayes was one of the 1849 emigrants to California who traveled via the Southwest route in 1849.

HAYNES, ASA (Diary)—M.
(1) Ellenbecker, John—*Jayhawkers of Death Valley*.
Haynes was a member of the Jayhawker Party of Death Valley fame, in 1849-50.

HEAP, GWINN HARRIS (Book)—M.
(1) *Central Route to the Pacific*.
Describes his Mojave Desert crossing in 1853.

HOGAN, GOUDY (Journal)—M.
(1) Hafen, LeRoy and Ann—*Journals of Forty-Niners*.
Hogan was a member of the Pomeroy Wagon Train who left Salt Lake just after the Sand Walking Co. (See Van Dyke, Seeley, and Pettit.)

JACKSON, WILLIAM H. (Diary)—M.
(1) Hafen, LeRoy and Ann—*William H. Jackson, Frontier Photographer*.
Jackson left Salt Lake for Los Angeles in December of 1866, traveling the Southwest route through Las Vegas, Barstow, the Cajon Pass and San Bernardino. On April 30 of the following year he left Los Angeles for Nebraska over the same route across the Mojave.

JAEGER, L. J. F. (Diary)—C.
(1) *Historical Society of Southern California. Annual Publications*. 1928. (Edited by Beattie, Geo. W.)
Jaeger, supposedly the author of this diary fragment discovered in a pile of debris in 1913, operated the Fort Yuma ferry on the Colorado. He had occasion, from time to time, to travel over the Colorado Desert (1855).

JOHNSTON, CAPT. A. R. (Report)—C.
(1) House Ex. Doc. of Emory's *Reconnoissance*.
(2) Cutts, Jas. Madison—*Conquest of California and New Mexico*.
Johnston was with General Kearny and the Army of the West. The day after completion of this report (1846), Johnston was killed in the Battle of San Pasqual.

JONES, NATHANIEL V. (Journal)—C.
(1) January, 1931 issue of *Utah Historical Quarterly*.
Jones served with the Mormon Battalion, and describes their desert crossing in six entries (Jan. 11-21, 1847).

KEALY, THOMAS (Letter)—M.
(1) Hafen, LeRoy and Ann—*Supplement to Journals of Forty-Niners*.
Kealy left Salt Lake for Los Angeles in November of 1849 "in company with four wagons, fifteen yoke of cattle, and all necessary supplies, with our various kinds of luggage, and in good spirits."

LORTON, W. B. (Letter)—M.
(1) Goodman, John B.—*Over the Salt Lake Trail In the Fall of '49*.
(2) Hafen, LeRoy and Ann—*Supplement To Journals of Forty-Niners*.
Lorton traveled the Old Spanish Trail; was at Mt. Misery with a portion of the Hunt party.

MANLY, WM. L. (Articles)—M.
(1) *San Jose Pioneer*, June 15, 1895—"The Manly-Rogers Reunion."
(2) Belden, L. Burr—*Death Valley Heroine*.
(3) *Inyo Independent*, Aug. 30, 1884—"Reply to Brier Article."
(4) (Woodward)—*The Jayhawkers' Oath*. (Contains most of Manly's articles for the *San Jose Pioneer*.)
Manly, according to his own version, was the great hero of the Death Valley episode of 1849-50.

MANLY, WM. L. (Book)—M.
(1) Manly, W. L.—*Death Valley in '49*.
Manly, by his own account, is Death Valley's outstanding hero.

MILLER, GEORGE (Narrative)—M.
(1) *Historical Society of Southern California Annual Publications*. 1919.
Miller, Rhodes, Van Curen and Lander made a tour of Death Valley in April of 1869.

MOODY, RANSOM G. (Account)—M.
(1) Hafen, LeRoy and Ann—*Supplement to Journals of Forty-Niners*.
Moody left Salt Lake in November of 1849 for Los Angeles, over the Old Spanish Trail, arriving at the Lugo Ranch in San Bernardino in early February.

MOWRY, SYLVESTER (Report)—M.
(1) Winter issue of *Arizona and the West* under title "Report On His March In 1855 From Salt Lake City To Fort Tejon." Edited by Bailey, L. R.
As indicated by the title, Mowry followed the Old Spanish Trail route. He was forced to deviate from the more direct trail to Ft. Tejon, going over the Cajon into San Bernardino for supplies, thence on to Ft. Tejon via Los Angeles.

NUSBAUMER, LOUIS (Diary)—M.
(1) Bruff, J. Goldsborough—*Gold Rush.*
(2) Koenig, George—*Valley of Salt, Memories of Wine.*
(3) Long, Dr. Margaret—*Shadow of the Arrow.*
Nusbaumer was one of the Death Valley pioneers of 1849.

ORMSBY, DR. C. M. (Letter)—M.
(1) Hafen, LeRoy and Ann—*Supplement to Journals of Forty-Niners.*
Ormsby left Salt Lake for Los Angeles toward the end of September, 1849, with the Jefferson Hunt Wagon train. He was one among those who turned back at Mt. Misery to follow the trail of Hunt's seven wagons into San Bernardino over the Old Spanish Trail.

ORMSBY, W. L. (Report)—C.M.
(1) Lang, Walter B.—*First Overland Mail.*
Ormsby was the "only through passenger on the first *westbound* stage" from St. Louis to San Francisco. This Butterfield coach followed the Southern desert route.

PANCOAST, CHARLES EDWARD (Book)—C.
(1) Pancoast, Charles Edward—*A Quaker Forty-Niner.*
Pancoast came to the gold fields via the Southwest route in 1849.

PATTIE, JAMES OHIO (Narrative)—C.
(1) Flint, Timothy (Edited by)—*The Personal Narrative of James O. Pattie of Kentucky.*
Pattie is supposed to have started his adventures in 1824; and during the course of these adventures he entered California.

PEARSON, G. C. (Account)—M.
(1) Goodman, John B. and Jessie H.—*Overland in 1849.*
(2) Hafen, LeRoy and Ann—*Supplement to Journals of Forty-Niners.*
Pearson left Salt Lake for Southern California in late September, 1849, over the Old Spanish Trail.

PETTIT, EDWIN (Portion of Biography)—M.
(1) Hafen, LeRoy and Ann—*Journals of Forty-Niners.*
Pettit was a member of the Pomeroy Wagon Train that left Salt Lake just after the Sand Walking Co. (See Van Dyke, Seeley, and Hogan.)

POOLE, C. H. (Articles)—C.M.
(1) Pacific Railroad Surveys, Vol. 7.
Poole was with the Railway Surveys group. (1853-1855.)

POWELL, H. M. T. (Journal)—C.
(1) Grabhorn Press release—*The Santa Fe Trail To California.* (Edited by Watson, Douglas S.)
Powell was a member of the Illinois Company, one of the groups (11 members) of 1849 emigrants en route to the gold fields over the Southern desert trail.

POWNALL, JOSEPH (Diary)—C.
(1) *Rushing for Gold.* (Under Robert G. Cleland's article—*From Louisiana to Mariposa.*)

(2) *Pacific Historical Review*—February, 1949.
Pownall was one of the 1849 emigrants who traveled the Southern route to the gold fields.

PRATT, ADDISON (Diary)—M.
(1) Hafen, LeRoy and Ann—*Journals of Forty-Niners.*
(2) Long, Dr. Margaret—*Shadow of the Arrow.*
Pratt was one of the Mormons in the historic Sand Walking Co. attached to the seven-wagon train who followed Hunt into San Bernardino. (See account of Jas. S. Brown.)

PRATT, ORVILLE (Journal)—M.
(1) Hafen, LeRoy and Ann—*Old Spanish Trail.*
Pratt records a complete trip over the Old Spanish Trail in 1848 and his is the only journal that does so.

PRATT, PARLEY PARKER (Diary)—M.
(1) March and June issues of *California Historical Society Quarterly*, 1935, Vol. 14, Nos. 1 and 2—*A Mormon Mission to California in 1851.*
Pratt traveled over the Old Spanish Trail; records a description of Bitter Springs and other points of interest.

PREUSS, CHARLES (Diary)—M.
(1) Preuss, Charles—*Exploring With Frémont.*
Preuss was Cartographer for Frémont in his First, Second and Fourth Expeditions (1844 and 1848).

RANCHO EL CHINO (Record)—C.M.
(1) Bynum, L.—*Record Book of the Rancho El Chino.*
Entries by members of various overland groups.

RANDOLPH, W. C. (Statement)—M.
(1) Hafen, LeRoy and Ann—*Supplement to Journals of Forty-Niners.*
Randolph was with a company of Packers, the first group to travel from Salt Lake to Los Angeles over the Mojave Desert in the fall of 1849.

RICH, CHARLES C. (Diary)—M.
(1) Hafen, LeRoy and Ann—*Journals of Forty-Niners.*
Rich, a member of the Sand Walking Co., was with one of the groups who packed down the gorge at Mt. Misery in 1849.

ROGERS, HARRISON G. (Journals)—C.M.
(1) Dale, Harrison Clifford—*The Ashley-Smith Explorations and Discovery of a Central Route to the Pacific 1822-1829.*
Rogers accompanied Smith on certain of the latter's expeditions. His first Journal was written in 1826-1827; the second Journal in 1828.

ROGERS, JOHN (Account)—M.
(1) *Merced Star* of April 26, 1894.
(2) Belden, L. Burr—*Death Valley Heroine.*
Rogers was Lewis Manly's scouting companion on the long trek from and to Death Valley to save the Bennett and Arcane families in 1849-50.

ROLLINS, JAMES H. (Account)—M.
(1) Hafen, LeRoy and Ann—*Journals of Forty-Niners.*
Rollins was a member of one of the Sand Walking Co. groups who packed down the gorge at Mt. Misery in 1849.

ROMERO, CAPT. DON JOSE (Diary)—C.
(1) Bean, Lowell John and Mason, William Marvin—*Diaries & Accounts of the Romero Expeditions In Arizona and California.*
Romero conducted his expeditions during the years 1823-1826. In June of 1823 he set out from Tucson (then in Sonora) to open a route of travel across the Colorado Desert into California. The following December another attempt was made, this time eastward from Mission San Gabriel via San Bernardino and the San Gorgonio Pass. (Included is the *Diary* of Don José Estudillo and the *Account* of R. Gonzalez.

ROSE, L. J. (Letter)—M.
(1) *Missouri Republican* of Nov. 29, 1859.
(2) Cleland, Robert G.—*The Cattle On a Thousand Hills.* (Appendix IV—pp. 306-315.)
Rose was a member of the ill-fated group of emigrants who, in the latter part of August 1858, at the Colorado River, were attacked by the Mojave Indians.

SEELEY, DAVID (Sketch)—M.
(1) Hafen, LeRoy and Ann—*Journals of Forty-Niners.*
Seeley was a member of the Pomeroy Wagon Train who left Salt Lake just after the Sand Walking Co., 1849. (See Van Dyke, Hogan and Pettit.)

SHANNON, THOMAS (Account)—M.
(1) *San Jose Daily Mercury,* Nov. 16, 1903.
(2) Belden, L. Burr—*Death Valley Heroine.*
Shannon was one of the Jayhawkers of the Death Valley episode of 1849-50.

SHEARER, MR.—M.
(1) Hafen, LeRoy and Ann—*Supplement to Journals of Forty-Niners.*
Shearer left Salt Lake for Los Angeles, over the Old Spanish Trail, in September 1849.

SMITH, JEDEDIAH (Narrative)—C.M.
(1) Sullivan, Maurice S.
    a. *Travels of Jedediah Smith.*
    b. *Jedediah Smith, Trader and Trail-breaker.*
(2) Neihardt, John G.—*The Splendid Wayfaring.*
(3) Morgan, Dale—*Jedediah Smith and the Opening of the West.*
(4) Dale, Harrison C.—*The Ashley-Smith Explorations and the Discovery of a Central Route to the Pacific, 1822-1829.*
Smith was perhaps the first white man to cross overland into California over the Old Spanish Trail route.

STANDAGE, HENRY (Journal)—C.
(1) Golder, Frank A.—*March of the Mormon Battalion, from Council Bluffs to California, The.*
(2) Bieber, Ralph P.—*Exploring Southwest Trails* (in foot notes to Cooke's Journal).
Standage was a private in Co. E of Cooke's Mormon Battalion (1846-47).

STEPHENS, L. DOW (Book)—C.M.
(1) Stephens, L. Dow—*Life Sketches of a Jayhawker of '49.*
Stephens was one of the 1849 emigrants crossing Death Valley, being a member of the Jayhawker Party. He also records a trip to Warner's Ranch, and tells of crossing the Colorado Desert to La Paz, returning—it would appear—over the Bradshaw Trail.

STOVER, JACOB Y. (Narrative)—M.
(1) Caughey, John Walton—*Southwest from Salt Lake in 1849.*
(2) Hafen, LeRoy and Ann—*Journals of Forty-Niners.*
Stover, of the Sand Walking Co., was in one of the groups that packed down the gorge at Mt. Misery in 1849.

STUART, CHARLES V. (Account)—M.
(1) Hafen, LeRoy and Ann—*Supplement to Journals of Forty-Niners.*
Stuart was with a company of Packers, the first group to travel from Salt Lake to Los Angeles over the Mojave Desert in the fall of 1849.

SWEENY, THOMAS W. (Journal)—C.
(1) *Journal* of Thomas W. Sweeny.
Sweeny made several trips to and from Fort Yuma and San Diego across the Colorado Desert in 1850-1851.

TALLACK, WILLIAM (Account)—C.M.
(1) Lang, Walter B.—*First Overland Mail.*
(2) Leisure Hour (London) under caption—*The Longest Stage Ride In the World.*
(3) *Historical Society of Southern California Quarterly*—1935: Vol. 17, Parts 2 and 3.
Tallack, the Englishman, made his Butterfield stage trip from San Francisco to St. Louis in the summer of 1860.

THURBER, ALBERT K. (Journal)—M.
(1) Hafen, LeRoy and Ann—*Supplement to Journals of Forty-Niners.*
Thurber, a member of the S. D. Huffaker train, left Salt Lake in November of 1849, enroute to Los Angeles via Cajon Pass and San Bernardino.

TURNER, HENRY SMITH (Journals)—C.
(1) Clarke, Dwight L.—*Original Journals of Henry Smith Turner.*
Turner crossed the Colorado Desert in 1846 with Kearny's Army of the West.

TYLER, SGT. DANIEL (Book)—C.M.
(1) Tyler, Sgt. Daniel—*A Concise History of the Mormon Battalion.*
(2) *A Concise History of the Mormon Battalion.* Rio Grande Press reprint.
Tyler was with Cooke's Mormon Battalion in 1846-47.

UDELL, JOHN (Journal)—M.
(1) Udell, J.—*Journal.*
Udell crossed over the Mojave Desert and the Cajon Pass. (1859.)

U. S. BOUNDARY COMMISSION (Diary)—M.
(1) Woodward, Arthur—*Camels and Surveyors in Death Valley.*
Material in Dr. Woodward's book is taken from *The Sacramento Daily Union* 1861 issues. They contain material relating to Death Valley and other sections of the Mojave, asembled by a member of the U. S. Boundary Commission.

VAN DYKE, JUDGE WALTER (Journal)—M.
(1) Coy, Owen C.—*The Great Trek.*
(2) Hafen, LeRoy and Ann—*Journals of Forty-Niners.*
(3) In the *Southern California Historical Society's Annual Publications* for 1894, Van Dyke has prepared an account entitled *Overland to Los Angeles By The Salt Lake Route in 1849.*
Van Dyke was a member of the Pomeroy Co., in a party of about 50 wagons traveling along the Old Spanish Trail behind the Sand Walking Co., leaving Salt Lake Nov. 3, 1849. (See Hogan, Seeley, and Pettit.)

WHIPPLE, AMIEL WEEKS (Survey Notes)—C.M.
(1) Foreman, Grant—*Pathfinder in the Southwest.*
(2) *Pacific Railroad Surveys,* Vol. III.
An account of Whipple's survey in 1853-1854 for a railway route from Ft. Smith to Los Angeles.

WHIPPLE, AMIEL WEEKS (Survey Report)—C.
(1) *Report of Lt. Whipple's Expedition from San Diego to the Colorado, 1849.* Senate Ex. Doc. No. 19. 1851.
(2) *The Whipple Report.* Westernlore Press. (Edited by Edwards, E. I.)
Lt. Couts furnished military escort for this expedition.

WHITWORTH, ROBERT W. (Diary)—C.
(1) Gracy and Rugeley (Editors) of "From the Mississippi To the Pacific; An Englishman In the Mormon Battalion" in *Arizona and the West,* Summer issue of 1965.
"During the first days of August of 1846, a sixteen-year-old Englishman and his 'partner' . . . found themselves on one of the longest and most grueling marches in the military history of the West—that of the Mormon Battalion. One of the two young Englishmen . . . kept a diary of his experiences."

WILLIAMSON, LT. R. S. (Reports)—C.M.
(1) *Pacific Railroad Surveys,* Vol. V.
Williams was connected with the Railroad Surveys group.

WOOD, HARVEY (Personal Recollections)—C.M.
(1) Wood, Harvey—*Personal Recollections.*
Wood, a member of the group of emigrants known as the Kit Carson Associates, came up through Mexico, traveled down the Gila, crossed the Colorado about the middle of June 1849. His journey across the desert followed Cooke's route.

WOODRUFF, ALDEN M. (Journal)—C.
(1) Foreman, Grant—*Marcy and the Gold Seekers.*
(2) Bieber, Ralph P.—*Southern Trails to California.*
Woodruff, a member of the Little Rock Company, followed the Southern trail to the gold fields in 1849.

WOODS, ISAIAH C. (Journal)—C.
(1) Rensch, H. E.—*From California Historical Quarterly.*
Woods crossed over the Colorado Desert, turning off at Vallecito to cross the mountains into San Diego. (1857-1858.)

YOUNG, SHELDON (Log)—M.
(1) Long, Dr. Margaret—*The Shadow of the Arrow*.
(2) Hafen, LeRoy and Ann—*Journals of Forty-Niners*.
(3) Edwards, E. I.—*Into An Alkali Valley*.
Young was a member of a group of the 1849 Death Valley emigrants. His "Log" gives us our first known written description of Death Valley.

INDEX